WREATH FOR ARABELLA

The Lady Arabella Stuart

WREATH FOR ARABELLA

BY

DORIS LESLIE

HUTCHINSON & CO. (Publishers) LTD
London   New York   Melbourne   Sydney   Cape Town

Printed in Great Britain at St. Albans
by the Mayflower Press (of Plymouth).
William Brendon & Son, Ltd.

CONTENTS

BOOK ONE
(1590–1592)
page 7

BOOK TWO
(1596–1603)
page 107

BOOK THREE
(1605–1611)
page 239

AFTERWORD
page 348

BOOK ONE
(1590-1592)

Chapter One

SCREENED by the window curtain the Lady Arabella and her cousin, Mary Talbot, were watching Mr. Morley. Turn about, hands behind, with his chin in his ruff and the wind in his hair, he paced the lawn below, unwittingly to entertain an audience.

"He revolves in circles," giggled Arabella, "while he counts my sins that he may write them in rotation to the Shrew."

A sugared almond bulging Mary's cheek caused obstruction to immediate reply. "Arbelle! The things you ..." Mary's titter turned into a choke. "The things you ... ough! ... you say!"

"Serve you right, you greedy, for eating the whole dish. Come to yourself, girl, come!" Somewhat strenuously Arabella patted Mary's back. "What things I say?" She grabbed the last of the comfits and conveyed it to her mouth before the spluttering Mary could forestall her.

"So rude." Mary wiped her eyes, repeating, "Rude. I didn't eat them all. There were but six. You ate the marchpane. You know what you say. But you'll never say it to her face."

"What'll you lay I don't?" asked Arabella.

"My turquoise ring," after some hesitancy offered Mary, "to your rope of pearls."

"Ho! So!" Arabella turned upon her, sharp. "Would you, i' faith! That's treason—or as near to it as winking. My pearls are royal heirlooms. I'd as soon lay odds on the old Queen's crown."

"O, lord!" gasped Mary, paling. "Hear her! *That's* treason if you like!"

"If I like! Did she not tell me to my face that one day I'd be wearing it?"

"Arbelle! She never did!"

"She did. To me and the French Ambassador's wife when I sat at the Queen's own table. 'One day she will rule here even as I, but I shall have been before her,' she said. And may I be drawn and quartered if I'm lying. Don't you believe me?"

In truth Mary did not, though she had heard, as indeed had all the family, from more reliable source than the Lady Arabella, how that the Queen had shown the utmost favour to this young and orphaned daughter of Her Majesty's kinsman, Charles Stuart, Earl of Lennox, on that august occasion three years since, when the child was first summoned to the Court; how that Lord Burghley had bidden her to supper at his house on that same night, and had expressed aloud the wish that the Lady Arabella was of some less tender years, that were she, say, fifteen, and with those eyes and such a mouth . . . and had rounded something in Sir Walter Raleigh's ear, who had answered, ' It would be a happy chance'. Whereupon the gentlemen had laughed a deal and tweaked her curls, and filled her with spiced wine till she was sick.

All this and more had been retailed to the artless Mary, who may have dared to envy Arabella's introduction into highest spheres: or maybe not. One might be disadvantaged to sit through endless banquets, and to suffer afterwards indisposition ; to be the youngest of all present and reminded of the fact ; to be placed above the salt but beneath the royal eye, and watched, while every mouthful that you ate turned sour in your belly from panic, or from poison, for any woeful thing could happen at the table of a queen, though surely never such announcement as the promise of a Crown to one who was so far removed from it. But : " O, of course I do believe you," Mary hastened to allow, " all the world *knows* that you'll be Queen."

" The world ! Who is the world ? Those cackling lickspittle courtiers, and my kinsfolk and yours ? Are they the world ? " demanded Arabella. " There's no voice, let me tell you, in England but her Grace's, and what *she* says sways the stars—and that," Arabella added, " is alliteration, a fault which Mr. Morley tells me may be forgiven in a poet, but never in a person. I might want to be a poet, though I'd never want to be a queen."

" I would," murmured Mary.

" You would not." A shadow veiled the laughter in Arabella's eyes. " To be banished or imprisoned. To be——" her voice faltered and dropped, " murdered, as my lovely Aunt Mary of Scotland was murdered. That's what could happen to me if the Queen keeps her word. God forbid ! "

" O ! . . . You sure *will* be murdered to talk so," breathed Mary. " Keep a curb on your tongue, Arabella."

" Who hears it but you ? And you'll not inform on me, will you ? Lest *your* silly head be cut off."

She was laughing again in her cousin's shocked face. Poor Mary. Arabella quizzically surveyed her: always so ready to rise to a bait. Mary's shape was spherical, plump as a ball. Her cheeks were round, her eyes blue and perpetually rounded. Her lips formed a pink circle of timorous O's, and her round chin had a round dimple in it. Even her farthingale was globular, patterned in an arabesque of moons, or were they silver cherries embroidered on a background of midnight blue brocade?

"Is that," asked Arabella, "a new gown?"

"O, yes, do you like it?" Mary brightened. Of gowns one could speak in safety. "My father brought it me from London, and my mother's tiring-woman, who has truly, Arabella, the sweetest taste in making up a——"

"Look!" Arabella made a grab for Mary's arm. "Look at Mr. Morley! He's at his prayers."

Incautiously she pulled aside the curtain to see the tutor take his stance under the dovecote on the flagged terrace, which, bordered by a yew hedge, divided the herb garden from the lawn. His eyes were up, his lips were down, and his fingers at the buttons of his doublet.

Mary, breathing warmly on Arabella's neck, tiptoed to peer over her shoulder. "What's he hiding over his heart? Do you think it's a locket from a lady?"

"Nothing so unlikely," retorted Arabella, "and I'm sure he has no heart. That's a rosary he dangles next his skin. I always knew him for a Papist."

"O!... A Papist!" uttered Mary, shying. She hurriedly drew back. "Be careful or he'll see you."

"And what if so? I'll not to my lessons till the week is out. I've a right to a vacation while my lady be from home. When she's here in residence much hope have I of holiday. I'm screwed to my books——" Arabella's self-extenuation was superfluous, for both she and Mary knew she would ultimately do the fullest penance for this, her latest misdemeanour, deliberate and defiant truancy—— "and sick to the stomach of schooling. My head," she put her hands up to it and rocked as if in pain, "is like to burst so packed it is with learning of dead languages that I forget my own.... Watch him now. I'll wager he prays for my damnation!"

And with immense bravado she leaned from the casement and shrilled loud in her childish treble to bring the doves in a flutter from their cote : "Morley ! Master Morley ! Have you abandoned the search ? "

He looked up. His long face, the longer for its neat-trimmed pointed beard, seen thus in some trick of light or shade cast by the uneasy wings of white doves, or reflection from the green of grass and hedge, had a faint greenish pallor like a drowned face under the sea.

Mary shivered.

"If ever I saw a living corpse ! O, how can you abide him ? "

"I accept him as my cross," Arabella answered carelessly. "One in a long succession of such burdens. There was Mr. Kynnersley before him. *Do* you remember Mr. Kynnersley who brought my Lady Shrew from Hardwick here, to Wingfield, on a summons of complaint when I refused my schooling for a week ? "

"O ! " Mary shied again, "then this is not the first time ? "

"By no means," boasted Arabella. "And I was three years younger then."

"What," Mary ghoulishly inquired, "did you receive from the Sh—from our lady grandmother as punishment ? "

"A rump so sore I couldn't sit. She all but skinned my buttocks with her birch. Put me across her knee, she did, as if I were her naughty page."

At which memory, or maybe in anticipation of similar chastisement yet to come, Arabella laid her hand upon the hinder region of her farthingale which distorted her young body out of all semblance of its shape. "But she'll not thrash me now. No, not since I've sat at Her Majesty's own table and been publicly acknowledged her successor. She wouldn't," Arabella said with more bombast than conviction, "dare to birch the backside of England's future Queen."

"O ! " Mary gaped at her. "Arbelle, you talk so big. You know what's said of Pride before a Fall ! "

"'Twill not be I who fall," flashed Arabella. "Or if it happen—" her grin was like a schoolboy's—"that I tumble, I'll bring my lady down with me, I swear. She lives for nothing else but for that day when she can point to me and tell them all ' *I* put her where she sits.' But I pray God that day will never come."

And she was trembling now ; her eyes, green-golden as the sea in sunlight, clouded. "'Tis a fearsome weight," she whispered,

" to wear the promise of a crown. Do you recall what happened to Jane, the Nine Days' Queen ? "

Mary nodded, drawing in a breath. Such talk as this alarmed her more than it impressed. It was not in her cousin's usual vein to dwell on gloomy matters—she who cared more for a jest than a sermon. But even as the goose-flesh rose on Mary's spine, Arabella's laughing voice dispelled it.

" Good Master Morley, do not waste your prayers on me ! "

Startled from his invocations, Mr. Morley with some haste refastened his doublet, then advanced a step, his head uplifted and his eyes askew in the last of the wintry sun that sank, red as a holly-berry, behind the shrouded hills.

" Madam ! " he protested in a penetrating monotone. " No prayer for your Highness's welfare can be wasted. That your Ladyship disdains your schooling is as grievous a slight to me, your Ladyship's instructor, as it is a direct defiance of my Lady Shrews-bury's command."

" Come, come, Mr. Morley. Would my lady command me to my lessons when I'm so sick o' the megrims and green bile that not so much as a crumb has passed my lips these five days ? "

" If your Highness's indisposition," stated Mr. Morley, chin upraised, eyes squinting more than ever, " be such as to render you unable to construe two pages of the Socratean dialogues, then 'twere best we summon a physician to your Ladyship. And may I tell you, Madam," the tutor's small beard quivered with the curb he put upon his swelling indignation, " my Lady Shrewsbury will hear from me how that your Highness has deliberately evaded——"
his wrathful gaze still focused on the mischievous face of his pupil framed in the casement above, Mr. Morley now advanced another step, tripped upon a loosened flag, and fell upon his knees. Even Mary had to laugh at this. Arabella held her sides.

" Sir ! Mr. Morley ! I pray you do not kneel. I'll excuse your ceremony, sir. Those stones are damp. You'll be riddled with rheumatics ! Rise, sir, do."

" O, Arbelle," tittered Mary. " You've sure plagued him enough. Now let him be."

" Hold your mouth," Arabella bestowed a silencing pinch upon her cousin's arm. " I entreat you, sir," she cried in great concern, " get up ! "

The goaded Morley got up, rubbing his grazed knee-caps.

"He'll have you marked for this," said Mary hopefully, and she too rubbed—her arm. "O! ... You do misuse your spite, Arbelle. I'm black and blue. I dread to think what her ladyship will say when Mr. Morley tells her."

"Tells her what? Did I cause him to fall? Did I spread traps for him?" Mary's meekness and timidity were a little too exasperating. Black and blue indeed! The girl was like a jelly: she *asked* to be pinched with that round look of hers—her 'O, this', and 'O, that', and her squeamishness. "Let him do his worst, then!" challenged Arabella, unabashed. "Let him come up here and *drag* me from my room. He won't!"

She ran to the door and turned the key, leaned against the oak, and regrettably, poked her tongue at Mary. "I've said it and I'll keep my word. I'll not to my lessons for a week. So may he break the door if he wants to fetch me out."

But Mr. Morley, who for the last five days had alternately upbraided, coaxed and threatened his young charge for her defiance of his tutorship, did not 'fetch her out'. Instead he took himself and his tale in—to Arabella's waiting-woman, Bridget Sherland, whose parlour provided, with the addition of a cup of mulled wine, an agreeable setting for exchange of confidence.

"For, Mr. Morley," Mrs. Sherland said, "'tis not, as everybody knows, the greatest pleasure in the world to be cooped up in attendance here at Hardwick, when I for one prefer a gayer life."

"As indeed you well deserve, Mistress Sherland." Mr. Morley passed his cup to be refilled, "with your—hem—your winsome personality and grace."

Mrs. Sherland acknowledged this effusion with a smile. She was buxom, she was orty, bright of eye, quick of tongue and of Irish extraction. Her hair, dyed the fashionable tint favoured by Her Majesty the Queen, towered in a cluster of red braids above her creaseless forehead under a velvet coif. The whale-boned corsage that embraced her ample curves upheld her in a stiff unbending posture where she sat, her farthingale of rose-coloured taffetas overspreading either oaken chair-arm.

Mr. Morley, seated on a settle, faced her across the hearth. A log fire burned cheerily to defy the clammy dusk behind the window panes. As Mrs. Sherland rose to draw the curtains, Mr. Morley covertly appraised her. She moved well, a handsome piece and to his taste, but even more so was her wine that added spice to Mr.

Morley's confidential humour. The closed curtains, the tapestried walls depicting dim scenes of the chase, where red-tongued hounds and green-clad huntsmen flitted in perpetual vague motion under the wavering glow of wax and firelight, lent to this cosy warm interior a sense of intimacy that prompted Mr. Morley to disburden.

"'Tis not the life that I complain of, Mrs. Sherland, but the meagre stipend which her ladyship allows me for the onerous responsibility and charge ——" Mr. Morley's speech, habitually weighted, gave significance to the most trivial remark and profundity to an obscure one, thus acquiring for himself among his associates at Hardwick the reputation of a scholar second to none in Derbyshire. Mrs. Sherland kept her silence as he paused.

" —a charge, Mrs. Sherland," Mr. Morley said, " that I need not remind you is one on which the strictest surveillance must ever be maintained."

Mrs. Sherland opened her lips but perceiving Mr. Morley had not done, she pursed them and encouragingly nodded.

" The post," continued Mr. Morley, and he sipped again, " which I am honoured to fulfil as tutor to her Highness, is an appointment that requires not only tact and forbearance, but a certain knowledge—as you know—of high diplomacy."

" Sure, sir, indeed." Mrs. Sherland sipped in her turn, looking down her nose. " Only high diplomacy could possibly arrange the all-important question of a royal m——"

" 'Sh ! " Mr. Morley laid a warning finger to his lip.

"Betrothal, sir, I was about to say," supplemented Mrs. Sherland, meek.

Mr. Morley leaned his back against the settle. His eyelids dropped ; he placed the empty cup upon the table at his side, and smilingly did Mrs. Sherland fill it.

" For," she added with a roguish gleam, " there can never be a marriage without first a betrothal, Mr. Morley."

" True, true ! " Mr. Morley's eyelids lifted ; he looked upon his cup. He raised it to his chin, and : " Madam, your good health," he offered affably before he drank again. " Which being so," concluded Mr. Morley, " sufficient for the day."

" And for the Duke of Parma it would seem," suggested Mrs. Sherland.

For this riposte Mr. Morley was not at all prepared. He stayed his cup and bristled.

"Madam! You surprise me."

"*I* surprise *you*!" Mrs. Sherland, with much sprightliness, protested. "Come, sir! You a diplomat and scholar, well versed in knowledgeable matters and the friend of knowledgeable men—even such a one, Mr. Morley, as is lodged not a mile from Hardwick at his brother's house——"

Mr. Morley compressed his lips till he looked to have no mouth.

"To whom do you allude, Mrs. Sherland?" he asked coldly.

"Why, sir, to that clerkly gentleman, the brother, I am told, of Mr. Harrison, who prowls about the place from time to time. They say he's popishly inclined, but that's not detrimental to his learning —nor his wisdom." And Mrs. Sherland gave a little cough.

"Madam," Mr. Morley turned a wary eye upon her. "I have no personal knowledge of any such a man. A clerk in Holy Orders? *And* popishly inclined?"

"'Tis only what I'm told, sir," answered Mrs. Sherland simply. "I've seen him once or twice. I thought maybe he came to visit you."

"And why, madam, should he come to visit me?"

"Why, sir, do scholars meet but to converse on subjects far above the common talk? *Two* scholars in one neighbourhood?"

Mr. Morley stroked his beard.

"Once for all, Mistress Sherland, have this clear. The man of whom you speak, whose name you say is——?"

"Harrison," murmured Mrs. Sherland, "as so I've heard."

"Whose name *I* have not heard until this moment," Mr. Morley with succinct emphasis replied. "'Tis a name unknown to me, and should, if I may be permitted to suggest, remain unknown to you. A Papist! Mistress Sherland, have a care!"

"I only wondered," apologetically murmured Mrs. Sherland. "Your cup, sir, is it empty?"

Mr. Morley drained and passed it to the lady's ready hand.

"Madam, an excellent wine."

"My pleasure, sir, to serve it to a palate of good taste." Bridget divided the last of the flagon between them. "But we wander from a more intriguing topic, Mr. Morley. Do you feign ignorance——"

Mr. Morley frowned and interrupted: "It is not my method to feign ignorance."

"*Or* show surprise ?" Mrs. Sherland here produced a dimple. "Your pardon, sir, I do repeat what is but old wives' gossip."

"No, no," protested Mr. Morley and his eye upon her lingered. "Not," he contradicted, "the gossip of old wives, but the apt corollary—shall we say—of—hem—of a young widow."

Mrs. Sherland's smile broadened to show remarkably fine teeth. "Well, sir, wife or widow, I've been both, but I'm not so lacking in my wits as not to guess what you already know. Is it not admitted that the Duke of Parma has presented his—credentials ?"

So enchanting was the lady's look that Mr. Morley's narrow cheeks, in sympathy, expanded.

"Since you will have it out of me, sweet rogue, I'll not dissemble. There has been some correspondence between the Duke of Parma's elder son and——" he drained his cup again and ruefully regarded it. Still smiling Mrs. Sherland rose, went to a corner cupboard and produced another bottle. "'Tis mild as milk, Mr. Morley," she wheedled. "Let me tempt you."

"'Ods body, madam, but you'd tempt an oyster from its shell," returned the now slightly inebriated Morley.

"You over-estimate my capabilities," simpered Mrs. Sherland, "but not the merit of my brew. Wait, now, while I fill the cups."

The cups were filled; more glances passed, and Mr. Morley was emboldened to a toast.

"'Merry met and merry part, I drink to thee with all my heart'! Nectar, Mrs. Sherland, distilled from the spittle o' the gods."

Mrs. Sherland's laughter tinkled at the compliment. "Och, sir! You blarney me! From the grapes o' France, and flavoured with a secret of me own."

"A secret," gulped Mr. Morley, "culled from the dew of your lips."

"A poet !" Mrs. Sherland cried with rapture. She raised her cup towards him. "To your muse !"

"*You* are my muse," quoth Mr. Morley. "You a-muse me."

"A wit as well !" declared the lively lady. "Sure, you have missed your vocation. You should take to authorship and write dramatic comedies to play before the Queen."

"Each to his taste, Mrs. Sherland," Mr. Morley modestly

replied. " I might use my pen to better purpose than to put words in the mouths of mountebanks. But I'll allow I have a taste for drama, and that my—hem—my muse could be more usefully employed than in correcting errata on a schoolgirl's script."

" Or," purred Mrs. Sherland, " in writing letters to the Duke of Parma."

" Letters ? " Mr. Morley drew himself up. " What letters, madam ? *I* have not written letters to his Grace."

" To his Grace's elder son, I should have said—or as *you* were saying ! " And now Mrs. Sherland sat beside him on the settle, her silken skirts against his padded breeks, her arm along the oak behind his head. The fragrance of the wine, the perfume of musk and amber that emanated from the folds of Mrs. Sherland's taffety ; the warmer and more pungent scent of Mrs. Sherland's armpit in close proximity to Mr. Morley's nose, all combined the further to beguile him, who forsook discretion and succumbed to Mrs. Sherland's smiles, and her teeth. Such teeth the woman had ! White as white seeds in reddest fruit. Such lips—ripe as strawberries, and as tasty—could he taste them ! But as he leaned nearer, she drew back. " Now, now, Mr. Morley, I have never known you randy, and—" her shoulders shook, " so fresh ! "

" You, my dear soul . . . would freshen an old salt herring," babbled Mr. Morley, whose head was now lighter than air. He basked in an effulgent rosy haze of Mrs. Sherland. He had never been so happy in his life.

" Is it true ? " cajoled Bridget at his ear.

" Is what true, angel ? " Mr. Morley, turning his eyes ceilingward, closed them in beatitude.

" That Prince Rainutio has been offered for her Highness ? "

" As true," gathering his ebbing wits about him Mr. Morley strove for caution, " as pigs, my dear, may fly."

" I believe you, since Rainutio is already married," said Mrs. Sherland, nodding ; and she poured more wine into his cup.

" Married ! Wha—what's married ? " inquired Mr. Morley. " Who is—marriage—that cannot be disholved ? "

" Is it possible ? " breathed Bridget. " You mean by dispensation of the Pope ? "

Mr. Morley waved his hand before his nose.

" By his Holiness' approval—and by—by—" he drank again. " By annulment—or by——"

18

"Is the Pope then so inclined?" asked Mrs. Sherland, and she steered the fumbling hand of Mr. Morley to her side.

Mr. Morley nodded, buttoned his small mouth, and kissed the air between the hastily averted lips of Mrs. Sherland.

"For shame, sir!" she tittered. "How unseemly!"

"Sweet sprite," sighed Mr. Morley. He raised his head most sternly to regard her. "*And* the King o' Spain and all o' Catholic Europe. One an' all," said Mr. Morley, "are inclined towards Arabella. You know why." He nudged the lady under her ribs. "You surely do know why."

"How should I know *anything*?" asked Mrs. Sherland, laughing softly; and despite her farthingale Mr. Morley was aware of the pressure of her thigh against his own. "A poor fool like me stuck in the mud o' Hardwick with never so much as a smell of the great world's doings. Me! Ha! Ha!"

"Haw! Haw!" echoed Mr. Morley, with delight. "You know as much as I, my dear, and that's no more than'll sit on a codpiece."

"Which—" fluttering her lashes the giggling Mrs. Sherland eyed him over,—"would, I swear, in some direction, be a-plenty!"

At this the flattered Morley was induced to fumble further, till Mrs. Sherland slapped his straying hand. "Sir! Pray remember your calling."

"When *you*—call *me*," he panted, "I forget it."

"But you don't forget," said Bridget, playing with his fingers, "what you've heard of Rainutio. Do you say the Pope is willing to annul the Prince's marriage?"

"Do I say! What have I said?" asked Mr. Morley, gazing at her eyes.

"Too much, and not enough for woman's curiosity," Mrs. Sherland snuggled closer. "Has the Duke of Parma not a second son?"

"Pretty creature. . . ." Again Mr. Morley sighed his contentment. "A second? . . . Yes, but he is now a cardinal, though I am told—never mind by whom—but I *am* told," he belched, "that he too may be absolved to gain the—pr-ize."

"God's life!"

The vehemence of her ejaculation brought the lady to her feet, and Mr. Morley almost to his senses. His jaw fell; he stared, and uttered faintly: "How? Why, madam—what—— ?"

"So *that's* their scheming felonies!" Bridget having filled him up to pump him dry, now gave vent to her repression. "'Tis as I thought and feared. I'll see her in her grave before they touch her. As for you——" She towered over Mr. Morley to snatch the cup from his hand, and with commendable effort restrained herself from hurling the contents of it in his face. "As for you, if you've hid lies behind your drink I'll pluck your beard out hair by hair, you spying toad!"

This attack, so untender, so unwarranted from one who, glance by glance and cup by cup, had artfully enticed him, caused Mr. Morley such a shock as, in a man of fuller blood, might have produced an apoplexy. He paled to his skull upon which the sparse hair lifted; he strove to speak, but his tongue shrivelled on his palate. He rose, sweating, from the settle, adjusted his ruff, pulled down his doublet, and stiffened at the knees to stutter: "Ma-Madam! You mal-malign me! Is this a fair advantage? I have told you nothing but what you yourself admit is common talk."

"Common talk!" It was as if a demon had possessed his smiling Sherland. "Yes, *I* know!"

"You know!" echoed the pallid Morley, round whom the room no less than the menacing form of his lady, dizzily revolved. "What do you know?"

"Yourself too well," Bridget retorted tritely. "I know too, that a snail leaves a filthy slime behind it on a wall. But these walls are thick, thank God, and strong enough to hold the Prince of Parma and the Pope and that white-livered Spanish Philip out o' them. Yes! And all his sneak-spies too and popish persons. And if you——" screamed Mrs. Sherland whose teeth between her parted lips now resembled nothing daintier, to Mr. Morley's frightened fancy, than a wolf's——"yes, *you*, whom I have never doubted had low dealings with those poxy papistical foreigners to feather your own foul nest and give them an inch to take their ell of Arabella, which since the day that she was weaned has been their aim—if you have had a finger in *their* pie, then, Mr. Morley, you had best be gone from here before you hang!"

She paused for breath as Mr. Morley, all but fainting, inly prayed to be delivered from this nightmare.

"Do I dream?" he muttered. "Madam, what is this? Have you run mad?"

With the reply that she had never been more sane, Bridget's hands urged Mr. Morley to the door. "When wine is in, sir, truth is out," she told him as she opened it. "And if I find you here, or there, or anywhere in Derbyshire hatching mischief, Mr. Morley, and talking behind bushes with suspicious persons, priests or votaries or what you may choose to call 'em, I promise there'll be such a muck o' trouble, Mr. Morley, that you'll wish yourself pickled in brine!"

The unhappy tutor, dragged from sweet coma to harsh consciousness, attempted reassertion.

"I swear, madam, you misjudge me. My tongue was loosened by your devil's brew. I have said naught of harm, and God knows I am guiltless of these evil accusations. I have repeated only what my Lady Shrewsbury divulged to——"

"Liar!" The strident Mrs. Sherland interrupted. "Is it likely her ladyship would talk to you, at all, of that which never should be spoken above breath? Wait till my lady hears of your tittling tattle—only wait! You had better be advised to pack your baggage, Mr. Morley."

Mr. Morley's teeth were all a-chatter.

"You'll not make mountains of so small a trifle, Mrs. Sherland, to lose me a good post? I too have a tongue in my head."

"Then keep it still, sir, lest it be cut out! Now go call the Lady Arabella to her studies. A fine tutor, you, to pander to her nonsense. 'Tis meself'll get the blame for her misdoings when her ladyship returns from Sheffield. . . . Will you go?"

And without further hesitation Mr. Morley went, or more correctly, bolted from the room.

Bridget now was in a quandary. Despite Mr. Morley's University degrees she had always thought him fool, never sharp enough for rogue. How could she convince her ladyship, with whom he stood in favour for his music—the fellow was a wizard with the virginals—that she harboured in her household one who hand-and-gloved it with the Pope, or if not with His Eminence himself, then with that Spider, Spanish Philip, or the whole muck of Popish princes on the Continent? How? Hell take the man and all his works!

With a foot upon the hearth she stood staring at the logs. One fell in a shower of sparks and died in white ash on the bricks. The room chilled, but Bridget, still warm from her outburst, made no effort to mend the fire. . . . It would be indiscreet, worse, folly, to go running to her ladyship the moment she returned, to start a hare with not a hound to hunt it. And what, at most, could be her hints ? That she had reason to believe this stranger at the gates—own brother to that mild Mr. Harrison—was no less than a paid spy, sent by Philip of Spain, or Parma, to pounce on Arabella ?

The notion was fantastic, and Lady Shrewsbury, Bess of Hardwick, whose tenacity of purpose and indomitable will was matched only by that other Bess of England, would give Bridget small thanks for her pains, and more likely ignominious dismissal for service consequentially bestowed. And rightly, too, deserved, if Bridget, with no substantial evidence for its support, dared offer so flimsy a tale. She knew what her ladyship's response to *that* would be : a look to freeze your marrow-bones, a contemptuous thin smile under the small beaked nose, and sarcastical concession.

" Your zeal in discovering a suppositious mystery accords well with your appetite for spurious romance."

That, or words to that effect, had been her ladyship's retort to Bridget's warning, sixteen years before, of those secret meetings between Charles Stuart, Earl of Lennox, and Elizabeth, Lady Shrewsbury's young daughter by her second husband, William Cavendish of Chatsworth.

Bridget recalled a certain journey undertaken by Margaret, Countess of Lennox, and her son Charles, who were travelling to Scotland to visit the boy King James, grandson of Lady Lennox. The royal party, at Bess of Hardwick's invitation, lodged on their way north at Rufford Abbey, one of the Shrewsbury seats.

Margaret of Lennox, mother of the murdered Darnley, and granddaughter of Henry VII, had been accepted heiress presumptive of England at the time when her uncle, Henry VIII, chose to bastardize his daughters, Mary and Elizabeth. It therefore mattered not a rap to Bess that six miles distant from Rufford lay the house of the Duchess of Suffolk, her dearest friend, to whose son, Mr. Bertie, by a second marriage, Elizabeth was more than half betrothed. Charles Stuart was the better catch, a Prince of the Blood Royal, and Bess Shrewsbury laid a pretty bait to land him.

Was it coincidental, accidental, or fate's own hand, if not my Lady Shrewsbury's, that brought Margaret of Lennox to bed with the colic at Rufford ?

So high ran her fever, so feeble her pulse, so frequent her violent vomiting, that the journey to Scotland was held up for five days.

In those five days Charles Stuart, Earl of Lennox, nearest heir to the throne if the sickly boy James, King of Scots, were discounted, came and conquered Elizabeth Cavendish.

She was wistful-eyed, timid, not yet seventeen, and defenceless as a flower in summer storm against that tempestuous wooing. They met in the woods around Rufford. Bridget blinked a moisture from her eye. . . . So little more than children ! He was scarce nineteen, but never were young lovers more in love. Bess of Hardwick's ruse had worked beyond her highest dreams. Those two were mated first : then wed.

God rest them both ! sighed Bridget, and rubbed away another tear as she remembered how she came upon them in a copse, and in each other's arms ; how that Elizabeth had begged her dearest Bridget to intercede on her behalf—" with my good mother, for I swear I'd sooner kill myself than marry bow-legged Mr. Bertie and his boils. . . ." How that Lord Lennox (nothing of the fop, his brother Darnley, in *his* metal. A lad born to be King, a prince indeed !) had commanded her, politely, to—" inform my Lady Shrewsbury of our intent. Mistress Cavendish has honoured my addresses. You, madam, must announce the news of our betrothal, for . . ." and here he swung his sweetheart round. Bridget saw their ghosts again standing in the dappled sunlight, ringed with woodland green : he in a doublet of dove-grey and gold, she in her silver-white gown. . . . " For," said Charles Stuart, and his boy's voice cracked with laughter and emotion, " I am in such case that I'll not wait upon the order of my mother, nor of the Queen herself ! I love— I want—Elizabeth, and we'll marry, come what may."

While Bess, inwardly triumphant, but seeming to be scandalized, heard with simulated horror Bridget's tale of a clandestine romance, she was compelled to vindicate herself to Lady Margaret, and protest her innocence of this unorthodox and shameless misbehaviour, this circumvention of propriety on the part of her Elizabeth, which had brought the whole affair to such a head.

Bridget Sherland, witness of that very glib apology in the room where Margaret of Lennox, recovered now from her indisposition, lay upon her pillows sipping broth, saw a gleam of humour flash across the convalescent's face, and :

" If I know anything of my son Charles," pronounced the Lady Margaret, " circumvention of propriety has been brought to . . . maidenhead."

Bess Shrewsbury received the quip with cackles. She had hoped, but not so readily, for condescension. It may be that Lady Lennox was as hopeful as her hostess. This Cavendish girl, a gentle, pretty creature, was also well endowed. Her father, the late Sir William, had owned vast property—and Chatsworth. The son of Lady Lennox was poor in purse if rich in blood. Lady Lennox rose from her sick-bed to call a blessing on the pair. Lady Shrewsbury, of lesser precedence, must follow her example, and the whole household after her in loud congratulation.

A clergyman was fetched and the ceremony solemnized. The impetuous young bridegroom carried his girl bride across the threshold of their chamber in traditional Scots fashion. . . .

There we leave them.

When news of this hurried marriage reached the cast-off Mr. Bertie, he went whining to his mother, who prayed that 'Bitch of Hardwick' would get her full deserts.

Her prayer was answered.

Word of the wedding of her kinsman to a commoner had been carried all haste to the Queen. Such offence to Majesty, who took it very ill, boded worse for everyone concerned. Bess of Hardwick was sent packing to the Tower, on a charge of treasonable connivance at the marriage of her daughter with a Prince of the Blood without the Queen's consent. After her, accounted an accomplice, followed Margaret of Lennox; but the two young people, cause of all the trouble, were, surprisingly, permitted to prolong their honeymoon in undivided bliss, if virtual imprisonment, at the bridegroom's house at Hackney.

While the incarcerated Countesses were chafing in the Tower, Commissioners appointed to look into their case found nothing treasonable in it. After a searching cross-examination which continued for some weeks, the Ladies Shrewsbury and Lennox were released by gracious intervention of the Queen.

The Queen certainly was gracious; she could easily have not been so disposed. The two unhappy matrons who trembled in the Tower might well have lost their heads because young Charles Stuart lost his heart.

There was quite a buzz about the Court, a breath, a stir, a waiting, for the promised heir-to-be. Another semi-royal prince to come to the succession? Semi-royal? *Wholly* royal, went the contradiction of Lord Burghley and Lord Leicester, and others of the Council Chamber who had ruled James of Scotland out of England's heritage by reason of the rumour he was not his mother's son. Mary Stuart, gossip gave it, had been delivered of a still-born babe. James must therefore be a changeling; but if he were not, the long-standing Act of Attainder that forbade those born without the realm to inherit land within it, still held, even if that land went with a Crown. Which being so, the wife of Charles, Earl of Lennox, might well produce a future King of England; and in view of the boy James's sickly health, of Scotland too.

But the child that was born to the Royal House of Stuart was not destined to be a King.

It was a girl.

A rap at the door roused Bridget from her reverie. He who stood impatiently upon the threshold did not wait for her to call him. He burst in.

"Mr. Cavendish!" Bridget bobbed. He took her by the shoulders.

"Mistress Sherland, hear this calmly. A courier has come to Chatsworth with the very gravest news."

"Gravest . . . ?" Bridget heard it calmly. "My Lord of Shrewsbury?"

"Is dead," said Henry Cavendish.

He was mud-bespattered from hard riding; his suit damp with rain.

"You are wet through, sir," Bridget said. "Give me your cloak." And she relieved him of it.

"Though he was not my father I can scarce remember any other. Still, one can only welcome this sad end to all his misery."

Bridget, shaking raindrops from his outer garment, paused to reprimand him.

"If that remark, Mr. Cavendish, is intended as reflection on the good grace of your mother, may I suggest that 'tis not only disrespectful but in the worst——"

He interrupted, quizzing her.

"Try not to be sententious, my good Sherland. The rôle of sermonizer never did become you."

His upper lip, under the slight moustache, was whimsical, so too were his hazel-brown eyes. Despite that he was in his fortieth year he had the merest suspicion of a beard and a skin like a girl's. Yet this eldest son of Lady Shrewsbury was a thorn in his mother's side, since by right of seniority and his father's Will he must eventually inherit Chatsworth.

Bridget hardened her heart as she looked at him. These Cavendishes! What witchery, she wondered, had they in them to melt stones? Arabella too, with Stuart blood for flavour, had that same spice of enchantment; and because, more than any of his family he resembled that Elizabeth, dead these eight years since, pining, it was said, for her husband, Charles Lennox, who preceded her of a consumption after eighteen months of marriage; because Henry Cavendish was impudent and gay; because he alone, of any, dared speak his mind to Bess, Bridget, who had so greatly loved his sister, must love him.

But: "You have as much compassion as a winkle," she told him, sharp as knives, "to make so light of such a grievous sorrow. My good lord gone!" She squeezed a tear out of her eye. "God save us! Lack-a-day!"

Henry cocked an eyebrow.

"Your dramatic sensibility, dear Sherland, does you credit. Yet I confess, upon my life, that I can't weep for death. What was *his* life, poor gentleman? Shackled to my mother, striving all these years for freedom, bound to her body—and soul!"

"Sir!" He had succeeded in shocking Mrs. Sherland. "Where's your shame?"

"I have none," said Henry lightly. "He who admits to shame admits to weakness."

Bridget pursed her lips. "Yet you, sir, have a weakness, that leads you oftentimes astray."

He smiled and sat on the settle, lazily stretching his legs.

"What is my weakness? Women—or wine?"

"You are too deep in both," Bridget returned tritely, "to be affected now by either. No, your weakness lies in your own good heart, which is stronger than your head."

"Would you label me a half-wit?" He laughed round at her and bent to the basket of logs in the chimney-corner to heap more wood on to the fire. "Here's a dismal hearth to dry me! . . . As for your recriminations, I refute them. If I had come to you in mourning black, weeping for him whose sorrows are now over, and who passed, we hope, in peace——"

"Amen! God rest him," murmured Bridget.

"I would," continued Henry, "be guilty of false sentiment, which is only a shade less pernicious than pure sentiment. Why weep for death? Why make so great a Thing of death, that soon or late must come to every one of us? I may be killed tomorrow in a brawl——"

"Heaven forbid!" ejaculated Bridget.

"And you may take the small—or the great—pox, and die within a——"

"Mr. Cavendish! That you can sit there with a grin on your face and my lord not cold," cried Bridget energetically, "gives me to think that I've mistook your understanding. Sure, your heart forsakes you! You're a cynic."

"Cynicism," declared Henry, adjusting a log with his toe, "is a wise man's sense of humour. Which reminds me that my niece, Arbelle, will never lack in such. Her tutor in a rare state—how she plagues him!—greeted me, pale as salt, with the latest naughty story of her doings."

"*Her* doings," echoed Bridget, red. "Let him look to his own, the slimy slug."

"What has he done," asked Henry coolly, "to provoke you? I thought that he and you were on the best of terms together. If his music, as I hear, can charm my mother, it should coax *your* humour, as the lyre of Orpheus induced the wildest beast to——"

"Hush, sir! If I tell you—" Bridget cautiously approached him—"you will scoff."

"I? Scoff?" He looked at her in mock reproach. "Dear lady, have you ever known me scoff—at you? Give me your confidence. I am all attention. Has Mr. Morley burst his bounds at last and taken fond advantage of your——"

"Listen!" Bridget interrupted, redder still. "I am in no mood for folly, Mr. Cavendish. I desire your good sense to bear upon a matter, sir, that needs it. If I take my fears and doubts to your good mother she—with due respect—will shout me down, or have me out o' doors. That whoreson knave—" she hushed her voice—"is up to no good, at all. Hearken, while I tell you——"

And she told.

Henry's face grew longer; he rose from his seat, brows knit.

"If," he said at last, "there's ground for your suspicion, I'll go myself and call on Mr. Harrison. In the meantime, guard your tongue. Repeat to none what you have said to me—not even to my sister Mary, who will, however, be so swollen now with her position as wife of the new Earl that she'll not lend an ear to any matter save her own importance. Nevertheless, be cautious. Tell my mother least of all. You are right, she'll have you out of here if you attack her Morley. This, though, I can give you for so much as it is worth. When I was last in London, Burghley spoke to me aside, bidding me beware of strangers hereabouts. The Pope, they say, is determined to secure our Arabella for a Catholic prince—Parma's son, or any son—the King of France himself if he were free."

"The devil! And I knew it!" exclaimed Bridget. "The Papists will stop at nothing to kidnap and carry her off. I'll have her guarded night and day——"

"Don't fret yourself. She'll not be here," said Henry. "First, she must attend the funeral."

"And I," said Bridget hurriedly, "must see to her mourning clothes."

"Yes," Henry nodded, "and her cousin Mary's too. They'll walk together in procession. And when the rites are over Arbelle will go to Court. The Queen commands her presence."

Bridget brightened. "Does she so? And why did you not tell me before? 'Pon honour, Mr. Cavendish, you would try Job's patience. To play the cat and mouse with me, and keep me dangling here when——" she hastened in a flurry to the door. "I'll overhaul her robes this very instant. Pity 'tis that she must go before the Queen in mourning black."

"Purple," corrected Henry. "You forget her royal state."

"I'm not allowed to," muttered Bridget.

He followed and stood before her, his eyes laughing down to hers that narrowed as his glance impudently raked her, top to toe.

"You ripen with your years," he told her softly, "as a peach upon a wall."

Her hurried breathing stirred the laces on her bosom.

"Over-ripe, sir, now," she showed her teeth, "I fancy."

"Never," he bent his head and kissed her full on her parted lips, "too ripe," he said, "for this." Then he took her hand from the door-latch and silently turned the key. "Or even . . . this."

*   *   *

The last rites of George Talbot, Earl of Shrewsbury, Bess of Hardwick's fourth husband and former jailor of the Queen of Scots, had been performed with grisly pomp at Sheffield. His widow, with whom, during the latter part of his married life, he had hardly been on speaking terms, now dutifully mourned him in full regalia of weeds. But the cortège had scarce returned from the family vault, before the ever-present feud between the Cavendishes and the Talbots was resumed.

First arose the question of the Will.

The extravagance of his heir or his heir's wife, Mary, had decided the Earl to appoint his two younger sons his executors. They in their turn, strongly backed by their Cavendish step-brothers, William and Charles, nominated their father's widow sole executrix, than which nothing could have been more satisfactory to Bess. She would now have the disposal of her late husband's property in her own very capable hands.

Before accepting this, her final suitor, Bess had taken the precaution further to secure, for the good of her Cavendish brood, the wealth and estates of the Talbots. Thus, while they were children, she had married her daughter Mary to Gilbert, the Shrewsbury heir, and her son Henry to Grace, Gilbert's sister. Despite that the joint ages of these four did not amount to sixty years between them, their marriages proved happier than that of their respective parents.

Lord Shrewsbury, Earl Marshal of England, 'my good old man' as the Queen was pleased to call him, in whose castles and whose custody she had consigned her cousin Mary, suffered as his wife's lesser half, although not uncomplainingly, for many years. Indeed, marital disagreement arrived at such a pass that Her Majesty thought fit to intervene. The rumours suggesting a liaison between the Earl Marshal and his royal prisoner, floated, it was said, by Bess, to inculpate her husband, had come to the ear of Elizabeth, who wisely paid no heed to scandal. She had some knowledge of the Countess, still more of her 'very good old man', and she drew her own conclusions. And while Lord Shrewsbury's honour might be brought to question, he could safely answer for it when he faced his Sovereign to declare himself : 'most graciously used by Her Majesty who expressed her desire to comprehend the controversies between him and the lady, his wife.'

With the details of these 'controversies' we are not here

concerned. His refusal, however, to live with one who called him 'Knave, Fool, and Beast to his face, and mocked and mowed at him', may not have been unjustified. Bess of Hardwick's temper was as hot as her ambition. Her hobby for collecting husbands and their houses, the bickering and quarrelling that ensued between the offspring of Shrewsbury and Cavendish, may have also had a share in the fluctuations of continued strife which culminated in the Earl's appeal for a divorce.

As for his alleged intimacy with the Queen of Scots, he indignantly denied that preposterous charge in an emphatic letter to Lord Burghley.

'These untrue surmises of me are invented by my Wife and her children. I therefore request your lordship this much; that they may have trial of their complaint against me, and by the grace of God my dealings shall be such as I wish my Wife and her Imps, who I know to be my Mortal Enemies, might daily see into these doings.'

It was the Queen, however, who saw into these 'doings'. The Shrewsburys were commanded to the Presence, where she sat them on stools either side of her and harangued them for an hour, finally insisting on a reconciliation.

The scowling couple, in face of smiling Majesty, must perforce patch their quarrel and agree to live in harmony thereafter. 'Whereat the Queen, with many good words did show herself glad thereof, and the Earl and Countess in good sort departed very comfortably together.'

This according to Secretary Walsingham, who drew up the Queen's Order to effect that: 'the said Earl should convey the said Countess to some one of his principal houses in Derbyshire, and shall allow the said Countess towards the defraying of the charges of her household, the sum of three hundred pounds.'

But royal jurisdiction notwithstanding, within two months they were at loggerheads again. Letters flew from the Countess to Burghley, the Lord Treasurer, and from the Earl to his gossip, Sir Henry Lee, in whom he confided that 'my son Gilbert says he is not over-ruled by his wife, nor does he countenance her or his mother against me in all their bad actions. . . .'

By which it would seem that the poor gentleman was grateful, even for such small mercy from his heir. Then, in the midst of these disputes and correspondence came the summons to Fotheringay.

He was ailing; he was old. His wife and her Cavendish sons, with the exception of Henry, the eldest, were avowed by himself his worst enemies. He was nearing his end, yet he must assist at another's.

There, in the last scene of that tragedy at Fotheringay Castle, he, who had been reviled as the paramour of Mary Stuart, received her as she mounted to the block.

That broke him.

And now he too was gone; estranged in life from the woman he had married and from his eldest son; unmourned in death by any of his children save his daughter Grace, and his step-grand-daughter, Arabella Stuart.

She sat beside his widow now on that homeward journey from his funeral, and in that first twenty miles of the jolting drive to Hardwick, her grandmother had not opened once her lips.

Arabella, cramped and chilly, with pins and needles in her foot, strove to hold her tears from brimming over. It would not do to let my lady see how much she grieved for one who was no blood-relation to her. But she could well remember him, his long gentle face with its forked silver beard, his high Talbot nose, and the comfits that he gave her when, with her mother, long ago, she stayed at Sheffield Castle.

Her mother. . . .

Through veils of distance she appeared, lily-pale, fair and lovely: she who used to sing her songs at bedtime.

One came to her now of ' Green-sleeves '.

> ' Green-sleeves was all my joy,
> Green-sleeves was my delight,
> Green-sleeves was my heart of gold,
> And who but Lady Green-sleeves. . . .'

She turned her head to gaze out at the sodden clouds, the grey, rain-drenched hills where forlorn sheep grazed in grass that seemed to spring like green water from the rocks. . . . ' Green-sleeves was my delight. . . .' She once had a doll with green sleeves given her by her Aunt Mary of Scotland. She remembered how her Grandfather Shrewsbury used to lead her to the Queen where she sat in her high chair in the great gallery at Sheffield, and the Queen would take her on her knee, brush her hair from her forehead and say in her pretty, slight French accent : 'She is all Stu-art, this one'.

Stu-art. . . . The Queen could not pronounce the name as it was spelt with an E and a W, and that was why, Arabella supposed, it was now spelt UART. . . . She must *not* cry.

" Are you cold, my Jewel ? "

Arabella quaked. Long-suffering had inured her to the knowledge that when her lady grandmother addressed her as ' my Jewel ', she applied a sugar-coating to a pill.

" No, I thank your ladyship." Then emboldened, Arabella dared to ask : " Are you ? "

The firm lips tightened.

" No."

Arabella stole a glance. Despite that curt denial one might believe the blood within that rigid body was congealed. The grim old face under its widow's coif, no less parchment-white than the starched ruff that framed it, looked to be moulded not of flesh, but stone. Yet in those frosted features, the clear keen eye, the harsh strength of the jaw, could be discerned the immense vitality and unwavering spirit that had spurred Bess of Hardwick along the stony path of her ambition.

The daughter of an inconspicuous country squire, John Hardwick of Hardwick House, she had outlived four husbands, each one of more social significance than his predecessor.

Robert Barlow was the first; him she married at the age of twelve, to be widowed at fourteen. He had, however, left her independent. She could now afford to wait and secure a better prize.

She did.

Sir William Cavendish, her second, had considerable means. In addition to the grant of Church property, and the manors of Childe-wicke, Cuffley, and Northawe in Hertfordshire, he had received further honour from young Edward VI, as Treasurer of the Chamber to the King.

On his marriage to Bess, and at his wife's bidding, he sold his southern estates in favour of others in Nottingham, Stafford and Derbyshire. In this, her native county, Bess decided to settle and persuaded Sir William to buy from the Leeches, who owned it, the manor of Chatsworth.

The place did not please the exigeant Bess ; it was damp, and un-modernized, rat-ridden. A new house must be built for her and her children. In due course, by the death of her brother without issue, she would inherit Hardwick. Meanwhile they must all lodge at Chatsworth pending the rebuilding of a mansion befitting a knight and his lady, the completion of which Sir William did not live to see.

Less than ten years after his marriage, he died, leaving Bess the mother of six children.

The loss of this most loved of her four husbands was the greatest sorrow of her life ; but it was not in Bess to sit repining. Vigorously did she take command of the work in hand at Chatsworth, directing labour, signing orders for more stone, for timber, cloth and tapestry, bedding, curtains, marble. Yet, though every minute of her day was occupied and her six small children demanded her attention, she was still young enough to find her widowhood a penance, and to crave as much for the nuptial rites denied her as for the glamour of Court life. She had known so little of it during these years of child-bearing. She must now take her place among the highest in the land. Another knight, or better, would present himself in time. And this time she had not long to wait. Within a year she was offered and accepted consolation from Sir William Saintlow, Grand Butler of England, Captain of the Guard, and former Seneschal of Waterford in Ireland.

The gloomy Queen, whose fanatical Catholicism had terrorized the country, was pleased to countenance the marriage, and conferred on Bess the honour of Lady of the Bedchamber. This post, that held with it less duty than distinction, did not at all impede her house-building activities in Derbyshire. She spent more time there than in London with her husband, who in his letters addressed her as his 'honest, sweet Chatsworth', and signed himself 'most lovingly hers with aching heart until we meet'. They were destined not to meet much longer : but her third widowhood had left her well-established, high upon the social ladder, powerful and prosperous. She had rebuilt Chatsworth, had acquired more land from William Saintlow, and retained her post as Lady of the Bed-chamber to the, then, young Queen Elizabeth.

Such office, even if it were but mainly nominal, surrounded all who held it with intrigue. It was Bess Saintlow's misfortune to find herself inveigled in a romance, not her own : the pitiful story of Catherine Seymour, sister of Lady Jane Grey.

Previously married to and afterwards divorced by Lord Herbert,

33

B

when the fate of Lady Jane shattered his hope of becoming consort of a possible heiress to the Throne, Catherine had later loved and wedded secretly one Edward Seymour, Earl of Hertford. He was the elder son of the Protector Somerset who perished on the block as did also Catherine's father, Duke of Suffolk. The horror of the axe that had bereft these two young people of their parents and Catherine of her sister, the innocent, uncrowned Jane, scared them into silence of their state. She was royal, he the son of one who stood for royalty. Both knew the punishment that must surely follow if the marriage were discovered. But for all their care it could not be concealed.

Catherine's condition became obvious. The scornful glances and contemptuous whispers of Court ladies must at all costs be suppressed, her virtue vindicated. Her husband, who could have cleared her, had been sent to Paris on a diplomatic mission. In whom then could the Lady Catherine confide ? One who must be trusted to advise her ; one whose own integrity stood high.

It was, therefore, to the widowed Bess Saintlow that Catherine took her tale and begged that lady's intercession with the Queen.

Bess was very loath to interfere. She guessed what Her Majesty's reception of such a tale would be. The Queen was known to bear a grudge against young lovers ; and this girl, the Queen's own cousin of the hated house of Grey, who stood so near her in the line of succession, had allied herself without the royal sanction to a Seymour.

It speaks well for Bess that in pity for the poor girl's plight, she braved the royal fury striving to placate it, and followed Catherine to the Tower for her pains.

The young husband was summoned back to London and imprisoned with his wife. Their two sons were born in the Tower, and seven years later Catherine died, of a broken heart, it was said ; but Hertford, her husband, married again, and was still alive.

It was this long-distant episode of two young lovers victimized, that Lady Shrewsbury, on the homeward drive from Sheffield, now remembered. . . . She, twice imprisoned, had twice incurred her Sovereign's displeasure, and for almost the same cause : the first, her revelation of a secret royal marriage ; the second, for her share in such a one. And the fruit thereof was hers alone to guard, to guide, to cherish : this, her daughter's daughter, born a Royal Stuart, the core and crown of her whole life's fulfilment.

Bess glanced aside to see a tear roll down the child's cheek. So! She wept for him who lay in Sheffield's vaults, and for whom his widow held no sorrow in her heart, no tender memory of courtship : she, whom he had used to nickname ' his sweet None '. She never had discovered what that endearment stood for. ' None'. Foolish, meaningless, pronounced to rhyme with ' cone ' . . . in those dim days when he had loved her as the Queen's favourites loved Majesty, and died for it.

Between these two Elizabeths there lay comparison, or so Bess liked to think. The one whose sovereign power was England and those vast new colonies named after her, presumed, virginity : the other, whose power was planted in a solid part of England, who had amassed wealth, owned many mansions—she rolled their names with relish on her tongue—Chatsworth, Wingfield, Worksop, Rufford, Tutbury, Welbeck, and Hardwick. That too would be rebuilt in her good time.

If the Queen had conquered half the world, had defeated Spanish insolence, held Philip at bay still weaving plots to vanquish her who was invincible, Bess of Hardwick had conquered her husbands, had established *her* sovereign right, to intimidate the Talbots and leave their lands, by intermarriage, to her children. She who saw beneath the whole ridiculous veneer of virgin Majesty, the jewelled raiment, monstrous hoops, dyed wigs and raucous oaths, saw also the woman, bereft of artifice, a heroine, yet unheroic ; vain and petty, vicious, glorious and great. So Bess of Hardwick might have been were she too born the daughter of a King. But even yet —beneath its folded lid, the hawk's eye glinted—even yet she might stand sponsor to a King ! Her thoughts soared upward, higher. She was not the Queen, but she might be the grandmother of one. . . .

The coach bumped and rattled on its way ; the rain swept in. At her side, Arabella cuddled closer in her fur-lined mantle. Was her grandmother fallen in a trance ? So still she sat, and silent as a witch. Arabella crossed her fingers to ward off spells and lurking evil, for you never knew. . . . It were best to be on guard with one so unaccountable and mumpish, who changed from day to day, or hour to hour : who could be gentle-sweet as honey with caresses in the morning, and hide the skin off your back before night : who would have the household call you ' Highness ', ' Princess ', and all this stuff of bowing head to knees when you went out or you came in, and yet would yell at you that ' by God's death, you were the veriest imp that ever was spawned from Satan.' Such oaths, so Arabella had been told, as should be only uttered by the Queen.

How dreary cold, unending was this drive! Conscious of a squeaking in her stomach, Arabella tapped her numbed feet on the rushes and yawned with hunger like a chicken with the gapes, the while her grandmother bitterly reviewed the loss of the Lennox estates. These, stolen from her grandchild by James of Scotland, had been handed, with the title, to the King's favourite and kinsman, that painted mammet, Esmé Stuart, Lord d'Aubigny, on whom he had conferred a dukedom. Nor could all her entreaties and schemes recover one inch of that land, Arabella's by right of heritage. But now, with the girl of marriageable age, she would leave no stone unturned, discard all scruples if need be, to gain her ends. She had hoped—the dream was past, but she had dared to dream it—that the King of Scots would have considered the possibility of a union between himself and his cousin, Arabella. He had played with the idea, and finally renounced it, to cause Bess lamentable shock when he proclaimed his intention of choosing Anne of Denmark. Still, there was time enough to see her ' Jewel ' righted, herself if possible more highly placed. Protectress. Regent. . . . Elizabeth was nearing sixty and ravaged with disease. It was said she had the pox, bequeathed her by her father. If the Queen died : if James of Scotland could be proved an alien by reason of his birth : if the Act of Attainder not yet repealed, should deny him England's throne, why then there was no other but her own beloved ' Jewel ' to ascend it !

The vehemence of her fancy brought a cold dew to her forehead. She took a kerchief from her sleeve and dabbed.

" My lady ! " Arabella touched her knee, excitedly to cry : " My lady ! in the road there ! Look—a hedgehog ! "

To Lady Shrewsbury's cold lips came the glimmer of a smile. Regardless of the rain, Arabella thrust her head over the side of the coach.

" I like," she said, " to poke a hedgehog and see it roll itself into a ball."

" So one might learn from these, the humblest of God's creatures," her grandmother unclosed her lips to say, " dissimulation. An art practised of necessity by Kings and Queens—and hedgehogs."

She shut her eyes, and, smiling still, the lady dozed.

IN view of Lord Shrewsbury's death his widow decided to keep Arabella at Hardwick until January. Although her granddaughter was no blood relation of the deceased, the meticulous demands of complimentary mourning should, and must, be carefully observed. But notwithstanding that Her Majesty had mourned her ' good old man ', and ordered the Court to refrain from any form of entertainment, she herself had gone dancing the day after his funeral. Nevertheless, Lady Shrewsbury was not sending her ' Jewel ' to Whitehall to be deprived of its fullest advantage. Within three months the girl could be presented and convention satisfied.

Ever since the Queen, at her own table had informed the wife of the French Ambassador that the child was her heiress, or words to such effect, Arabella's life had been conducted in accordance with the great future to which destiny—and sovereignty—had called her.

At Hardwick, by her grandmother's command, she was given precedence at every function ; addressed as ' Highness ', schooled as all Princesses of the Blood must be, in languages, living and dead. She conversed very prettily in Latin. The Queen had praised her French when she was twelve. She was now fifteen, yet despite the dose of penny-royal administered daily by her grandmother, she showed no sign of her approaching womanhood. Long-legged as a filly, small-boned, with the awkward grace of unripe youth, she gave promise of some beauty in the exquisite bone structure of her face, the curved blunt-cornered mouth, the perfect skin, and those strangely coloured eyes of hers, not green nor grey, but a mingling of both, gold-flecked. She had a curling mane of gilt-brown hair ; Bess ordered her maids to let it fall loose on her shoulders, and so she seemed younger still.

Lady Shrewsbury did not intend to accompany her granddaughter to London. The Queen had looked somewhat coldly on Bess since the source of those slanderous reports regarding her husband's conduct with the unhappy Mary Stuart, had been so wrongfully ascribed to herself and her ' Imps '. She therefore sent Arabella in the care of William, her second and favourite son ; not Henry. He had been deprived of that honour by reason of his callous behaviour towards his mother during her bereavement. They had, in fact, come to harsh words in respect of the Will and her distribution of the property. He had his own axe to grind—so Bess did not hesitate to tell him—with regard to the portion of Grace, his wife, and the dead Earl Marshal's daughter. Certain jewels that had belonged to Grace's mother, the first Lady Shrewsbury, Bess, very properly, retained. Henry always had been difficult. Beneath his fastidious taste and daintiness of person, he hid, his mother sadly feared, a subtle cunning. His open championship of her late husband, his disregard of all that she had suffered as wife of one who sought—O monstrous !—to divorce her, she who was as unimpeachable in virtue as Lucretia, rankled deep in the heart of Bess. So Henry Cavendish did not go to Court in charge of Arabella.

In addition to Bridget Sherland, Bess had secured the service of a second gentlewoman. The girl must have two ladies in constant attendance, and Anne Bradshaw, who came of good Derbyshire stock, was selected. In her early twenties, and too plain, Bess inferred, to be flighty, she had the dark faithful eyes of a spaniel, a wart on her cheek, was pale and lean and submissive. She would prove a suitable successor to Sherland in the event of that lady's retirement, which in view of certain rumours Bess had gleaned, and that reflected somewhat shockingly on Bridget's private life, might well be expedited. The woman had less reserve in her amorous pursuits than a tom-cat, according to good Mr. Morley's innuendoes. Yes, even to the length of bold intrigue, or so Mr. Morley delicately put it, of ' an interlude ', with Henry. . . . Another reason why her ladyship did not wish him to escort her precious ' Jewel '. But at present Mrs. Sherland could not well be spared. She was required to train that prim and proper Bradshaw in her duties.

So, when all was ready and everything in order, Arabella well-supplied with three dozen new gowns, hats, perfumes, gloves, and costly presents for Her Majesty, Bess sped the parting entourage with final strict injunctions, and Arabella with embraces, on to London.

There had been some changes in the pageant of the Court since Arabella, three years before, was first presented. The Great Armada, with its wreckage, had swept most of the chief actors from the scene. Leicester, the prime favourite, who for five and twenty years had dominated Elizabeth's emotional existence, was dead

So too was Walsingham, her Lord Chancellor; and Sir Christopher Hatton, once so charming and gay, who used to dance so delightfully, was dying. Only Burghley, the moving spirit of her realm, at seventy, remained, and Raleigh, that intrepid rover of the sea who in a few years had been raised to wealth and power, knighted, made a Captain of the Guard, and a Vice-Admiral.

Black-browed, dark-eyed, broad of shoulder, narrow-hipped and tall—Her Majesty had always favoured high men—he knelt, a magnificent figure in bronze velvet slashed with gold at the feet of his goddess, 'Virginia'. He brought her strange offerings from those far-off lands where he had hoisted her flag: tobacco, potato. She sniffed wryly at the one, bit at the other, spat it out and rated him roundly for breaking her teeth, then flung him another estate.

But he, whose quick genius had animated the Fleet that had so recently crushed the Armada, he whose daring exploits had resounded throughout the whole of England, was not proof against the subtle poison of a Court filled with paradoxical discordances, where the Tudor rose of culture bloomed on a dung-hill of tainted scandal that held him like a lion, bound with silken cords, tamed to lap the favour of a Queen. His goddess called him 'Water'. She was always finding nicknames for her Chosen. Other gallants of the Court who may have been misled by a whispered word, a long, low-lidded glance from those, as yet, unfaded eyes, to think himself her next choice, saw in this latest jest of the Queen on Raleigh's name, a dig at a slice of his character . . . 'Weak as Water-Walter', chuckled that daring young spark, Robert Devereux, Earl of Essex, into his sprouting beard.

He was not yet twenty and she was fifty-three, when Elizabeth, who had known him as a child, first began to know him as a man.

His meteoric rise took the wind out of all sails. His audacity delighted 'Gloriana'. Where those others might tremble before her, he stood to argue, cajole, and demand what he willed: Knight of the Garter, Master of the Horse, and he wished now to command the Queen's armies.

The wars that were agitating France, in consequence of the attack by the Catholic League with Paris on its side and Spain for its support against the Huguenot King Henry of Navarre, had caused Elizabeth some qualms. What if the Catholics and her old bugbear Philip were the victors in a Holy War? She saw her kingdom jeopardized, and in self-defence she more than ever rigorously ran to earth suspected Papists. If Henry IV was a pauper he also was a Protestant, and to show her approval she sent him a large sum of money and a small force under Lord Willoughby, which acquitted itself with tremendous success and went a long way to settle the Huguenot King on his throne.

The example of that young hot-head of Navarre, to whom a good fight was better than wine or fair women, fired the youth of Elizabeth's Court. The blaze of excitement that had been kindled by the mighty defeat of the Armada, still smouldered. A party was forming among the more dashing young gallants, led by the favourite Essex. The Spanish had landed in Brittany. The Queen sent an army to meet them. If the Channel provinces passed into Philip's hands they might well be used as a base for another attempted invasion. Henry of France, having agreed to support her, not only failed his word but had the presumption to ask for more English soldiers to come to his aid in Normandy. He named Essex commander of the expedition, and Essex stood with his followers burning to fight, ready to go where he led.

And: ' I love them ' he wrote to his Queen in one of his many extravagant letters. ' I love them for my own sake, and for my virtue's sake. . . . I love them for my country's sake, for they are England's best armour of defence and weapon of offence.'

But though he charmed her heart away with airy words, though she might sit with him all hours of the night while her ' Water ', Captain of the Guard, stood locked outside her door gnawing at his nails; though her long lithe fingers played with his chestnut curls as he knelt at her feet to kiss them, and implore her to send him with his men to France and bring her further glory, Elizabeth stood firm. He must not go. In truth she was so utterly infatuated with her pretty boy that she could not let him go. Though he glower, storm, and sulk, she would be adamant. He *must* not go. . . .

He was still sulking when Arabella, for the first time in her life, met him at the Palace of Whitehall.

*   *   *

On her arrival in London, she was lodged at the town house of Lord Shrewsbury, in Coleman Street. Owing to the recent death of the Earl Marshal and the duties that entailed upon Gilbert, now head of the family, neither he nor his wife, Arabella's Aunt Mary, were in residence to receive their niece. Thus William Cavendish, her temporary guardian, not only took charge of her, but of the whole household as well. In this he was ably assisted by his younger brother Charles.

Both these Cavendishes had been knighted, nobody quite knew why, unless it were that they had charmed the Queen, were handsome, gay, accomplished. Who could tell what whim would sway the fancy of that capricious, indefatigable goddess of the Court, named, not ineptly, Gloriana : she, whose courage and clear-sightedness had overcome innumerable crises, to emerge triumphant in her golden age ? So these two Cavendish brothers may each have captured, for a moment, that wilful, fiery imagination, to rise ' Sir Charles ', ' Sir William ', to lead her in a galliard, to be promised heaven alone knew what rose-coloured fantasies, and then . . . forgotten.

They, however, had their knighthoods, and each had inherited his mother's limitless capacity for taking out of life every ounce, and more, of life's advantage. Their interest, therefore, in their young and royal niece may well have been inspired by consistent optimism. As with their mother, so with them all hope of elevation was centred in this girl, their sister's child.

She, always ready to respond to warmth, adored them. They stood only second in her favour to her Uncle Henry, and him she adored most of all. She was at that age which is lavish with its love ; when ebullient emotion is never quite controlled, when tears well beneath shrill cadences of laughter. None guessed what volcanic upheavals stirred those small flattened breasts under the stiff brocade bodice. While conforming outwardly to pattern, she was tormented by a frightening awareness of herself, and of a world to which it seemed she had but just awakened. The smallest things of sight and sound were multiplied. A bird's song, the lilt of a harp, a drift of snow upon a hillside touched by the reddening sun, would lift her to the skies : a harsh word would cast her to the depths. But she *must* love—everybody. It was sweeter to love than to hate ; she knew no half-way measures, no tolerance of ' liking ', save in the case of Mr. Morley, and him she could almost love because he was such easy game to quizz. She could even love her cousin Mary whose silliness provoked her to a pinch or two, at times. And she loved *dear* Bridget Sherland, for all she could be shrewish and a scold. But the latest candidate for the heart of Arabella was the gentle, undemonstrative Anne Bradshaw. . . .

Arabella's summons to appear before the Queen seemed to be considerably delayed; for although she was commanded to the Court, she had not yet been given the formal invitation without which she could not be received.

She had now been in London over a week and had scarcely been allowed outside the house, though, to be sure, there was no lack of entertainment taking place within it. Friends of her Uncle William, mostly gentlemen but very often ladies, were constantly coming and going and staying till late in the night, drinking and playing at cards. But to these assemblies she was not admitted. By Sir William's order she was kept strictly to her own apartments, and these were dark and gloomy with their low-ceiled rooms and great heavy-tapestried bed. She missed the view from her windows at home; there you looked out on green country, the wide-spreading park and the hills. Here you looked out on a street so narrow you could almost shake hands with your neighbour in the house across the way. But there was always something to see or hear from her casement. Cries of apprentices shouting their wares to deafen you; gaudy signs swinging above shop doorways; the coaches that swept by, and litters bearing haughty high-nosed ladies in wondrous gowns to Moorfields, there to watch the archers at their practice; the ceaseless parade of fine gentlemen in bright slashed doublets and gay shoulder cloaks, with high-plumed hats on their heads and rosettes on their shoes; a troupe of tumbling dwarfs on their way from Bartholomew Fair; a street-singer, or a strolling jester in his cap and bells, and whining beggars exposing withered limbs and horrid sores. To these she would throw a coin or two, and laugh to see them scramble for the money in the dirt.

And then came a day when beneath her window two lads passed, loud in talk together. She leaned out to look after them, and in a trice one had snatched at his sword to threaten his companion.

Arabella called excitedly to Anne: "A street fight! See! They're at it. . . ."

And they were, with clash of steel and a nimble darting this way and that, until the smaller, slighter of the two dropped his blade, clapped a hand to his arm, and doubled himself, squealing.

Arabella, quick with pity, bade Anne: "Bring the poor young gentleman up here. He's hurt."

When Anne hesitated, she stamped her foot. "I *will* have him brought up! I'm sick of sitting here, never speaking to a soul save you and Bridget. Besides, he's wounded and 'tis only Christian charity to tend him. Bring him up."

It happened that Bridget Sherland had gone out that day to pay a call, and Anne was not yet sufficient mistress of herself, or Arabella, to refuse that imperious command. So up the young gentleman came, and with him his friend, who somewhat curtly announced :

"My name, madam, is Northumberland. And my companion, for whose plight I am responsible——"

"Can speak for himself," interposed the other with a flourish. "Stuart. Ludovic, Duke of Lennox, at your service, madam."

Arabella gasped.

"Stuart ? That's my name. Arabella . . . My father was Lord Lennox. So you must be my cousin."

"God's death, Percy, d'you hear that ? " uttered the pale young gentleman ; and down he flopped on a stool in a faint.

Here was a to-do, with Arabella in a great concern, his friend shaking him rudely by the shoulder to tell him : "Go to, you ass ! You can't gull me," and Anne Bradshaw fluttering beside him, to force between his teeth a bitter dose that speedily caused him to revive and knock the phial from her hand, and splutter : " 'Struth, madam, would you poison me ? What evil-tasting stuff is this ? Percy ! Here ! I'm bleeding like a pig."

Whereupon Anne fetched a basin of warm water, rolled up his sleeve, and bathed a very small cut above the elbow that showed barely a trickle of red, for all he set his teeth and whimpered and begged her not to torture him, while his comrade callously pronounced his hurt no worse than a scratch from a pin.

"A scratch do you call it ? " blubbered Lennox, sitting up. "I hope you know you might have killed me."

"Pity I didn't," muttered the surly Northumberland.

"And," Ludovic anxiously examined a trifling stain on his doublet, "my new suit is ruined. You beast ! "

"What," Arabella asked with haste, "was the cause of your quarrel—or mustn't I know ? "

"You may certainly know," stated Northumberland, scowling. "There has been no question of a quarrel. 'Twas merely a chastisement. *That*—" he jerked his thumb in the direction of the huddled Lennox—"was too cocksure about a point in duelling, so to prove *my* point——"

"You drove it in my arm!" piped the Duke. "Ow!... It hurts."

"Serve you right."

"To do me wrong!" Ludovic sprang to his feet. "My lord! You go too far!" And he lunged forward as if to come at his opponent with his fists.

"Not again!" cried Arabella, darting in between them. "You'll only get the worst of it."

"He would indeed," growled Percy, "but that I'd sooner fight a flea."

"Do you hear him?" squealed Lennox. "He called me a flea!"

Arabella smothered a giggle.

"He didn't. He said——"

"He said enough for me to rip his guts—and I will too!"

He made another lunge, this time in attempt to kick the Earl of Northumberland's shins, and would have received retaliation if Arabella had not caught him by the belt and dragged him back.

"For shame, cousin! Where are your manners—to behave so uncivil in a lady's chamber. Sit down. You here, my lord," she directed the glaring Percy to a stool. "And you here, cousin, out of harm's way. I'll sit between, and if you fight, you'll have to fight across me. Anne, if you please bring a flagon of wine . . . And here," she offered her comfit-box, "is something to soften your tempers."

While the Duke refused wine and ate sweets, and the Earl refused sweets and drank wine, Arabella, well-pleased with her success as peace-maker, took stock of her virulent guests.

Ludovic, pink and white as apple-blossom, with flaxen hair and a voice that rang the changes on a treble and a croak, might, though his age was indeterminate, be younger, she decided, than herself. Northumberland, however, was considerably older, with a long stormy face, holes in his hose, and ears that stuck out like a bat's. But his eyes, deeply set in their sockets, were a clear, direct grey, and they looked at you straight, and one could forgive much in a Percy.

Arabella had studied her history. She knew he was descended from the famous Harry Hotspur, but she did not know that his father had been imprisoned in the Tower for conspiring in favour of Mary, Queen of Scots; and that he had been found with his brains blown out and a pistol in his hand and none could tell if it were suicide or murder. Which tragedy might have had effect upon his son to turn him moody as the devil, and suspicious of all men.

It seemed that Ludovic was acquainted with and kinsman of Arabella's cousin, James of Scotland. Here was more of interest and a bond.

"Is His Majesty tall or short?" she wished to know. "And is he handsome?"

"Hideous," said Ludovic, "he slobbers."

"Slobbers?"

"His tongue is too big for his mouth, and when he drinks it all slobbers over. I'm his page, and I have to wipe wine from his beard. . . . Ugh!" He pulled a face, then picked a sugared almond from the comfit-box and nibbled.

"I don't think," Arabella told him primly, "that you should speak so disrespectful of His Majesty."

"I can say what I like. He loves me. My father, Lord d'Aubigny, was his dearest friend. He made him Earl of Lennox first and then a Duke."

"*My* father," said Arabella, growing warm, "was Earl of Lennox. So I should have been the Countess—and not you!"

"I couldn't," tittered Lennox, "be a Countess if I tried. And anyhow the King has favoured *me*."

Arabella reddened to her ears. "Is that why you fainted," she asked him through her teeth, "when I told you my name?"

"I didn't faint."

"Then more shame on you for causing such a fuss."

"Madam," Anne Bradshaw thought it time to intervene. "His lordship was overcome from loss of blood."

"Blood!" Northumberland snorted, set down his cup which Anne had refilled, and leaned forward across Arabella to say: "He has as much blood to lose as a jelly-fish."

"My lord!" Ludovic jumped from his stool, fairly gibbering with rage. "I'll not sit here to be insulted by an oafish, ugly, whoreson——"

"Hush!" cried Arabella. "Cousin! Guard your tongue."

"But he *insulted* me!" shrieked Ludovic. "You heard him! First he cuts my arm——"

"And next time I'll cut it off." Northumberland rose to his feet, fixed his eyes upon them, and delivered his apologia in jerks.

"Madam. I hold myself responsible . . . for my young friend's misbehaviour. I am not fitted to the rôle of wet-nurse. His mother, who resides in Scotland, entrusted me with the unwelcome charge of him at Court. I am recently come from my Northumbrian home, where life is rude. And rough. We are not so pretty in our choice of words as London gentlemen. This one has learned too much of his coarse language—from my tongue. I fear my—guardianship has done him little credit."

"Guardianship!" echoed Lennox wrathfully, "fine guardianship to teach me dice and sword-play, not to mention alchemy. Yes, cousin," he turned to the astonished Arabella, "they call him 'the Wizard' here in London for his knowledge of the stars, and spells and——"

"Hold your peace!" rasped Lord Northumberland. "I beg your Ladyship will pay no heed to his romancing." His gaze shifted upward to rest on Arabella, and behind his scowl she could discern a twinkle. "I thank your Ladyship for your—forbearance, and hope that at the worst you've been—diverted."

"I have indeed," Arabella bubbled into laughter. "I have not been so diverted since last May Day frolics, when my uncle's jester played the fool and walked on his hands upside down! In truth, my lords, you are comedians, and I think would make your fortunes at a fair. But I know," she added in a hurry, "that is far beneath your calling. And I'm happy to have made acquaintance," she glanced from one to the other, "with you both."

Percy bowed. "Madam," a dark flush stained his forehead, "does me too much honour. Undeserved."

"And me too," shrilled the Duke. "I am beholden to you, cousin, for your kindness. I'll return it."

"I look for no return," she answered quickly, "save to trust that I shall see your lordships here again."

Ludovic, cramming comfits in his mouth, scrunched and gulped and asked her: "When do you come to Court?"

She shook her head.

"I do not know. I have been in London these ten days and am not yet invited."

"The Lord Chamberlain," Northumberland said awkwardly, "shall be reminded of your Ladyship's arrival."

"I," Ludovic declared, "will remind the Lord Chamberlain of her arrival. 'Tis my duty to do so. She is *my* cousin, not yours.

I thank you for your comfort, Arabella," he smiled, showing dimples, " and your comfits. But I sadly fear that I have ate the lot."

"You are welcome, Cousin Lennox. This has been a great adventure. I trust your hurt will soon be healed." Then she held out her hand to him; he knelt and took and kissed it.

" 'Tis healed already for your sweetness. . . . Am I pardoned ? "

So prettily and bashfully did he look up at her that, looking down at him, she knew he was.

She watched them from the window walk along the street, Lennox hanging with affection on his elder's arm, in perfect amity together. She stared amazement. Truly the ways of London gentlemen were unconformable. . . . To brangle and spar so crabbed and splenetic, so peevish, ungallant, and moody ; and then in a moment turned shy as two lambs, blushing to stammer, and down on the knee !

Nor could she tell which of the two had most vexed . . . or surprised her. The gauche, gruff-voiced Earl of Northumberland, with holes in his hose, and his clear direct look, yet so sullen : or Lennox, her cousin, who though she admitted was rageful, had the face of a seraph and spoke very dainty, when he ceased at the end to be rude.

Meanwhile, Anne Bradshaw was dismally conjecturing what Mistress Sherland would have to say to this when she returned.

Mistress Sherland had so much to say to ' this ' that Mistress Bradshaw might have found herself without a situation.

" To bring two brawling young cubs out of the street into her Ladyship's parlour ! "

"They were not cah-cubs," sobbed Anne. "They were no-oh-blemen."

"Fine noblemen ! That viper, Esmé Stuart's spawn for one, and a traitor's son for the other. Where's your sense ? "

William Cavendish, at first disposed to uphold Bridget in her outcry against the weeping Anne, changed his tactics the next day when a messenger delivered to the Lady Arabella Stuart an invitation from Her Majesty the Queen.

There was, however, no transcendence of the fact that Mistress Anne had shown a grievous carelessness and failure of her trust, in admitting strangers to the house.

"They weren't strangers ! " loudly insisted Arabella, hot in defence of her Anne, "and I won't have her blamed for my fault. Only think, Uncle William," she sprang from her stool to perch on his knee, " only think ! That he should prove to be my kinsman —my own cousin——"

" Who has stolen your earldom and lands," growled her uncle.

" I don't mind," she answered equably, " and I wouldn't want to live on my land if I owned it. I want to live at Hardwick all my life."

Her uncle pinched her cheek. " You won't say that in ten years' time, I'll warrant."

Nevertheless, he decided this chance introduction could not have been better achieved.

When James of Scotland handed the title and estates of Lennox to his distant cousin, Esmé Stuart, then Lord d'Aubigny, he had, perhaps as a sop to his conscience, suggested Arabella as a future wife for his kinsman's son. The Queen, however, would not hear of any such alliance, nor indeed would Lady Shrewsbury, who had higher aspirations for her ' Jewel '. But William Cavendish now reasoned, if a marriage with a royal European Prince could not be politically effected, Stuart, Duke of Lennox might be reconsidered ; or failing him—young Percy of Northumberland.

*　　　*　　　*

It was Friday the 13th that Arabella went to Court, but anticipatory excitement overcame that ominous portent, though Bridget, who was frankly superstitious, produced, as antidote to evil, an amulet composed of a dried toad-skin stuffed with spice and powdered seed pearls. She tied it on a silver ribbon round Arabella's waist, next to her skin, before she dressed her in the gown her uncle chose : a thick cream silk with velvet sleeves spangled in black—the dress in which she had her portrait painted. A girdle of jewels clasped the prim little square-necked bodice ; her petticoat fell in softest folds over the springing hoop, and the only touch of colour other than her jewels was a scarlet fan that hung from a golden cord. Her hair, drawn back from her forehead, swung long and loose upon her shoulders under a veil of finest lace. She had a triple necklet of pearls and little red shoes with gold heels, and Bridget touched her lips with ruby salve, and vowed there would be none so fair among all those haughty beauties as her Sweet.

Escorted by her uncles, she drove in a coach to the river, thence by barge to Whitehall.

The night was cold, but fair; a young slip of a moon lay on her back among the stars. Arabella furtively turned the silver coins she carried in her purse, and hoped her uncles would not see her bow nine times for luck.

Wrapped in her ermine cloak, she sat in the bows and watched the blossoming lights on either bank. London seemed to be in gala dress under its blue velvet mantle. An impudent breeze, like an invisible urchin, ruffled the water's surface into a million star-lit wrinkles, touched with gold from the flickering torches. Above the stench of Thames refuse she thought she could smell flowers : too soon for primroses, but winter aconites and snowdrops would be peering under hedges, and the breath of them was springlike drifted on the wind from Surrey meads. Other barges passed before, beside, behind theirs, to and fro. Half the town was on its way to the Queen's Palace and the other half come out mid-stream to watch.

So great was the press of river traffic that they had to wait a full half-hour before their barge could be pulled in to Whitehall Stairs ; but for Arabella that was all part of the evening's magic, the air full of whispers and light laughter, and such a wealth of colour and glitter of jewels springing out of the darkness under the torch flares as never was seen. Like brilliant birds of Paradise the ladies and their escorts clustered on the steps, their high-pitched voices drowned by the harsh cries of watermen touting their boats for hire, with an ' Eastward Ho ! ' and ' Westward Ho ! ' to deafen you.

Through the gardens where lanterns swung from the bare trees, twinkling rays of emerald and ruby, topaz and sapphire, to cast a rainbow path across the lawns, she went, keeping close to her Uncle William, and glad of his hand for guidance in that crowd ; and so, by way of a long stone passage lined with men of the Queen's Guard, and through a succession of vast apartments, hung with tapestries and pictures by great foreign masters, they came at last to the Presence Chamber. Here again they were halted by the stream of guests before them, while the Lord Chamberlain called the names of those about to be presented.

She stood there dazzled in the blaze of a myriad candles, and half-sickened by the smell of body-sweat and perfume. Faint

49

strains of unseen music accompanied intermittent scraps of conversation, subdued laughter, rustle of silk, and the unceasing stentorian repetition of the Lord Chamberlain's announcements. She heard her own name called, and those behind pressed forward the better to observe her as she went.

She was not in the least afraid. Why should she be? The Queen had received her kindly on her former visit to the Court. Was not the Queen her cousin, and was she not, too, a Princess of the Blood? But for all that, her heart beat to burst itself under the tight-fitting bodice. Bridget had laced her far too close for comfort. Her head swam. The tapestried walls seemed to dip and curtsy to her; the gold and scarlet uniforms of the Queen's Guard made her blink. She had never seen so many jewels. Everything sparkled. The very curtains were studded with precious stones that gleamed like devils' eyes. Her feet sank into scented woven rushes as she walked. Why did she walk alone? Why did everybody stare? Why was there such a hush, as if the whole Court had been struck dumb?

Then, of a sudden, from the minstrel's gallery in the Great Hall, a boy's voice rose, sweet and gay, singing to his lute. She knew the song—an old one, said to have been sung by King Henry VIII, the Queen's father.

> ' O Love, Love, on thy soul God have mercy
> For as Peter is princeps apostolorum
> So to thee may be said clearly
> Of all fools that ever was, stultus stultorum.'

' Of all fools that ever was!' She must not be a fool and feel so dizzy. She had heard tell that strong men swooned away when they looked upon the Queen: her face shone like the sun, they said.

In a gilded chair raised on a dais, surrounded by her Maids of Honour, roped with pearls, bediamonded, sat Elizabeth. Her gown, alarmingly low-cut, was peppered with jewels in a design of peacock's feathers; an immense collar of stiffened lace rose from her shoulders, leaving exposed her shrivelled throat and bosom; an absurd little miniature crown surmounted her false red hair, dressed high and coquettishly curled.

Yet despite the sagging contours, the harsh lines from nose to mouth, the daubs of paint that pitifully simulated youth to challenge age, the ghost of youth still hovered, lost, forlorn, in this grotesque travesty of maidenhood. It was as if by sheer force of her consummate energy, she, who had been denied the beauty her soul craved, as much as it craved and had won for England a succession of unparalleled achievements, projected now upon external vision a nimbus of her Ego, self-created. Beauty, disturbing, elusive, lay in the movements of her long eager hands, in the fierce blue of her eye where humour lurked and tenderness, and cruelty; and in the firm smiling lips, tight-closed to hide the blackening teeth.

What secret dual personality dominated that extraordinary being whose blade-like intellect and masculine intensity of purpose had fenced with the chicaneries of kings, to turn the fate of Europe : who in a word, a moment, could command the greatest brains of her kingdom, pour out extempore speech in Latin to dismayed ambassadors, and in a second be overcome with flutters, aping the girl to ogle some bewitching boy, avid for his flattery: who swore great oaths, tore her food to pieces with her fingers, roared with laughter at a ribald jest, and yet whose elegance and wit was unsurpassed by any woman of her generation ? Did her childhood's precocious passion for that handsome opportunist, Thomas Seymour, destroy her life's maturity to plant within her roots the restless unassuaged pursuit of love ? Was she a demi-virgin who sublimated famished instinct in the stupendous task of governance ? Or was her life a sham and she a figurehead, reflecting glory through the ages from those master-minds behind her throne ?

None knows, nor ever yet has solved her mystery.

As Arabella, second lady in the land, knelt before the Queen, the piercing eye was veiled behind that painted mask, while the voice, metallic, querulous, bade her : " Rise, girl ! Stand upon your feet. Let us see how you are grown."

Two fingers, gemmed to the knuckles, were thrust under Arabella's nose. She knew that she must kiss them, but at the touch of those shy, soft lips Elizabeth snatched her hand away and repeated : " Stand ! How high are you now ? "

Arabella stood; and the sharp glance under the heavy lids lifted to explore that young lithe body as if to strip it of its clothes. Beneath the glow of candleshine the girl's bare neck and shoulders gleamed, marvellously white, against the harsher white of satin that like the closed cup of a lily enfolded the budding breasts.

"Yes." The Queen nodded her head. "Yes. . . . One day, God willing, you may be comely and of some better shape. As yet you are green. A spring onion!"

There was an instant's pause; the watching Court released, and the child lost, a breath. A lady tittered, and another; the Queen smiled behind her lips. Her Maids of Honour dutifully giggled, and, after that moment's shock, Arabella giggled too. Spring onion. Very comical. . . . And now she was completely unafraid. Her Grace had cracked a joke—never mind at whose expense; and though she blushed at having caused so much attention, Arabella believed she was approved. She curtsied as her grandmother had taught her, low to the ground. The Queen's face relaxed. She said wryly: "'Tis a pretty conceit to laugh at yourself, and one that we might envy. . . . Essex! Take the Lady Arabella to the dance."

From a near group of courtiers one advanced to bow before her. He too wore white, with a touch of red and black—how strange that was to be sure!—as if they had been costumed for a couple in a masque. He was so tall that she must stand upon her toes to reach his arm.

The Presence Chamber faced an archway that led to the Great Hall. From her seat the Queen upon her dais could watch the dancers. The centre of the floor had been cleared of rushes, and the oak polished till its surface was slippery as glass. The bright stiff dresses, flash of jewels, the multi-coloured doublets, formed a brilliant arabesque against that vivid background of tapestry and curtains. The music thrummed a lively measure, and boys' voices sang:

> ' My love, he loves another love
>   Alas, sweetheart, why does he so? . . . '

"*Not* aptly chosen!" murmured Essex, under cover of the song.

She looked up to see him looking down. His eyes, amber-tinted, danced as gaily as his feet. "Who taught you your tricks?"

"Tricks?" . . . She had heard talk of him, but never thought that he could be so young.

"You turned the laugh to yourself, sweetheart. Was it wise?"
This alarmed her.

" Then did Her Majesty make mock of me when she——— "

He interrupted swiftly : " The Queen's humour may not be questioned, Arabella."

> ' Harder heart did never
> Two kind hearts dissever . . .'

sang the minstrels.

Essex hummed the refrain, swung her to him, whirled her round, and left her breathless.

" Arabella " . . . He whispered it as if they shared a secret. " Such a fancy name ! Did fairies attend your christening ? "

She shook her head and answered soberly :

" I have not been told so, but they might have come. My waiting-woman, Mrs. Sherland, says a very small man with grass green hair and squirrels' eyes stood by my cot the night I was born. But I think that she imagined it. I don't believe there *are* such things as fairies."

" I do." His voice teased her. " And I see one now. You dance as light as the queen of them all, and are ten thousand times more beautiful."

Was it true ? Had he said it ? . . . Did she dream ?

" Why," he murmured, watching the colour fly into her face, " have you been kept from us so long ? Does your grandmother wish to spite us that she withholds your Sweetness ? "

The music faded and the dance was done. She curtsied—her foot slipped, and she—O horror !—fell upon her back.

Her shame was worse than death.

She thought she heard the sniggers of those who stared, to jeer. Her farthingale encumbered her recovery ; and the more in the whitening panic of embarrassment she struggled, the more did she know herself abased, until he, for pity, needs must pull her up and dust her down as if she were a toy. And then she saw him laughing, that she must laugh with him in her relief while she stammered her apology. He cut her short.

" But, Madam, you should know that the pas seul par excellence for women, is the chassé horizontale ! And now all the beauties of the Court will match their step to yours. You set the fashion."

And without more ado he tucked her hand in the crook of his arm and walked her away to a window-seat.

There she sat while he leaned against the embrasure and stared at her. She could not meet his eyes, she was so hot. To cool herself, she laid her cheek to the glass of the leaded pane and looked out at the river twinkling below. On the far bank lights shone from Lambeth Palace. Barges lay moored in the shadows. The night was very still out there, and dark and comforting. She wished she could go home. . . . She had no place here in these great noisy rooms, and not a word to say. To stumble and land on your back. To behave so gauche and clumsy. To disgrace herself and her uncles . . . if they watched. She hoped to heaven they did not. He must think her a bumpkin, a gowk. . . . A spring onion.

She heard him laugh below his breath.

"Poor babe! . . ." And down he sat beside her, took her by the shoulders, and turned her face to his. "Why do you hide it? How old—or how young are you, Arabella?"

"I am fifteen, my lord."

"Almost a woman. Yet you look no more than twelve. Will you be a beauty? . . ." (but had he not already said she was ten thousand times more beautiful than the fairy queen?) "I think you never can be plain with those eyes that change their colour like a cat's, and a mouth that's not yet ripe for kisses, but when it is, God help you!"

A hot flame overswept her, to set her tingling with delicious new sensation. Surely to feel so strange was wrong, was sinful. . . . She eyed him with suspicion, not knowing what to make of him, who turned each word to jest, yet sure that she must reprimand him for his insolence. She drew herself up.

"I . . ."

And there she stuck, defenceless, full of trembles. She, who could bait her tutor to a fury, defy her grandmother, order her ladies 'do this', 'do that'—and act as mediator in a brawl— (and where were those two, she wondered with a glance around: no sight of them)—must now be tongue-tied, strangled, with not a word to throw to him who dared to mock her as if she were a wanton, or a woman . . . with a mouth not ripe for . . . She caught her underlip between her teeth and he, watching her, laughed softly.

The musicians in the gallery began to play again. He took her hands and pulled her to her feet.

"Now come dance the galliard."

She swallowed, slid a glance at him, and had it on her tongue to say that she would not. She knew etiquette forbade her to dance twice with the same partner. She should not show him so much favour. . . . His beard was honey-gilded, and he handsome as a god. If only she were older, or did not look so young! And as if he read her thought he stooped his head to whisper in her ear: "Come, sweet, though you look twelve, you'll soon be twenty. What would you say to me if you were twenty now?"

What indeed? That he presumed too far above himself? That his state was below hers, that his arrogance offended? But it didn't. Her agitation deepened to the knowledge that his words, his looks, his touch, were sheer enchantment: he a wizard, and herself bewitched, dissolved in ecstasy. O shameful! Shameless! . . . From head to toe she burned, and all the while he watched her with eyes narrowed, lips provocative, and tilted upward in his silent laugh.

"Well? Why do we wait?"

His eyebrows followed the upward tilt of his lips like the wings of a bird in flight.

As he led her out, one barred their way and stood before her bowing.

"So your Ladyship has come to Court."

She knew him in a second. And what a transformation! Nothing now of the slubberdegullion in his dress; his doublet, cloth of gold, his hose impeccable, his hair trimmed and his ruff starched; indeed he looked himself to have been starched, so stiffly he stood to attention.

"Your lordship has already been presented to the Lady Arabella?" the lazy voice of Essex intervened.

"Yes." The young man flushed; and Essex smiled.

"Too sad that you're too late, my lord. Her Ladyship dances with me."

Northumberland glowered, darkening.

"I would not aspire to supplant my Lord of Essex," he sullenly rejoined. "But I claim the right—to pay my duty—to her Ladyship."

While he was nothing of a courtier, raw and red, and the junior of him who now held highest place of any man in England, he would not be put down because Essex was set up; nor could

Arabella like him less for that, but she did not wish to be the subject of contention. So:

"May I not," she offered, anxious to placate, "dance with you both, my lords?"

"There is no dance performed—in public," Essex drawled, "that can share in equal parts a lady's favour. Madam, you must choose."

She was in great trouble now. To choose. . . . There could be no question of choice, and she knew it: and Northumberland knew it, and Essex, Prince of Court charmers, he knew it, to some maids and all women's undoing. What then possessed her at this moment to deny her heart's assertion? Was it an impish streak of mischief, or instinctive coquetry aroused, to play the one against the other?

"*I* crave the honour, Arabella, of this dance," shrilled a boy's treble voice at her side.

Thankfully she turned to see Ludovic, resplendent, making a leg in full rig of turquoise and silver—his hair shining gold, his face tinted, his lips reddened and shaped to a cupid's bow, and such a mincing grin upon his face that she must laugh to see it. Her laughter broke the discord and pealed above the music as it faded to its end.

"The dance is over," said Essex, very cool.

The group was now attracting some attention. Couples, dispersing towards an inner room where refreshment was laid, paused to watch and whisper. Ladies smiled behind their fans, and William Cavendish muttered to his brother, "I'll swear she's not so green as Her Grace will be green-eyed!"

Her Grace was watching, to tap a toe upon the dais and her nails on the chair-arm; to lift the jewelled pomander, shaped like an orange, that dangled from her waist and to sniff it while she flashed an eye at those around her; to rise and step down among her company who formed an aisle as she passed through the arch-way, into the Great Hall, her Maids of Honour following behind her like white birds: the doves of Venus.

The musicians tuned their viols; the harpist struck a chord, and Essex bowed to Arabella. "Madam, may I have the honour now?"

"No, you may not!" All heads were turned, every voice but Elizabeth's hushed. With lips drawn back, forgetfully, to show her darkened teeth, her words grated through the silence of the room. "*We* wish to dance. . . ." And to the minstrels' gallery,

she raised a hand and called: " To your recorders, gentlemen !
We will dance the passamezzo."

The company stood apart to watch, Arabella, agape with
admiration, between Essex and Northumberland. Her Majesty
appeared to be transformed. Not now an horrific old creature
with rouge in her wrinkles and her head in a wig, but a nymph,
radiant and lissom, swaying, bending, turning, with eyes up at
his lordship, pointing the toe, eyes down to the curtsy and round
at her guests in a look that commanded approval. They gave it
freely ; not a maid nor matron present could excel the Queen in
grace. As the dance ended the murmurs of applause rose to a
crescendo. The Queen, all smiles, nodded gratified acknowledg-
ment and kissed her finger tips to sycophants who fawned. The
air was full of compliments. . . . " A miracle wrought by God,
Heaven-sent to joy us. Diana skims the stars to out-skip Terpsi-
chore ! "

This staggering impromptu, spoken for all the room to hear,
was uttered by one who had his eye on a clear field to favour :
one who set his worth high above that of Essex, his good friend ;
higher even, and more worthy to step into his uncle Burghley's
shoes than Burghley's son, the dwarfish, hump-backed Cecil.

Exquisite, academic, delicate of feature, artist in life and living,
Francis Bacon, whose fulsome flattery tripped no less a graceful
measure on his tongue than ' Diana's ' foot upon the floor, knelt
to kiss the ground on which she walked. Essex raised an eyebrow.
Did the fellow think he could add wine to ' Water ' by pantomimic
repetition, or something near to it, of that apocryphal affair of
Raleigh's cloak ? Which, if it had actually occurred, neither he
nor Francis could remember, since each was in his nursery at the
time. Howbeit, his performance now occasioned a sensation to
arrest ' Diana's ' progress. Her eye lingered, and then languished.
. . . A handsome youth, of gentle mien, and charming diction.
She had heard some talk of him. Had he not a flair for poesy,
or was it politics ? His appearance, too, so point device. . . .

Her smile stayed.

Another conquest ? Jealously asked those who had aspired,
to be sunk.

Elizabeth passed on, and Essex imperceptibly exhaled.
Whew ! . . . For a moment he had thought Her Grace might, in this

57

happier mood, have called for a sword to knight him where he grovelled, the posturing ass!

But Her Grace had forgotten his name. She was later to remember it, for all posterity.

The music played again, partners formed to take their places for a round dance, the Antick Hay. Arabella was partnered with Northumberland, Lennox with a sulky-mouthed golden girl, a Maid of Honour, whom he presented to Arabella as Mistress Elizabeth Throckmorton.

Though Lennox stepped, Arabella granted, gracefully enough, he looked for all the world like one of those little toy manikins dressed as courtiers in tinsel, and sold by street vendors for two-pence: and he was too small and a deal too young for Mistress Throckmorton, whose height and figure overpowered him. Moreover, the lady's eyes were for ever straying, till it seemed a signal passed of smiles, and of eyebrows twitched and shoulders shrugged, between herself and a distant gentleman who leaned against a pillar looking on.

"Who is he?" inquired Arabella of Northumberland. "I seem to remember his face."

Sir Walter Raleigh, she was told.

Well, to be sure! She had sat next to him at supper with Lord Burghley. How splendid he was, how haughty and grand with his black beard, and those sombre dark eyes. A noble gentleman, in brown velvet and gold and the handsomest legs in the room.

And now, notwithstanding that Northumberland moved unwieldy and slow as a cart-horse, trod on her toes, breathed down her neck, perspired till the sweat took the starch from his ruff and moistened her palm, she was happy: the music rollicking, and the dancers joining their chorus to the minstrels'.

'. . . She thumped it on her way
With a sportly hey de gay.'

Hands across, twice round, back again, twirl about, two singles, set and turn, round again. . . . Repeat!

Arabella laughing, panting, dragged her partner by the hand, prancing on before him down the length of the Great Hall. "Hurry! We are all behind. . . . *Hey de gay, hey de gay*!" And down to curtsy.

Pouf!

She rose from the bob with a stitch in her side, her colour high, and her lace veil round her neck instead of on her hair. "Mercy me! I've lost a bodkin. Never mind. . . ." For he was crawling on his hands and knees to find it. "How you are hot, my lord!"

He was; but not wholly from exertion. He took his handkerchief and mopped his face and got upon his feet and mumbled: "I hope to find your bodkin when this crowd clears from the floor. Can your Ladyship describe it?"

"'Twas of gold filigree, set with seed pearls, but no matter. I've another that will hold my veil in its place." And she made attempt to rearrange the length of gossamer. "A curse upon the thing! Can you?"

Too much to ask of him. His fingers shook and were entangled in the lace; his forehead oozed. She laughed. "I' faith, your lordship has ten thumbs! Well, I must go uncovered."

As she removed the second bodkin from the veil, her hair, glinting in the candleshine as if gold dusted, tumbled curling round her face. She loosed a sigh. "I'm thirsty."

"There is," he tore his eyes away from her, "refreshment in the Ante Room. Will your Ladyship . . .?"

"Indeed I will. I could drink a hogshead."

They found the Ante Room deserted but for the servants— and the Duke of Lennox. Arabella asked for orange water, and Ludovic, critically picking over silver dishes laden with sugar-meats, fruit, cakes, and eringo—the candied root of sea-holly— vouchsafed in whispers: "I warn you, there is never much variety, nor much of anything to choose from here. Her Grace is more ready to receive, than to offer entertainment. Do you like ginger-bread?"

While Arabella admitted that she did, she felt bound to reprimand him.

"You should not say, even if you think such things."

"What things?"

"That Her Grace—" she pursed her mouth, and Lennox, filling his with marchpane, finished the sentence for her.

"That Her Grace is close-fisted? So she is—as everybody knows."

"O, do hush!" Arabella cast a nervous glance at the wooden-visaged lackeys. "Suppose we should be overheard?"

"Who is to overhear—save my good friend Percy?" And he bestowed a hideous grimace on that gentleman, who now returned with a servant bearing cups upon a salver.

Ignoring Ludovic's attention: "Orange water for your Ladyship," he offered glumly; and filled a beaker of canary for himself.

"This," Ludovic was nibbling a stick of eringo, "is good. The first bite may be bitter, but 'tis tasty. Have some."

Arabella had some, agreed that it was tasty; and had more.

"Shall I tell you a secret?" With a sly glance at the smouldering Northumberland, he put his lips to Arabella's ear. She drew away and frowned at him.

"I wish you wouldn't whisper."

"I'm not whispering. . . . Look at Percy, how he glares. Do you know that old mangy lion in the Tower, whom they call Edward the Sixth? Well! Isn't our friend here the very spit of an old lion with the mange? All of an itch and full of growls. But let me tell you," giggled Ludovic, "for he's so modest, that *he* never will—he is a poet!"

"*Are* you, my lord?" Arabella asked, impressed.

She thought indeed he must be, for only a literary genius could sit so silent and so moodish, and withal so patient, to be baited even more than she would dare bait Mr. Morley. But when to her question he turned an eye upon her with that of gloom and wrath in it to make her flinch, she added hastily: "'Tis wonderful to be a poet. Do you know Mr. Spenser? And have you read ' The Shepherd's Calendar'? 'Tis excellent good verse."

"Your Ladyship mistakes," he answered harshly. "I am not a poet."

"Yes, he is," insisted Ludovic, wide-eyed. "He is a man of *greatest* parts. You wouldn't think it by his rough outside which belies his inner Muse, but I assure you he possesses the most delicate perception! I wish that you could read a verse inscribed to *whom* I must not say, but 'tis dithyrambic. All of his heart, which is pierced by a dart on account of a lady, fairer and rarer, whose name it is Ara . . . *Ow!*"

This abrupt termination of the recitative was occasioned by an icy shower of canary wine flung full in Ludovic's face. His pent exasperation thus relieved, the sorely-tried Northumberland bowed to Arabella, turned upon his heel and left the room.

"Dear, dear!" cried Arabella in a state, "his lordship *is* irascible, no question."

"Irascible!" shrieked Ludovic, "he is a fiend! You do not know to what extent he rages. Small wonder they name his family the Fighting Percys. . . . Here, you!" he turned to a grinning lackey, "bring me a napkin. Quick!"

The fellow hurried to obey. Ludovic snatched the damask from him, and: "Let me wipe you," Arabella offered kindly, for he presented now a parlous spectacle. Tears of rage gushed from his eyes and mingled with the wine-drops on his cheeks; his cupid's bow was blurred, his lace ruff limp, his brand new doublet spattered.

"The whoreson swine!" he stormed. "I'll tell my mother how he has misplaced her trust. I'll not lodge in his house at Blackfriars—not I—another night! I'll take myself and my servants to the Mermaid Inn. The Filth! The Buzzard! I'll see him sizzle on a grid for this, I will! The King of Scots shall hear how I'm insulted. He'll be brought to the block. My father would turn in his grave to know his son was so scurvily used. My father was his friend, but I am now his enemy! I'll make him pay with his own blood for every drop of *this* he's spilled on me. By God, I will!"

"Indeed," Arabella dried his face and straightened her own, "he is most wickedly to blame. But cousin, so are you. In truth you plagued the poor gentleman to that extent I wonder he did not clap your ears. After all, he is your elder."

"Not so much my elder. He looks older than his age."

"And you look a deal younger than yours."

Ludovic folded his lips.

"I do not tell my age."

"And I don't wish to know it," retorted Arabella, "but I'll warrant you are old enough to have learned yourself more sense. . . . Your ears are wet."

And so vigorously did she scrub them that he wrenched himself away, indignantly to splutter: "So you maltreat and turn upon me too! . . . My suit is spoiled."

She gave his shoulders a none too gentle shake. "'Tis only your complexion that is spoiled, and that can soon be renewed—from a paint-pot."

"Cousin." He drew himself up to his very small height. "I resent the implication that I paint."

"Well, don't you?" she persisted, cruelly.

He wrinkled his nose at her, grinning.

"No. My valet paints me. He's an artist. My father—God rest his soul—brought him back with him to England when he returned from Paris. In Paris all young gentlemen are rouged." He smoothed his curls. "I wish I had a mirror. Do I look a fright?"

"Yes," said Arabella, giggling, "to scare the crows. I've seen your double stuck on two sticks in a barley field."

Ludovic flushed scarlet.

"'Pon honour, cousin, if you were not a girl——"

"More's the pity I am." And now she did not make attempt to hide her laughter, "for I'd love to squash your prettiness flat with one blow from my fist—if I dared—but I daresn't!"

"Would you so! I'll wager you'd dare more than that." He gaped at her, half-admiring, half-incensed, and wholly captivated. "I wish you *were* a boy. What games we'd have together! Will you marry me?"

Her mouth fell open with the shock of this.

"Will I . . . *marry* you!" she gasped, "and you scarce out of swaddling clothes!" Her laughter pealed again. "Lord-a-mercy, cousin, you must be crazed."

"With love of you I am—i'faith I am," he earnestly assured her, "and think! You would redeem your title and estates, and I would have you as my friend for life. You may call me Ludo. All my friends call me Ludo." His eyes sparkled. "I'll write tomorrow to my King. If he gives consent we will not have to ask Her Grace. We are both Scottish."

"I am not," said Arabella proudly. "I am English."

"Why," his jaw dropped, "so you are—born on English soil. I had forgot. But what of that? We can still marry."

"Yes, but not each other."

'Ludo' seized her hand and squeezed it hard.

"Nevertheless, I've asked you first. I am not yet a man, but when I am I'll ask for you again."

She smiled upon him. Sure, the boy had charm. . . . He had, indeed, that siren charm of the Stuarts, bequeathed to every one of their line, save the King of them all in Scotland.

"I thank my lord and cousin for the honour," she said demurely, "'Tis the only offer I have ever had."

"So *you* think," he answered darkly. "But I know better, for I keep my ears wide open; and that is one advantage in looking very young, since," he smirked, "one's elders never heed a little boy. I can tell you," he continued, narrowing his eyes and looking at that moment, Arabella thought, not very young at all, but very old, "that you have half a dozen foreign princes on their knees before the Pope, praying him for his consent to wed you. . . . You may not know it, but you are the most desired of princesses in all Europe."

She was sure now that he raved, and told him soothingly, "You're overwrought. You had best go to your bed."

"Not I, my dear," he dimpled, "with no bedfellow. I'm going to dance with you."

"No, we'll go seek my Lord Northumberland, and you," she told him firmly, "will apologize."

"*He* will!" flared Ludovic; then, coaxingly, he kissed her finger-tips and turned her hand palm upward in his own, and kissed that too. "Dear cousin, though you're bitter, like eringo, you *are* sweet! Come, dance with me."

But they found the dancing over, the Queen retired to her room, no sign of Northumberland, and her uncles waiting in the Hall, none too pleased at the delay, to take her home.

Back again along the waterway where all lights, save that of stars, had died upon the darkness and the voices of the wherrymen were silent; homeward through the solemn night, bereft of colour now, and any sound beyond the plash of oars and whispers, close, confiding, in the mutual security of secrets hushed beneath the ghostly canopies of barges; homeward, dazed and drowsy, cuddled in her cloak, just a little sad with the aftermath of jollity, went Arabella.

Opposite her in the stern, her Uncle William dozed, and her Uncle Charles, full of wine and half-unconscious, snored. The boatman had to haul him out as if he were a sack, to deposit him inside the coach that awaited their arrival at the Bridge.

"A lovely night," sighed Arabella, her head upon the pillow. "A night for fairies". . . .

And a night for dreams, in which she, very strangely, danced with one whose face was hidden, but she saw him dressed in white with a touch of red upon him: red as blood. And he offered her to eat of eringo, the sea-holly. "You'll find the first bite bitter, though 'tis sweet, and may, God willing, make you comely, and of some better shape. . . ."

She stretched her hand to take it and screamed to find the titbit was no tastier than a spring onion . . . and as green.

Chapter Three

FOUR months she stayed in London, yet so swiftly did the days follow one another, it was as if she had but just arrived in Town when the time came for her to leave it.

With the quick adaptability of youth she had accepted her exuberant new life as one accepts a climate. True, the wayward royal temperature might, and did, blow hot and cold to smile or frown upon this Tudor bud, who, all innocently, had become a source of irritation in the constant prick of its reminder that the choice of England's future Sovereign must lie between a fifteen-year-old girl, and Mary Stuart's son. And certain too, the Queen did not bestow upon her any favour ; had in fact, before the Court, to Arabella's lasting shame, seen fit to reprimand her on that not-to-be-forgotten one occasion, when, prompted by her Uncle William, she had taken precedence at Greenwich Palace before all other ladies on the way to Chapel, following behind the Queen's train-bearers that Her Grace must turn and order the Master of the Ceremonies to send her to the tail of the procession. And there were other grievances, such as that most deplorable occurrence when on a gala night, which included among the guests the Kings of Denmark and Sweden, Arabella had appeared in a new satin gown of amber and gold with a border of pearls, to be told by the Queen in whose Privy Chamber she was honoured to sup, that she would not be permitted to sit down at table in so unbecoming a dress. The shade, the Queen vowed, turned her bilious. . . . All those who heard laughed : Arabella retired, and went home in tears with her uncle.

Nor did the offer, too rashly made in attempt to console, that he take her to the playhouse incognita, masked, to see a young player of the name of Will Shakespeare, whose performance had been praised by Mr. Bacon—meet with any response, nor blot out her dreadful disgrace. She cared not a button for players. She wanted to sup with the Queen, and later to dance with Lord Essex. . . . She would go to no plays, but to bed ; which she did, to cry herself sick with her hurt.

Yet despite these jars and transgressions, and the disconcerting moods of the goddess who presided over Arabella's destiny, she was never more than temporarily affected by caprice. The gossips, however, were vastly entertained. Those Cavendishes—so set above themselves to push to the fore this royal sprig of theirs, had been pushed back ! And well deserved. One would think to hear them that the Lady Arabella was already God's Anointed. It could not be too pleasing for Her Grace to know her spoken of, and in full company, as ' Highness '. But what made Her Majesty mad as jumping beans, her Maids of Honour whispered, was when my Lord of Essex turned his eyes upon the Lady Arabella. Yes, and he would lead her once too often to the dance. " Nor not my Lord of Essex only." This from Bess Throckmorton, " What of Henry Percy of Northumberland ? I'll warrant she has led *him* to the dance, to set him up as rival to her kinsman, that little painted puppy, Ludo Lennox."

Then was it true, the others asked her eagerly, that Percy of Northumberland had dared approach her uncle for her hand ? Yes, it *was* true. Mistress Throckmorton had it from Sir Walter, and he if anyone, should know. These Percys had the daring of the devil ! Would she take him—or rather would the Queen permit she take him ?

The Queen emphatically would not; and sent her Lord Treasurer to call upon Sir William.

Seated there before him in his black velvet doublet, his silver hair like a halo round his head, the saintly old gentleman laid the flabbergasted William on the rack.

Did Sir William know that Lord Northumberland had offered his addresses ?

Sir William did not know, expressed surprise, was shocked. Could Lord Burghley doubt him ? Would he have kept such matter of importance to himself and risk Her Grace's disapproval ?

Lord Burghley stroked his long white beard, the while his frosted eyes searched the eyes of William Cavendish in a deep probing look. Then into his beard Lord Burghley dropped a smile.

65

"Needless to say, Sir William, you never would encourage a betrothal that had not first passed the sanction of Her Grace."

"Betrothal!" William, goggling, thumbed his lip. "There has been no talk of a betrothal. She is yet a child. He——"

"Is of an age," interposed Lord Burghley, with a downward glance at his shoes, and in one of them he twiddled a toe against a twinge of gout, "when," he proceeded smoothly, "youthful ardour comes to boiling pitch. And when a young man, uncurbed, hot-headed, who since his earlier vicissitudes in Paris has lived the life of a recluse, deep in alchemistic interests and research, a young man whose head is in the stars and who studies, I am told, astrology, tells horoscopes, writes verse," again that hidden smile, "when such a one forsakes his fortress in the wilds of the North, to plunge into the delights—and delusions of the Court, he is like to take love's fever somewhat hardly."

"The dissembling cub!" burst forth the worried William, "to put me in this awkward plight. I swear upon my oath, my lord, that I had not a notion, nor, I'll stake my life, has her High —hum—has Arabella, that the lad is so inclined."

"The young lady," said Lord Burghley, soft as silk, "shows a delightful, shall we say, insouciance towards the admiration she arouses in . . . *all* sexes."

"H'm!" William rubbed his nose. "She has lived so guarded in my mother's care that she appears, and is, much younger than her years."

"Which being so," agreed his lordship gently, "it might be well to remove her from importunate propinquity until she shall attain her years," he hesitated, "of . . . discretion."

William gave a start that almost jumped him from his chair.

"My lord! Am I to understand Her Grace desires the Lady Arabella be——"

"Safeguarded."

Lord Burghley rose from where he sat, and so did William. It was his turn now to search that old, cold face, which screened heaven knew what of cunning and of courage; of ceaseless unswerving devotion to his country's cause, and to his Sovereign who so aptly named him 'Spirit'. He was: her guardian spirit, without whose guidance, she, and the England that she loved as never had she loved a man, might have sunk, a rudderless ship, on the tidal wave of war and political crises. And now she sent

im here, or was he come of his own choice, to point sheathed
barbs in silken threats—at whom? At Arabella? At his mother,
t himself, or at his schemes and dreams? Was he friend or foe,
or prophet? He might well be one, with that patriarchal beard
nd so disarming courtesy, that held God alone could tell what
depths of guile.

William cleared his throat, "Your lordship——"

His lordship raised a hand; and William, uncomfortably, was
silenced.

"I think, Sir William, you must know with what deep affection
nd esteem Her Grace regards the Lady Arabella. It is not only
because an amorous youth has professed himself inflamed by, and
desirous of her Ladyship's manifold attractions——"

And watching that calm, narrow face, William thought: The
old fox! Whose tail now is he twisting?

"But," Lord Burghley continued, "there are other reasons
why her Ladyship should be returned to Hardwick."

"Reasons?"

It was as if this old man with his white beard, cold eyes, and
oily words were weaving spells about him to lull his senses and
deprive him of his wits.

"I put it to *your* reason, sir," and behind those mellow tones
could be discerned a sting. "There has been talk for some time
past of foreign powers and their interest in the Lady Arabella.
The Prince of Parma still remains . . . persistent."

"I trust, my lord, that you—that we—that all attempts from
that direction have been crushed. Such a marriage would be as
odious to us as to Her Majesty."

"Worse than odious, Sir William. Dangerous!"

William began gently to perspire. Anyone would think that *he*
was responsible for Popish interference on the subject of his
niece's marriage, and, moreover, plotting to deliver her into
an enemy's hand. The Prince of Parma. . . . What to gain from that,
save Philip's favour and the Pope's? Did Burghley take him for
a traitor—or a fool?

"My lord," William stood up very straight to look the Lord
Treasurer full in the eyes, nor did his own falter for the chill of
the look returned. "May it please you, deliver to Her Majesty my
assurance, which speaks as well for my mother and my brothers,
that we would sooner take with our own hands our beloved

67

child's life than see her allied to any foreign Prince, no matter he
be Catholic or Protestant, nor any man save him whom Her Grace
may choose."

And William sat down again.

Lord Burghley nodded, passed a hand over his lean cheeks as
if to wipe them clear of all expression, and turned to William a
face empty as a mask.

"Sir, may I know if you have heard tell of one who lodge
in the neighbourhood of your good mother's house at Hardwick ?
The name, I think, is Harrison."

"Harrison ?" A sinking sensation occurred in William's
stomach. What in Hades was the old man after with his questions ?
"Yes, my lord, I know him; or rather I know of him. He is the
brother of a neighbour who, from time to time, he visits."

"Is that so ?"

"A seminary, I believe." William knotted his slender brows
"I have not seen him."

"A seminary . . . Ah!" remarked Lord Burghley; and
placing his finger-tips together he nodded over them. "A seminary
That proves his worth as scholar."

On the first finger of the Lord Treasurer's right hand flashed
a ruby, which in the leaping firelight looked like a small red eye
William stared at it, and boiled. Was it his lordship's policy to
play him like a fish upon a hook ? To land him into this unhappy
circumstance without a word of warning. . . . Harrison !

"I swear that I know nothing of this Harrison," said William
urgently, "save what local talk may give, which as your lordship
will appreciate, goes in at one ear," his smile was a trifle sickly
"and out at the other."

"May I suggest, Sir William, that should any talk, local or
otherwise, regarding this same Harrison, be overheard, you will
close your ears upon it—for retention."

But William would have no more veiled innuendoes from this
muted trumpeter, the Queen's mouthpiece. If such were his
intent, then be damned to it! Come out into the open, he
prayed silently, for God's—or Arabella's sake. If she stood in
danger who but he had the first right to know it ?

"My lord, you speak in riddles. I am, *pro tem.*, my niece's
guardian. If you have any knowledge concerning her that you
withhold from me, I crave your confidence."

68

Again Lord Burghley nodded above his finger-tips, and the red eye of his ring sent out a ray, red-tinged.

"Such knowledge as I have," he said quietly, "is surmise. But I repeat her Ladyship must be safeguarded."

William held his patience.

"She never stirs outside the house, unless attended by her gentlewomen or her tutor."

"A Mr. Morley, I believe?"

"Yes, my lord." The old ferret! So he knew that too. "A scholar of Cambridge University, and Master of the Classics. A man in whose trustworthiness we have the utmost faith."

"Sir William," the old gentleman stood over him, tall, lean, and very courteous, "I too, in my time, have had faith in the trustworthiness of those about me—and in highest office. Yet I have learned from my experience that the most virtuous may sometimes be pursued by vicious means."

"Does your lordship insinuate that——"

"Insinuation, sir," Lord Burghley interrupted, "is the devil's rhetoric; not mine."

Give the devil his due, thought William wryly. Spare your rhetoric, speak what you know. But he said: "My lord is a great diplomat, the greatest that our country to this date has ever seen." And his eye, unflinchingly, met that of his inquisitor, who smiled.

"Sir, you honour me above my state. I ask no more than that my work shall be well done. I may be over-zealous," his smile, not now hidden, broadened under the drooping moustache, "a meddlesome old busybody, poking my nose into affairs that are beyond my province. Let my excuse be that I believe my time of service must soon, perforce, be ended. . . . No, Sir William, let us not deny it. I have lived my threescore year and ten, and all I ask of God and of myself is that when I do retire, I shall leave my Sovereign's house in perfect order."

"Indeed, my lord, no doubt of that," said William, moved; and he was reminded, oddly, of a withered tree that stood in the orchard at Hardwick. His mother had forbidden the gardeners to cut it down, for every spring one branch upon its bare limbs blossomed, silver-white. And thinking of that tree, he bowed his head and took that wrinkled blue-veined hand outstretched to him, in his, and wrung it, closely.

"I thank your lordship for your trust and for your warning. The Lady Arabella shall be more than ever—watched."

Lord Burghley made as if to speak, but reminded of his toe he winced instead, and went limping to the door. There he turned.

"Of all infernal visitations," he said blandly, "I think the gout the worst."

William expressed himself concerned to see his lordship such a sufferer. "The waters of Buxton, I am told, if not a lasting remedy, do bring relief."

His lordship twinkled.

"A more drastic treatment is to refrain from drinking wine, so Dr. Lopez tells me."

"Lopez?" The name was new to William.

"Her Majesty's physician. A Portuguese Jew, fled from Spanish persecution. Very gifted. Quite a necromancer in the mysteries of medicine, if science and magic march together—which being two lines, neither parallel," the Lord Treasurer covered his head with a black velvet cap, "must be, as Euclides would demonstrate—absurd. My duty, sir."

"Your lordship's servant."

But as the door closed upon his visitor, William stood for a full minute gazing at it blankly, biting at his thumb, before he rang a bell to summon Bridget.

*   *   *

While news went buzzing up and down the Court that Her Majesty had commanded the Lady Arabella to return to her Derbyshire home, speculation fluctuated as to whys and wherefores. Was it because Lord Essex had been heard to declare that only a gazelle could match the girl in grace, and that were he not already pledged he might be tempted to aspire? Or was it because Northumberland already had aspired, to be firmly reprimanded for his impudence, and now sought consolation in his studies?

These, so rumour gave it, were concerned with casting spells. Small wonder he had earned the name of 'Wizard Earl'. In the new house he had bought at Blackfriars he had a room fitted with strange devices, maps of the moon designed by himself, signs of the zodiac painted on a frieze, and all kinds of scientific instruments. He dabbled in potions, claimed alchemistic knowledge, neglected his estates, and was greatly addicted to tobacco: that the worst of all. His rooms, it was reputed, stank of the evil-smelling herb which he smoked to soothe his temper, not of late improved by Her Majesty's rejection of his suit to Arabella. Moreover, some said he was in favour with the Pope, and that alone would damn him in the eyes of England's Queen, to say nothing of his presumption in daring to approach Lord Burghley for the hand of Her Majesty's cousin, even though she were a cousin twice removed. But all hope of that, according to the Maids of Honour, had been effectually quashed by the Queen's dismissal of ' Her Highness ' from the Court.

The Queen doubtless realized, so went the whispers, that the Earl was indirectly descended from Warwick, the Kingmaker, and if allied to one so near the Throne as Arabella Stuart, he, or his heirs, might prove a future menace. It looked as if Her Majesty were determined to consign the Lady Arabella to spinsterhood, at least for so long as Her Majesty lived. Had she not refused the match broached some years ago by the Earl of Leicester between his son, the three-year-old Lord Denbigh, and her Ladyship ? And heaven knew how many foreign princes, not to mention James of Scotland, had been cast out by Majesty's command. . . . "Poor girl ! Too bad that she must sit and spin her life away with that abominable old witch, her grandmother, at Hardwick," twittered the Maids of Honour, who may have a little envied the attention paid to one so young and far above themselves in rank : whose gowns had cost a fortune, and whose hair was natural curling, not frizzled and not dyed, according to the fashion : who was as simple in her manners as a dairymaid, and yet had caught the fancy of every man—and boy—whom she contacted.

"And so would you, my love," Bess Throckmorton confided to one Margaret Ratcliffe, who despite that she appeared in a new ' whyte sattin gown all embrodered upon good cloth of silver ', which cost her father a hundred and eighty pounds, had not created near so much furore as did the Lady Arabella in the amber velvet that the Queen had so disliked. "Yes, so would you—and I—if we were pushed to the fore for our royal blood, which after all is but a drop distilled from her great-great-grandfather, and come to that "—Bess Throckmorton had it on the most reliable authority— "there was some question of the girl's bar sinister, by reason of the Lady Margaret Lennox having for a time been bastardized by her uncle, that dreadful old horror, Henry VIII."

But then he was rather given to clamping the bar sinister on his nearest relatives, as witness his own daughter. . . . Well! least said of that *now* the better.

Thus these damozels, who so eagerly made cat's-meat of every scrap of gossip to which they could apply their dainty claws, tearing it shred by shred until its flavour staled, and they searched around for fresher stuff to chew. They were soon to have their bellies full of spice, that, caught up and tossed hither and thither and out of the Court, rolled in city gutters gathering more dirt at every street corner, and in every inn and tavern, to be finally exploited by the Globe Theatre Players in gags upon the stage. . . . My Lord of Essex had been discovered clandestinely married to Sir Philip Sidney's widow, the daughter of Sir Francis Walsingham!

What would Her Grace say to this?

What indeed? Her trembling Maids looked to see the roof of Whitehall Palace torn from its rafters and flung into the Thames, so forceful was the state of outraged Majesty.

Doctor Lopez hurried to concoct a soothing draught. And in humbler quarters, along Southwark way, a high-browed, solemn-faced young play-actor, who it was said himself wrote verse though not of much distinction, convulsed his friend Kit Marlowe and other cronies at the Mermaid, with the daring and extempore observation that, " the Lady would be well advised to :

' Sigh no more, men are deceivers ever,
One foot on sea and one on shore,
To one thing constant—never! ' "

The Lady, however, continued to sigh, and in such gusts that a veritable hurricane was wafted through the door of her Privy Chamber. Outside in the Coffer Room, her Maids, jostling each other for an ear at the keyhole, clustered in the prettiest palpitations while the ceilings shook, and the very guards, not excluding their stalwart Captain, were seen to quake.

So did his lordship, down upon his knees to kiss the hem of his Lady's garment and swear by all that he held holy, this marriage meant no more to him than a convenience. His soul was dedicated to the Goddess of his heart. He was crazed with unrequited love to such extent that his adoration for so ' incomparable, exquisite radiant, divine '—(the string of adjectives was inexhaustible)— ' and glorious a Being,' had completely turned his brain.

The Goddess of his heart was half inclined to think so. The first storm of her fury abated, she forced herself to take him at his word. This marriage of convenience, she stipulated strongly, must not in any way encroach upon the personal relationship of Majesty and servant; and she left him sobbing. But before the door had opened on her own apartment he was after her, to entreat Her Grace would grant him this one boon—that he might be allowed to prove his constancy and lay down his life, if need be, for her beloved sake! Would Her Majesty not reconsider her decision? Henry of Navarre had sent further appeal for an army to aid him in Normandy. Was Her Majesty still determined not to join the fight?

And watching her eyes, Essex saw a lightning flash leap up behind their faded blue; he seized his moment.

"Will Your Grace run the risk that you and France be overpowered by the Catholic League . . . and Philip?"

In a trice she was turned to steel, while her protean mind, discarding trivialities, bristled to the challenge. Philip! That whippet-hound who dared to pit his strength against her own, and make himself sole master of the world! She stared before her, beyond the pretty youth who stood forgotten, waiting with held breath for this, his chance.

What visions did her transitory genius evoke? What complexities of statecraft would she weave from his artfully contrived insinuation? And while he watched her, Essex marvelled. This, then, was the secret of her power over men and over nations; this, her mercurial and startling unexpectedness, that, between a second and a second, could transform her from a fluttering mass of femininity into a stern-faced woman of affairs, embodiment of wisdom stored, of indomitable energy and grandeur.

"So!" She brought her eyes to his. "You leave me no alternative. I'll run no risks, and you will play no pranks. Two months I'll give you for your limit. Henry owes me money, not repaid."

Once more he knelt to kiss her feet. Her face relaxed. She twined her fingers in his hair.

"God's death!" The familiar oath shot from her lips with a laugh that caused her Maids, straining their ears at the keyhole, to wonder what sudden twist of humour had sweetened—or soured—Her Grace. "Your wife will have no reason to adore me if I send you to France within the first week of your wedding. Widows on a second marriage squeal for their rights, but maids fight shy of theirs—as we are told. We speak from lack of knowledge." She closed her lips to smile.

And Essex, having won his point, now waxed hysterical. Her Grace was over-gracious. . . . "Most fair, most dear, most excellent!" he babbled, while outside the Maids of Honour clapped their hands to their mouths to choke back their titters. "Beloved Sovereign! The two windows of your Privy Chamber are the poles of my sphere, and when my task is done I will return to that Heaven to be consumed like a vapour by the Sun that draws me up to such a height."

"Dear fool," she told him, melting, "take your soldiers, and don't overleap yourself in horseplay."

At least there would be no more honeymoon delights for Sidney' widow and his bride; no ardours shared between a common subject and her Queen. . . . "May God," she said, "protect you."

He covered her hands with kisses, and, still kneeling, watched her pass; then sprang to his feet and rushed to the door that led to the Coffer Room. Like a flock of white birds the Maids scattered Bestowing a triumphant glance around, Essex kissed his finger-tips to each in turn.

"Which of you beauties will give me a gage to wear in my cap when I go to join Henry in France?"

He had won! And those who had laid wagers against the chances of his going—they had lost.

Arabella was home again at Hardwick when Essex and his band of followers set out for Normandy. She heard stray news of his exploits. He had come to the aid of King Henry in the siege of Rouen, where under the very walls of the city he saw his brother killed. He had exceeded the time limit of two months granted by the Queen. He had been careering wildly across the country with no heed for his life, bent on any kind of battle. He went dressed as a common soldier and carried a pike. He led his men into the most reckless danger. The Queen was furious, and ordered him home, but before he returned it was said he had gone round knighting sundry on the field as if he were their king!

All this Arabella heard in scraps of talk between her uncles at the table, and enlarged upon by Bridget to the wondering Anne

74

Bradshaw. . . . In the quiet of her chamber she prayed God to guard Lord Essex and bring him home in safety from the wars.

*   *   *

During her granddaughter's absence from home, Lady Shrewsbury, deprived of her charge, had found other and more urgent occupation. A latent scheme, of a sudden sprung to life, had been put into immediate activity. It was not in Bess to stand upon an impulse. She obeyed it.

The old house at Hardwick had grown too small, or her family, with grandchildren, too big, for the accommodation she required. Bess decided she must build again : a decision that may likely have been prompted by the ever rankling reminder of a gipsy's prophecy, foretold her in her youth, that so long as she continued to build houses she would not die.

She was past seventy, yet very far from dying. Her amazing vitality, now rekindled, dominated as before an army of workmen, this time at her gates. Though the foundations of the new Hardwick had been laid some ten years since, the re-erection of Chatsworth had ousted all other interest. But with the completion of the family seat, the Dowager turned the full force of her constructive energy upon the building of a mansion fit to house a future Queen of England. With that aim in view and spurred by her possessive mania, if she did not actually set the bricks with her own hands, she stood over those who laboured, to direct them.

From the windows of the old Hall she could watch the steady growth of this new Hardwick. The echo of hammers upon stone was music to her ears, and a ceaseless source of irritation to Mr. Morley's. He found the noise distracting, not only to himself, but to his pupil. Her Highness's attention, he reported, was beguiled from her book to dwell upon irrelevant proceedings. He therefore asked permission of her ladyship to conduct his pupil's studies in the garden. The weather being fair, the Lady Arabella would doubtless profit by the sunshine.

Her ladyship expressed her full approval of the proposition. Fresh air was good for all young growing things. The girl of late had looked a trifle peaked.

Smilingly she watched her ' Jewel ', with her tutor, cross the greensward followed by two pages carrying books and a lexicon. The little cavalcade passed between yew hedges and retired out of

75

sight. . . . Bess nodded to herself. Excellent, most admirable Morley! Always so conscientious and careful of his charge. How ridiculous of William to pay heed to that old woman Burghley's croakings. And what, after all, had they proved to be? No more than a packet of pins! Burghley had not forgotten nor forgiven that deplorable misunderstanding between herself and her late lamented. But then Burghley had been poor Shrewsbury's bosom friend—or professed to be. One never could fathom his sentiments, nor untwist the coils of that serpent mind. And this attempt to poison her own and her son's against her servant, who played so sweetly on the virginals, indeed on any instrument—a veritable bard, and no mean poet—was a dastard's trick.

Had she not proof enough of Morley's rectitude and capability? Witness only how Arbelle had advanced in learning since he had replaced her former tutor, Mr. Kynnersley. The girl could now, not only write, but converse, in fluent Latin; was well learned, too, in Greek, had more than a smattering of Hebrew, in which Kynnersley had never led her past the alphabet; and as for her Italian, Morley, who was not given to over-praise, had declared her accent to be indistinguishable from one born a native of the country. . . . Burghley. Pah! The old man was in his dotage. That Irish prattler, Bridget Sherland, might be led away by idle talk, but her son William should have better sense than to lend ear to an old man's postulations with regard to the brother of her neighbour, Mr. Harrison.

Fed on fantasies, William, like a zany, needs must call upon the gentleman, only to find that his brother had not lodged with him for near upon a year; that he was deep in his research on a translation of the Bible from the Greek, at Cambridge University: a godly man, a clerk in Holy Orders. And what a wild-goose chase to make William look a fool, which undoubtedly he was, to be so undermined by that old dawplucker, Burghley, and his fears. Superbly ignoring that she and the Lord Treasurer were of one age, Bess chose to regard him as at least twenty years her senior, for age, to Bess of Hardwick, was discounted. Her years carried no weight; her hair, though white beneath its dye, sprang as virile and luxuriant as in her youth; her figure remained upright, her health as sturdy as the will that disdained the common weaknesses of flesh.

So, having thus dispelled any lurking symptom of uneasiness evoked by William's repetition of his recent talk with Burghley

Bess summoned her architect to discuss with him the plan he had submitted for a colonnade under the windows of the Long Gallery. And there must be many windows. . . . More glass than wall if need be.

Meanwhile, Mr. Morley, having seen his pupil settled in the shade of a yew arbour that faced a small enclosed Dutch garden, and was sufficiently remote from the clanging and the banging to permit the removal from his ears of the lamb's-wool with which he had stuffed them as protection against the din, opened a volume of Cicero and bade her Ladyship construe. He felt disposed, he said, to take a walk where in quiet he could meditate. It was necessary that he, a scholar, should have that modicum of peace which of late had been denied him. He would return in half an hour.

"And I am sure your Ladyship," Mr. Morley with unwonted cordiality suggested, "will agree that 'tis pleasanter to pursue your studies in God's fresh air than in a room."

Her Ladyship agreed. It was—a great deal pleasanter : but most pleasant of all to find herself alone. Even the two pages had been sent back to their quarters, lest their presence, Mr. Morley cautioned them, disturb her Highness.

She sighed with the sense of relief and freedom accorded by Mr. Morley's absence, nor did the now distant clangour of the builders incommode her. She liked to hear sounds of activity about the place ; a welcome change from the hush that habitually pervaded Hardwick. She was glad too of the arbour's shelter that screened her from the sun which blazed down unstintingly on lawns and parterres. The dazzling colours of the herbaceous border shimmered in the heat. Bees sipped in every honey-cup. She watched a blue butterfly, like a winged harebell, alight on a sprig of marjoram. . . . How much happier the butterfly, carefree, dancing on a sunbeam, than herself, who was for ever guarded. Yes, were they not guards, these guardians of hers,—her grandmother, uncles, her ladies ? Better far to be a peasant, at liberty to wander where she willed, than a princess, unacknowledged, misliked by the Queen. No denying the Queen did *not* like her ; but how she had offended, save for that one fault when at Greenwich on the way to chapel she had taken precedence—and had she not the right to do so ?— Arabella could not understand. And she was grieved. She would have loved the Queen, her cousin, if the Queen had shown her just one glance of kindness. And now, here she was, sent home in virtual disgrace.

If only she could have been allowed to dance, or even speak with Lord Essex once again, and bid him God-speed. She had a fancy that of late he had avoided her. Was he offended too? He had now gone to the wars and she would never know, and perhaps would not set eyes on him again.

She sighed and blinked, swallowed an ache in her throat, and stared at the open page before her.

' *Frons, oculi, vultus, persaepe mentuntur* ; *oratio vero saepissime* ' . . . The brow, the eyes, the face, often deceive us, but most of all the speech. . . . Yes, she had learned that much at Court. But how cruel to sit here reading Latin when she longed to be out walking with Anne!

' *Fronti nulla fides* ' . . . There is no trust to be placed in outward looks.

What a dreadful old cynic is this Cicero, reflected Arabella. 'Tis as if a perpetual malaise had curdled his soul to turn the milk of human kindness in him sour, for all he speaks so sweet. . . .

The noonday sun poured in upon her where she sat. She laid a hand over her uncovered head. It burned; she would be sunstruck. And moving farther along the seat into a particle of shade, she unfastened the front of her square-cut bodice. These unbearable hot stuffy clothes! Why could not one go in gossamer . . . like a fairy? 'You are ten thousand times more beautiful than the queen of them all'. . . . Her head nodded, her book slid from her lap. Startled from that second's drowsiness, she stooped to retrieve it. . . . And a shadow fell across the grass.

A man, one whom she had never seen, stood before her.

Instinctively her hand flew to her breast to refasten the jewelled clasps of her corsage, while her eyes, screwed against the sun, took note of him. He wore the dress of a stone-mason, with clay on his shoes, no hat on his head, dust-begrimed breeches, and a sleeveless leather jerkin over his soiled shirt.

"What do you here?" demanded Arabella. "Go back to your work. You have no right to trespass in this garden."

"Madam," and his voice and the bow that went with it stamped him high above the status of a stone-mason. "Have I the honour of addressing the Lady Arabella Stuart?"

"That is my name." But even as she answered him her heart missed a beat. What did this civil-tongued fellow want with her? Despite the blue stubble of beard on his chin, his lean face and his delicate long-fingered hands bespoke a refinement belied by his clothes. His hair, close-cropped, shone black as jet.

She rose from her seat.

"Why," she persisted, " do you approach me here ? I will call my servants."

He advanced a step. " I crave your Ladyship's indulgence. I am a messenger."

" A messenger ? " She caught her breath. Could it be possible that Essex . . . " From whom ? "

" From one who desires your Ladyship's favour."

Was the creature mad ? She cast a scared glance about her ; no sight, no sound of any person near. Even the distant hammering had ceased. The men were at their dinners.

" To whom do you allude ? Who are you ? *What* are you ?"

" What I am I have already told your Highness. What I will, is to obey the command of him who sends me here. I am but the servant of his Grace."

" His Grace ? " . . . A Duke ? A Prince ? Had she met with any such in London who would be so bold as to send a messenger in this rude guise to force admission into Hardwick's privacy ? Yes, one ; and one only. He was bold enough to brave a dragon, even her old grandmother, to gain his ends. Her heart beat faster. If it should be . . . She had spoken scarce a word with him before she had left London, but she dared to think that he had looked upon her from a distance, kindly.

" Is he," she breathlessly inquired, " one with whom I am acquainted ? "

" No, Madam." And watching the involuntary fall of her lips at that negative reply, he smiled, repeating : " No. That is to say, not in person, though his name, if I would tell it——"

" Why then, do you not tell it ? "

Her fear had vanished. She would put this impudent rascal in his place. He was without doubt an impostor, one of those workmen yonder, who had presumed above himself thus to approach her that he might boast of his audacity among his fellows. Well, she'd have him in the stocks for this—if he were in his senses. And if out of them, what then ? She might be murdered before help could come. But : " I have only to raise my voice," she told him crisply, " and my servants will run and seize you. I am not alone."

She was ; yet if she could call his bluff while she played for time with one eye on a means of escape, she might make a dash for it, slip past him by the yew hedge, burrow into that and out upon the other side, when she would be within easy distance of the house. And as if he guessed her motive he approached still nearer, blocking her exit from the arbour.

"I beg your Ladyship be not alarmed. I confess that I am come in this disguise——"

"So!" What little breath was in her body left it. "You admit you are not what you claim to be. By the Lord," she gasped, "you're brazen!" And now her heart was beating so loud against her ribs that he must hear it. "Who has sent you to me? I *will* know!"

"One, Madam, who has waited—and with what patience—for a word—a token from your Highness, and receives none."

Decidedly, she thought, he must be mad; yet the knowledge that she was here alone, unguarded, with a lunatic, did not lessen her discomfort. Where was Mr. Morley? Why did he not return? Should she scream in the hope she would be heard? Caution restrained her. . . . No, she must humour him. And forcing a smile, while she edged away, still with one eye on the alley, she said pacifically: "If you would but tell me from whom you are come, I would better understand the purport of your message."

His answer gave her little satisfaction.

"Madam, has your Highness not in your possession a miniature portrait of yourself?"

Heaven restore the fellow, and save me! prayed Arabella.

"Why, yes," she wet her lips, "many miniatures have been painted of myself."

"The most recent," he prompted, to sink her, "is the work of a Mr. Hilliard, I believe."

She suppressed a start. Then he was *not* so mad. Covertly she watched his face: thin to a degree, oval, pock-marked, and such very black hair. . . . And: "How," she asked him, carefully, "do you know so much of my affairs?"

"Madam, it is my duty to know the confidence of the Prince, my master."

"Who is this Prince, your master?"

While she summoned all her courage to fence with him, she could not help but feel exhilarated at the piquancy of this extraordinary encounter. If she came safely out of it, if she were not stabbed or strangled where she stood, what a tale she would have to tell her cousins !

Motionless, he watched her closely from beneath his lowered eyelids.

"Madam, I'll not prevaricate. I am here at the bidding of the Duke of Parma. You are acquainted with the name ? "

"Yes ! " she flung back at him, hotly, "an enemy of England and a friend of Spain. You'll be hanged for this."

"Your Highness——" his lids lifted and his eyes, dark, narrow, smiled down at her. "Old sores have long been healed. Philip of Spain has accepted his defeat."

She blazed at that. "A fine acceptance ! With his Spaniards swarming like cockroaches in France to take our ports. And you —you dare approach me by these underhand foul means, to speak for him—or for his Prince ! " Indignation now consumed all thought of danger. "Well, sirrah, if you are what you claim to be and not as I suspected escaped from a madhouse, return this message to your master. If he wants my portrait, or——" her curled lip folded tight against her teeth—" if he wants *me*, let him come for both himself. I mislike such offers, sent by messenger. Moreover, the Duke of Parma is an old man. He should be ashamed at his age to——" She stopped aghast. The wretch was laughing, silently, but openly. Her temper rose to the boil.

"Ay ! You may laugh ! I'll warrant you'll not laugh when you're brought to the scaffold for a traitor."

But though his laughter faded, she was certain that her threat had carried little weight. Eyeing him doubtfully, she saw his thread of a mouth quirk at the corners. Did he mock her ? She drew herself up. "I mean what I say. You and your Prince run the gravest risk by resorting to such trickery to gain my ear, unknown to my guardians."

"Madam, you mistake my master's motive, and my own. Let me be brief."

"I wish you would," she retorted. "You have beaten around bushes long enough."

"For some time past," he told her, "negotiations of which you, by reason of your youth, were unaware, have been attempted to effect a marriage between your Ladyship and His Grace of Parma's son, Prince Rainutio."

For a moment she was taken off her guard. Then, with quick

recovery from this surprise, she answered, pat: "The Prince of Parma's son is not my only suitor." Had not Ludovic of Lennox said that half the royalties in Europe were on their knees before the Pope to ask her hand in marriage? "But why," she demanded, "did you not at once explain your errand? Prince what-you-may-call-him and I—" she began wildly to improvise, "have exchanged a mort of correspondence on the subject of my marriage. . . . I refused him." And frantically she wondered if she would stand condemned for such a bare-faced lie, but for the life of her could not withhold a final thrust: "I do not care for foreigners. They smell."

Ah! That shook him. His eyebrows shot up to his hair, and biting back a giggle, she seized upon her moment to enlarge. "I am not unmindful of the honour the Prince bestows on me, but, sirrah, you must surely see that I am very young, not yet of marriageable state, being still kept to my schooling." Her lips smiled as she gazed at him, large-eyed. "Yet my tutors have taught me somewhat of foreign policy, since the time when William of Normandy invaded our land until the present day. I know, for I have learned much of Spain—and Spaniards—that during the Armada, your master, the Duke—" she dropped her smile to glare at him—"was King Philip's right hand. Was it not the Duke of Parma who stood with an army at his heels in the Netherlands, waiting to cross under cover of the Spanish fleet to England? But he was prevented by our great commander, Drake. And you—" the arrogant young voice shrilled, quivering with rage—"you dare to come to me who am of English birth with such an offer from your Prince. Indeed *he* must be mad to jump at such a hope and send you to me in this outlandish guise! Did he take me for a mooncalf to imagine I'd be wheedled by your flattery and make a bolt for it with you—to him? And what then? Carried off to Spain, or God knows where. I'll say, sir, that you have been mistook in me and in my sense. You may tell your Prince I will have none of him, nor of his son. . . . Take your tale to my grandmother. Take it to my uncles. Take it to the devil if you will. But if you value your life, I advise you, don't bring it to me!"

She paused for breath, her eyes, yellow as a cat's, fixed on him in a look that caused his own to narrow once again, in something more than recognition of a young girl's courageous handling of a situation that might have baffled sterner heads than hers.

"By my soul!" The words broke from him on a deep intake of breath. "The Prince shall know what he has missed, and what England will have missed—if your Highness does not follow the succession."

"And you," she flashed, "shall know the penalty for treason. And that *will* follow, sure, when I inform on you!"

Head to knees, he bowed to her, as though she were the Queen.

"For such sweet treason, Lady, a man would die a thousand deaths. . . . God save your Grace."

And before her eyes he seemed to melt away, so swiftly did he go, backing from her presence to turn and dart behind the yew hedge. She ran forward, out into the blazing sunshine, tripped over the hem of her petticoat, and was saved a tumble by the outstretched hand of Mr. Morley.

"How now, Madam! What is this? I left you at your studies."

"Morley!" She grabbed his arm. "Did you see that man? Follow him—quick! Behind the hedge there. Call the servants—have him seized."

Mr. Morley's pale eyes protruded in amaze. "Madam! There was no man here."

"There *was*, I tell you! . . . Let me go." For he had taken possession of her wrist and held it in a vice. "Let me run after him if you will not."

"I beg your Highness to compose yourself. You are dis-traught. The sun——"

"You're wasting time. He mustn't slip us. Will you——" She struggled in vain to free herself from his bony grasp that felt dry to the touch as a lizard's skin—"let me *go*!"

"Come, Madam," Mr. Morley, with immense magnanimity entreated, "come with me into the house."

"I won't!"

"Yes, Madam, you will." And retaining his hold he walked her with him along the yew-lined alley.

"But he spoke to me!" screamed Arabella into Mr. Morley's passive ear. "He asked me for a miniature—said he came from the Prince of Parma—I tell you he was standing there. You must have seen him."

She renewed her struggles, while with a slight increase of speed, Mr. Morley continued to walk, and, blandiloquently, talk.

"Your Ladyship must be hallucinated. For these last ten

minutes after my return I have perambulated up and down this alley. I can swear there was no living thing, save the birds and butterflies—and your Ladyship—in sight."

"You lie!" shouted Arabella, shockingly. "If you don't release me this instant I'll—" She gave another ineffectual tug, "I'll bite you!"

She made as if to do so, but was circumvented. With his free hand, Mr. Morley gently, but firmly, cupped her chin and stayed his step. "Madam, you are sadly indisposed."

"I am not indisposed!"

"I fear, indeed, you are." Mr. Morley anxiously surveyed her. Tiny beads of moisture dampened her forehead. Her face was scarlet, her eyes bright. Mr. Morley turned his own to heaven, sighed deeply, and walked on, dragging his writhing pupil at his heels. "Your Ladyship," with arch-angelic patience he pronounced, "is in a fever. Pray, Madam, do not indulge in these contortions. You will do yourself an injury. Be calm. Hold your breath. Count twenty."

"I tell you," yelled Arabella, unpacified by Mr. Morley's exhortations, "that I saw him! You must have seen him too."

"'Twas my mistake," confided Mr. Morley to the air, "to bring your Highness out into the noonday sun to——"

With an adroit and final twist Arabella disengaged.

"You can't tell me you didn't see him if you were walking up that alley. I can repeat word for word what the man said."

"Then come, Madam, and repeat it to her ladyship."

And as if galvanized to action, Mr. Morley took her arm in his and marched her across the lawn into the house.

Yet when they reached the staircase that led to Lady Shrewsbury's apartments, Arabella found she had no fancy to undergo a cross-examination by her grandmother, and to have her word denied by Mr. Morley. Wrenching herself free again she ducked to avoid retention, and, her skirts raised for flight, flung back at him: "No! I'll not face my lady with you at my side. What I saw and heard was true, and you know it!"

"Madam", with renewed urbanity Mr. Morley smiled. "Allow me to set you right. I see now a solution of this mystery. Did you not feel drowsy in the heat?"

"Well . . . yes," she admitted, "for a second."

"And in that second you dozed."

"I tell you——"

"Pray——" Mr. Morley raised his hand, "let me tell you that in that second when you yourself admit to drowsiness, you slept and dreamed. Do you not know that a dream can encompass an eternity and take the dreamer round the world in half a second?"

"I didn't dream." But she was beginning now to wonder if she did. In any case her grandmother would sooner credit Mr. Morley's explanation of this improbable experience, than believe her word that it had taken place.

"Very well," she temporized, "if you can swear you saw no man approach the arbour within ten minutes of your appearance there, then maybe . . . I did dream."

"Yes, I think so. And now let me advise your Highness—go to your room and rest. I will excuse your studies for today."

If this generous concession were intended to conciliate it lamentably failed. Restraining an urgent desire to inflict violence upon the mellifluous Morley, Arabella turned from him.

"I thank you, sir . . . I will."

Glancing back across her shoulder, she saw him gazing after her with every expression save that of tenderest solicitude obliterated from his countenance. Then, shaking his head and again sighing deeply, he proceeded up the staircase.

Scowling, Arabella stood to watch him go before she gathered her skirts and ran to Mrs. Sherland's parlour. There she blurted out her story into Bridget's ear; nor, till she had finished, did her waiting-woman offer any comment beyond much head-wagging and an explosive oath to the effect that: "By God's Beard, she would see the scoundrel pickled, torn to pieces—disembowelled——" and so on.

"And Morley says I dreamed it, but I didn't. He was *there*. How could I have dreamed his talk of Parma, or his clothes—all clay-begrimed—his hair, so shining black?"

"Glory be to Jesus!" ejaculated Bridget. "Black! Did you say black?"

"Yes. Jet black, as if it had been plastered thick with tar."

"Aho!" Bridget nodded with such energy that her front of false curls slipped unheeded from her head and fell on the floor in the rushes. "If 'tis the man I think him, his hair *was* the colour of hay; but I wouldn't doubt," she added grimly, "that he's dyed it. Had he a lean and pawky look? Sharp featured?"

" Yes, and pock-marked."

" Heaven help us ! I'll stake my life 'tis he—the hell-born, diabolic, miserable—*ah* ! " Baring her teeth, alarmingly, Bridget raised her hands to clench them. " If I had him here before me I'd tear his tongue out by the roots—but I'll have him on the rack for this, don't fear ! "

" Mercy on us ! " Arabella cried. " Bridget ! Do you know him ? "

" Ay," Bridget swallowed. " I know him, the malefic, blood-sucking rat."

" But who *is* he ? And what," persisted Arabella, " does this mean ? "

" It means, my precious," Bridget, rising, went to the door, conspiratorially opened it, peeped, and returned to sit again. " It means that you will go to Tutbury tomorrow."

" Tutbury ? " Arabella was more than ever in a puzzle. " To my Uncle Shrewsbury's house ? But why ? "

" Because 'tis far removed from here."

" Her ladyship will not permit that I should go. It is not my vacation time."

" Sure, we can make it your vacation time."

And now Bridget appeared to be in highest fettle, continuously nodding and breaking into chuckles, when catching Arabella's eye she would turn preternaturally grave, to mutter words disjointed, and, to her gaping audience, incomprehensible.

" That'll teach the old witch whose head is screwed on and whose isn't. Out in the sun, forsooth ! My Lady shall have fresh air. Hah ! There'll be fresh dungeon air for some to breathe when this day's work's unravelled. To think the danger that my sweet escaped—if it were not the bravest—would you believe that it stood there bold as the O'Brien, my ancestor on my mother's side, who cut the horns off the devil's head when he met and challenged him in mortal combat on the field in the Valley o' the Black Pig, and may I be put to the torture if I lie to ye ! There it stood—a tigress—" here Bridget, overcome, jumped from her stool to implant a sounding kiss on Arabella, " slinging his villainies back into his teeth. As for the other, that pelf-licking, falsifying Judas— I'll have him plucked ! Give him the rope and he'll hang him*self*. I always said he would. So meek and mild butter wouldn't melt, and him playing on the virginals and warbling to the lute, and my lady setting him above the angels. We'll pack your bags. You'll start off in the morning, but *not* to Tutbury. . . . Methinks Sheffield would be safer, being more distant still. Your aunt has been in residence these few weeks at the Castle. Or . . . no! We'll keep you here another night, and maybe longer. Yes, we'll keep you in your room until you're fit to leave it. There's two can play the devil's game and one of them's meself. By holy faith," and Bridget fell to laughing, "if you're not now, you will—indeed you *will* be indisposed!"

"Bridget!" Arabella eyed her with alarm, "do *you* think that I am sick?"

"Sick enough, my pigeon, to enjoy a posset of my brew." Bridget drooped an eyelid; and Arabella blenched.

"What! Will you poison me?"

"Do you hear it?" Bridget's eyes rolled heavenward. "Do you hear the nursling that I dangled at me breast impute me with these poisonous devices? Me, who has watched and waited like a ferret at a rat-hole—hah! the joy to know meself was right and that old cockatrice—though my tongue be slit for saying it—was wrong!"

"The saints defend us!" panted Arabella, "has all the world run mad? Bridget, what do you know of this stranger? For I can swear, whatever Morley tells me, or my lady, that I spoke with him."

"And who would be after saying ye did not?" Crossing her arms over her ample bosom, Bridget gleefully hugged herself. "And I'll say you dealt with the black toad for what he was, knowing what you are—a Royal Stuart, born to be Queen, as you will be without their puffed-up damnifying—— Where is your Uncle Henry?"

"Why, Bridget," quavered Arabella, "how strangely you speak. Where should my uncle be but at his house at Chatsworth?"

"Pray Heaven that he be not at Tutbury, for 'twill mean a loss of time to send . . . Now to bed with you this instant, and not another word." A superfluous injunction, since Arabella was scarcely given half a chance to speak one. "How my sweet stares! Does it think its old Sherland has gone twisted too? Not so twisted but that I'll twist the head of——" Bridget put her hand up to her own and found her false front missing. "A pox!" quoth she, "I've lost me hair!"

"Here," Arabella, giggling, stooped to pick the bunch from off the floor. Bridget snatched it from her, and : " There's someone," she cryptically muttered, " who will lose more than his hair over this day's circumstance, I'm thinking. To your chamber with you now, and ask no questions, for you'll get no answers. Go to bed. . . ."

She went to bed, attended by Anne Bradshaw, no less mystified by these untoward proceedings than herself. For what with Bridget popping in and out of the room to nod, and to whisper, and chuckle, and vanish, finally to reappear with a posset which she begged her Ladyship to drink, the two were in a rare perplexity.

" For 'tis certain," Bridget, with astonishing antinomy informed her, " that your Ladyship *did* sit too long in the sun to induce a fever of the blood. This, I promise you, will cool it."

Arabella had her doubts, not only of the dose prescribed, but of Mrs. Sherland's best intentions, that now seemed illogically to have swerved from her own to Mr. Morley's point of view. A stormy scene resulted, whence Bridget emerged triumphant by dint of holding Arabella's nose while she forcibly administered the mixture, until the greater part of it was swallowed ; and whether or no it were natural fatigue following upon the day's excitement, or the effects of the posset which tasted excessively bitter, that caused Arabella to fall fast asleep, none, not even Bridget, could tell. The fact remains that sleep she did, and was sleeping still, when her grandmother, after her interview with Mr. Morley, came to inquire what ailed her ' Jewel '. Nor could any drastic treatment, such as the shaking of the patient, and the slapping of her cheeks, and the clapping of her hands, and the contents of a bucket of cold water thrown upon her where she lay, disturb her lethargy. Slow and heavy was her breathing, very flushed her face, and her grandmother distracted.

The girl was in a stupor, or a trance. Morley had spoken of her drowsiness and recounted her strange dreams. God forbid this formidable coma of the body did not presage a worser sickness of the mind. What had the child to eat or drink that could have induced so unnatural a palsy ?

Mistress Sherland swore upon her life that the child had not ate nor drank since breakfast ; but Anne, when questioned in her turn, was non-committal. As far as she knew, she gently emphasized, her Ladyship had taken nothing to eat or drink—of her own will.

" Of her own will ! " barked Bess. " Explain yourself."

88

"I—madam——" Anne attempted to explain herself, when Bridget deftly intervened.

"Mistress Bradshaw, madam, was about to say that her Highness has taken neither bite nor sup, having no will nor appetite for either."

Most strange and unaccountable! Morley, then, had obvious good reason to report the girl so sadly indisposed that she had been unable to pursue her studies; mouthing and drowsing over her book, and starting up to point at visions, which Morley, who had never left her side, was prepared to stake his oath, were entirely delusive.

And now the house was in an uproar while conjecture rang the changes on the nature of the sickness, varying from the plague to the small-pox and every kind of fever, finally deciding on the verdict pronounced by Mistress Sherland: the Lady Arabella was bewitched.

"Bewitched my——!" Disgracefully the Dowager discarded that suggestion; when put about Bess did not mince her words. "Dizzard!" She turned to rail at Bridget, who appeared to be uncommonly subdued. "Keep your addle-pated Irish farragos to yourself. Don't air them in my presence. If anybody in this household is bewitched 'tis I, to have kept one so witless in my service all these years—sprung from a race of savages, born in the bogs of Dublin."

"I was born, madam," corrected Bridget, honey-mouthed, "not a mile from Hampton Court. My mother 'twas who——"

"Your mother was a witch and begot you o' the devil! Out of my sight!" thundered Bess, "you sicken me. Mistress Bradshaw," she addressed the trembling Anne, "go tell the Master of the Horse to send a fellow off to Buxton for the doctor. To Buxton. Do you hear me? Hurry!"

Mistress Bradshaw hurried, and Bridget wrung her hands, and on her knees invoked the Deity and all the saints to restore her precious Highness; and Bess continued to hurl abuses at every member of the household, from the scullion, peeping round the buttery door, to have his ears cuffed for his presumption, to the steward, stout and pompous in black velvet and a yellow ruff so wide and stiffly starched that his head seemed as it were pilloried. And while the Master of the Horse hastened to obey his lady's orders, speeding his trustiest groom and the swiftest stallion in his stables off to Buxton; while Mr. Morley conferred with the secretary, one John Starkey, a young and recent graduate of Cambridge, upon this disastrous event and its prognosis, which Mr. Starkey, who claimed to know a smattering of medicine, suggested might be very grave indeed; while all this and more was taking place at Hardwick, Henry Cavendish arrived from Chatsworth.

In the Great Hall hung with armour, coats of mail, shields and yawning helmets, Henry waited for his mother to appear. The oreille—a recess containing two tables furnished each with napery and silver plate, and the huge salt-cellar that divided the rank of those about to sit above or below it—was already prepared for the diners. At the lower end of the Hall were placed the trencher-boards, but those who sat there ate and drank from pewter cups and dishes. The serving-men and pages stood at their posts; and the steward, looking, Henry thought, uncommon flustered, was putting the finishing touches to the tables in the oreille. The musicians were assembled in the gallery, and everything appeared to be in its customary ostentatious order, save for the absence of the hostess.

"What's to do?" inquired Henry of the steward. "Where is her ladyship, and where the dinner? For I am here, I think, in time to eat it."

The steward opened his mouth, but no word issued; indeed he looked to be struck dumb as the voice of the Dowager resounded through the Hall: "There'll be no dinner, nor no guests today. Take away the dishes. Take them! . . . *Take them!*"

The steward, whose mouth, still open, resembled nothing so much as that of a landed codfish, pointed his gold-headed stick at his underlings. And while they and the pages bumped into each other in their haste to dismantle the tables, Bess called to the minstrels, who at her appearance had begun softly and sweetly to play "Cease your noise there! Put up your lutes. I'm in no mood for your twanging."

A scurry above indicated that the lady's order was obeyed. A scared head popped over the gallery's rail, to be speedily withdrawn, as Bess, who had now arrived within reach of a lower table snatched a pewter cup as if to hurl it. "Go, all of you. Leave the dishes. *Leave* them!"

The servers scuttled, the pages fled. The steward, striving to uphold his dignity, followed with stately steps that broke into a run as Bess called after him: "Clotpoll! You have forgot the salt Come back!"

His face empurpled, and breathing down his nose, the steward came heavily back to bear away, one in each hand, the huge salt-cellars.

" Jobbernowl ! " croaked Bess, " not both at once—you'll drop them. You—page ! Here ! "

Too late.

One salt-cellar crashed with a clanging of metal on stone. The salt was spilled—disastrous omen ; and then, every hair on his scalp uprisen, the steward in his desperation dropped the other.

Henry took advantage of the tumult that ensued to help himself to a dish of roast quail, which, in the flurry had been overlooked. And when the steward had been roundly dealt with and dismissed upon the spot ; and when a page, more courageous than his fellows, who had lingered to see his superior debased, had in his turn received a due chastisement, to be sped, howling, Bess, her widow's coif awry, her farthingale crooked, advanced upon her son.

" Why do you come here at such a time, on such a day, to plague me ? "

Henry raised his eyebrows.

" How does this time and day, good madam, differ from any other time and day ? The sun is setting and my stomach sinks."

" Then you can go feed it on curds in the buttery. I see you have made short shrift of the quails. Two pence each they cost me, and you've ate a clear dozen." Bess kept a weekly full account of her expenditure, for though lavish she was thrifty, and knew to a farthing the price of every item bought for and consumed by her large household.

" Why," she again demanded, " are you here ? "

" Firstly, madam," Henry, bowing, kissed his mother's hand, " to assure myself that your ladyship enjoys her usual robust health. I am delighted to find you in high spirits."

" High—'Ods Blood ! " Bess all but choked. " You see how I'm a-jangle—in no fancy for your jibes."

" Madam," protested Henry, " that you mistake my salutation does distress me. Are you troubled ? " Releasing her hand, he courteously urged her to a seat, and giving her no moment for reply, continued, silken-voiced: " If my arrival is ill-timed I humbly beg your ladyship to pardon me, but my need is great and my mother generous."

Bess, seated, favoured this preamble with a look at her son to bore holes. " Come to your point. Don't burble. If your need is money you can spare yourself the asking. You will get none, for I've none to waste—on wastrels ! "

" Money, madam, is with me an ever-present need, but not my present mendicancy. No. My request of your ladyship's good favour is," he paused, his head aslant, " the loan of a milch-cow."

" What in the name of the prophet," Bess exploded, " do you mean by such a——"

"Madam," Henry gazed at his irate parent with moderate reproach. " My good wife Grace is ailing. She lacks appetite, grows thin——"

" Is she with child ? " rapped out Bess.

" Alas," he sighed. " I fear not."

" Just as well, for such a pair of fools as you and she would breed a sawney. What else does she lack beside appetite—and sense ? "

" The best cream milk," Henry apologetically ventured, " which the physician has prescribed for her—two full quarts a day, that I had hoped, madam, to obtain from your good——"

" Torment of Hell ! " shrieked the Dowager, " what have I to do with this ? Do you think that my old shrunken teats could give her suck ? "

" Madam," Henry redundantly assured her, " you do malign yourself. Though you be as fecund as a Ceres or Amalthea to feed the gods, your bounty could not well provide my poor wife Grace with that two quarts of full cream milk, *per diem*, which——"

" You blabbering jackass ! " fumed the justly provoked Bess. " Have you no Chatsworth herds that you come to me with talk of milch-cows, while Arbelle lies stricken to the death ? "

" Arbelle ! Stricken ! " Startled from its natural quiddity, Henry's face expressed profoundest horror. " Stricken," he repeated. " Why ? What with ? "

" How the devil should I know ? " Bess rebutted. " If I could know I'd cure her. She sleeps. She will not wake. We've shaken her and pommelled her, but she lies there in a stupor. Morley thinks she's had a sunstroke, but I myself believe she ate of toad-stools in the garden. Morley swears she didn't. Yet he may have turned his back when she was at her studies."

" *Are* there toadstools in the garden ? " asked Henry doubt-fully.

Grinding her two remaining molars, Bess appealed. "Heaven send me patience with this boggart! Yes. There *are* toadstools in the garden. Or she may have caught the plague. That Irish Jezebel, Sherland, vows she is bewitched, but I would sooner think the woman has been at her with some of her own barbaric sorcery. God help us!"

"That," Henry judiciously considered, "might be possible."

"How?" His mother turned her gimlet eye upon him. "Do you believe Bridget Sherland so inclined?"

"To witchery?" Henry pondered. "Yes . . . maybe."

"Merciful Powers!" His mother in a ferment rose. "And you admit it! 'Tis common talk you fornicate together. Well!" She uttered a sound between a laugh and a snort. "You, if anyone, should know."

Henry's upper lip slid sideways.

"Yes, madam, I do know, but not from such imputation as you do cast upon the lady's virtue."

"Virtue?" bellowed Bess. "The woman's wanton. If it were not for the love she bore my dear dead girl, I'd have her duck-stooled in the village pond for all the lads to jeer at."

Henry stroked his beard to mask a grin.

"Good madam, my poor belief that Mistress Sherland is possessed of witchery does not, in fact, condemn her for a witch."

"Your words," blazed Bess, "condemn you for a liar! I've suffered shame enough from the tales of your lecherous debaucheries that cry scandal to your name to make it stink from here to Derby Town. 'Tis known throughout the county that you've begot your bastards—and if Sherland's not their mother, then, by God, I am not yours!"

And the silk of her voluminous farthingale hissing as if beneath its folds it housed a colony of snakes, the much affronted Dowager stalked over to the window. There she stood to cool herself and watch vainly for the doctor, who she knew could not arrive before nightfall. The westering sun had turned the sky to molten brass, and sliding a gilt sword-thrust through the leaded panes, lit the marsh old face outlined against the mullion to a cameo fineness.

"I have sent," she said, "for a physician." Her voice thickened. "I gave promise to my dear one on her death-bed to cherish . . . if I should have failed my trust. . . ."

From under the puckered lid an unwilling slow tear trickled;

and at that small sign of weakness, the first in all his life he had discerned in her whose spirit so tenaciously defied the inexorable challenge of her years, Henry, conscious of a tightening in his throat, went to lay an arm about her shoulders.

"It is not in your soul," he said, "to fail. But I think you take too many cares upon yourself."

Discarding his caress she turned on him; but the glint of humour spreading a fan of wrinkles round her eyes, belied the frown between those fierce old brows.

"You," she told him hardily, "whom I know to be a fool and believe to be a liar, may have some better understanding of feminine distempers than a wiser or worthier man. Go then, see if you can wake her—for I have tried and can't."

Thus bidden, Henry, nothing loath, betook himself to his niece's room to be received at the door by Bridget, who in whispers and with much display of eye-winking and teeth, informed him "All is well. She is restored, praise be! Anne is with her. No harm done. She's sweating lovely. Come aside. . . ."

The words that passed aside in Bridget's parlour between Henry and herself are not recorded, and the nature of the patient's illness still remained obscure, though the doctor was of opinion that the symptoms, with unnatural sleep and much resultant vomiting, resembled an attack of sweating fever.

This Bridget was disposed to doubt. "For," with glib assurance she reminded Bess, "I recall the self-same symptoms in her Highness's affliction, which your ladyship may remember did attack the Lady Margaret of Lennox, when she lay at——"

"That," spurning the suggestion Bess made haste to interpose "was due to a surfeit of lampreys. Did her Highness eat o lampreys?"

"Not, madam," admitted Bridget, "to my knowledge."

"I wonder what is to your knowledge," muttered Bess with a sharp upward glance at the unwontedly meek Mrs. Sherland And to her son Henry she said: "You can take your milch-cow and your niece with you to Chatsworth. The doctor orders change of scene and air."

It was, however, not to Chatsworth that Arabella went. True in accordance with the Dowager's command, Henry Cavendish departed with his niece, she in his mother's coach attended by her ladies, he mounted, riding at the wheels, the baggage-men before the grooms behind, and a herdsman in the rear driving a fat red cow. But no sooner was this singular procession well beyond sight of the Hall, than Henry bade the coachman turn about sharp and take the road to Sheffield. The herdsman and the cow were ordered on to Chatsworth, and when Arabella asked the reason for this change of plan and route, she was offered little satisfactory enlightenment.

So, with some quizzing of the ladies on the part of Mr. Cavendish, the entourage proceeded on its way, halting by the roadside to eat of abundant provisions produced from a hamper secreted beneath Bridget's petticoats, and which contained roast capon, cold viands, and pies enough to stock a pastrycook's establishment, to say nothing of four bottles of canary, three of sack, and a sufficiency of ale for the servants.

After which feast the merriest humour prevailed; and when the journey was resumed the coachman on his box rolled from side to side as if his coach were a galleon a-sail on the sea, the while he urged his horses forward with a lusty rendering of:

> 'Corin was her only joy
> He loved her not a pin'.

This, with improvisations of his own, served to convulse Mrs. Sutherland and scandalize Anne Bradshaw, and reduce Arabella, who had taken her fair share of sack, to laughter almost as exuberant as Bridget's, though what there was to laugh at in such a silly song she had no notion. Until at last, overcome with the fun and the sun, and one cup too many of wine, she went from laughing to crying, and sleeping it off—with her head on Anne Bradshaw's shoulder.

But when at sundown they arrived at Sheffield Castle, she, still a trifle top-heavy, gleaned no more than the haziest notion as to why she was there, uninvited; nor could further query of her uncle elicit more than the ambiguous reply: "Be thankful that you're here, my girl . . . for here you're going to stay."

Chapter Four

AND there she stayed while summer passed. The creeper on the castle walls flamed red in glowing sunsets, and fell in rusted heaps to lie forgotten till the gales came shrieking like witches on All Hallows E'en, down chimneys, and in and out the battlements to tear from the tossed tree-branches the last of their golden wealth. She stayed when the dead leaves rose again, whirling madly on the heels of the winds with a faint brittle sound as of elfin bones cracked, in the wild dance of Autumn's death.

And through those misty, sun-lost mornings, Arabella and her cousins, the Talbot girls and the Cavendish boys, went riding to the chase with their falcons belled and hooded on their wrists. Over stubble field and pasture, through copse and undergrowth and out again full gallop, across the wine-pink heather, they followed the startled coveys to the end of a good day's sport. Then the homeward turn at a jog-trot, their feathered catch slung limp across the saddles, their peregrines, bloody-beaked and proudly perched upon the glove; and a great orange moon peering over the hills to give promise of as good a day tomorrow.

Those few months at Sheffield Castle brought to Arabella joy never known before of youth's companionship, the lack of all formality, the unrestrained delight of games permitted: blind-man's buff and hide-and-seek up and down the great hall, in and out the tower rooms. Or they would play at club-kayles, striking the ball with a mallet into a wooden hoop for forfeits—a garter or kerchief to the girls, a kiss demanded from the boys—the boisterous young sons of Charles and William Cavendish, who often came to stay a week or two, and were gay and full of quips as their Uncle Shrewsbury's Fool. A right merry Fool was he, with a face like a pie and a hump on his back, and an indefatigable fund of good humour. He would gather them round him and sit in their midst wearing his green and red motley, asking them riddles, or cutting a caper, or singing a song, tuneful or sad, or comical, tragical, farcical, rude; whatever your choice, he would give it. And with all these diversions the weeks fled apace, and still the Lady Arabel lodged with her Aunt and Uncle Shrewsbury at Sheffield.

Henry had basely left his sister Mary to deal with their mother in this direct contradiction of her order; and if he gave his sister any inkling of his reason in removing their niece from the neighbourhood of Hardwick, he told Bess no more than she would care to hear.

Mary found 'Arbelle improved in health and vigour.' She was 'merry and ate her meat well. . . . She danced with exceeding

96

ood grace and behaved herself with great proportion to everyone
1 their degree.'

Letters poured back and forth from the new Countess at
heffield Castle to the old Countess at Hardwick Hall, while daily
.rabella dreaded the summons to return. But it seemed that
·ess accepted and approved of the reports tactfully presented by
·er daughter; or it may be she was now so fully occupied with
1e rebuilding of her house that she was glad enough to shift the
·sponsibility of her charge to Mary's younger shoulders for a
.me. She insisted, however, that Mrs. Sherland should render
1onthly bulletins in person as to the condition and well-being of
·er 'Jewel '.

Thus Bridget journeyed to and fro, bringing back the latest
·ossip she had garnered.

It was Christmas when Mrs. Sherland, big with news, returned
·gain from Hardwick. Morley and my lady were heading for a
·lit, so she with satisfaction announced to Arabella.

"And he has asked—the impudence!—to have his stipend
·aised, but if I know my lady she will sooner put him down than
·art with a groat a week more to his wage. I left them hammering
·out together in the gallery, and would have had my ear to the
·eyhole," Bridget brazenly confessed, "but that young Mr.
·tarkey was prowling round about so very pious—S'truth! and
·1at reminds me!" She clapped her hand to her heart. "If I've
·1islaid it now——" And opening her corsage she began a fevered
·earch, digging down between her breasts, lifting up her petticoats,
·) expose, unblushingly, her plump white thighs. "Now where in
·1e devil did I put it? Somewhere safe upon my person in case
·f robbers on the road——"

"But what _is_ it?" Arabella asked, amused at Bridget's antics.

"A letter. May I die if I thought I didn't put it in my pocket!"

A flag of colour flew in Arabella's cheeks. From whom could
·e this letter? If she dared hope again that one whose name was
·ever long outside her thoughts had sent a thought to her . . .
·Oh, Bridget, you _must_ find it. Have you lost—don't say you've
·ost it!"

"No, here 'tis."

From her stocking Bridget dragged a folded parchment. "It
·lipped my garter with which I bound it, thinking were I set upon
·long the way no thief would lift _my_ petticoats. For _I_ am not

97

sixteen ! . . . Now wait, will you ? " As Arabella sprang to grab
" 'Tis your granddam who has opened it, not I. You're in luck
way. 'Tisn't every girl in England has a letter from a King."

" A King . . ." In drenching disappointment Arabella floundered
" What King ? I don't know of any King who'd write to me.

" Do you not ? " Bridget smiled broadly. " What of you
cousin James of Scots ? Is he not a King ? "

" My cousin ! " Her face lit up again. Her dear Aunt Mary'
son . . . her Cousin James.

He, her dead father's nephew, who since her birth had chose
to ignore her, and had confiscated her estates and hereditary titl
to bestow them on that first in his long line of favourites, Esm
Stuart, the father of Ludovic, now with effusion, and suddenl
wrote :

' Although the natural bonds of blood, dear Cousin, be suffi
cient for the good entertainment of amity, yet I will not abstai
from those common offices of letters, having now keeped silenc
till the fame and report of so good parts in you have interpelle
me. . . . Now bearing more certain notice of the present plac
of your abode . . .'

Arabella, reading aloud her letter to Bridget, who stood, al
ears and eyes agog, paused to knit her brows over the stiff crabbe
writing.

" How can he know my *present* place of abode ? The lette
was sent to Hardwick."

" There's more known of you and your movements," Bridge
told her slyly, " than you can know yourself."

" Maybe. But 'tis not very pleasing to think I am spied upo
by my cousin—King James o' Scotland or nothing ! "

Bridget twitched her nose and looked along it. " You ma
be glad one day to have a cousin who's a King. You've not ha
much to thank for from one here, who is a Queen. Read on, m
chuck."

Her chuck read on.

"——Um—um—' of your abode. I will the more frequentl
visit you by letters, which I would be glad to do in person, expectin
also to know from time to time of your good estate by your ow
hand. And now after my heartiest condemnation——' "

" Lord ! " Arabella interrupted herself to exclaim, " I never di
see such a—it can't be ' condemnation ' ! "

"Let me look." Bridget peeped over her shoulder. "*Comm*-endation, child. Where's your sense? And you a scholar."

"'*Comm*endation. I wish you '," proceeded Arabella, "' my dear Cousin, of God all honour and hearty contentment.

From Holyrood House the 23rd December 1591.

Your loving and affectionate Cousin,

James R.' "

Well!

Here was news enough to feed the family at Sheffield with dinner-table gossip for a month. The King of Scots had written to Arbelle and expressed the hope to visit her in person. He might at any time come riding through the gatehouse with his savage Highlanders behind him in their swirling kilts, playing on the bagpipes and dancing reels along the drive.

This fantastic picture was offered Arabella by Gilbert Cavendish, Sir William's eldest son, who greatly joyed to tease her. Rising promptly to the bait, "Highlanders aren't savage!" she retorted. "'Tis known that the Scottish are a far older and more civilized race than the English. And is it likely they'd come dancing?"

"More than likely. Dancing and yelling their war cries. As for civilized," scoffed Gilbert, "can you call it civilized for men to wear petticoats up to their knees?"

"They don't!"

"They do. And when the wind blows—Lord! The sights that may be seen!"

"Go hang yourself!" screamed Arabella. "My father was a Scot and I am half a Scot—the better half I'll say. The other half that's English is as mongrel as yourself—or my spaniel bitch whose mother was served by a greyhound."

The argument might have continued indefinitely if her cousin Mary Talbot, grown more globular than ever, had not waddled in between them to soothe the one and scold the other. "O, hush, Arbelle! You know he loves to plague you. Gilbert, hold your peace. I'll tell your father of the way you speak so disrespectful to Arbelle, as if she were a kitchen-maid and not a Princess born."

"Princess born or kitchen-maid 'tis all the same to me. Both are born of women and have women's parts alike," laughed Gilbert. "What say you, my pretty?" He tweaked a curl of Arabella's hair. "I'll swear you were born to pleasure a man the same as any other girl, though you do carry a crown on your head."

99

"You——!" Arabella fell upon him with her fists. "You pig-faced snite! I have no crown on my head, nor am I likely to carry one—see!"

"Hey now!" Dodging her blows he caught her hands and held them fast. "Here's a shrew, i'faith! Has your head no crown to it then, that it goes topless?"

"O come, Arbelle, for shame!" cried Mary in a flutter. "Gilbert, let her go! Come, cousin, to my room." She put her arm through Arabella's, and dragging her away, whispered: "I have a secret to tell."

The secret Mary had to tell was not, however, readily confided, for although she with much mystery, declared: "I know why the King of Scots writes to you so intimate and friendly——" it took not a little persuasion to urge her into telling more than that.

"Do you so? And why?" Arabella feigned complete indifference.

"O . . . Why?" Mary rubbed her cheek against her shoulder, looking coy.

"Yes, chatterpate!" Arabella gritted her teeth, then showed them in a smile. "Why?"

Mary pouted.

"I am not a chatterpate. And I do know why. Only . . ." She sucked her rosy underlip, glanced aside and up and down, "only I'm not supposed to know. I overheard."

"And what did you overhear, my love?" Arabella leaned towards her while her hand stealthily crept up to the soft under-flesh of Mary's arm. "Only tell me, sweet, and you shall have my veil of silver gauze—to cover your gawping face!"

"O, to be sure!" whimpered Mary, "you can be mighty generous when you want to know a thing or two. . . . Take your hand away from me, Arbelle! I won't be pinched. I'll tell my mother how you pinch me!"

"Run quick and tell her then," smiled Arabella. "I have not touched you yet, though I promise you I will if you don't tell *all* you've heard. Eavesdropping."

Her fingers threateningly hovered and Mary gave a yelp, then tumbled out her words in a torrent. "O! . . . I . . . I heard that the King o' Scots told someone who wrote it to Lord Burghley who told it to my father and my father told my mother——"

"Lord sakes!" cried Arabella, "told and told and told—*who* told?"

"I'm telling *you*," squealed Mary, "that the King of Scots has said that someone of the name of . . . O, his name has slipped me now!"

"Tell it!" Arabella seized her little finger, "or I'll bite this off."

"O, Arbelle! You look at me so savage I'm inclined to think that Gilbert's right. The Scots *are* wild, truly."

"Only when driven half demented," Arabella said in a cooing voice, "by the imbecility of gentle creatures like yourself. Have you forgotten your reward, my silver veil?"

"'Tis your promise I'm to have it?"

"Yes and yes and *yes*—if you'll go on."

Mary went hurriedly on.

"Well, my father told my mother—no, Arbelle, don't come at me again—I'm trying to remember my father's very words. . . . O, yes! I do remember now because it was the selfsame name as yours, Stuart—which is Ludo—which is—would you believe! The *oddest* name. Ludo*witch*! Yes, that was the name, and my father said he told the King of Scots that he was 'sick with love and longeth after Arabella', and the King said that if he doesn't have a child he'll make this Stuart his successor and marry him to you!"

"Marry him to *me*! The devil he won't!" Arabella jumped from her stool, her face flaming. "Marry Ludovic? That baby doll! So now we have the reason for my royal cousin's friendliness. And if you," she turned precipitately upon Mary who ran screaming to the door, "if you," said Arabella, dashing after her, "have been telling lies, I'll——"

Mary gulped.

"O, no Arbelle, I've told you all I've heard, but if you don't believe me, go ask my mother."

"So I will!"

And so she did, to beleaguer Lady Shrewsbury with questions. Who had brought this rumour from the King of Scots to couple her name with that of 'Ludo' Lennox? Why was she not told what she *should* be told? Why must she learn it from the mouths of sucklings? She was half sick of mysteries. There were too many in her life. She had been patient long enough; had been brought here from Hardwick by her uncle for no apparent reason, and had out-stayed her time—if not her welcome. Her demands for explanation of this disposal of herself had been cast aside with lies or bald half-truths. Now she must know what all, it seemed, but she herself, *did* know.

Firstly, that stranger, who last summer had come upon her in the garden unawares—" That was no dream," she stormed, " and Morley knew it. And Mrs. Sherland too. Only my grandmother is gulled, not I. . . . Who was he ? "

" Tush, child ! " Lady Shrewsbury, unprepared for such unruly demonstration from one who hitherto had seemed so tractable, summoned all her tact to cope with it. " Your head, my love, is full of fancies. You've been ill."

"Not that old tale again ! " cried Arabella. " It has been overdone. I was never ill, or if you like Bridget can tell you just *how* ill ! . . . What are these plots and secrecies around me ? I am not a child now. I am sixteen. You were married and a mother before my age. Sweet Aunt . . ." and Arabella, down upon her knees, was pleading. " Tell me, if you know, who was the man that came to me in a disguise that would not have deceived a sparrow. I know he wasn't what he seemed to be, nor could he deny it. But why should he have come to *me* ? Why not to my lady, or to you, or to my uncles ? "

Looking down into that turbulent young face, Mary Shrewsbury sighed. " How can I tell more than you can tell of designs against your person ? Since ever you were born, foreign powers backed by Spain have plotted, one with the other to marry you to this or that Catholic Prince. The Queen has rejected all proposals."

Arabella's eyes widened.

" Proposals ? Is it true I have had proposals of marriage ? "

" Certain suggestions have been made—" Lady Shrewsbury glanced uncomfortably aside, " of which Her Grace does not approve ; and although *we* might, it would not be politic to risk the consequence of any lapse of guardianship on our part."

" Yes, " said Arabella bitterly, " my grandmother has always guarded me as I were made o' gold."

" That, my love, is her fond duty," again her aunt's gaze slipped away. " But her ladyship will not be warned. . . . There is nothing more to tell."

" There is ! There is everything to tell ! " Furiously Arabella jogged her aunt's elbow. " You say ' we ' might approve. Who do you mean by ' we ' ? My uncles and yourself ? Approve of what ? Of whom ? If a marriage has been suggested between me and any man, no matter whether he be prince or ploughboy, I should be told of it. It is my right to be told."

She paused, and, searching her aunt's clear precise features, the thin folded lips, those light secretive eyes, Arabella wondered : Could it be possible, as Bridget once or twice had hinted, that her Aunt Mary was a Papist and held the Mass in her chamber with a priest ?

" O, God ! " she burst forth, " Lady ! What do you hide from me ? You and my uncles, even your daughter Mary, know more than I do of concerns around myself. . . . And now this letter from my Cousin James."

" Dear child, that is only natural interest——"

" There is no interest," Arabella quickly interposed, " save *self*-interest in Kings. And does he dare to couple the name of his kinsman, my usurper, Lennox, with—' longeth after me ', forsooth ! " Her laugh turned on a note of hysteria. " That little painted popinjay ! That strutting ape ! "

If there and then the girl had sprouted horns and a forked tail, Lady Shrewsbury could not have been more greatly troubled. This unsuspected personality released and rampant up and down her chamber, bore nothing of resemblance to the pretty and docile family pet, in whose future the family's hopes and desires were centred. Here was a raging virago, with eyes that blazed, and a tight mouth obstinately sealed, when it did not open to take you up and put you down with pert remarks and over-sharp perception. Nor could all her guarded answers satisfy the questing mind of Arabella, which now fixed fast upon a secret, harried her aunt as a puppy hound, unleashed, will harry a hare.

It was therefore with no regret and some relief that the Countess received peremptory word from her mother. Arbelle must be returned at once to Hardwick Hall.

She had been advised by Bridget : " You will find some changes here." But she was not prepared to find the daily routine of the life to which she was accustomed, entirely subverted by elaborate precautions devised for her safe-keeping.

Hitherto she had been accorded her own suite of apartments ; now she must share her grandmother's, not only by day, but at night. Her bed had been placed in an alcove in the Dowagers' room. Her studies were conducted in the Long Gallery—and this the only welcome change—not by Mr. Morley.

He was gone, and replaced by the secretary, John Starkey, who conversed with her in Latin, read to her in Greek, stood over her while she laboriously translated Hebrew from the Talmud, duly chaperoned by both her ladies. Nevermore was the Lady Arabella to be left unguarded in the presence of her tutor.

At the gates of the old Hall the great new building rose. Week in, week out, and month by month, the hammering persisted. In summer's sun or ankle deep in snow, the workmen toiled. The seasons came and went and the redoubtable Lady of Hardwick, well seasoned too, still sturdy to combat all weathers, watched commanding, with one eye on those who laboured, and another on the windows of the old house where her treasure, her ' Jewel ', was locked in a casket of which none but Bess of Hardwick kept the key.

And none but she, had she so chosen, could have told the reason why the Lady Arabella was now retained in virtual imprisonment. Her walks in the garden were watched, and a serving-man, John Dodderidge, a bull-necked brawny fellow, over six feet high, had been appointed to attend her Highness and her ladies when they took the air.

But Morley was gone. . . . For that one small mercy Arabella could at least be grateful ; though why he had gone, whether dismissed or of his own choosing, she was not likely to know.

The sad truth of the matter Bess kept to herself ; nor to herself did she care to admit it. She had erred in her judgment of Morley Yet although he had asked for a rise in his stipend, that impertinence alone would not have been an inexpiable lapse. She made it plain to him, however, that she would employ none in her service who expressed dissatisfaction. He must agree to her terms or get out This ultimatum notwithstanding, Morley demanded an annuity to the tune of forty pounds a year. To such presumption and audacity unprecedented, Bess returned the only answer possible.

Mr. Morley went.

It may be he premeditated his dismissal, since his bags and belongings were ready packed when he made that reprehensible suggestion.

Shortly after his departure Bess received the blow that shook her to her depths, delivered in a letter from Lord Burghley. H

with suavity and many flourishes, informed her ladyship of ' Certain
spies who lurked in the most innocent Apparel in the neighbourhood of Hardwick Hall, and indeed around the person of the
Lady Arabella. It was Lord Burghley's duty to enjoin her ladyship
that she ensure the strictest supervision of her charge.'

Bess, though shattered, was hard put not to return Lord Burghley
as good as he had given; but she wisely waited till her ' Jewel '
was safely housed again at Hardwick, by which time her ruffled
temper and her fright were both, in part, allayed. Her state of
mind, however, shows clearly in the context of the Dowager's
reply to the :

' Honourable Good Lord,
      ' I was at the first much troubled to think that so wicked
and mischievous practice should be devised to entrap my poor
Arbelle and me, but I put my trust in the Almighty and will
use such diligent care as I doubt not to prevent whatever shall
be attempted by any wicked persons against the poor child.
I am most bound to Her Majesty that it pleased Her to appoint
your Lordship to give me knowledge of this wicked practice.
. . . I will not have any unknown or suspected person to come
to my house. I have little resort to me; my house is furnished
with sufficient company. Arbelle walks not late; at such time
as she shall take the air it shall be near the house and well
attended on. She goeth not to anybody's house at all; I see
her almost every hour of the day. She lieth in my bedchamber. . . .'

Bess stayed her pen. ' Well attended on.' Yes. Never again
to be allowed alone at her studies in the garden. . . . Morley !
That double-dyed fiend ! . . . The ink spluttered to blot the page
as she determinedly resumed.

      ' About a year since there was one Harrison, a seminary,
that lay at his brother's house about a mile from Hardwick
whom I thought then to have caused to have been apprehended
and to have him sent up, but found he had a license for a
time. . . . My son William Cavendish went thither of a sudden
to make search for him, but could not find him. I write thus
much to your Lordship that if any such traitorous and naughty
persons (through Her Majesty's clemency) be suffered to go
abroad, that they may not harbour near my houses, Wingfield,
Hardwick, nor Chatsworth in Derbyshire; they are the likest
instruments to put a bad matter in execution. . . .'

The furrowed old face hardened. She had been warned by both her sons of this same Harrison, and even by that strumpet Sherland, but she had refuted any such idea; had scorned their hints. Yet might he not have been that very man who approached Arbelle last summer in a workman's dress? . . . 'Most innocent Apparel' . . . Blind! The gnarled hand tightened in a spasm to crack the quill. She had been blind, had placed her trust in one to be betrayed. Morley doubtless was in league with Harrison. Never in her life had she known her judgment fail. . . . And he had played so sweetly on the virginals, conversed with such intelligence . . . to gull her! But none, Bess swore, should know she had been fooled, unless it were that ferret Burghley, who had nosed her secret from her, and to whom she must, perforce, explain her situation and write what must be read, not only by the Queen's Lord Treasurer, but by the Queen herself.

From the innermost depths of her iron-cased heart broke a stifled groan; then the old head under the widow's cap, jerked up as if pulled by a wire. Selecting a new grey goose quill from one of several upon the table there before her, Bess fastened her mouth to check a shake in her chin, and wrote the words that must be written.

'One Morley who hath attended on Arbelle, and read with her for the space of three years and a half, showed to be in hope to have some annuity granted him during his life, alleging that he was so much damnified by leaving of the University. . . . I understand he was most discontented, and withal of late, having some cause to be doubtful of his forwardness in religion (though I cannot charge him with Papistry), I took occasion to part with him. I have another in my house who will supply Morley's place very well.

I beseech your Lordship I may be directed from you as occasion shall fall out. To the uttermost of my understanding I have been, and will, be, careful. . . .'

So careful, that gazing from her window at those great grey rock-hewn walls, while her ears sickened to the sound of iron blows, Arabella had the strangest thought that when those sounds were silenced and when those walls were built, they would take shape to hold her there within stone arms imprisoned; as now and in the future, and for all time to come.

BOOK TWO
(1596–1603)

THE walls rose high and higher; the many windows, paned with glass, gleamed behind the park trees bronzed as the eyes of deer in a thicket, reflecting throughout the seasons each sunrise and sunset. And still the hammer blows at Hardwick struck echoes from the hills in that victory year of 1596.

The sluggish tide of war with Spain, that during the past decade had advanced and retreated back and forth to menace England's shores, quickened now to tempest pitch.

It was an ill wind that blew four Spanish galleons from the Breton coast to Cornwall, there to pillage and burn Penzance and scuttle away before retaliation could be offered. This occurred in the summer of '95 ; a touch and run raid no doubt, but enough to shock England and England's Queen. Her Land's End had a chink in its armour. Yet while she railed at her Sea Lords, Gloriana if not alarmed unduly, was depressed. There had been trouble enough at home over that unfortunate affair of her trusted physician, Lopez, the Jew, who the year before was hunted to the scaffold, accused of high treason by Essex.

And what, after all, had been proven more than a shrieking confession dragged from him by means of the rack ? Who would not confess to treachery to save himself such torment ? Elizabeth never would be quite convinced of her good physician's guilt, but he had paid the hideous penalty in full; an old man, bent with torture, strung up to be cut down and disembowelled, alive, and in his death gasps swearing to his innocence and the love he bore his mistress. She had been merciful to his poor wife, had handed back to her all his goods and chattels that lawfully reverted to the Crown. She, however, kept the ring her ' dear good doctor ' wore, and which had been given him—as deduced from evidence in that mock form of trial which passed for justice—by his master, Philip of Spain. So Lopez had been convicted for a spy com-missioned by Philip to poison her, his Sovereign. She would have sooner seen him poisoned by his own hand than have it on her conscience that he, so old and frail, must die indirectly by hers.

She wept for him, and wore upon her finger the splendid ring of diamonds and rubies that might, or might not, have been Philip's.

And now he, her arch enemy, that green-toothed rat, was gnawing at her coast again. Well, vermin could be crushed, and *had* been crushed, sunk in their burning ships, mauled in all the glory of their much vaunted Armada by the onslaught of her valiant sea-lions, Drake, Howard, Raleigh—who so shamefully had played the fool with that baggage, Bess Throckmorton, and in consequence had been punished and then pardoned. . . . But what a captain, what a sailor, what a man! And Essex, too, who had climbed somewhat above himself with his latest temerarious petition to be given full command of her galleons and her seas.

Reluctantly she gave it. He would never cease to plague her till she did. He was now preparing to set out with Howard on another new exploit, this time against Cadiz. A fine expense! Henry of France had already cost her a fortune in money and thousands of men, and so much gratitude he showed for it, that, so her agents reported, he was about to throw in his lot with the Catholics and embrace their cursed faith: this the worst blow of all. To think that Navarre, the gallant desperado, for whom she had always held such fond regard and high esteem, as much for his handsome looks as for his courage, should turn traitor to the church of his adoption; and traitor thus to her, his cofferer, his saviour, his *patronne*, from whom for years he had drawn good English gold to finance his crack-brained adventures.

Pacing her Privy Chamber alone, unwatched, and wigless, her greying hair still showing tawny glints, she swore that by God's Soul there was no truth in man, no, not in any one of those who licked her feet, save for what they spewed upon the lip—worth what? No more than a dog's vomit. She knew them all. There wasn't one who 'loved' her for more than she could give in wealth and honours. Not one, save—yes, *that* one, her fading 'Spirit', Burghley, sick and aged, tottering, but loyal down to his dreams. And his son Cecil, that puny hump-backed dwarf, with his so delicate lovely face, his polished manner, and a mind to match her own, quick and rapier keen to press a point—he too, she judged, was loyal, loving her for what she represented, not as England's Queen, but England's immortality. To him she would assign his father's place in her good time. And meantime, what of Philip?

What indeed of Philip ?

High in the desolate mountain peaks of Guadarrama, where he had built himself a stronghold, his Escurial, he perched, a lean and hungry spider, weaving a ceaseless web of plot to conquer England and place on England's throne a Catholic King . . . or Queen.

There, at his littered table, cankered, old, half-paralysed, covered with sores that rendered him loathsome even to his doctors, who could scarce contain their retching at the stench of him, he sat, defying the remorseless onslaught of his slow, awful death, the while he planned another Great Armada. This time he would not fail. This time he would live to see that proud, unconscionable Woman, his dead wife's sister, vanquished, and her ships, her commanders, her men, *his* prize, his prisoners. She, whose hysterical laughter still rang in his ears—as a girl she had always laughed at him—would laugh at him no more.

He shivered with the ague. His palsied hand endeavoured, painfully, to guide the pen that scrawled his name on the sheaf of papers there before him. But above the fevered cacophony of his mind, one motive, one recurrent theme, resounded : to labour for God's glory, that England be restored to the one and only Faith, by one only means and to one end. . . . Over that sallow-sick face flittered a gleam like the light of a taper turned on a crumbling skull. The swollen tongue came out to moisten the scabbed dark lips that smiled. . . . One only end, which he, through all these years, had dogged undaunted.

She, that child, that girl, kinswoman of the martyred Mary, and England's rightful heir, they kept her close, had foiled him, but not for ever. No ! He still might hope. The Parma brothers each in his turn had been named by His Holiness as a possible means to that end, through alliance to this Arabella Stuart. It had come to nothing. Parma's spies had bungled shamefully, or the girl was too well watched. What of these reports from one Middleton, an English priest . . . or was it Harrison ? No matter.

The trembling hands crept to a locked drawer of the writing table where he sat, hunched. A key was turned, a parchment found and scanned. Yes, here ! The confession of the Jesuit, one James Yong, extorted on the rack in the presence of the Lord Keeper Puckering, Mr. Fortescue, Chancellor of the Exchequer, Lord Buckhurst, and others. Yong purported to have overheard a conversation between two agents in Spain's employ. . . . 'If we had *her* the most of our fears were past, for if anyone could hinder us in England it is the Princess Arabella. . . .' Why? The craven curs! Philip crashed his fist upon the desk. Why should Arabella hinder them, when with his next breath the treacherous fool admits 'she is England's greatest fear, lest she be proclaimed Queen when Her Majesty should die. . . . And certain cunning fellows have promised to convey her by stealth out of England into Flanders, which if it be done, the promise is she shall shortly visit Spain. . . .'

Yes, Spain for her sanctuary: Spain's King for her protector! But Burghley, that old fox, had laid his snare and crushed the scheme in its beginnings. Let it go. There was more afoot than the croakings of black-hearted cowards who betrayed with shrieks a sacred trust, rather than submit to a few hours' searing of their miserable flesh. . . . So this one and that one, this Yong, this Harrison, or Middleton, and others, one Morley, the girl's tutor who had succumbed to certain questions applied by English methods, would . . . again that dreadful smile . . . be questioned closer still. And here. In Spain.

Meanwhile he had more to do than brood upon a blunder. French agents in Paris had been better occupied, and to some advantage.

Once more he searched among his documents, and unfolding a paper from a packet neatly bound with a narrow red ribbon, King Philip, smiling, read:

'The Minister Sully has been overheard to express the views of the King of France. . . . The King, said Sully, has discussed with him which Princess of Europe he should choose for his wife if his marriage with Margaret of Valois were dissolved. "I should have no objection," he said, "to the Infanta of Spain, provided that with her I could marry the Low Countries. . . ."'

A-ah!

In the paroxysm of his fury, Philip spat a blood-stained slime; his face dripped sweat. A shrinking page approached him with a basin. The King waved him back. "Leave me. . . . Leave me!" The Infanta! His beloved Isabella, who, by dispensation, he himself would marry sooner than any man but he should know her loveliness. . . . Did that damned heretic Henry hope to ravish *her* as he dared hope to ravish the Spanish Netherlands ? A heretic, turned apostate, that he might force entry into favour with His Holiness. What further devil's insolence was here reported ? . . . The pus-rimmed eyes peered closer.

" 'Neither would I refuse the Princess Arabella of England, since it is publicly said that the Crown of England belongs to her, and were she declared presumptive heiress to it.' "

Heiress to that God-forsaken island ! Yes, if through her the right of succession could revert to Spanish claim and this boasting braggart, Henry, be brought to heel, who for arms and money might be bribed : and subjugated.

Philip rose from his great chair, and shuffled through a narrow door into his oratory to kneel before the altar where his priests, in their glittering vestments, performed their holy work. He prayed that the earthly duties to which he had been called might be carried to a glorious finale. He must live to see that frightful Woman done to death or saved from everlasting torment by renunciation of her pharisaical profanities. He must conquer all the Netherlands. He must win that weakling, James of Scotland, to the Faith. He must marry his daughter. No man on earth was fit to touch her sacred body but himself, God's Chosen. . . . He must assemble his ships and launch yet another Armada, and vanquish once and for ever that poisonous fog-bound plague-spot, that England of abhorrent memory, and the unspeakable Woman who ruled over it : his sister Queen whom he had known in her young girlhood, and whom—Pity of Christ !—he had so desired, so hated : and loved.

His eyes rolled up to show the whites. He mouthed and mumbled while his priests circled round him, and the tender faces of pictured saints gazed down. He clutched his crucifix, he cried aloud and kissed the tortured Figure. He saw visions and fell prostrate in his ecstasy. The priests chanted their benediction and got him on his feet, and returned him to his lair and his First Lord of the Seas, the Duke of Medina Sidonia.

Elizabeth too was at her prayers, in Greenwich Chapel, when, on a quiet Sunday morning, the distant boom of guns drifted up the Thames across the sea from Calais. The Archduke Albert,

Governor of the Netherlands, had sprung a march on Henry and was in possession of the coast.

She leapt from her seat to interrupt the Bishop in his sermon and swear that by God's Son she would save the town from Philip's clutches!

She lost no time. The shocked Bishop continued his address to a diminished congregation.

Down the aisle swept the Queen. Her startled Maids, her gentlemen, less startled than intrigued, followed after. The Bishop raised his hands in despair and a blessing. At the church door the Queen turned with an order: "Despatch a messenger to the Lord Mayor of London to impress a thousand men without delay and send them off to Calais. Now. At once!"

But the next day her excitement had abated. When Henry's Ambassador asked for more assistance she offered it on one condition; that England alone should garrison the Port of Calais with an army to meet the Spanish Netherlanders. . . . No! Henry emphatically rejected the outrageous proposition. He would 'sooner be bitten by a dog than scratched by a cat.' A few days later Elizabeth was mortified to see the town carried by storm and the Spaniards dumped upon the beach across the English Channel.

It was Lord High Admiral Howard of Effingham who recommended, at this crisis, that England should anticipate Philip's preparations and attack his threatening fleet before it left their ports. In this, Essex, renouncing his temporary command of the seas to wiser and cooler judgment, ardently seconded him, and took over an army of fourteen thousand men, while Howard fitted out the ships to carry them.

Toward the end of June the English fleet manned with these formidable numbers, sailed into the harbour of Cadiz. They had caught napping Medina Sidonia, to take him and his galleons by surprise. With shouts of 'Entramos! Entramos!' Essex threw his hat into the sea and was for jumping after it to land his men in boats, but that Raleigh with some pressure, managed to restrain him. The bombardment must be effected from the water.

The Fleet gave voice.

From every deck the cannon barked. The town was set afire. The infuriated Spaniards returned volley after volley from the shore in fierce reply, to little purpose. Their ships were sunk a anchor and the town, burgeoning with loot, fell in a matter of hours. It was an overthrow complete and deadly, astonishing to conquered and conquerors alike.

Throughout Europe Elizabeth was lauded to the skies. The victors, with their ships beflagged, came sailing up the river into London, crowned with laurels, their pockets stuffed with Spanish gold, their sea-chests full of treasure.

While Raleigh divided the naval honours of the fight with Admiral Lord Howard, Essex was the darling of the day. He had led the final attack on the city to rout the Spaniards on their land. The streets rang with cheers for him; every steeple pealed its joy-bells. The Queen danced in her Palace on the Thames, and in his Palace on the Guadarrama Mountains, Philip prayed, and itched, and clawed his flesh, and damned to perdition his flabby First Lord, the Duke of Medina Sidonia.

*   *   *

Throughout that summer and well into the autumn the victory celebrations continued to fill London Town with gaping folk, who from nearby villages had flocked to see the sights.

The Lord of Misrule romped through the streets with a hundred lusty followers, decked in liveries of green and yellow, with bells on their garters that jingled as they danced mounted on hobby-horses, dragons, and other fearsome creatures. Through twisting alleyways, up and down the river banks, along the Strand, they galloped, their pipers piping, their drummers drumming, right into the church : and though the minister be at prayer or preaching —what of that ? Out again and through the churchyard, dancing to their homes, there to feast and frolic until sundown. And that was on a Sunday, and it went on all through the week. Nor was it London and its environs only that took part in these revels ; from all over England came those more privileged than country oafs to pay homage to their Queen. And among them Arabella.

For the first time in four years Her Grace had summoned her to Court. A great event, and perhaps to Arabella an answer to her prayers. Life had been dreary enough at Hardwick under the restrictions that, ever since her return from Sheffield, had been so firmly enforced. True, she was permitted on rare occasions to revisit her Aunt Shrewsbury, a welcome change ; yet even there she had been kept under restraint, and watched. But she had her faithful adherents, Anne, Bridget, and John Starkey, who still tutored her long after her schooling days were past.

She enjoyed to read with him. He did not ram his knowledge down her throat, that from sheer repletion her lessons, half-digested, would regurgitate *ad nauseam*, as so often was the case with Mr. Morley. No, John Starkey, with an obvious enjoyment of his tutorship, led her past the scheduled road of routine to enchanted byways. Thus, having mastered Greek and Latin, she was, for her delight, presented to Dante, Petrarch, and Boccaccio. She wept with Beatrice, laughed at the naughty tales told in that villa at Fiesole, till her tutor deemed it wise to close the book and introduce her to less equivocal, more modern, English writers.

Here was fresher field for thought. She revelled in the newly published ' Faerie Queene '. With Amoretti she pursued the poet's great love-passion in its varied stages of despair, to hope and triumph; nor was she the less absorbed to know this happy versifier to be the friend of Essex.

To the Lady of Hardwick Mr. Starkey rendered panegyrical reports of her Highness's advancement. He found the Lady Arabella most studious, intelligent, receptive; her taste for poesy pronounced. Were University degrees permitted to the gentler sex, no question but that the Lady Arabella would have taken highest honours.

Oblivious to, indeed all unaware of his employer's frosted eye, the rhapsodic Starkey continued his hosanna. Her Highness was exceptionally gifted. He would submit to Lady Shrewsbury a verse the Lady Arabella had composed. Her ladyship would certainly agree that here was no mean poet, but a very Mistress of the Arts. Publication would be certain if under a pseudonym the poem could be——

" Go ! " The Dowager pointed to the door. " And do you, sirrah, fill her head with any such farragoes, I swear I'll have yours in the pillory, if not upon a pike ! "

A threat that caused the earnest Mr. Starkey to stifle his emotions while his pupil, in his heart, he continued to extol.

And Bess considered. . . . Much use to a girl to be Mistress of the Arts. Better she were mistress of a man ! Yet how in the devil to get her back into the Court if the Queen were not anxious to receive her, was a problem.

The problem, however, soon resolved itself. The Queen, it

seemed, *was* anxious to receive her, and forgive past misdemeanours with an invitation to attend upon Her Grace.

Bess went ahead with preparations. Hardwick echoed to the pattering of tire-women's feet, and the click-clack of their shuttles as the spinners, at their wheels, whispered that the Lady Arabella would look lovely as a lily in this gold, and sweeter than a white rose in this silver. . . .

The joy-bells were still ringing their message of good cheer, the streets festooned with flags and strung with garlands, when she knelt before the Queen on the last night of that glorious July.

The month's festivities at Court had reached the peak of jubilation in a Masque. This by command of Elizabeth who, as tribute to the heroes of Cadiz, had ordered the presentation of a ship at sea with masquers dressed as mariners to man it. Neptune, in full apparel of fish scales and seaweed, rose majestically from out the cloud of gauze that passed for waves, attended by twelve ocean nymphs and tritons.

The ship, a masterpiece of stage-craft, wobbled insecurely on a platform with sails swelling in the breeze promoted by spasmodic efforts of lackeys in the background, armed with bellows. A lavish spectacle, the more realistic for a thunderstorm that shook the roof and cracked the skies to scare the girls, and cause Her Majesty to cry that Jove himself looked down to bless the revels.

The counterfeit effect of sound, the mock flash-lightning of torches, were submerged in nature's violence. The Queen was charmed. The mummers more so. They had been spared much intricate display of noises off. And that not a syllable they spoke could be heard above the din and the frightened shrieks of pretty creatures, did not at all distress them since none was quite word perfect in his part.

Surrounded by her Maidens, Elizabeth sat smiling. Arabella, seated next to her aunt, Lady Shrewsbury, smiled too. Never had she beheld such wealth of colour, costume, such graceful poses or such dainty nymphs. While others, who by frequent repetition of mountebank impersonations, had been rendered ultra-critical if not a trifle bored, Arabella was enraptured.

The tritons' palpably puffed cheeks, achieved by paste stuck on and painted over, the indeterminate sex of sirens, recognized by the blasé as boys, thrilled her with awe and delight. Neptune's wig, his roseate complexion, his magnificent presence, his mumbling voice that rose now and then to a roar, was to her the height of Thespian achievement. Notwithstanding all the classic dramas she had read, she had never yet witnessed a play, nor been within sight of a player. How boldly, between thunder-claps, Neptune defied the elements, straddling a dolphin, brandishing his trident, while with impassioned ardour he declaimed:

> ' Come away, come away,
> We grow jealous of your stay,
> If you do not stop your ear,
> We shall have more cause to fear '.

Amazing! Quite a poet. She did not know, and likely, nor did anybody else, that the verse had been devised and jotted down upon the moment by the young Ben Jonson, as yet unfamed, unnoticed, who stood behind to prompt his boon companions.

The Queen clapped her hands and loudly applauded: " Bravo! Bravissimo! Brave Neptune! "

So fiery was her wig, and so bejewelled, that it seemed as it were bursting into flame. She blew kisses from her finger-tips, she hailed him: " King of the ocean, as we are now Queen of the seas! "

Neptune, highly gratified, stepped from the back of his dolphin to climb on to the deck of the ship, that creaked beneath his weight and looked to topple over. Perspiring tritons rose from gauze waves to steady it. A flash of lightning lit the sea-king's face and called forth more screams from the ladies. Neptune smiled reassurance, and when the thunder rolled away, prompted from behind by Mr. Jonson, he delivered his finale.

> ' We leave that climate of the sky
> To comfort of a greater Light
> Who forms all beauty within sight.'

Acclamation was unanimous.

" Excellent! "

" Most worthy god! "

" A fine declaimer! "

" Bravely spoken, Neptune! You have well-learned your lines."

" No lines, no words, however brave, can do justice to the beauteous light of my most dear, admired Sovereign."

Arabella glanced aside. . . . Yes, there he was, posturing before

Her Grace, first among those who came to offer their felicitations, gratitude : and platitude.

She bit her lip. Was it possible Her Grace could swallow all this blather ? Her Grace apparently could, and did, and asked for more. She beamed. She tapped her fan coquettishly upon the shoulders of her kneeling gentlemen. She glittered like some ageless golden fairy. . . . 'But you are ten thousand times more beautiful than the queen of them all' . . . Would he remember ? Would he give one look in her direction ?

No.

The masquers backed from the royal Presence and disappeared behind the now deflated sails of the ship. The Queen, with her Maidens, stood. In unison all the guests stood. Her Majesty called for a dance. Graciously she laid her hand upon the arm of Essex, but the eye she turned upon him was not gracious ; it was cold.

He led her out. The Court watched with admiration, genuinely stirred by the grace of that incredible defiant figure whose years, as always when she danced, slipped from her like a grey discarded cloak.

"One might," Mary Shrewsbury's whisper tickled Arabella's ear, "believe her endowed by magic to transform herself. She's sixty-three."

Sixty-three ! So old, yet never old. Despite the painted wrinkles, the crude wig, the blackened teeth, every movement of that slender, reed-like body, each gleam from those burning blue eyes, expressed an unquenchable love of life and living. Yes, she was, and would remain, for ever young.

Lady Shrewsbury's smile was a thought one-sided. She had not been raised to favour, had not once been invited to the Privy Table. She was tolerated merely for the blood-relationship she bore to Her Majesty's kinswoman; and the knowledge rankled. Moreover, it had reached her ears that the Queen suspected her of 'Papistry'. . . . She could deny it, bring witnesses to prove the charge unfounded. . . . She hoped, she prayed such need would never be. There were odious dark ways employed to trace the shadow of a 'Popish' charge. What ! Must one's prayers, one's sacred privacy, be watched, condemned, and brought to light by torture unendurable ? May Heaven protect all those who worship at their secret shrines. May God, entreated Mary, protect me.

Her fingers strayed to her corsage for comfort. Behind the glitter of her jewels, between her breasts, lay the precious emblem of her Faith. Her lips moved silently; then fortified, she turned again to Arabella with softness in her voice.

"Observe, although she honours him, how Her Grace has eyes for everyone but Essex. They say that she does not at all approve of this adoration the people fling upon the hero of the hour. And why should she approve, when Essex claims the due that should be Raleigh's?"

"All who fought at Cadiz," Arabella returned quietly, "are heroes." But her heart cried: Only he deserves what has been given, and more than any one of us can give.

She did not see herself ridiculous. She did not see herself in love. The hero-worship of a school-girl had grown with her unfolding, imperceptibly from bud to spring-time blossom. She had been fed by Mr. Starkey on romance, was filled with poesy. But while her spirit sang. neither she nor those around her realized that she had crossed the threshold of youth's womanhood, with all its strange perplexities, its lightning fevers, passionate obsessions, and eager, indestructible beliefs. There was about her still the look of a bewildered child dreaming on the borderland of life envisioned, and life lived.

The summer storm was over. In the Great Hall the Queen's guests danced, Arabella with Northumberland, who the year before had married Dorothy, sister of Essex.

Between gyrations, Arabella made a little speech.

"I am rejoiced to know your lordship is happily espoused."

"I am," he answered, very short, "*not* happily espoused."

"Oh! . . . I . . ." Her mouth opened a little. Embarrassed, she blushed. "I have heard that newly married gentlemen in love are apt to deny their hearts—a—affection as a—as a lad who robs an orchard hides the apples he has stolen to enjoy in secret. Your words do contradict you."

And having got that out she slipped a smile, looking up at him as he looked down.

"You have not changed."

"Me? . . . I . . . Indeed I have. I am a woman grown."

"Not that. You never will be. Will your Highness sit? This room is stifling."

She would have sooner danced than sit with him who, as ever, showed so churlish an outside; yet maybe, she reflected—always ready to excuse—that is only a disguise to hide himself. She remembered he had always appeared bashful, with nothing of the courtier in his poise, nor in his words. She laid her fingers on his offered arm and felt the muscles under the encrusted satin harden to her touch. Glancing down she noted that his left hand had tightened too, and was clenched against his sword-hilt. What a tormented gloomy creature, to be sure! He seemed to be at constant war between himself and unseen persons.

Eyes followed them; exchange of whispers passed among the Queen's Maids. . . . " He has not forgot his first infatuation. Was ever man so faithful ? "

" Or so faithless. His wife's a shrew."

" Pity 'tis he could not take his choice."

" He'll take it an it please him for she's as green as ever, and looks no older than she did five years ago."

" Lord ! What a gown ! Cloth of gold and strewn with pearls. It must have cost a fortune."

Young Lady Mary Howard pulled a face. " Wonder the Queen don't strip her of it, as she stripped mine from me." . . . When she had dared appear in velvet as fine as any the Queen possessed.

" Well ! She must be twenty, and still spinning St. Catherine's wheel. Her Grace won't let her marry."

Which knowledge must have comforted the Maids.

Seated in an oriel window overlooking the river, the subject of these generous conjectures gazed out into the dark : a night of stars and grape-bloom shadows that held a strange dream-like solidity, as if at any moment they might rise from the silvered water and march in shapes along the Palace walls. Yet nothing stirred. The waiting barges with their lanthorns fixed, stood motionless ; no sound of voice, no cry of bird nor beast disturbed that silence, the more gentle for the contrast to the distant strains of revelry within, of laughter shrill, discordant, and of men's voices slurred with drink.

Leaning her elbows on the window-sill, Arabella covered her ears. " I love," she said, " to watch the dark. 'Tis full of magic. I love to watch the river sliding its way to the sea. I would like to follow the river. It is always moving. Does it never sleep ? "

She spoke so softly that he who stood beside her must bend his head to hear.

"I marvel," his breath quickened with his words, "that you retain your crocus-sweetness in this hothouse Court . . . of shams."

Unwillingly she turned with a question in her eyes and a doubting smile on her lips.

"Shams, my lord?"

"Hypocrisies. Or false gods . . . if you will."

Her smile deepened.

"But I will not, my lord. False gods do not exist save in imagination. Though I think," she added musingly, "there is in every one of us a false god, if not false image, self-created."

"In fact a thousand devils," he sardonically agreed, "each striving for supremacy, as the one eternal ego . . . would you say?"

She had no wish to say if he would take words from her, to twist them with such dry insinuation.

"I have not," she answered, coldly, "much knowledge of the ego."

"No? You do not believe with Plautus, then, ' *Ego met sum mihi*'?"

His tone half-mocking, half-derisive, piqued her.

"Certainly I don't believe 'I am my own commander'. God alone is that."

"Yet have you not admitted a god within yourself?"

"A false god, yes."

"Can one discriminate between the false and true?"

She shook her head. "You pass beyond my range. I'm no philosopher. Nor am I misanthropic."

"You consider me a misanthrope?"

"I do not," she gleamed, "consider you at all."

"H'm!" The corners of his lips turned down. "*Touché.*"

He sat beside her. His eyes deep in under his shelving brows weighed heavily on hers. She looked away; and struggling between resentment and politeness engaged in small-talk.

"My lord, do you hear aught of your protégé, my cousin?"

"Which cousin?"

Was ever man so taciturn and rude?

"Why, my cousin Lennox."

His face closed.

"Nothing to his credit. The King of Scots has honoured him so far above himself that he looks to be Ambassador in France."

"But that is surely to his credit? He must have earned the honour."

"I suggest that honour credited is seldom earned."

"And I suggest," she answered hotly, "that such an observation does *dis*credit you, my lord! Will you now escort me to Lady Shrewsbury, my aunt? She will be searching . . ."

"*I've* been searching and I've found!"

He whose name was at that moment her unspoken thought, caprisen between Northumberland's assertion and her defence of it, stood bowing.

Northumberland's hand slid to his sword-hilt. Arabella curtsied. Lord Essex kissed her fingers.

"My most humble duty, Madam."

"My lord, you startled me. I did not expect—"

"Her Ladyship," Northumberland said harshly, "has asked me to escort her to . . ."

Airily Lord Essex waved him off.

"I will escort her Ladyship. You had best go seek your wife. When I last saw—and heard her—she was deep in talk with Cecil. Discussing you."

She did not see the sullen red flare in the other's face as he received that taunt. She did not see his threatening step towards him who offered it. . . . Nor did she see him go.

* * *

The summer weeks sped by, and with each day a new horizon lifted, constantly re-forming and vanishing away in a flux of swift impressions touched by the first breath-taking pangs of youth awakened. She was lost in the warm intoxication of discovery that in the eager flight of hours, drugged reason, duty, judgment.

Her wonder-charged reception of his sophistical advance was a delicious rare experience for him. He fostered it, to lose himself, a little. But while he knew that in her innocent defencelessness he could have had her for the asking, since throughout his meteoric arrogant career he had seized and taken where he willed, he chose to dally. Sense, or sentiment, or maybe the danger that environed his approach to one who by all tenets should be unapproachable, restrained him. And that too was an experience: disturbing.

For the first time in his all-conquering pursuit of pleasure he was halted. True, in a world of surface flippancies and puppet courtiers, who, in the whim of a moment might be raised to the sunlight of favour or cast to the nethermost shades, one could not afford to offend. But not wholly did consideration of himself, and the consequence of royal animosity suppress him. To play the lover unconfessed, to watch her shy response, her provocative retreat, was an unbelievable temptation that chafed his manhood sorely to resist. Yet he resisted. Nor, until the Court had moved to Richmond, where the formality of routine enforced at Whitehall relaxed to a holiday humour, did he achieve an assignation. And even that was not bespoken ; nothing said that if repeated could be possibly pronounced as indiscreet.

" Her Majesty will ride at eight o'clock tomorrow morning. Does your Ladyship ride with her ? "

Yes, her Ladyship would ride. And when Essex with a long look bowed and left her, she went flying to Anne Bradshaw.

" Anne ! The Queen rides tomorrow morning. I have said that I'll ride too. But I am not invited. I *must* ride tomorrow morning."

Anne's spaniel-dark eyes lifted from her tambour frame, and at their wordless question Arabella crimsoned, defiantly to add " I presume, since my Lord Essex is Master of the Horse, he would not have asked me unless he were instructed by Her Grace. . . . And I am cramped for want of exercise."

" Shall we," Anne offered gently, " go take a walk now, by the river ? "

" Walk ? " Arabella pointed to the window. Under low-lying clouds the river, mist-enshrouded, twined like an oily grey serpent between its rain-blurred banks. In the drenched meadows the Queen's herds huddled beneath the trees for shelter from the downpour. " Walk in this ? "

It was Anne's turn to flush.

" I tell you," with renewed assertion Arabella emphasized, " I *will* ride tomorrow morning."

" If Lord Essex has suggested that your Ladyship shall ride then——" carefully Anne sorted silks, " he doubtless will arrange it."

" But what if he—— "

At that eager withdrawn supposition Anne raised her head, and for the thousandth time she wished that Mistress Sherland had not been detained in London to attend on Lady Shrewsbury, who by tacit understanding was reported indisposed. The Queen had no included Mary Shrewsbury in her entourage at Richmond, where Arabella had her quarters in the House.

"Lady," Anne re-threaded her needle, "is it of so much matter that you ride tomorrow morning with Her Grace?"

"Yes. You know how I enjoy to . . . Anne!" She knelt to twist Anne's face to hers. "Of what are you thinking so shut in yourself? I have observed of late that you and I—and 'tis not my fault, I'm sure—are not so easy with each other as we should be. What do you hide from me? What have you heard? Come out into the open if you have aught to say—and say it."

"What should I say that is not said? And what should I hide from you, my dear? . . . My very dear." Anne let fall her needle to take the girl's chin in her hand. "My only prayer is for your happiness."

"Why?" Arabella rose from her knees and moved away. "Why should you pray for my happiness when I am happier now than I have ever been? Tell me," she said coaxingly, "what you have heard. I think I guess. That Ratcliffe girl, and Mary Howard, and every one of the Queen's Maids are whispering my name to couple it with Essex because, forsooth, he likes to dance with me. His step suits well with mine. You know——" she seized Anne's wrist to shake it. "*Will* you leave your broidery a minute and attend? You know there is no more in his regard than the attention of a—of one who by virtue of his high estate must——" She gave a little breathless laugh—"must show discrimination to myself—politely. After all I am Her Grace's cousin."

"I know," Anne murmured, peering closer to her work as if her life depended on the shading of a rose. "I know 'tis dangerous to play with fire."

"Of all exasperating creatures!" Arabella cried. "You never speak except to vex me. Who would play with fire to be burned? Not I!" Again that held-in laugh. "I'm mortal scared of hurt, and I'm no stoic. But I'll ride tomorrow morning come what may!"

And ride she did, following behind Her Grace's palfrey, mounted on a roan grey mare, dressed in a habit of hunter's green velvet, with Essex ahead alongside the Queen, and a view of his back for her comfort.

The rain of the day before had passed. September sun shone from a flax-blue sky, and burned to copper flame the beech and oak-

125

leaves. Rowan-berry clusters pierced the green, scattering scarlet droplets in the hedges for the birds' delight. In every orchard red-gold moons peeped from burdened apple-trees ; in stubble fields the corn stood stacked for harvest. The freshened air, with its tang of wood-smoke, first herald of autumn, whipped the colour into Arabella's cheeks, while her heel spurred the grey mare, daringly to overtake the Queen and out-distance those behind her.

Under low-hanging branches, over fallen tree-trunks, avoiding by a hair's breadth a herd of startled deer, Arabella rode full tilt, leaning forward in the saddle to urge the grey mare on. Her hair, loosened from its bodkins, tumbled from under her plumed hat in a cascade of curls. She was lost in this miracle of living, of swift movement, of escape. . . .

" By God's Soul ! Has the girl or her horse run mad ? "

Elizabeth, herself no shirker of hard riding, curbed her white palfrey which was in a fret to join that headlong gallop. Under her lowered hat-brim the Queen's eyes slid round to Essex. His chin was up, his nostrils flared. Between his parted lips his teeth gleamed in soundless laughter. He half stood in his stirrups. . . . A stripling, a boy again, as when she first had seen him.

" I' faith ! Her Ladyship rides like the wind ! "

" Or the devil." Abruptly Elizabeth wheeled in her tracks, calling to her followers : " Turn about—all of ye ! Essex, you ! Go overtake the Lady Arabella."

Like points of steel her eyes beneath the shadow of her hat darted this way and that way, at every face, stabbing to silence the excited chatter of her ladies ; to stifle the amused asides of gentle-men, who muttered that the broth was on the boil. Her Ladyship, it seemed, had cooked her goose.

" She surely must have lost her head ! " gasped Lady Mary Howard.

" No, my love ; her heart."

Elizabeth Brydges gave a twist to her tip-tilted nose, that a everyone, and in particular her sister Maidens, knew had been somewhat disjointed since the advent of the Lady Arabella to the Court.

Cobham, the Lord Chamberlain, looked glum. There'd be trouble brewing over this tomfoolery. He'd advise Her Grace—if she would need advising on that score—that this young harum scarum be sent home to her granddame before further mischief were done. The Queen was rampant, and small wonder. . . . The anxious Cobham edged his horse to gain Her Grace's side.

"Your Majesty—hem—ah! A most regrettable occurrence. Her Ladyship's mare is somewhat—ah—mettlesome. I will speak to the Groom of the Stables. He should not have mounted her Ladyship on such a——"

"Her Ladyship knows how to ride, and she'll soon learn how to fall."

The Queen closed her lips and smiled.

The Lord Chamberlain stared between his horse's ears and hemmed again. Here was a coil, and no mistake! But why send Essex off to bring the girl to heel?

The Lord Chamberlain was not the only gentleman who wondered why; or what capricious fantasy had seized Her Grace, to snatch at vanished Spring before the ruthless fall of Winter's snows engulfed it.

Unseen but all observant, flame-like as Autumn's touch upon the dappled leaves, her spirit may have hovered, poised, above the thud of hooves to steal a secret.

"Lady! . . . Will you out-race me too?"

A flying glance behind; a girl's clear laugh.

"Come, catch me if you can!"

Over rabbit-haunted hillocks, up to the hocks in bracken, intoxicated by her laughter and the glint of streaming hair, he followed that fearless figure where she led.

Having tested his horse's wind, he gave full rein, knowing himself the heavier weight, his mount the heavier steed. By Jupiter! The girl rode like a demon, downhill, and lying forward on the grey mare's neck with a wave of her hand and a shout behind to him. "Come on! You haven't caught me yet!"

Not yet. . . . And nowhere near it! The grey mare went like the blown dust devils kicked from her galloping heels. Setting his teeth he dug his spurs. His horse, infected by that madcap lead, gathered himself to outstrip it. Was this her idea of a jest?

She had now come to the foot of the hill with a level of greensward ahead, but that headlong flight had begun to tell even on very Arab-bred sinew and muscle. He gained; and as he neared he saw the whip-hand raised to cut the mare over its flank, and then a sudden swerve, a flash of grey and green, and she fell sideways, down, and rolling over to lie where she was flung.

He saw no more till he knelt beside her in the grass. Her eyes were shut, her eyelids quivering, her face still flushed and warm, with tiny beads of wet about the brow where the fair damp tendrils strayed.

"Child! . . ." Fear thickened his voice. "Are you hurt?"

Sliding an arm beneath her, he raised her up with a frantic glance around for running water. There must surely be a stream. . . . He saw the mare, dark-streaked with sweat, standing quietly enough some paces off, nuzzling a tussock. He turned again to her whose head lolled upon his shoulder, and laid a hand over her breast above her heart. A wild fluttering responded to his touch; her whole body seemed to shudder. Then her eyes sprang open and laughter curved her lips.

"I've won!"

"You have." Still kneeling, he dropped her hand. "By a trick."

"My horse had tired. You'd have catched me. I'll allow it was a trick . . . a scurvy trick. I learned it when I used to go out riding with my cousins years ago."

She sat up smoothing her disordered hair, her eyes mockingly in his. "I've lost," she said, "my hat."

What lunacy could have possessed her to play this game with him? . . . Relief, anger, the fierce urge of his blood aroused by that wild chase, her dewy tremulous mouth that framed those breathless phrases, all conspired to lessen his control. Yet he managed to articulate: "You might have broke your neck."

"My neck is strong." And white as milk, that glimpse of it between starched ruff and velvet.

Entangled in her habit, she struggled to her feet. He caught her hands to help her. "I know, my lord, 'twas an unfair advantage."

Saying that, she looked at him, her upper lip folded short against her teeth, and in her eyes two dancing imps. Tightening his hands on hers, he drew her nearer.

"I wonder," he said huskily, "if you know just how . . unfair."

Her face paled; very still she stood while her eyes, gold-flecked and shining, half doubtful, half expectant, questioned him. Greedily he drank her in. So strange a mixture of sorcery and innocence her tumbled hair, those freckles like a schoolboy's on her nose, tha

ripe blunt-cornered mouth, that smile, magnetic, tantalizing. . . .
Good God ! Was ever man so tempted ?

Then, as if to test him further, she stripped off the jewelled
gauntlet from her right hand, rubbed her wrist, and wincing, said :
" I did not fall so well as Gilbert Cavendish, my cousin, would have
wished, or as he taught me . . . I think I've sprained, or twisted
this." And she held her hand out to him as a hurt child might, for
comfort.

At that confiding gesture he gave way, and with a short
cry took her, to slake himself with kisses on mouth and throat
and breast. But at her instinctive first recoil from the storm she had
so wilfully aroused, his arms slackened and fell.

" Forgive me. I am mad."

" I love . . . I love such madness."

On her bruised parted lips she laid two fingers and spoke
through them. " No man has ever touched . . . nor never shall
touch me again. No man but you, my lord, so long as we two shall
live."

With something like a groan he turned from her.

" You don't know what you say. I am married. I am bound."

" And I'm forbidden marriage."

Her chin lifted. There was that in her poise, her tone, the
expression of her eyes that for one shadowy moment seemed to
harbour a reflection of another, whose imperious proud spirit rose
between them. And almost as if she, too, were conscious of that
ghostly intervention, she shivered, to add inconsequently : " A
grey goose is walking on my grave. You said——? "

" I would have said . . . that you're too young. Only a fledgling,
unschooled, untutored in any worldly knowledge, would dare give
utterance to such preposterous . . ."

He paused. She was gazing at him with that half-smile, her
eyes still faintly mocking, while she repeated the caressing movement
of her fingers to her lips. He had purported to be brutal and had
failed. She saw through his over-emphasized protest.

Dismayed, he turned from her. This foolish passion-bud must
be crushed in its first flowering : he must tear from him those
clinging fibres that so insidiously had twined about his heart. . . .
His heart ! A low bitter laugh escaped him. He had thought
to have no heart, or that his appetite for tainted interludes had
rendered him case-hardened. And now this ! . . . This swift revival,

this tingling flare of feverish elation to give him back a little of his boyhood's faith, beliefs, and ecstasies.

Yet resolutely he repelled the aching urge within himself to rediscover all that youth craves for, its dreads and hopes and dreams, and all that she—with what guileless impetuosity—now offered; not to save his skin, which had toughened in the sordid game of subterfuge, but to save hers.

He stood staring at a point above her head to tell her steadily "Your Ladyship must not forget that we are both our Sovereign's servants."

"If I forget, then why should you remember?"

He could feel her eyes drawing him and dragged his own away from that smile, from those lips. And how he steeled himself to speak the words he never knew.

"Will your Ladyship allow me to remount you? Your horse is straying."

She sighed, a broken sigh, and still gazing at him, her eyes clouded now, she whispered: "I thought . . . I dared believe you were inclined somewhat to . . . like me. Since first I saw you there was never any other. Only you."

This could not go on. If she had made a study of the subtle arts of torture she could not have more cruelly succeeded. Yet still, so much is certain to his credit, he resisted, with unimagined self-denial to repeat: "Can I persuade your Ladyship to mount?"

In silence, sobered, hurt, with every now and then a puzzled glance at him who sat so stern and upright in the saddle, she rode home.

The sun stood high in heaven; a lark soared up exultant. All the trees were full of feathered song, but not another word was passed between them. So close they rode together that their shadows merged in one, to follow, darkening, behind them in their tracks.

Chapter Two

I t was a nine days' wonder in the Court that the Queen had shown such lenity to the Lady Arabella's hoydenish behaviour when riding with Her Grace. The polite fiction that her Ladyship's horse had bolted, and that only her superb equestrian skill had saved her from more serious consequence than a sprained wrist, served to smother curiosity until fiction, to all intent and purpose, became fact.

The Groom of the Stables had been roundly dealt with, and the roan grey mare, by order of Lord Essex, Master of the Horse, reserved for his lordship's use and delivered to his house at Wanstead.

Thither he too repaired on plea of ill-health. He suffered from convenient attacks of ague.

According to report his lordship was leading the life of a recluse; had assumed a totally new character, no longer the pleasure-loving dilettante, but a grave and pious man, content to live quietly at home with his long-suffering and virtuous little Countess. He attended her to church, knelt with her in prayer on the cold stones of St. Paul's, the most exemplary of husbands.

But this amazing transformation bred more chatter in Court circles than ever did his lordship's livelier habits. And in a month or two of his retirement, gossip, headed by that pietistic Dowager, old Lady Bacon, mother of Francis and Anthony, both bosom friends of Essex, had brought to light a motive for this sudden change of front. These guileful pretences were a cloak to hide some new intrigue, which, of course, involved a woman. One whose name among that galaxy of beauties must be hushed; a famous name, a name of highest rank. Mystery surrounded it. The Maids of Honour fluttered, and not a girl among them ceased to pray that *her* name would not be tarred.

But it was no Maid of Honour of whom the venerable Lady Bacon, who loved to have a finger in everybody's pie, wrote from her country house at Gorhambury on plea of acting in his lordship's fondest interest. Was he not as dear to her as her own sons?

On his share in this unhappy situation Lady Bacon did not waste much ink. His lordship's amours were a byword. Moreover it was known to be a gentleman's prerogative to indulge his fancy for the fairer sex, providing always that he did not endanger his or her good reputation. And the character of this nameless lady, so the zealous Dowager had been informed, was, until this recent sad occurrence, irreproachable. Not so now: by no means.

Vituperation spluttered from Lady Bacon's pen. No words

were harsh enough to give expression to so ' unchaste and impudent a creature, of such incorrigible unshamefacedness. . . .'

The indignant mother of the estimable Francis, whose friendship with Lord Essex she had always viewed with doubt, lost little opportunity of pressing home her point. 'She hoped, she prayed the Lord '—alluding to the Deity and not to the recipient of her objurgation—' would speedily by His Grace amend or cut the woman off before some sudden mischief would befall him.'

She then reminded the vexed Earl ' that fornicators and adulterers would be judged by the wrath of God '; and ended with a warning . . . ' Remember and consider your great danger hereby of soul and body, and grieve not the Holy Spirit.'

He replied at once with a strong denial of the accusation, protesting: 'Before the Majesty of God the charge is false, unjust, an invention of my enemies, and that since my departure from England for Spain I have been free from incontinence with any woman.'

" That'll muzzle the old Bitch ! " Thus Essex, fuming at his writing-table to call down curses upon all such saintly hags, who preached so loud against that which they were too blood-dry to practise.

Meanwhile, at Whitehall, the quakings and the shiverings persisted among the damsels of the Court. Lady Bacon's confidential correspondence did not maintain its confidence for long. If Essex thought to muzzle his ' old Bitch ', she could still give tongue, alarmingly.

The purport of her diatribe to Essex filtered through, arousing further flutters among those gentle ones who had hourly expected to be called before the Queen.

The Queen, however, appeared serenely deaf to whispered scandal. If his lordship needed rest, he deserved and he must have it. The ague was a most distressful malady. The ladies breathed again, and turned their glances towards the Lady Arabella. Did she carry her arm in a sling, poor dear, to hide the heart on her sleeve ?

Then in the midst of all these twitters, came the rumour, hot on everybody's lip. The King of France was in negotiation for the hand of Arabella !

Was it true ? Why had she not been approached ? Must she always, all her life, be but a pawn upon the chequer-board of

Kings and Queens ? 'Twas a monstrous imposition, an impertin-
ance, even to *discuss* the disposal of her to this one or that one,
without a by your leave. And the King of France was married.
How could he obtain release, if, as she had heard, he had embraced
the Catholic Faith ?

"How sick—how sick I am of these incessant secrecies ! Why
am I so cursed as to be born the Queen's kinswoman with no will
of my own—a peg on which to hang their plots, and in the end
by all their scheming—to hang *me* !"

So Arabella, raging like a whirlwind up and down her aunt's
bedchamber in the house at Coleman Street, where once again,
when the Court returned to London, she was lodged.

Mary Shrewsbury, suffering from a streaming cold, sat with her
feet in a tub, her head in a towel, and the pungent vapour of hot
mustard in her nose. She was in no mood to attend to her ram-
pageous niece.

Behind her chair stood Bridget, holding a basin of broth, the
while with much silent lip-message and eye-winking, she disgracefully encouraged this revolt.

"I . . . a'tchew ! . . . Arbelle, pray have codsideration for by
ate," entreated Lady Shrewsbury. "Is this the tibe to cub at me
with questiods ? My head aches like the dabbed."

"Does it ? I'm the most selfish animal to plague you, but if
you were in my place——"

"I'm not, thank God. Though I'll dare swear there is no girl
in England would not edvy—ah—ah—t'ch'you !"

"Envy *me* ?" So shrill and high was Arabella's laugh that
Lady Shrewsbury, between sneezes, again besought her : "Be not
so noisy, love. Yes, edvy you. Bridget ! A clead handkercher for
by's sake . . . Ah . . . T'chew !"

"*Envy* me !" repeated Arabella, unmoved by her aunt's anguish.
"Me ! who have been imprisoned for four years at Hardwick, who
am not allowed a moment's freedom, who must not speak to any
man without I'm slurred. O, yes ! I know ! Am I a dummy, think
you, that I *don't* know ? And now I'm to be handed over to that
free-eater, Henry of Navarre. A happy choice ! Not only is he old
enough to be my father, but as everyone will tell you, he cannot
keep his hands off any woman under seventy. A profligate and
avowed Papist . . . As . . .um . . . as I have heard." Her aunt's
besmudged eyes had darted her a look to run her down. "How-

ever . . ." Arabella hastily amended, "his Grace's predilections are none of my affair. I hold my own beliefs, and my husband, if ever I'm allowed to have one, will hold his. But I will not marry the King of France—no, not though by refusing him I lose my head for 't!"

"H'm! H'm!" coughed Bridget gently, "your Highness has never seen His Majesty. I hear from all accounts he's handsome as a god, and in his prime. A man of greatest parts."

"What's that to me? So let him keep his parts, or display them to French madams. I am English born. France has always been the enemy of England. This present truce won't last. 'Tis only because Her Grace has favoured him—the Lord knows why—that our armies are not camped across the Channel now! It is common knowledge that Navarre is heavily in debt, and the Queen finances him to drain dry *our* Exchequer. Why should I be married to a pauper?"

Lady Shrewsbury removed one foot from the tub and shook it. "Ah! It burds! I've had enough. This inferdal rheum will kill me. I feel stuffed. And Arbelle, I beg you do not air your views outside these walls. 'Tis unbecubig id a girl of your age to express political opidions. Nothing yet has been arranged. You do predmeditate. I don't know how you seized upod this talk of marriage. 'Tis only in the air. Now leave me, pray."

"Forgive me, precious Aunt! How thoughtless, cruel, unkind I am. A monster. . . ." She bent over the distressed Countess warmly to kiss her cheek and plead: "I want to go back to Derbyshire. Why should we stay in London? The Queen has shown me little enough affection. She invites me to the Court only for appearance' sake because she cannot disregard her relative' existence. She'll be glad enough to see me go. I think she hates me."

"Be silent, girl!" Sharply Mary withdrew her second foot. "Bridget! Quick—a towel. As for you——" She twisted in her chair, sternly to regard her unrepentant niece. "Have you no shabe to let your tongue give utterance to such wickedness? I'll not listen to it. Leave the roob!"

Arabella left the room to run to her Uncle Gilbert's. There, with added vehemence, she regaled that gentle gentleman with repetition of the scene which she had just enacted to her aunt.

Lord Shrewsbury, a man of fewest words, though much con

rained—there were some who called him hen-pecked—by his
ood wife's dominance, was not unobservant. To him it seemed
nce Arabella had returned from Richmond that she appeared to
e possessed; was ever, as it were, upon tiptoe: would start up
a the middle of a quiet conversation to interrupt with some entirely
relevant remark. Most disconcerting. Or she would sit and
rood with a book in her hand and not a page of it turned. He
ad timed her once when, after dinner, she, he, and his wife had sat
ecorously round the fire. For a full half hour, with that book
efore her, gazing down, presumably intent, she sat, still as a mouse.
le judged her to be studying, till, to his consternation, he saw
aat she was holding the volume upside down.

And worse! but this he had deemed wiser not to mention to
is wife, he had come upon the child unaware, seated at a table,
rriting. Certainly there was no harm in that. His mother-in-law
eported that Arbelle wrote verse and read the poets. Good! He
miled at the down-bent head, noting the white nape of the neck,
le loosened curls of fawn-gold hair under the lace coif. Pretty
reature. Gilbert Shrewsbury cherished quite a father's fondness
or her; but the intangible emotion that seized him while, un-
bserved, he watched was anything but fatherly.

And so disquieted did he become that, to save himself from
ome outrageous folly which tempted him to place a kiss upon the
ender whiteness of her neck, Gilbert—although it went against his
rinciples—approached nearer to the table to see what so engrossed
er. And leaning over, for the life of him he could not help but
ead the words that she had scrawled.

'Will you continue thus to torture me by silence? Must I be
or ever banned by you? What have I done to deserve such——'
nd having seen thus much, Gilbert, with an uncommon thumping
a the region of his heart, let forth a not entirely paternal exclamation.

"By my——! What in hell is this? Have you a secret? Or
secret love?"

How she jumped! And in what a flurry she covered with her
and those tell-tale lines to smudge the ink. And such a colour in
he face she turned to him—and those eyes of hers dilating, golden
s a cat's, half-dazed: and then her voice, low, breathless:

"My lord, I have no secret. No, nor any love. Or perhaps,"
he added with a look to turn him dizzy, "perhaps that's not quite
rue. I have a love . . . for verse. And yes, this *is* a secret that your

135

lordship has surprised. Dearest Uncle, never tell my aunt. I'm writing poesy."

How pat and with what confidence her voice regained its normal tone. And, as if he had not been disquieted enough, she needs must leave her chair to go to him and stand upon her toes with her hands on his shoulders and her face upturned to his. " My lord, I pray you do not tell my aunt, for in truth I'm bashful of my foolish versifying. 'Tis the feeblest stuff. But with practice I'll improve. And who knows but I may be a poet yet ? "

What could he do but stroke her cheek, still most paternally and force himself to disengage and promise : " I'll not tell."

But if those lines he read were verse, then what was prose ?

With a sickish sense of something not quite right, not as open and amenable to decorum as Lord Shrewsbury's high principles demanded, and with a lurking memory of that paternal—or avuncular—excess of pure affection this unaccountable sweet child had aroused in him, he lay awake that night recalling it. Recalling too, the outburst in his chamber when she had ramped and raved to him of some, he hoped, unfounded scheme to marry her to Henry of Navarre. The first he had heard of it : and hearing was more than ever in a state. Navarre ! And she the Queen of France exiled from her friends, her . . . relatives, placed on a foreign throne and unapproachable ? The only throne he hoped that she might occupy was England's. And how she had besought him : " Uncle save me from these plots to marry me to this, that, or the other prince or king or man—whatever ! If I must marry let him be of my own choice. Take me away from here. I do detest the petty spites and gossip that surround Her Grace's Court. I long to go back to Derbyshire. I want—I must go home."

Why did she want to go home ? Back to the deadly dull routine of Hardwick Hall and the indomitable governance of that old . . . Hem !

Close beside him his good wife Mary slept, or so by her deep breathing, he believed. And conscious of a tickling in his throat that Lord Shrewsbury devoutly hoped did not presage an attack of Mary's rheum, he moved to the edge of their great fourpost bed. Sinking his head in the pillow he allowed his thoughts to drift in a nebulous comforting fog. But from the first snore of soundest sleep he was startled into wakefulness by what seemed to be a rock hurled between his shoulders.

" Ah ? . . . Yes ? . . . Hum ? " queried Gilbert from his pillow.

" Arbelle," whispered Mary. " I am anxious."

" Damn Arb——" Lord Shrewsbury restrained himself. " Why, my dear, should you be anxious ? And why poke me in the back when I was just dropping off to——"

" Don't drop off. I have to speak with you."

" What ? Now ? "

" Yes. Now. She'll be the death of me," said Mary, sitting up. " I wish you could have heard her in by roob this eveding."

Lord Shrewsbury had heard her in his room that evening, but he was not prepared to lose his sleep by saying so.

Drawing apart the heavy curtains, Mary fumbled at the bedside table for a tinder-box. She lit a candle, and her husband, blinking, resignedly turned over to inquire :

" Must you have light to speak, my dear ? "

" I can't speak in the dark. And I can't sleep for this forbidable cold. But much you care."

" My angel ! " protested Gilbert feebly.

From under her pillow Mary produced a handkerchief, attended to her nose, and looked with much disfavour on her spouse, who, his head a little sideways and his jaw a little dropped, had returned to his forgetfulness.

" Wake, will you ! " Mary prodded him again.

" By all means." Lord Shrewsbury lifted up an eyelid. " Did I not say so, love ? What is it ? "

" Arbelle is seized," said Mary cryptically, " with a Spring Fever."

" She appeared to be uncommon well at . . . ah . . ." Gilbert swallowed a yawn, " at bedtime."

" Not that kind of fever. A worser kind. Will you attend ? I tell you this is serious."

" Serious," his lordship repeated. " Is it ? "

He was aware, bemusedly, of some alarm.

" I' faith, sirrah," his wife declared, " you're as much help as a platter of porridge. Can you not see the danger that lies in this unfortunate infatuation ? So far they've banaged to keep whatever is betweed them frob Her Grace. But it can't go od for ever. Did you know she writes to him ? "

Returning his head to his pillow Shrewsbury licked his lips

that were suddenly dry, and muttered : " Writes ? To whom ?
. . . Pish ! The romantic folly of a schoolgirl. I should not fret
myself if I were you."

"I don't. *She* does. And she's dot a schoolgirl. You forget
that she's turned twenty."

His lordship wished he could forget. . . . Turned twenty.
Well !

Under the bedclothes Mary drew up her knees and folded her
arms around them.

" So thid she grows. Have you not noticed ? Her collar-
bones stick out. She suffers. She feels deep. And she *is* deep.
I dread to think what bisery she'll brig upon herself if she follows
her heart and not her head, poor child. . . . Shrewsbury, do you
hear ? "

Yes, Shrewsbury heard, and hearing closed his eyes. He'd
heard enough. His wife was saying : " So ! We bust excuse her
to Her Grace and take her back to Hardwick before more bischief's
dud. You," Mary persisted, " bust arrange it. Yes, tomorrow.
You bust ask Her Grace's clebedcy. It will not be refused. Her
Grace, unless I'm much bistaken, will be glad to see the back of
her. I've never," Mary mused, " got to the bottob of that tale
o' the horse."

Sleep, so much desired, so cruelly wrenched from him, descended. Through slumbrous waves of darkness : " Horse's tale ? "
Gilbert murmured. " Very goo'. . . ."

" Then that," said Mary firmly, " is decided. A curse upod
this cold. If I were not so stricken and unsightly I would conduct
the case myself. Cad I trust you to be diplomatic ? Arbelle is ill.
She must go home. You understand ? "

" Wha . . . ? . . . Ah . . . "

His lordship snuggled deeper. From him issued, presently,
a prolonged unmistakable sound.

Mary blew out the candle and leaning towards her husband
stroked his nose.

" Shrewsbury," she whispered, " you are snoring." And
louder she repeated : " Shrewsbury ! Don't snore ! "

She sank her head and smiled in the darkness ; and very soon
she too began to snore.

*　　　*　　　*

138

If the nature of the Lady Arabella's illness that necessitated her immediate withdrawal from the Court aroused some speculation, it was stifled. The Queen, with adequate concern, accepted Lord Shrewsbury's apology and the diagnosis of her Ladyship's physician. The Lady Arabella was suffering from a semi-tertian fever. It would be advisable that she return to her native air. The atmosphere of London was ill-suited to her Ladyship's condition.

At Hardwick Arabella found her grandmother disposed to view her reappearance with no little acrimony. Had her ' Jewel ' disgraced herself again ? One could believe it better than this poor excuse of illness. Bess saw no sign of an indisposition. What she did see, however, and seeing did deplore, was a pert and wayward humour, a high-handedness, a deliberate defiance of that sovereignty by which Bess ruled her roost. The girl had not been in the house an hour before she demanded that she be allowed her own apartments. She was too old now to sleep in her grandmother's room.

Too old ! . . . When Bess was sufficiently recovered from the shock of opposition to speak her mind, she spoke it roundly, and with enough strong purpose to have brought forth tears of penitence from any other than the changeling who stood before her, unabashed.

" May I remind you, madam, I am not a child now. I have the right to insist upon my privacy."

" What's this ? Do you dare question my regard for you and demand privacy from *me* ? From me ! " Bess choked. " A fair return for all the love and care and money, which ever since your mother's death I have bestowed on you—an orphan, penniless— the guest of charity. *My* charity. I see," Bess uttered awfully, " how I have nurtured in my heart a snake. Too old, forsooth, to lie in my bedchamber ! I'll warrant there's more behind this boldness than your tongue admits. Though you strive so subtly to deceive me, I am well aware what prompts you to your scheming. Privacy ! From whom ? From careful eyes that watch to save you from yourself—or from a man ? *What* man—" raged Bess —" has brought you to such a pass that you must hide o' nights —alone ? Ha-hah ! I know your Stuart breed, 'tis hot and lusty and will out ! Why am I accursed to be the granddam of a whore ? For such you are in heart, if not, yet, in body. Here's perfidy. Ingratitude. You slut ! "

When from lack of words and breath to shout them Bess collapsed, Arabella, who had braved, unflinching, this tirade, made answer in those gentle tones which, although intended to extinguish wrath, do invariably produce reverse effect.

"Madam, if it is ingratitude to demand the right of privacy accorded to the meanest servant, then I am ungrateful. But I swear upon my maidenhead that I am not a whore!"

It was a startling experience for Bess. While she summoned all the Powers from above to her command, she realized that now or never must decide the issue of this apocalyptic moment.

Masking her dismay behind a tactical compassion: "Alack, my love," Bess offered winningly, "I fear the doctor is *not* mistaken in his findings. You are indeed unwell. Your excitation is aroused from some serious disorder. Let me advise——"

"I am not disordered," with unparalleled effrontery Arabella interrupted, "as your ladyship must know. As all the world must know. I did not return from London for any other reason but my own. The condition of my health served me merely for excuse."

With an inward cyclone storming Bess surveyed this flesh of her flesh, if such it were, and not an imp from hell in human shape: this, her bond-slave, turned recalcitrant, a mutineer, to grapple with authority in attempt to wrest the rod of empire from one whose hand had hitherto securely held it. Yet the skies did not fall to blast the puny speck whose bleating voice upraised as lamb to lioness, shook the mighty Bess of Hardwick to her foundations. No lightning struck the creature where it stood, simpering . . . Yes, positively simpering!

Bess put her lips together, and because her legs seemed now to be unable to support her, she sat down.

"Arbelle," striving to conciliate and re-form her scattered forces, with monumental self-repression Bess manœuvred, "the victim of disease is not always, by God's mercy, conscious of disorder. Sickness, like the green bay tree of evil, flourishes in richest soil. Therefore, in pity for your case, I overlook your humoursome contrariness, and pray that heavenly guidance may protect my precious Jewel."

Perceiving that her 'precious Jewel's' underlip bulged ominously outward, Bess nodded to herself and complacently observed: 'If she weeps I have her!'

But Arabella did not weep; although something very like a sob tore at her throat and her eyes were suspiciously bright, no tear fell from them.

Changing her tactics, Bess attempted rough persuasion.

"Come, wench, ask pardon for your sauciness and we'll overlook this breach of——"

"Breach of what?" So violently did Arabella take the words out of her mouth, that Bess for all her hardiness could not repress a jump. "Breach of mealy-mouthed submission to years of tyranny? If I be guilty of such, then the Lord be thanked that at last I'm in my senses to see how I am placed."

And in a moment the hurricane of pent emotion, now released, submerged her. To the horrified Bess the girl appeared to have been seized by some demoniac power, uncontrollable. She yelled, she stamped, she swore the Queen's own oath. "By God's Son, I *will not* be commanded do this—do that—and treated as a suckling! What! Am I a puppet with sawdust for a heart to be put down and taken up, to dance to *your* tune—or stuck in a box with a lid on't till I'm pulled out to make my bow and mouth your words, and gratify the whim and vanity of all who think they own my very soul, because they've bought it with their *charity*?" That thrust had evidently pricked her to draw blood. "What charity is here?" shrieked Arabella. "A prisonhouse that grudges me a bed, a chamber, be it never so small—an attic up in the roof, where I can sleep and dream, unwatched. That's all I ask. Is it a great thing? Is it a crown? A throne? Those may, God willing, be denied me, but a little small room with a table, a stool—and I'll not ask for bounty. You may starve me, beat me, let me go in rags. What do I care for these?" Her hand wrenched at the rich broidered folds of her gown as if she would tear them apart. "You may give me charity, but the pride that is my father's breed with which you taunt me, can refuse it. I'll take no charity more than will let me lie o' nights on a pallet of straw, alone. Outside these walls you may watch me where I walk. You can plant servants as you'd plant your green bay trees, as sentinels on guard. God knows I'm used enough to that, and I'll not squeak a protest. Your ladyship has been my mistress all my life. But henceforth—and I will have you hear me what I say—henceforth I'll be the master of my*self*!"

And having hurled as did David, the stone from his sling at

Goliath, Arabella dashed, now sobbing undisguisedly, but still tearless, from the room.

Master of myself. . . .

Stonily Bess stayed where she was left, repeating tight-lipped : " Master."

Not mistress, be it noted. Master ! Merciful heaven, the girl was half a boy. Unmaidenly. Deprived of all the delicate refinement of her sex. . . . Then beyond, above, her agitation rose a prouder thought. No vacillating Stuart had spoke there, but the fighting Tudor of her ancestry, that Welshman upstart, the usurper King.

And from her shattered depths something deep within the gaunt old Dowager sprang seething up against her will, to laud this royal militancy, the while she sought about for means to save her face.

The child was deranged. She had long suspected it : a weakness gathered from the Stuart side. Incipient insanity. Was not Darnley given to similar febrile display, to rend the air with his blubbering and howls ? Or so she'd heard. Well, one must shrive, forbear, forgive this poor unfortunate who so evidently knew not what she did.

As for her unprecedented fancy for a bedroom—that might be reconsidered. *Any*thing, Bess decided, might be reconsidered, sooner than again be forced to undergo such turbulence. " Horrible ! Most horrible ! " ejaculated Bess.

The sound of her own voice was reassuring. She would not be robbed of her supremacy, her absolute faith in herself, by the demented ravings of a devil. For what other than a devil had so possessed the girl, to turn her brain ? The situation, horror-fraught, *was* horrible in that it pointed to the unmistakable condition of the child's state of mind. Arbelle was mad ; unquestionably mad. She must be placated, and at once. The moon this week was at its full, and the girl moonstruck to lunacy. The north room would be prepared without delay. It opened on an antechamber where Sherland and Bradshaw could sleep and watch for further symptoms. Such a mountain made of molehills ! To scream and rage so violently for a bedchamber. . . . Dear God, if that were all !

Determinedly Bess rose. Her face was set, and saved. None to see it could have guessed she suffered, nor divined the bitterness of this accepted transmutation in the balance of her power.

Youth had given tongue with its first battle-cry, and Age had answered to outcry it. Youth, crude, stumbling, egotistical, had dealt a blow but not a death-blow. Never! Youth, whose eyes had opened on a world that in its purblind, utter ignorance it believed had been created for itself, battered cruelly at the door of Age, but not to break it down. No, never would that door concede more than an open inch. . . .

While Bess that night dwelt long and deeply on her trials as custodian of this ungovernable spirit, which, beyond all power of credence had been released to desecrate her orderly domain, she, intrepid, and still undefeated, seized upon a straw. . . . A straw among the bricks and mortar of her great new Hardwick Hall.

What could have been more opportune than that just at this unlooked for crisis, the house which for so long had been in process of erection, stood erected, waiting to receive its owner and its owner's servants, movables . . . its owner's ward?

Rising from her bed, Bess went over to the window to draw aside the curtains and peer between them at the dawn.

Upon the topmost turrets of the mansion at her gates, the first red glare of sun struck sparks from the gilt-emblazoned letters of her name. E.S. for Elizabeth Shrewsbury.

There, and for all time, she had set her seal. The hammer strokes were silenced, their work done, and this, the offspring of her own creative genius, outshone her dreams. 'Hardwick Hall has more glass than wall.' On the many windows of her palace gleamed the rose-torch of a new day. Her day . . . and all her days yet to be granted. She must not die. What was the warning a gipsy once had told her in her girlhood, long ago? That while Bess of Hardwick went on building houses she would *never* die!

And gazing up at those ornate gold emblems of her name and her supremacy, Bess saw in them the finished token of her enterprise. Salvation! A straw, infinitesimal but none the less significant, appeared to her wakeful fancy to be wafted towards her on a beam of light. And with an involuntary upward gesture of her hand Bess grasped the air. The House, and those gold letters that signed it hers, would live along the ages, would endure for generations, when Youth lay dead and rotting in its shroud. . . .

Turning from the window, Bess called her woman to her. She would dress and go about her business.

A few hours later she announced to Arabella her intention.

"You will pay a round of visits to your aunts and uncles pending our removal from the old house to the new."

No concession had been granted : no weakening of purpose nor of will. No bedchamber, no privacy assigned. The House had served its first turn as a means to victory : a doubtful victory, but for Bess a triumph. How ludicrous to have allowed so small a matter as a fit of foolish tantrums to lose her a night's sleep ! The case was plain. The girl must go. There was much to do and few enough that Bess could trust to do it. Arabella's presence about the place in this rebellious mood would only hinder preparations. In the spring when all was ready, her ' Jewel ' could return, and, as Bess hoped, chastened.

Arabella accepted her grandmother's decree with a submissive acquiescence that joyed the heart of Bess. God be thanked, the girl was come to her senses again. The seizure had been a passing madness only. . . . And let someone other, prayed the Dowager devoutly, have the care of her, for I'm too old to suffer torment for my sins, before I must.

She shed tears, but not of grief, to see her go.

Chapter Three

THE round of visits to Arabella's relatives began at Chatsworth with her Uncle Henry, and ended in the summer of the succeeding year at Sheffield.

It was there, in her aunt's household, that she renewed her studies with her former tutor, Mr. Starkey.

He, who for the past year had been instructor to the younger sons of William Cavendish, was once again ecstatic and more than ever worshipful. Mr. Starkey was, in fact, in love.

And Arabella knew it.

Her recent contact with the Court and courtiers had sharpened her perception and enriched her self-esteem. The admiration she attracted from every gentleman save one, she had valued at its worth, which wasn't much; nevertheless she was not now so raw that the symptoms Mr. Starkey all unconsciously displayed, were lost upon her.

No. . . .

While winged with magic he went soaring to the stars, little did he realize that if he were her lackey he could not half so well have served her purpose. As a scholar and a gentleman of high if poor estate, he might, so Arabella reasoned, have his uses.

We should pity Mr. Starkey.

For so erudite a person, well grounded in philosophy and languages, both dead and quick, we find him, in the study of his records, somewhat dense. Or was Arabella singular in cunning?

With what earnest application to Greek verse, which she detested, did Mr. Starkey's pupil inflame his academic heart? With what zeal she followed where he led her through divers courses of revision in those classics that he deemed it wise she should pursue. How fluently and sweetly did she converse with him in Latin, or read aloud, and with what subtle humour, the comedies of Plautus, daintily pronouncing: ' *Amor et melle et felle est fœcundissimus* ' . . . to ravish him. Yet while he strove to keep his status and his head, as guide, philosopher and if not close enough for friend, at least mentor, he made attempt to warn her against the gaieties of London life: " Which like noxious weeds untended in a garden, stifle the growth of that fairest flower, Knowledge."

" Indeed, indeed," she murmured, her eyes on his, " I am athirst for all that you can teach me, Mr. Starkey."

No man was prouder of his charge: no pupil more engrossed.

Mary Shrewsbury, from her distance, watched and wondered. What fresh devilment was here, that the girl preferred the company of this unprepossessing Starkey to her own, or even to her daughters'? She had three. Mary, devoted slave of Arabella, and Elizabeth. Alethea, her youngest, was not yet of marriageable age, but the other two were ready to be suitably espoused. She had planned to bring them to the Court in attendance on their cousin, to further their advantage. And now here was Arabella at her books, favouring above all others of her family and household, Mr. Starkey. . . . Why?

Mary well might wonder why. Mr. Starkey had little charm to recommend him. Prematurely bald, such hair as grew upon his head was of no colour; his eyes were weak, and pale and protruding, as were his rodent teeth. He had no chin and wore no beard to hide that sad defect. But if Lady Shrewsbury found him the most tedious of gentlemen, Arabella, seemingly, did not.

It was near upon the time when she must return to Hardwick that she, with diffidence, approached him.

"I have to ask of you a favour, sir. I think your interest is mine."

"Yours, Madam, utterly. Your Ladyship must know that I——"

"Yes, yes, I know. You always have been faithful."

"I was about to say that if it be within my power, Madam," stated Mr. Starkey, whose voice betrayed a tremor that belied his guarded tone, "I would——"

"'Tis but a simple matter, Mr. Starkey. You will be taking a vacation—at Eastertide, I think?"

"Yes, Madam, to visit my mother at Chelsea."

"And Chelsea is a village within easy ride of London?"

"Yes, Madam. What——?"

"I have a letter that I wish you to deliver. Ask me no questions, but keep your counsel, Mr. Starkey, for my sake."

She smiled at him.

"For your sake!" Shedding caution, Mr. Starkey panted: "For your sake, Madam, I would climb Olympus and defy the gods!"

"You are not asked to climb a mountain, Mr. Starkey, nor would I ask you to incur the wrath of gods, or even a mere mortal. You are asked only to deliver this."

She handed him a letter, sealed.

He read the superscription and his face turned ashen white.

"Madam! To what am I committed?"

"To my service, Mr. Starkey. 'Tis imperative this letter reach its destination. He to whom I write it is my friend. And more than ever do I need a friend—at Court. I have one here in you. But you are not all powerful."

"God knows that if I were——" broke forth the anguished gentleman, "there could be no favour great enough to grant your Ladyship, but——"

"There is no 'but' in this request. And the favour that I ask is such a small one that I do not understand why you assume it great. Only I pray you grant it me . . . and then forget it."

She laid a finger to her lips as if to fasten there a secret, and turned and went from him with one last look around her shoulder to strike the poor man dumb.

Forget it ! . . . Staring down upon that bold scrawled writing, the knees of Mr. Starkey shook. The whole of Mr. Starkey shook. To what folly was he partnered ? What intrigue ? Holy Heaven ! How had this come about ? Forget it ! He never could forget it. He had failed in his duty. He should have made more stern endeavour to repress such dangerous connivance. What had her Ladyship to do with him whose name was scarcely lower than the Queen's ; whose reputation, gloriously public as it was privately equivocal, could profit nothing but dishonour if coupled with a girl's ? And that she, his Lady, should stoop thus to employ her chaplain and her tutor in questionable practice, was to Mr. Starkey not only a profound humiliation, but Gehenna. What had he dared to hope, to think, to dream ? That she, of her grace, had bestowed kind glances on him, shown herself eager as a starved young bird, for the crumbs of knowledge with which it was his joy to feed her ? And had sent him soaring up to heaven to be cast in a moment to hell ! . . . Mr. Starkey groaned aloud. His thoughts, confused and crowded, rushed upon him with hideous vision of disaster, in which he gladly would have sunk to save her soul. Then even while in ghastly stupefaction he gazed upon the damning evidence he held, the door was slowly opened, and in the aperture, her face appeared, wreathed in smiles.

" Mr. Starkey ! H'st ! " Her words were hushed to draw him with her in delicious intimate conspiracy. " If he should not be at his London house, take the letter to his Wanstead residence. I will tell you all some time. Enough to say at present the case is urgent. Mr. Starkey, you must know how much I value your good will . . . *and* your discretion."

And through the open door again she vanished.

Had Mr. Starkey known it there were greater matters pending for Robert Devereux of Essex than a letter from a girl.

Since his lordship's fit of ague he had remained retired, more to the chagrin of Elizabeth than of Sir Robert Cecil, between whom and Essex, since Cadiz, somewhat strained relations had existed.

The astute son of Burghley had not joined in the general

acclamation accorded to the popular idol, who had snatched laurels from older heads that by right of long and loyal service should have worn them. Moreover in the absence of the favourite, Cecil was in fair running for the post of Secretary, and he did not much desire the return of Essex to the Court with his bag of love-tricks ready to be played before the Queen.

It was therefore to the surprise of all the world that the two were seen together driving in perfect friendliness, and a coach, to Essex House, where they were met by Raleigh. What passed between the three has never been recorded, but the result was plainly amicable. The discussion having turned, supposedly, as all discussions did, upon the Spanish question, and Philip's mania to be revenged for the disaster of Cadiz, the three were seen to leave the house together, arm-in-arm.

They had been drinking: for this we have good Mr. Starkey's word.

". . . And were in highest fettle. As I approached the gates," so he recounted it to Arabella, "they came up. I recognized his lordship; indeed I had the honour to graduate in the same year with him at Cambridge. But his appearance since that time has sadly changed."

"Why?" With studied nonchalance Arabella asked. "Did he not look well?"

"Well enough, yes, Madam, well enough," grudgingly admitted Mr. Starkey, "a trifle sallow, ill-complexioned, golden-bearded, thin——"

"I know his looks, but I am told—have heard—he has been ill."

"The high spirits of his lordship," said Mr. Starkey, very glum, "did not betoken illness, but a levity to be deplored in one who holds so great an office. He laughed——"

"Laughed?" Arabella turned upon her tutor, blazing. "Why should he laugh? At whom? At what?"

"At—at nothing—" stuttered Starkey—"at nothing I could see to warrant it. I handed him the letter."

"You handed him the letter!" incredulously echoed Arabella. "How? Before those others, Cecil—Raleigh? Good heavens! Fool! You clumsy fool."

Fool. . . . Her fool! Gaping like a cod-fish, Mr. Starkey gulped. "But, Madam, Sir Walter—and Sir Robert—they made no question

148

of my presence there. They stepped aside as I advanced. My words were these——"

"I do not wish to hear them. You can swear that the letter was received?"

"Madam, on my oath. His lordship slipped it in the pocket of his sword-belt. That I saw with my own eyes."

"Pray God your sight is not defective, Mr. Starkey. I thank you for your service."

She held him out her hand. He stooped his lips to it and trembled. What ridicule had he not braved for her? What odious humiliation!

Wincing while he watched her go, he recalled his reconnoitre at the gates of Essex House, where, in the lavender dusk of evening he had waited, undecided. Should he enter—should he not? Framing speeches to explain his mission and himself. He had brought no servant with him, and, lurking in the shadows, muffled, in his cloak, ran greatest risk of being taken for a thief. Then, when he had at last determined to approach and wake the porter who was dozing in his box, the sound of voices raised in high variety of mirth brought the porter to his feet, and Mr. Starkey to attention.

They emerged, those three together. Thankful for the gloaming Mr. Starkey stuck his chin into his ruff, pulled his hat over his eyes, and stepping forward had intercepted the advance of the linked gentlemen. Their zig-zag progress and loud laughter had given evidence enough to Mr. Starkey that all three of them were slightly in their cups. Superior in his sobriety he spoke, addressing him who laughed the loudest.

"My Lord of Essex, I believe."

"Believe nothing that you see, an' still less that you hear." Essex dropped his arm from Raleigh's to clap his hand, alarmingly, upon his sword-hilt. "And who may you be, sir?"

"My name is not unknown to you, my lord, if disremembered. I am come with a message to——"

"Hold hard, Robin!" hiccoughed Raleigh. "From the stink of him, I tell ye, he's a Spaniard."

Mr. Starkey held himself in dignity.

"I beg you to believe I am an Englishman, Sir Walter."

"Hey! You know me too?"

Mr. Starkey bowed. "As who does not?"

"Can't you see the man's a dun? What do you owe him, Robin?"

It was the third, who silent until now, had spoken. The porter's flare flung an amber light across his face; and notwithstanding his discomfiture, Mr. Starkey had admitted admiration. The calm beauty of that frail countenance more than atoned for the crooked shoulders and humped back that it surmounted. Even the insult offered in those clear clipped tones lost something of its sting.

Mr. Starkey bowed again.

"I am no tradesman's menial, Sir Robert. I hold degrees as high in honours as yourself. I am a Bachelor of Arts and Master of——"

"Dramatics it would seem," broke in Cecil smoothly. "And since our names to you are so familiar—what is yours?"

"Unknown to you, sir, and of no importance. My mission——"

"'Ods Blood! Are we to stand all night here quacking with this fellow?" demanded Essex. "He talks big but he lies low. Here you, sirrah, I know you for your master's man. You may go tell the pawky knave that he's cut my suit awry to lose my custom. I'll not pay him a farthing. Look at my doublet—how it rucks. See this sleeve?" And Essex drove his elbow in Mr. Starkey's jaw with force enough to break his rodent teeth.

"I—I pardon your mistake, my lord," had gasped the wretched Starkey. "You will, I hope, regret it when you read what here is written—and from whom."

Secretively he handed him the letter.

Grinning, Essex took it with a skew-eyed glance at the arms upon the seal, which in the twilight he could not discern; but lifting the note to his nose, he sniffed, then rammed it in the pocket of his belt, and laughed still louder.

"By God's Beard! I've been mistook. You're Cupid's messenger, and not my tailor's. From what angel you are sent I've yet to know—but here, sirrah, is an angel for your pains."

And in Mr. Starkey's face he flung a coin.

Never in his life had Mr. Starkey suffered such debasement. . . His soul ached.

Watching the three pass out of sight he had assured himself that they were gone, before he stooped. The gold piece lay where it had fallen on the flagstones. Mr. Starkey groped about and found and, being of a thrifty mind had saved himself a tip, to bestow his rdship's largesse on the porter.

*   *   *

In the summer of that year Mary Shrewsbury conducted her ro daughters and her niece to London. Bess, whose sole pre-ccupation at that time was the moving of her household from the d Hall to the new, gladly gave consent to let Arabella go, on ndition that she be content to stay. No sudden change of mind,) fit of tantrums to return before she had arrived, would be lerated, Bess commanded sternly. Though the fractious Arabella mained in chastened mood, mild, docile, obedient, she never iew for how long this sweet temperance would last. Bess entirely pproved her daughter's strategy in thus promoting the fair chances ˙ Mary and Elizabeth to capture eligible husbands, as well might : when it was known they were appointed Maids-in-Waiting to .e Princess Arabella. Neither Bess nor Mary had considered the ossibility of Her Majesty's refusal to accede her young kinswoman .is concession.

The blow when it fell was the more shattering, in that while .e Queen pronounced her pleasure in welcoming the Lady Arabella › the Court, she denied her cousin's right to demand a Maid-in-Vaiting. Such honour could only be conferred on a Princess who as acknowledged heir-presumptive to the throne.

Burghley, with customary tact, delivered the royal order to ord Shrewsbury, who received it with the uttermost dismay. The ˙ueen had spoken, and on a breath went the cherished hope of .e Cavendish family; and indirectly also of the Talbots.

Arabella, on the Queen's word, had been struck out of the iccession! Yet—and this again from Burghley to alleviate the iock—Her Grace had named no other in her stead. The people f England and their leaders would rather, Burghley hinted, acclaim ; Queen an Englishwoman born on English soil, than a King of :otland, born an alien, no matter he were nearer to the Crown. ith which the old man, beaming comfort and benignity, departed.

When Gilbert hurried to his wife with the purport of this rry interview upon his lip, verbatim, Mary swooned; but she :covered soon enough to prepare for fresh attack. Her daughters ill could bask in some reflected glory. Not she, but Arabella, iould present them to the Queen.

151

Mary, had she known it, could not have chosen a less auspiciou
time to launch her girls upon the seas of matrimony. A wee
after the arrival of herself and her retinue in London, her husban
announced that though the Court remained at Whitehall, festivitie
would henceforth be suspended. Mary began to think that no
miscalculation balked her plans, but spiteful fate.

Fate had, however, more to do than single Mary Shrews
bury for ill-favour. News had come from secret agencies i
Spain. A naval expedition on a grander scale than any previou
Armada Philip yet had ventured, was preparing in the harbou
of Corunna and Ferrol.

The canker of revenge consumed the soul of Philip with eve
fiercer appetite than did the foul disease that ate his body. H
knew that he was dying, but he would live to see the loathly Woma
who challenged his great Empire extinguished.

English spies reported to Elizabeth how the King of Spai
sat working day and night in his Escurial, out-racing time wit
no time to be lost on either side. An attack upon the Isle of Wigl
was imminent. The fighting spirit of Elizabeth awoke to dange
The trivial pretences of her womanhood were shed, and, all he
masculinity re-sheathed, she called in council her advisers.

Essex, restored to health but not entirely to favour, was in th
sulks again : this time with Francis Bacon, who early in the yea
had published a slender book of Essays that aroused much con
troversial discussion. None who read it guessed those satirica
reflections were destined for immortality   While critics cackled
Essex scowled. His friend had dedicated the first volume to h
brother Anthony and not to him. He, England's idol, had bee
slighted.

But Francis, unaware he had offended, wrote him a letter, fu
of sound advice :

'Win the Queen ; if this be not the beginning of any othe
course, I see no end ... Remove the impression of your natu
to be opinionative and not ruleable; upon this string you ca
not on every apt occasion harp too much. ... There is non
of many years ascend near you in competition. The disposin
of places and affairs concerning the wars, will of themselve
flow to you, but —' and here the cool voice of elder judgmer
spoke a warning to young arrogance —'whereas I heard you
lordship designing to yourself the Earl Marshal's place or plac

of the Master of the Ordnance, I did not in my own mind like of either. Of the places now void I would name to you the place of Lord Privy Seal. It is a fine honour, worth £1,000 by year, and it fits a favourite to carry Her Majesty's image in seal who beareth it best expressed in heart. . . .'

Had Essex followed this shrewd counsel his future tragedy might have been avoided. Yet with total lack of foresight he needs must argue with Elizabeth for some petty post required for his friend, Sir Robert Sidney. Her Majesty's denial of the grant, resulted in his exit from her presence in one of his high tempers.

Saddling his horses, he announced his intention of retirement to Wales. Elizabeth, infuriated, swore to 'pull down his great heart'. Then, because she knew that if he left her now when she most needed him she might not get him back, she despatched a messenger to intercept him on his way. Essex haughtily returned, to be met with honeyed words and promises from Gloriana. And he emerged her Master of the Ordnance, the very post that Bacon had advised him to refuse.

Elizabeth had sunk her pride to sink the Spanish ships. This hare-brained reckless boy of hers was worth his salt as leader, and any pettifogging post she had to give. Who but he could lead the expedition against Spain? Who infuse an army with the courage to follow where he led through every danger? Witness his manœuvres at Cadiz. No sailor, certainly, but what a lion-cub —and what a soldier! Let him but repeat the triumph of his previous adventure, and Philip in his web would cease to spin. . . She chuckled, then crushed her hands together as if in them she enclosed a noxious insect. Delightedly she heard of the reunion between her 'Water', Cecil—on whom she had conferred the coveted post of Secretary—and Essex, at his house on the night that poor John Starkey was so woefully received. . . . A formidable trinity of friends. Raleigh, long outcast in consequence of his affair with Bess Throckmorton, was now pardoned and again appointed Captain of the Guard. He ordered, on the strength of it, a suit of silver armour.

To and fro between the coastal ports and London, from Chatham via Sandwich down to Plymouth, Essex journeyed.

To his 'Most dear, most excellent beloved Sovereign' he rhapsodically wrote, to thank her for: 'Your Majesty's high and precious favours, for whatsoever I could be able to do as Your Majesty's servant, subject, creature, humble vassal, I did owe it and a great deal more beside. But as I am tied to Your Majesty by more ties than ever was subject to a Prince, I will strive to be worthy of your gracious favour with more industry than ever did man upon this earth.'

Industrious he was; unceasingly he worked, to the detriment of play. The neglected ladies of the Court might sigh in vain. Not a glimpse of him was any one of them accorded, save when, with face stern set and eyes fixed forward veering neither right nor left, he passed to and from the Presence Chamber, always travel-dusty, booted, spurred, his armour glinting underneath his cloak.

And: " O Arbelle," so Mary Talbot sobbingly complained, " what cruel mischance sends England into war again at this gay season ? Gay ! My faith, it is no longer gay. Of all sad, bedraggled towns I think London is the dirtiest and smelliest, and ugliest—and not a gentleman within ten miles o' the place. Nor is it likely we shall ever go to Court while Her Majesty is holding audience with War Lords."

To this Arabella answered nothing.

Since her arrival at her uncle's house she seemed to have not a care in the world, beyond the working of a pair of gloves for the birthday of her cousin Gilbert Cavendish ; or so she said.

" And I had hoped so much," whined Mary, " to meet the Earl of Pembroke here in London. He came to visit us at Sheffield and played at tennis, and O, Arbelle, he's handsome as Apollo. He praised my eyes. He told me they were pieces of blue sky cut out of heaven. Yes, he did ! You needn't look so sceptical. There's others than yourself can please the gentlemen. My mother said he has a fancy for me. I *must* be matched before Elizabeth. I'd die of shame to see her married before me. . . . Gracious sake, Arbelle ! If those gloves are for Gilbert they would fit him twice. His hands are small as a woman's."

" I make allowance," Arabella said, " lest his hands grow."

" But he's a man," persisted Mary, " and should by rights be done with growing now. And what device is that you work upon them ? Let me look."

" I won't," Arabella snatched the glove away. " I'll not have you blabbering to Gilbert when you see him that I'm making him a present. I want to give it him for a surprise."

"O, you know I wouldn't blabber," Mary wheedled, "let me——"

"Go to—go find Elizabeth!" cried Arabella angrily. "Go seek Bridget or your mother, or someone else to plague. Have you nothing more to do than sit and chat?"

"O, Arbelle, you are so tart," retorted Mary, "I'm not surprised that with a tongue as sharp as yours, you're still a spinster. I had an item of great news to tell you," Mary nodded, pursing up her lips, "but since you are so nasty, I'll keep it to myself."

"What! Keep a secret to yourself and not tell me, when you know we always tell each other *everything*?"

Arabella's tone was syrup-sweet: the look she turned upon the pouting Mary, even sweeter. Mary melted, approached her and sat upon a stool. Her blue eyes, round as marbles, glanced at and glanced away from the embroidered glove on which Arabella had resumed her work.

"O . . . a coronet!" breathed Mary. "But Arbelle, you have forgot. Gilbert doesn't wear a coronet. And why do you give him quarterings that are not his? And what are——"

"What and why, and why and what!" cried Arabella, very flushed as she hastily concealed the glove. "Your sight's awry or else my sewing's crooked. That was no coronet you saw, but a stag's antlers. Come, honey-bird, your news."

"O . . . I forgot! O, now . . . yes, I remember. I declare I'm green with envy. Has not my mother told you?"

Arabella's toe began to tap. "Told me what?"

"Why, that Lord Hertford offers his three grandsons for your hand if you will take them."

"Take them all!" Arabella pealed with laughter. "All three? If that's your news, well then I hope it chokes you!"

"O, mercy me! There's never any pleasing you. I thought you'd care to hear it."

"So I do. That gives me three more irons in my fire, but I doubt I'll ever heat 'em. They are my cousins—very distant. Their mother—no, it was their grandmother if their father is Lord Beauchamp—died in prison because she loved a man and married him, poor soul!"

"How can they be your cousins?" Mary asked. "They are not mine."

"Nor, sweet dolt, is Queen Elizabeth. I'm not prepared to

draw you up a tree of genealogy to point the Seymour claim in kinship to me and to Her Grace, but you can take my word for it, they *are* my cousins—far removed. They descend from the same royal source, right back to Henry Tudor."

This information, carelessly delivered, served its purpose to impress.

"O, Arbelle! I had forgot you were a Tudor."

"I am not. I am a Stuart, but I've a strain of Tudor blood. So have the Seymours. It's not a happy heritage. Their grandmother was sister to Jane, the Nine Days' Queen. And they were royal Tudors, and were cursed for it. As it seems," said Arabella bitterly, "am I."

"Cursed!" Mary drew a scared breath. "Arbelle! You're bold to say so."

"I wish I were. I am not bold enough. But—" Arabella smiled secretly, "I may be bolder."

Then to drown the question that rose on Mary's lip, "What further news, my love," she asked, "can you give me of these Seymours, and how do you glean your gossip? At the keyhole?"

"I am not so sneakish," returned Mary, very prim. "I heard my father tell my mother when they thought I was asleep over my book."

"As no doubt you were, and dreamed it."

"No, I didn't! I heard my mother say that the old Earl of Hertford would give the eyes out of his head to see you married with his grandsons."

"And damned to everlasting for a bigamist?" Arabella cried in feigned alarm. "There's no law in the land can marry me to more than one at once! I think you've got this wrong," she teased, "you're sure it's not the old gentleman himself who asks for me? He might well be warming, in his dotage, for another wife."

"No," Mary answered her in all good faith, "I know it isn't he."

"Then why not his son, Lord Beauchamp? He's not more than forty, if as much."

Arabella took the glove from its hiding place beneath her farthingale and began to stitch again. Her lowered lashes hid the laughter in her eyes. She loved to bait poor Mary.

"Why, Arbelle, he's married!" exclaimed Mary, very shocked.

"So is Henry of Navarre, and the Prince of Parma, and the whole bunch of them. But do they care for that? Divorce is easy here in England. My Great-grand-uncle Harry made it so. I don't think much of what you tell me, and I will hear no more. I'm sick to the stomach of second-handed offers."

She drove the needle in her thumb, and swearing, dropped the glove. But as Mary bent to pick it up she made a grab and seized, and sat on it. Then, squeezing out a speck of blood from the needle's prick, she sucked the place and sighed: "I wish that I could find a man who'd come to me himself, and if he were a beggar or a chimney-sweep—I'd take him."

This was too much for Mary.

"O, Arbelle! You never would! A chimney-sweep?"

Arabella nodded, wrinkling her nose. "Or the Queen's own executioner could have me if he loved me. To be married to one who wanted me as woman and never as Princess, would so rejoice me that I vow, were he a leper, I'd go to him in gratitude, sleep with him in a ditch . . . and be his wife." Her voice shook, but not now with laughter. "I think I'd make a good wife for a man. I'd work for him, do simple homely things for him. I cannot cook or bake, but I could learn. . . . Lord! How you stare. What's wrong in that?"

"I'm surprised," gasped Mary, "that you confess yourself so wanton. Sleep in a *ditch* with a *man*! For shame, Arbelle!"

Arabella smiled at her.

"Not for shame, my sweet. For love. . . . Go now and find Anne for me; tell her that I'll take a drive. The sun is out, and will not stay in."

With Anne beside her in the coach, her page running at the wheels, and John Dodderidge, her servant, riding on ahead, without whose escort she was not permitted to go forth, Arabella was driven to Cheapside.

She wished, she said, to buy material for a new gown.

While she discussed with Anne the stuff and colour she would choose, debated whether or no it should be satin or brocade, and what sempstress here in London she could call upon to make it, her eyes strayed everywhere, observing.

The sun blazed down from a molten sky; the huddled houses shimmered in white-hot transparency. Dirt and refuse, black with

flies, lay rotting in the gutters. Arabella held a jewelled pomande
to her nose against the stench, while Anne deplored: " Madam
such a day as this is likely to breed fever. The heat is quite insuffer
able. The smell——"

" Is not uncommon for this cesspool of a London," Arabell
interrupted. " But for all the murk and dirt and stink of it, there'
no city in the world that has such charm—at least for country foll
like you and me."

Anne had her doubts of this, and of her lady's mood. Behind
her airy talk of gowns Anne detected a withdrawn excitement
a hurrying of glances that searched the faces of pedestrians and o
every gentleman who trotted by with clatter of hoof and clink o
steel, their horses kicking dust and dried mud from the cobbles
Anne, bred and born among the hills of Derbyshire, had littl
liking for, and saw no charm in this murky, dirty London wit]
streets so narrow that the gabled windows of the houses almos
met overhead enveloping the byways in a preternatural gloom
further darkened by a succession of grotesque signs. Moreover
one had to shout to be heard above the creaking of loaded wagons
the rattle of wheels, the hoarse cries of apprentices who intercepte
their approach with demands of: " What d'ye lack, ladies ? Wha
d'ye lack ? "

But worse than all the pandemonium was the sickly pall o
smoke that overhung the city, rising from the sea-coal furnaces o
soap-boilers, brewers, lime-burners, and the like, which cause
Anne acute discomfort. Her eyes poured water, her throat itched
her stomach heaved. Her lady, however, seemed unaffected b
this formidable fog. She exclaimed delightedly at all she saw
pointing out to her companion the Puritans in their sad-coloure
suits, wide-brimmed hats and snowy bands ; stout, neatly coife
market-women ; rosy-cheeked dairy-maids, fresh from nearb
villages, skipping their way among the loiterers, with pails slun
from a wooden bar across their shoulders, their voices cheeril
calling as they stopped at each door to dispense the contents of thei
buckets into the housewives' jugs.

The coach came to a halt at the sign of the Blue Boar in Cheap
side ; but even as John Dodderidge assisted the ladies to aligh
a commotion aroused, not by their arrival but another's, seized th
onlookers. In an instant it was as if all Bedlam were let loose. Th
apprentices ceased to yell their wares and darted forward, cheering

The street-vendors left their barrows, the dairy-maids their trade, to follow after them, jostling, pushing, dancing with the rabble, joining arms to form a cordon around a coach and four that had pulled up outside a goldsmith's shop.

Eager heads appeared at every window; and upsprung from foetid alleyways all the beggars in the town, with dogs barking at their heels, joined in the mêlée; even the sober Puritans appeared to be infected, uniting their cheers in chorus to the cry of: "Essex! My Lord Essex!... God save his Lordship!"

To her unspeakable alarm, Anne found herself severed from her lady and clasped round the waist by a bearded giant whose leathern apron proclaimed him a blacksmith, whose hand brandished an iron, still hot from the flame, and whose breath, redolent of wine and onions, assaulted her shrinking nostrils as he peered into her face to bawl: "See how they run, sweetheart! He holds 'em in his pocket, as I hold you in my——"

Merciful heaven! prayed Anne, deliver me. . . . Frantically she struggled. The blacksmith held her closer. "My Lady!... Dodderidge!" screamed Anne, "John Dodderidge! Where are you? Page!... My Lady!..."

But no single voice, and certainly not Anne's, could be heard above the clamour of a multitude. And, in that surging tumult no face could be distinguished, nothing seen save a confusion of bodies, of arms waving, of gibbering, ape-like mouths emitting cheers.

"There he goes! There he goes!" shouted her ruffianly cavalier; then, to her indescribable relief, he detached himself, and still brandishing his iron to threaten the unwary, rushed in among the mob.

Anne wrung her hands. "O God!... my Lady! Page! Page! Where are you? Find my Lady . . . Find her!"

Carried along like a straw in a whirlwind, pushed and jostled, terrified, she managed to obtain, between the bobbing heads, intermittent glimpses of the coach that had caused this cyclonic upheaval; the champing horses; the sunlit flash of gold-studded harness; the Earl's coachman in his scarlet livery with a broad grin on his face, his whip cutting the air to hold at bay those who might in their excitement come too near. She had a fleeting view of the Earl, unruffled, debonair, laughing gaily at those who greeted him

with cries of: "God save your Grace! God save your Lordship
God speed you to the wars!"

"My Lady!" Once more Anne raised her voice in agonize
appeal. "John Dodderidge! Page! My Lady! Where . . .
where is my Lady?"

Her lady at that moment was in a goldsmith's shop. She ha
seized her chance, in this massed epilepsy, to slip her guardians an
make a dash for it. Having recognized the arms upon the coac
as it drew up before the sign of the Green Dragon, she forestalle
him.

When he entered she was speaking with the owner of the shoj
who in view of such good custom had immunized himself from th
enthusiasm of the crowd without, to attend upon activities withir

"Rings, madam? By all means. Although I do not deal i
precious stones—for I am not a jeweller—I can offer you a diamor
of rarest quality, set in gold."

"A diamond? I do not care for diamonds. They are tc
bright, and much too costly for my means. A topaz now. . .
Have you anything of topaz?"

"Topaz, madam? Yes, I have a marvellous rare topaz. A
happy choice, too, is the topaz." He produced a tray glitterir
with rings, and continued without pause. "The topaz, so says S
Ambrose, augments and diminishes its virtue as the moon wax
and wanes. Here, for example, is a topaz of much interest. It
worth——"

"I thank you, good people, I thank you! But I entreat you a
—disperse. Don't raid the shop. Goldsmiths are the least tolera:
of tradesmen, being ever on the jump lest they be thieved. Goc
folk, good day to ye! God bless you all!"

She had control enough not to betray herself. Holding h
vizard before her face, she accepted the goldsmith's hasty apolog

"Your pardon, madam. I must bolt the door. . . . Your lordsh
honours me."

Nor did she turn when the goldsmith, bowing nose to knee
approached his latest customer.

"At your service, my good lord. What is your lordship
pleasure?"

"I can wait my pleasure. You are already engaged with th
lady."

She sneaked a glance at him through her mask's eyelet holes

see him staring at her, puzzled; and in the cheek concealed from him appeared a dimple.

"Here, sirrah! Master Goldsmith! . . . I will take this topaz ring. What is the price of it?"

The goldsmith returned to attend her in a fluster.

"I thank you, madam, for your patience . . . the safety of my stock . . . you understand? In their excitement at this close view of his lordship the mob might run amok and steal my wares. The topaz ring, madam . . ."

Essex advanced a step, slid a look at her sideways; and smiled. "I know the colour of your hair, like leaves burnt gold in autumn. I know your height," he whispered, "and I think that I know you."

She tuned her voice to a falsetto. "Your lordship takes advantage of my ignorance to claim acquaintance with me."

He twinkled. "Keep that up. This fellow's all agog to hear the worst. Do you think a mask can hide your face from me? I know each feature of it. I remember more of you than I ever could forget. . . . Don't drop your vizard. But why in the name of mischief are you here?"

"My lord mistakes me, surely. Does he know my name?"

"Do I not? You've signed it on my heart." Then with provocative inconsequence he added: "Did the messenger who brought your letter tell you I mistook him for a dun?"

Disregarding his advice, she lifted her mask to gaze up at him in widening reproach.

"My letter . . . you did not answer it."

"Was it safe to answer? Hide your face again," he murmured, "'tis too tempting."

Her voice came muffled through the velvet, urgently.

"When will I see you? When?"

"I hope . . . before I sail." His careless smile razed her; but she was too far gone to quibble with his words. Her pride shrank beneath the stunning shock of that reminder.

"Yes! Before you sail! When? I must, *must* see you once before you sail . . . I have worked a pair of gloves for you."

"Dear heart, we don't wear gloves in action."

"You shall wear my glove in your cap for luck."

"Madam." With a discreet cough behind his hand the goldsmith claimed attention to his trinkets. "Will you then take the topaz?"

She turned. " What ? . . . oh, yes ! The topaz. I will send my page to fetch it. What is the price you named ? "

The goldsmith, who had named no price, promptly added treble to its value. If this fair incognita had not the wherewithal to pay, Lord Essex, he decided, could, and with the least persuasion, would.

" Very well." Arabella laid a gold piece on the table. " Here is a deposit on account. My page will bring the balance. Put it aside for me."

The goldsmith, fawning, scribbled a receipt. It seemed he had misjudged her. She had the cash—he hoped. If not, he had the ring, and more than the full worth of it already in his hand.

" Madam, may I know your name ? "

" Anne Bradshaw," glibly answered Arabella. " You'll remember it ? "

" I shall not forget, good madam. My most grateful duty, madam. I am always at your service, Mistress Bradshaw. A thousand thanks, good——"

" Here you, sirrah ! Unlock your door and let the lady pass. I'll conduct her to her coach," commanded Essex. . . .

And all the way home :

" O, Madam ! Madam ! Madam ! " wailed Anne. " How could you give me such a fright ? How could you do so, Madam ? "

" For heaven's sake," snapped Arabella, " stop bemoaning. Here am I, safe and sound, thanks to his lordship, who rescued me when I was tumbled in the gutter." She began to giggle. " How they yelled ! My dress was all but torn from my back. I marvel that I wasn't robbed, and would have been so had he not arrived so timely."

The worried Anne stayed silent, and wondered which of the two—her lady, or her lady's page—had lied. The boy had sworn he saw her Ladyship gather her petticoats and run, pushing and even pommelling her way, to gain the goldsmith's shop. He had at once run after her, and being little, dodged and doubled under and between men's legs, to reach the door, to find it locked against him. That for his tale, which John Dodderidge had sourly supported. The sight of both could not have been deceived. More trouble brewing for her Ladyship, Anne unhappily reflected, unless she held her tongue ; and for her lady's peace of mind, if not her own, she must. Did the girl realize her danger ?

She did not; or else she joyed in it.

During the days that followed, to less perceptive eyes than Mistress Bradshaw's, she appeared to be on tenterhooks, alternatively in the highest spirits, or glum to desperation. She spent much time at the window gazing out upon the street: was sharp-tempered, or, conversely, gay, affectionate, or shrewish, and over-generous with gifts. For what reason, suddenly did she announce to Anne: "Here's a scatter-brain I am not to have told you! I have bought you a topaz ring. . . . You remember that day you lost me in Cheapside?" Was Anne likely to forget it? "I found the sweetest token of my love for you. The goldsmith is keeping it for me on deposit. . . . Send the page with my purse to the sign of the Green Dragon."

Then, lest Bridget should be jealous, she must despatch the lad upon a second errand. "To the mercer's hard by the goldsmith's, at the sign of the Blue Boar. Choose there to match this colour—" she produced a scarlet ribbon—"ten yards of watered taffety. . . ."

But on his way out she intercepted the boy at the door, thrusting into his hand a sealed packet. "Take this to Essex House. Give it to the porter at the gates. . . . Here's a little something for you. And if you talk of my commissions to any soul alive, I'll . . ." she bared her teeth at him most frightfully, "I'll not only dismiss you from my service, but I'll have you pilloried. It is not pleasant to be pilloried with the sun glaring down on your head to strike you mad. You've seen the pillory at Charing village? Yes? Well, that's for you, my lad, unless you do my bidding. But if you carry out my orders as I wish, I'll give you a new suit with silver buttons. Now be off and back within the hour." She cuffed him on the ear, then kissed her finger-tip and laid it on his cheek in compensation. "That's my brave boy. Go!"

He went, adoring. She knew that she could trust him. His father had served her father as page, and his father, her grandfather in his turn. His name was Owen Tywdder: and when he grew up and married, and if he had a son, his son would serve her in his place. It was traditional.

Having despatched him on her errand she must hold herself in patience until her call should come, though there was little she could gather and feed upon for comfort. Since that mad ride in Richmond Park and her unashamed confession, she had spoken with Essex, privately, three times. . . . Three times in all, but each moment of them treasured. Yet nothing said that could not have been shouted high for all the world to hear. Only for one instant in these last few weeks had he revealed to her that he was not entirely unmoved, nor so replete with royal favour that he could not favour her. Or was she self-flattered into thinking so?

On his return from Plymouth they met at Whitehall in the Coffer Room, as he came out of the Presence Chamber where he had been detained in conclave with the Queen.

The Maids of Honour were as usual twittering of what they dared imagine passed between Her Grace and him behind those doors; and peeping at the keyhole.

Arabella, who had that day been summoned to the Queen's Privy Table, awaited the Lord Chamberlain's instructions. This honour, offered by Her Grace to her young cousin was, Arabella realized, a formal and perhaps unwilling invitation. She knew also, however much the Queen might disapprove of and disfavour her, that if received at Court she must be, perforce, accorded royal courtesy.

In the wide embrasured window-seat she sat aloof and watched the Queen's Maids at their antics. She guessed the purport of their whispers and surmises; their slinking looks betrayed them. Fools! Did they not know whatever public gratitude—or secret gifts—the Queen bestowed on Essex, could never be a fair enough exchange for all she owed to his integrity—his valour! She burned with pride for him. She could suffer his long absence at the wars, knowing he would gain more victories for England. He was unconquerable, his leadership assured, his men as dauntless as himself in face of danger.

He came from the Presence at last, and those girls clustered round him, chattering like starlings, hanging on his arm, offering themselves to his caresses like so many bare-faced doxies. Her outward calm disguised her inward fuming. So tightly she clenched her hands that her nails drew blood from her palms.

Laughingly he disengaged, and passed on to where she sat. The Maids of Honour stood apart and enviously watched, but etiquette forbade them to intrude upon the private talk of one who was by right of heritage acknowledged second lady in the land.

"How soon," she asked him, "do you sail? I must know."

He gave a shrug. "If I myself could know——"

"Do you command the Fleet?"

" I am a soldier, not a sailor."

Her eyes glowed up at him. " You are a pirate ! Will you bring back treasure from the Spanish Main ? "

" I will . . . and pour it in your lap ! Shall I deck you with the jewels from Philip's crown ? If I could ! "

" Hush ! Those girls—they watch us. They can read your words. They'll have you up for treason."

" Is it treason to adore——? "

" Will you stay your tongue ? "

" Only upon your lips."

She crushed her hand against her corsage and whispered breathlessly : " Did you receive the gloves I sent ? "

" I did. And though my men will mark me for a Jemmy-Jessamy, I'll wear 'em, sweet, for you."

Her lips parted.

" Were they well worked ? And do they fit ? "

" As good as my skin ! And every stitch you sewed in them is one thread the more . . . to bind us."

She said softly : " How I shall think of, and will pray for you ! "

" Don't you ever think and pray," he asked in mock despair, " for anyone more worthy ? "

" There is none worthier." Her face, love-warmed, was lifted up to his to dazzle him, and despite his chaffing banter he was stirred. Such unfeigned adoration would turn the head of any man. If he could take her at her word ! In all his life he had never been deflected from the course of his desire. Yet this girl and her witchery, her unafraid directness, had hit his heart to torture him with vague insistent scruples. Why ? . . . Why, when he had never needed scruples in his pursuit of a woman, should he now renounce what any man would seize, and in renunciation, suffer insensate longing for that which must not be ? . . . He would be wise for her who had no wisdom for herself ; and on that resolution he irresolutely murmured : " When I come back, maybe . . . we'll meet again."

Any half-promise rather than commit her to her madness : or to his.

" We will meet," she told him tremulously, " before. We must. We shall. You see how I am shameless ? Do you despise me ? O, Essex, I admit I have no shame. I think it is more shaming to deny my love than to confess it. I know that you are loved by every woman, but I'll swear that none can understand you as I do. I believe you to be tender and yet—may I be bold enough to say it?—for all your strength, a little weak. Yes, weak enough to need one who will be faithful. Not just another woman, but your friend. No more than that."

No more? When all her young ungiven body yearned towards him to infuse his blood with feverish temptation.

He stood besieged, the polite veneers of hypocritical pronouncements torn from his lips to frame words that never should be uttered. Then, while sense perished in the fierce delight that overswept him at this tantalizing glimpse of her surrender; while God alone could tell to what desperate sweet impulse he might, in that intolerable moment, have sworn himself and her, the doors of the Privy Chamber were flung wide for the entrance of the Queen in all the glory of her bejewelled splendour. Two silver-clad pages held her train; her eyes flashed round the Coffer Room—at her Maids, who fell apart, and ceased their whispering to curtsy; at Arabella, who rose from where she sat to sink in billowing obeisance of gold brocade and amber; and at the bowing Essex.

"So! You! Still here?" In staccato shrill discordance the Queen's laughter scraped the air. "We rejoice to see you can find time for relaxation from your duties. We believed you on your road to Plymouth this last hour. By God's Son!" and now that glittering, inexorable figure quivered with the tense suppression of her fury, "is this how we can hope to draw our holy Philip's fangs? Does the King of Spain stand dallying to fingle-fangle with the girls, while his fleet prepares to sink us? Why are you not gone?"

He stayed unmoved, his eyebrows whimsically up, his eyelids down, and answered coolly: "Craving Your Majesty's indulgence, I go so soon as my men and my horses are prepared."

"Why are they not prepared?"

He looked at her; his smile, half impudent and wholly calculating, held a hint of mockery beneath his suave reply.

"The order has been given to make all speed . . . Your Grace."

She parried his look with one that would have caused another man less certain of himself and her, to quail. Curbing the volley of abuse that gathered like a thundercloud to burst, the Queen turned from him to Arabella.

"We are enchanted to receive our cousin at all times," the pinched mouth tightened till she seemed to have no lips, " save

166

at such time when active service claims our gentlemen. Essex, go! and may God hasten you upon your way."

The Queen swept on and out into the Gallery, thence to the Council Chamber. The Maids, subdued, and fearful of what new frenzy might assail Her Grace in such strained humour, followed. Arabella, still outwardly sedate, though more than ever nettled at this last rap of royal insolence, stepped into place on the heels of the procession.

"Wait!" His whisper stayed her. "I promise you we'll meet before I go. How or when or where I cannot tell, but you must trust me. . . ."

On this then, his promise and the oft-repeated resurrection of that last encounter, she must dwell in secret and again possess herself in patience till he came.

'Trust me.' Was it a promise? Could she doubt him? She could. She did. . . . Did not. Swinging from the dizzy heights of hope to darkest hopelessness, she dreamfully envisaged her fulfilment. She was his! But was he hers? The incessant hunger of her heart would be appeased. It must. She believed him not insensible to her unabashed invasion of his fortress. If only she could break that citadel, storm the battlements that held him from her and withheld her love!

So through those scorching summer days while the Council sat in long debate, and the elaborate preparations for the attack on Spain matured, she waited for his call. She would be ready, even though her heart's resolve destroyed her.

Her summons came a week before he sailed.

"O, Arbelle—" her cousin Mary, whom jubilance had rendered more than ever incoherent, thus delivered it—"here's news! We are invited, my father and my mother and Elizabeth and me—and you, first of all, which I forgot to say—to a banquet given by Lady Northumberland, his sister, at her house in honour of Lord Essex. Only think! What great personages will be present! The Queen herself may grace us. My mother says the Earl will not be there——"

"You mean," with a dry mouth, Arabella interposed, "that Essex will not——"

"No!" Mary cried impatiently, "Northumberland. He's not on best of terms with Essex, and my mother says that Lady Dorothy, his sister, has chosen just this time to entertain while her

167

husband is engaged upon his duties as Lord Lieutenant of the Border. They fight like cat and dog, I'm told."

In swift revulsion from abysmal disappointment to heights immeasurable, Arabella soared : and sat, with not a word to say. But Mary spoke enough for two.

"I am not sorry Lady Dorothy will entertain without her husband. I misdoubt him. I've heard that he holds discourse with the devil. I've only spoken with him once, but such rude sarcastical comments he passed on me, I was like to die. I don't care for moody gentlemen, and everybody says he is a wizard. O, I wonder if Lord Pembroke will be there ? Do you think my mother can be persuaded to buy me a new gown ? I have a taste for blue and silver. My apricot satin with the red velvet front is better suited to my grandmother than me. Blue is more my colour, to match my eyes. Lord Pembroke praised my eyes. O, I hope I may wear blue. What will you wear, Arbelle ? "

She would wear concealment for a cuirass, and feign indifference, boredom, as if nothing in the world could please her less than to attend the banquet arranged in honour of Lord Essex by his sister. . . . She vowed that of all entertainments, feasting was the most to be deplored. Her stomach turned at the sight of too much food. She could not drink more than a beakerful without she was disgraced, having too light a head for wine.

Her Aunt Mary scolded her for this lukewarm reception of Lady Dorothy's advance. "You should be grateful. The season is almost at a close, and stuck here in this London ditch we might be in a mausoleum for all the jollity we've had since you arrived. Now what of our dresses ? . . ."

Mary was made joyful by her mother's gift of a blue and silver gown, and Elizabeth by one of gold and ivory. But Arabella declared she would buy nothing new. She had gowns enough, she said ; and dismayed her ladies by insisting upon white.

"All white," she wished to be, "with no touch of colour, and no jewels. I'll be in white from head to foot."

"Sure ! You'll look like a bride before your time," protested Bridget.

Arabella smiled. "White suits me well, but I'll wear a crimson flower."

Red roses. . . . Like three dark stains of blood they nestled at her bosom. The satin folds spread over the wide farthingale caged her body in a sheath of white : her low-cut corsage was sprinkled with pearls ; from under a chaplet of roses gleamed her gilt-brown hair.

"You look as cool as spring, and hot as summer !" Bridget cried when she reviewed the finished product of her handiwork.

Anne kissed her, whispering, "There will be none so beautiful tonight as you, my dear. . . ."

Others may have thought the same when they saw her enter the great room in Russell House, St. Martin's-in-the-Fields, which for some years had been Northumberland's town residence. Surcharged with happiness, she appeared to shimmer in white flame. The supple satin of her gown reflected the iridescent light of candles and flambeaux. In contrast to the brilliant jewels and costumes of the guests, she shone starlike.

The gathering of friends that Lady Dorothy had assembled was selective and not unduly large. No more than thirty sat at the long table in the hall. Essex, acting host in his brother-in-law's absence, took the head, with Arabella, first in rank of any lady present, on his right ; her Aunt Shrewsbury on his left, Mary blissfully beside the Earl of Pembroke, and Elizabeth between him and the Earl of Kent. Essex, splendid in ruby velvet slashed with gold, paid court to Mary Shrewsbury, while Arabella found upon her right hand, Robert Cecil.

This, other than a formal presentation, was her first meeting with Lord Burghley's son ; and had she been less preoccupied with her emotions she would have delighted in that keen intellect, canopied beneath the calm explicit suavity of speech. She took no note of it, heard but did not hear, saw without seeing, for her sight was blurred. Of all that company her hostess only was definable. Ardently she searched his sister's face, detecting in the clear precision of her features, a strong family resemblance to him on whom she dared not look lest she betray herself to her Aunt Mary's watchfulness. The narrow table divided them, but could not hide her heart that must, she thought, be bursting from her bodice.

She focused her eyes again on Lady Dorothy, and reddened at the look that met her own. She had surprised a smiling question on those curved lips that tilted upward, as did his. How like they were, those two : the same quick turn of the head, the self-same whimsical yet penetrating glance. Did this enchanting lady, whose shallow laughter pealed as musical and well-timed as the viols of the minstrels in the gallery, unscreen her ambuscade? Would she afterwards discuss with mockery, decry, encourage, disapprove his choice? Was she enemy or ally? . . . Time would show.

Cecil in his smooth voice was saying: "What a harsh omission on the part of Providence it is, that not until tonight have I been favoured."

"Favoured?" He too was smiling. Could everybody read her secret? Did he guess that she was lovesick as any kitchen-slut for the steward's condescension? His small pointed mouth under the fawn smudge of his moustache seemed to give point to his words. She leashed her errant thoughts, repeating: "Favour? By whom and why tonight, sir?"

"That is what I ask. Is it not unkind that your Ladyship so rarely deigns to grace us here in London with your presence?"

Impatiently she crumbled a roll of bread beside her dish; even from Cecil the same parrot repetition of fair phrases offered to every woman, who in man's esteem, was no more than a receptacle for the sugar-plums of flattery. She hitched a pettish shoulder. "My presence here or anywhere, Sir Robert, as you," she faintly stressed it, "of all gentlemen should know, is insignificant."

He raised his damask napkin and patted daintily that smile from his lips.

"I cannot accept so modest a denial. Your presence, Madam, here or anywhere in England is of paramount importance—to the State."

She turned to him in wonder and alarm. He held between his fingers the leg of a fowl, and digging his teeth into the flesh as if bent upon no other business, he masticated slowly.

Her tone sharpened.

"In what way can I be counted of importance—to the State? I beg you to explain yourself, Sir Robert."

"Surely your Ladyship needs no explanation. Your royal blood speaks for you. There are those who may, but none who can with reason, challenge it."

She paled. . . . This from him! What could such avowal, so lightly spoken, yet insidious, portend? People said his crooked body housed a mind as fluent and unscrupulous as that other Crookback, Richard, who had done to death his nephews in the

Tower. Caution restrained her answer, while she fenced. " Sir Robert honours me above myself. It would be foolish to deny that all my life I have been haunted by my heritage, and by the fear of it ; but I can swear I have no higher aspiration than that to which my orphanhood and poverty compel me. I am beholden to my grandmother for this very gown I wear, and for the grace with which Her Majesty receives me, I never can give gratitude enough."

His smile played upon his lips again, lighting the beauty of his face to melt her. No. This man could not be false : could not be less than the Queen herself acknowledged—her honoured and most honourable Secretary. And suddenly, beneath the shock of his deliberate suggestion, she believed she could discern the thought behind it. James . . . her cousin James ! England's heir-presumptive by right of seniority, but not by right of English law. He was an alien ; and this hump-backed dwarf beside her, this administrative genius with England in his soul, would move heaven and earth to see an English Queen and not a Scottish king upon the throne.

It was as if a message passed from him to her ; but the urbane serenity of his countenance revealed no perceptible impulsion, no minutest flicker of an eyelid, to pique conjecture ; while under cover of the table-talk he murmured :

" Madam, only God can see into the future. Our lives are fortuitous—haphazard as the wind that plays with puff-balls. Yet the contrivance of human wisdom provides for human wants. If at any time your Ladyship is in need of counsel from one whose experience may profit you in whatsoever small degree, I trust you will not hesitate to call upon my duty."

But her last extempore speech had left her speechless. She had no more to say : nor could she cope with the precise oration of a Cecil. He had his father's cunning and twice his father's brains, and more than all his father's suavity. And she wondered how he dared to be so meaningful : or did his words mean nothing ? Strange enigmatic creature, with his hidden careful smile, his patient, melancholy eyes, his pitiful bent body.

Across the table Mary Shrewsbury strained ears for this low-spoken dialogue, the while she exchanged flippancies with Essex.

Till that moment Arabella had not ventured more than monosyllabic responses to the polite attention which, as host, he must bestow upon each lady seated near to him. But with the circulation of the wine, his words and glances sparkled ; the merriment increased. Some of the men already were far gone enough in drink. The board creaked beneath the burden of its dishes. Swans, white-mantled in their plumage, were paraded by the steward and his lackeys to whet repleted appetites. And when the plucked feathers that concealed the roasted flesh were gathered up in handfuls and flung about, to fall tenderly as snow on jewelled heads and doublets, the acclamation of approval hit the rafters. A great feast, and more to come : pasties of venison, turkeys stuffed with prunes and chestnuts, jellied larks and chickens' breasts with saffron sauce : baked woodcocks soaked in muscadine, and every kind of sugar-meats : 'kissing-comfits', syllabubs, pies, and bowls of fruit : grapes, purple figs and apricots, roasted pears and brandied cherries ; then more wine to wash all down and so begin again.

Most of the men were sliding from their seats before the meal was over. Young Pembroke, Mary's partner, very green in the face, was lugged away by two small pages, but not in time to save an overspill before he reached the door. Others, in similar plight, were more successful in their exit. The scraping of viols could not be heard above the laughter caused by the entry of the Fool in cap and bells, slipping in and out among the lackeys, cracking jokes, with whispered ribaldries behind his hand.

Arabella, spooning strawberries steeped in wine, prayed the feast might end before it turned into an orgy. The banquets she had hitherto attended had been held in the presence of the Queen or of her grandmother, and with due formality ; but this was nothing short of saturnalia Anxiously she watched her hostess give the signal for the guests to rise ; many of the gentlemen could not, without assistance. Those who could, dispersed to relieve their over-laden stomachs while the more temperate, or stronger-headed, took their places for the dance.

The first was a pavanne to the music of hautboys and trumpets, a stately procession led by Essex and Arabella ; but the dignity of this performance, ill-suited to the mood of merry-making, soon gave way to the boisterous galliard. The fun waxed faster and more furious. The indisposed, recovered, returned to pick their partners for the French Brawl, which ended in all joining hands in a round gallop.

His arm supporting Arabella, Essex steered her to an alcove in the arras. Breathless, she fanned herself. " Lord ! I'm giddy ! I cannot dance these jigs and high lavoltas. I've twisted my side."

" And you've twisted my heart," murmured Essex. " I saw
ow Cecil buttered you. What mischief was he hatching ? "

" None," her colour mounted, " except to hint that one day
ll be Queen."

" By God ! So did he ! I always knew him for a fox." This
xplosive answer and the beacon flame of anger in his eye warned
er to retract.

" I have been fed from birth," she told him quickly, " on hints
ke these."

" Then you had best forget them. Such hints—or hopes—are
ot for you."

The suppressed fury in his tone, and the look he turned upon
er, slashed her cheeks with scarlet. Was all the glad anticipation
f this hour to be slain in one harsh moment ?

" I have never held such hope, nor wish to hold it," she retorted,
ung. " I would liefer lie in my coffin than sit upon a throne."

Her voice, although high-pitched with hurt and indignation,
as smothered in the music of pipe and tabor, the stamping of feet,
ne general noise and confusion. In the midst of it and in a sudden
arp hostility, these two faced each other, strangers, who but an
istant since were lovers undeclared.

Her temper flying : " I am sick of hope dinned into me," she
ied, " by those who glut themselves upon ambition. Their
urpose is not mine. And as for you—I am amazed that you
elieve me party to, or capable of such false——"

She broke off on a note of hysteria ; her fingers tightened round
ne sticks of her closed fan. There was a little cracking sound,
oud to her ears in the fallen silence that, despite the room's hilarity,
nclosed them.

She turned from him to be caught back.

" Must you mistake my meaning ? I too would sooner see you
a your coffin than on England's throne, unless—" he paused
nd said, close-lipped, " unless the throne were shared by one who'd
ake the weight of it upon his shoulders."

She shut her eyes against the sickliness that overswept her.
)id the serpent of intrigue that spoke with his voice insinuate itself
ito her Eden . . . or her fool's wilderness ? This, then, the favour
ne besottedly believed he had bestowed on her, resolved itself, as
id all such favours, into self-gain . . . or worse. Did she signify
o more to him than her high rank and its golden opportunities ?

Did he seek, through her, a future more dazzling to the opportunist than all her present Majesty's endowments? Was she the prize to be cached as a dog will bury a bone, and dragged out from its hiding-place to be exhibited in his own time, as his cypher . . . or his consort?

"How you start at shadows!" The breath of his words caressed her cheek. "You must learn, sweetheart, that the sport of life, as with every game of skill, holds in it a strong element of chance."

Fighting her weakness and the battery of charm he trained upon her: "Chance is a jade," she answered scornfully, "with 'Miss' before her name."

His face bent down to hers; his eyes were eager.

"By the Lord! A man would tilt with death to win you in life's tourney!"

The music halted. The dancers scattered to their seats. Lady Dorothy, wine-flushed and slightly swaying, called for a coranto.

"Come on! We'll dance till morning, and then not dance again until my brother sails up the Thames with Philip's fleet in tow."

Shouts of applause and a hasty regathering of partners greeted this announcement. . . . "Let us leave these fools," Essex whispered, "to their follies." And taking her hand, he led her through the hall-screens out on to the terrace.

There, embalmed in the night's tranquillity, all doubt and fear, suspense, was swept away. The noise within sounded remote as the rise and fall of the river's suction on its pebbled beach. The torch-flares shed a wavering path across mist-enshrouded lawns that sloped gently to the unseen water's edge.

She leaned against a parapet and gazed out upon those undertones of darkness where all colours died, and ghostly flowers gave up their perfume to the air. In that moon-silvered mystery the agitation of her heart was stilled; for now that it had come, this long-sought moment, the torrent of her happiness dissolved her. She was spent. While conscious of his nearness, and of her blood's response to the fires she had roused, she stayed detached, observant and so still that a moth, grey-winged and frail, settled on her hand and, incuriously, she felt a kinship with this soft fairy creature. Perhaps it took her whiteness for a flame, and like herself was seared, intoxicated, helpless. . . . Was it sleeping? Was it dead? It fluttered, moved, was gone, the strange swift thing, haphazard, transient a love. But what was love? A meeting and a parting, an interlude, a passing out and then forgetfulness? She crushed the roses at her bosom till the petals fell in a red shower at her feet.

She heard him say defiantly: "So be it! Let the Fates decide. You've asked for this."

Fiercely he took and swung her round, straining her to him with the relentless savagery of appetite tormented, and not to be assuaged by the hunger-search of mouth to mouth, of sight-blind touch and warm sweet juice of tongue. Her stunned senses, reawakened, met his frenzy with a gentle madness to return it, until his arms fell from her, and half reeling, he groped for the edge of the parapet.

"I'm lost," he said, "you've sunk me. Are you satisfied?"

Her teeth gleamed in the darkness.

"Never satisfied, my love . . . my dearest love. Lose yourself in me again. I have not asked, I've *ached* for this!"

"You don't know what you say," he answered roughly. "You cannot understand—how can you?—that your wilful childish pursuit of me is but a whim."

"No!" she caught his hand to her heart. "It is no whim. Feel. . . . Am I a child? Call me abandoned, wanton. Yes, I am! I *have* pursued you. Is that wrong? Only let me offer you my love —you can reject it."

He was racked. Her reckless generosity ensnared and tempted him beyond his strength. She epitomized the theory he had always held of women, that they were more rabid, more courageous in their urgency than men. But despite his own compulsion he must care for her, who was so careless of herself.

"Listen!" His face down-bent to hers was deathly pale in the moonlight. "What would it profit you—or me—to tell you that your unfearing damned insistence breaks me—cuts me open— gladdens me—that I could shout to highest heaven, 'Here's a comrade!'—fashioned with every grace to joy the lusts of man? I've never known another of your mettle, to match mine."

"Egoist!" she flashed at him, "is that all I am? Your match? O, indeed I'm that and more. Essex!" She flung her arms around his neck, "Essex, take me. I am yours." Then, because he stood in silence, unresponsive, her heart narrowed. "Don't you," she whispered, "want me?"

"Not want you! God! . . ." A groan escaped him. "D'you

think I'm made of marble? But how *can* I take you? Oho, you're glib, my girl. Take—take! 'Tis easy, yes? You and I in our positions. Lose our heads to scrunch a sugar-plum. Can I risk your happiness and maybe more, your life, because you, in your innocence—or ignorance, which is it?—have honoured me above my worth. I am not worthy. Listen, will you!" Goaded by his passion he began to shake her. "Would you have me second-hand? I'm tainted. I'm old before my time. I've wallowed in bought pleasures. You see, I also can be honest. I have a wife. I've had a hundred women. And you're fresh. O, rare! Not want you? . . . Have you seen a spray of blossom flung across a wintry sky in April with snow falling to perish it? But it won't perish. It blooms on, defiant, fearless, till it grows into a small green apple. You are like the blossom and its fruit. And I'm the worm to blight you." His voice broke. "My sweet. My charming. . . . Are you bent upon your own destruction?"

"I would be proud," she told him softly, "to destroy myself for you."

His eyes peered down at her. He said, wondering: "In all my life I have never met with this. You're less of a woman than a boy, and the best of both. Half girl, half Ganymedes. Hear, then. I'll give you truth for truth. I'm crazed with want of you. And if that is love, then I do love you. If to think with foresight for your sake is love, then I do love you. If to deny what soul and body crave—and *only* for your sake—then that is love. And if I never speak again I tell you now that for your sake I'd die for you. And I may yet die for you."

"No, no!" she breathed, "live for me. Without you I shall die."

"Why do we talk of death?" He took her face between his hands and laid his mouth to hers. "Is this death? Is it? And is this? Beloved, past all hope, beyond desire, and beyond regret, I love you, and I want you as man should want his woman and—Christ's pity!—as man should want . . . his wife."

She gave a little cry and buried her head in his doublet. Her hand fluttered over his heart and paused. "How fast it beats," she whispered. "Is this hurry all for me? Essex, you said . . . wife. I cannot be your wife, but you have said it."

A wave of tenderness engulfed him. His throat swelled achingly. "What can I say to this? You probe my depths. . . . You touch my very essence. You have separated what I thought to be myself from something better than myself. And before the living God I swear to dedicate that better self to you."

A footstep on the flagstones struck her answer from her lips. Both turned. One stood there in the moonlight cloaked for travel, booted. The brim of his steeple-crowned hat cast deep shadow on his eyes—like a wizard's hat, thought Arabella, and was that gold-tipped stick he carried a magician's wand? She shivered.

"It seems I am come to my house too late to partake in the revels my wife arranged in my absence. Had I known your Lady-ship would grace my table I would not have loitered on the Border." He advanced and stood before her bowing, hat in hand. As he raised his head his eyes slid from her to Essex, then back again, while his slow voice sharpened. "The nights are cold in Northern England, but hot here. . . . Your Ladyship is wise to seek the air."

This lengthy introduction had given her sufficient time to cover her embarrassment.

"I am glad to greet my Lord Northumberland. I was greatly disappointed to find you were not present to receive your guests."

He smiled.

"I beg your Ladyship to favour me with one last dance before the night is done. But first I have to change out of these riding clothes and into gala dress. My good brother will attend you till I come."

She saw how Essex weighed that other with his eyes. What had he seen, or heard? Enough in all conscience to convict them if he chose. But would he choose?

"My lord," she offered her hand and told him fulsomely, "your absence marred my pleasure, but now no guest will dance more gaily. I will await your lordship in the ante-room. Essex, your arm, or I shall slip upon these stones. The moon is clouded. It grows dark."

"Dark," Northumberland repeated; and in the gloom he spread around him she could have sworn that it grew darker. And as if he took the thought from her, "It will," he said, "be darker yet. The stars foretell, this month, of moon's eclipse. . . ."

Chapter Four

THE unhappy circumstances that affected, not only individuals, but all of England, might well have been averted if the investigations of a scientist born centuries before his time, had been accredited as something greater than witchcraft. Advice from a meteorological expert, if followed, could have delayed the hapless start of the Fleet that, under the command of Essex, set out to conquer Spain. Instead, none listened to the croakings of the 'Wizard Earl' who prophesied disaster, and who, according to report, sat with his familiar, the aged Dr. Dee, in the latter's house at Mortlake, before a crucible and furnace to conjure up the devil.

Wild stories circulated. Northumberland had entertained the Sea Lords to a supper, where again he warned them to postpone their venture until the stars gave fairer prospect for the voyage. Foul winds would rise with the moon's eclipse; this would be seen to better advantage in Southern Europe than in Northern climes. Spain, no doubt, had already been forewarned. There were astrologers of good repute among the Spanish priests. It would be well to wait. . . . Postpone!

Thus he urgently advised, while the doubting company seated at his table drank his wine, and inwardly condemned him to the stake. Not a man among them, with the possible exception of Cecil, saw in Northumberland's delphic utterance anything but evil. In vain he argued, to be dubbed not only 'Wizard' but an enemy: one who consorted with spies. Witness his knowledge of the black arts practised by inquisitors . . . Philip's priests, forsooth! He looked to be convicted for a traitor if not worse; and had those in highest office been less occupied with preparations for the voyage, his stars might soon have prophesied his end.

However, when the Fleet set out, Northumberland stayed in, and behind locked doors regarded gloomily his charts and globes and instruments. Neither they nor his own judgment were amiss. The news when it reached the Council Chamber was alarming. True, the weather had been sultry; a fog had descended on the city like a shroud, but the city was accustomed to such visitations, though how an eclipse of the moon could affect the course of the winds, and cause a south-westerly gale to strike the overloaded vessels with such force that most of them were driven back to harbour within two days of leaving it, not Northumberland himself could have explained. The Council deemed it wiser not to ask him.

Further news, and equally disquieting, soon followed. Raleigh had parted company with Essex, and joining up with the St. Matthew and St. Andrew, steered for Cape Ortegal. Essex, raging at this desertion, which he believed to have been prompted more by jealousy of his command than by good seamanship, ordered his crippled fleet to put into Plymouth for repairs.

The better part of their provisions had been lost, the rest rendered useless by exposure to salt water. A bad beginning, and for Essex made no better by the knowledge that his enemies at home, to say nothing of his enemies abroad, were gloating over this calamitous reverse. But who could control the elements? Who could foresee—he might have wished that he had taken the advice of one who did foresee—that, so he wrote to Cecil: 'The most extreme storms and contrary winds would meet with us to lay open my ship's seams that her decks and upper works gave way, and her very timbers with her labouring did tear like laths, so as we looked hourly when the orlop would fall and the ordnance sink down to the leak. Then only did I suffer myself to be overcome. . . .'

And now he must bide his time while his men patched up the damage. His own flagship had sustained so much that he had to send her into Chatham to be partially rebuilt.

On August 17 Essex with his reconditioned fleet set out again, arriving a week later at Cape Ortegal, to find Raleigh there before him. No time to brood on that. Misfortune still pursued them. In a short gale that lasted only five or six hours, St. Matthew and St. Andrew lost their masts and were thrown out of action : these, the two main ships upon which Essex had relied to support his fireboats in their attack upon Corunna and Ferrol.

Not disposed to run the risk of losing any others, he decided to waylay a treasure transport from the Indies, taking the port of Terceira on the way. Word reaching him, however, that a fleet under the command of the Adelantado was sailing for the Azores to protect the Spanish treasure, he changed his plans, foolhardily to chase them. He wrote a long excited letter to Elizabeth of his intention. Her reply, if not condemnatory, was ambiguous.

' This at the present makes me feel like the lunatic man that keeps a smack of the remains of his frenzy's freak, helped well thereto by the influence of Sol in Leone,'—an oblique allusion to the stars, or to Northumberland's prophecy. It was the month of August. She went on to tell him that he vexed her—' too much with small regard of what I scape or bid.' She warned him not to ' venture wonders where approachful mischief might betide you . . . After your perilous first attempt,' (he took that reminder hardly), ' do not aggravate that danger with another.'

He kept her letter, and, with his usual impetuosity, paid no heed to it. Terceira, the citadel of the Azores, was his objective, but the island was too well guarded for immediate attack. He judged it best to lie in wait for the Adelantado and his convoy, and having dealt with him could make an easy capture of the treasure ships. Fayal was selected as a vantage point of observation ; yet once again he reckoned without Raleigh, or the knowledge of one with the salt of the sea in his veins. While Essex reconnoitred, idly cruising, Raleigh stole a march upon him to attack and take Fayal.

Another blow for Essex. ' Approachful mischief. . . .' Yes, he'd had his fill of that ! He began to doubt himself ; but still more did he doubt Raleigh. Again and again the fellow disobeyed his orders. He would make him pay for his contempt. His toadies, envious of Raleigh's repeated successes, urged him to extremes : court martial, execution, or the rope. Essex wavered. Unwilling admiration for one whose courage equalled, if it did not surpass his own, overcame his anger. ' Yes, I'd do it,' he was heard to say, ' *if* he were my friend.' He could forgive. He did ; and Raleigh offered an apology which was accepted, and which gained Essex nothing ; no prize, no prisoner, no credit. Raleigh was in possession of a town. Essex, too, must take a town, or if not, scuttle himself and all his ships. He could not face the Queen's scorn if he appeared before her empty-handed.

Off he went again to hunt for Spaniards, and skirting Terceira, decided he would take, en route, San Miguel. Another act of folly. That island lay east of Terceira, and while his ships manœvered to no purpose, the vast treasure of the Indies slipped past him into port.

That was the end !

Mortified to desperation, shivering with fever, he sailed home, to be greeted with the news that the Ferrol Fleet had taken advantage of his wild-goose chase after treasure, to descend quietly on Falmouth. Only a miracle had saved that unprotected coast from invasion. A storm, those same unfavourable winds that had hit the English ships on their way out, now drove the Spaniards back on their way in.... Saved! Yes, but at what a cost. Loss of prestige, friends, and favour. How would Majesty receive him?

Majesty received him with the iciest displeasure. She accused him of gross mismanagement, extravagance, and waste of time; nor did she fail to remind him that he had wheedled from her this command against her better judgment. Had she not been so misguided she would have promoted Raleigh in his stead. . . . A bitter cut. She would not hear a word in his defence, and may have taken a malicious pleasure in his stammering excuses. She would yet tame her 'rash temerarious' youth; but she was not at all prepared for his reaction when he fled her presence vowing never to return.

Sick with disappointment, the ague, and indignity, he retired to his country house at Wanstead. From there, as his fever and his temper cooled, he wrote sorrowful reproaches to his Queen.

'I do carry the same heart as I was wont, though now overcome by unkindness as once I was conquered by beauty.'

Wryly he re-read those lines before despatching them. 'I do carry the same heart as before.' True enough. His heart had not changed for one who was almost old enough to be his grandmother. 'Overcome by unkindness'. Substitute 'unkindness' for fate or circumstance . . . or a young girl's enticement. In his solitude and, as he believed, forsaken, he dwelled upon his mighty self-denial; and only he and his God knew what depths of agony he suffered by that same self-denial. Was not this the greatest of all sacrifice, his deliberate removal of his person from the delightful temptation of hers? For by so doing he believed that he had choked the magpie chatter that linked his name with Arabella Stuart's.

She, he learned, was still about the Court which had returned from Nonesuch to Whitehall. If he could let her know of his sad case! Sorely tempted to write a letter that would bring her to his bedside, he had the sense to choose the safer course.

Impassioned words flowed from his pen to the Queen. He may have grinned as he wrote:

'Since I was first so happy as to know what love meant I was never one day nor one hour free from hope or jealousy. . . .'

Hope? No, not for him. There was no hope. But jealousy? . . . He recalled a most unpleasant twinge that, like rheumatics, had

unaccountably attacked him even when she was a child and he ha
snatched her from Northumberland, that oaf, married to his sister
What a marriage! Neither faithful. But, come to that, was he
The Greeks were wiser. They married their wives and took for
lovers the exquisite *hetairae*. Marriage after all was no more than
convenience. His wife had justified her marriage by giving him an
heir.

His pen ran on.

' . . . Hope, jealousy. And so long as you do me right they ar
the inseparable companions of my love. If in the sweetness of
your own heart you do nourish the one and in the justness of lov
free me from the tyranny of the other, you shall ever make me
happy. . . .'

Charmed by these tender avowals, Elizabeth was persuaded to
ask after his health, and followed the inquiry with the hint that she
would welcome his return. Her Accession Day was near at hand
There would be celebrations. Would his lordship's ague permit
his presence at the Court?

But Essex, determined to wring from Gloriana more than a
noncommittal invitation, kept to his room, and sighed for Arabella

And then one day, without a word to herald her arrival; no
message and no messenger, and only one small page in attendance
on her, Arabella came. It was unbelievable. Stupendous! His
wife—profoundly he thanked God for it—had left Wanstead for
his London house. And here she was, this girl, muffled in a hooded
cloak, a basket on her arm, a vizard to her face, standing in the
doorway of his room. His man had shown her in without a word
She whispered to the boy, who slunk away; and to Essex, her eyes
unmasked and shining:

"I had to come," she said. "I heard that you were ill. I've
brought you fruit. I told the porter at the gates that I was the wife
of the mercer at the sign of the Blue Boar. My poor husband having
sickened of a fever sends me to your lordship with some samples
in his stead." An impish smile crossed her face. "I took the chance
this forenoon to escape from Mistress Sherland. My Uncle Henry
is in town. I left them playing at cat's cradle in my chamber. And
how unfortunate that my poor Anne was taken with the megrims
I offered her a glass of wine to cure them, and may I die if she didn't
fall asleep! . . . Don't look so shocked. They served me with the
same trick, once. But Anne had only half the dose they gave to

me. . . . O, Essex!" Setting down her basket she sped into his arms. "Heart! Can you believe how dreadfully I suffered when I heard that you were drowned?"

"Drowned!" So that was how they'd taken the Island Voyage disaster—with his death : and may have wished for it. He chuckled. "I'm still here, but you've no right to be. My foolish, reckless . . . What a risk! You know if you're discovered you're disgraced."

"Don't scold. I had to see you. What if I am discovered? At the worst there can only be a scandal, and that, for you, is nothing of a novelty." She gazed at him, her head aslant. "You're thinner . . . O, my soul!" she pleaded, "come back to Court. Come back to me. I'm sick with wanting you."

Her hood had fallen from her hair ; he brushed her curls across her face to tumble them, and murmured : "How you do delight to maul my heart-strings."

"Do I so, my dearest dear?" She leaned her forehead against his doublet, sweetly coaxing. "I only want you to come back. The Queen chafes and lours and is so waspish she drives us to distraction, and all for love of you. There never was a man more greatly loved, but—" she linked her hands behind his neck—"because I love you most of any, I dared to hope that if you'll not return for her, you will for me."

In the dilated pupils of her green-gold eyes he saw himself in miniature, a fairy's size, gay-coloured, slashed with red, the white ring of his ruff against the melting black. He sighed : "Delicious!" and sought her ripe blunt-cornered mouth with his. "O, rich! . . . Now let me drink and drink! But what"—his hands gripped fiercely at her shoulders—"what in Hades or in Heaven else am I to do with you?"

She trembled ; then two dimples came and went in either cheek. "You should know that, my lord."

A laugh burst in his throat. He crossed his fingers. "*Retro me Sathana!* Are you Eve or Devil?"

Silently she looked at him in that endearing way of hers, like a puppy-dog about to bite in fun, nose wrinkled, upper lip caught back against her teeth. And all his blood leapt in his veins to meet that something lawless, ever young and of the vagrant, that he recognized in her to match its twin that dwelled within himself. Gleefully he took her hands, and, widening her arms, brought them close against his sides, straining her body to his.

"You make me want to go a-gypsying," he muttered, "to sleep with you beneath the stars, to throw aside our makeshift finery and run as wild and as naked as God made us. Shall we? . . . Shall we?"

"Shall we not . . . O, heaven!"

The visionary prospect he unfolded was too radiant. She swayed; her eyes were closing when a small sound brought her to her senses and her glance, bedazed and frightened, to the door. She saw it open slowly. Her page stood there.

"My Lady!"

"To hell with you!" ejaculated Essex.

"No," she intervened, "he has my orders. Your major-domo must be on the prowl."

"So he is, my . . . Mistress Bradshaw," piped the boy.

"Bradshaw!" Essex doubled. "How you do misuse that poor girl's name!"

"Since I dare not use my own I must. . . . My lord," she pulled her hood over her head, took up her vizard and basket, and raising her voice, mimicked the broad accent of the London folk. "My husband bids me thus advise you that these are the best variety of samples he can show. But if my lord will honour my good man with a visit to his shop, your lordship can take his pick of what he fancies." Then drawing from the basket on her arm a rosy apple, she flung it at him, whispered: "Catch!" . . . .

He caught it. She was gone.

The baggage! He took a bite out of the apple and munched while he stood staring at the door that closed behind her. Then, head back, he laughed again to crack his sides. By God! This girl of his had won where the Queen herself had failed. He would —O, yes, he *would*—return to Court.

He did; to find his girl had flown. Her latest escapade had been discovered, and by none other than her Uncle Henry, who in the absence of the Shrewsburys had been appointed unwilling guardian of his niece.

He had seen her re-enter the house with her page in the dress of a citizen's wife; and though he hitherto had chosen to take the line of least resistance in respect of his mutinous charge, Henry felt it now his bounden duty to command the situation.

Protests, tears, hysterics, genuine or feigned, were of no avail.

Henry stood by his decision. He would take her home. Yes, back to Hardwick: this the penalty for her disgraceful misbehaviour. He was responsible for her good name. It would seem that she had slurred it. As for the trick she had played upon her waiting-woman——

"The same," she told him pertly, "as once was played on me."

He looked at her in silence, unrelenting, his eyes cold.

Unused to such a stern reception from one on whom she always could rely to take her part and fight her battles with his mother, she was dashed; but for the moment only. Furthering defiance she persisted.

"Is it a felonious offence to venture out upon a shopping expedition with my page?"

Henry raised an eyebrow.

"In disguise?"

"Why, damn my soul, sir, to perdition! May I perish——" she declared, "if my dress was other than the one I always wear when visiting the shops."

"I have yet to learn," said Henry, very cool, "that there are shops at Wanstead."

"Wanstead!" Her eyes opened, and her mouth; her colour dwindled. "Who said that I had been to Wanstead? What a lie!"

Henry eyed her squarely. "Is it?"

She began to bluster.

"If my page has slandered me I'll slit his tongue. I'll——"

"Your page has not been questioned."

"Then who has?"

"None but your own conscience—and," drawled Henry, "mine."

"Yours?" She stared at him.

"I owe it to myself," he said, "to drag you from a ditch when you fall in it."

"I have not fallen."

"No, not yet," he cuttingly retorted, "but you will."

At that she crumpled, dropped upon her knees and broke into a storm of tears.

Gravely Henry watched her. Was she play-acting, or did this *rise* denote a chrysalis emergence no less painful, if more poignant, than the cutting of a tooth? While he sympathized with and could comprehend the emotional complexities of the adolescent who soared so hopefully on sprouting wings to flounder in recoil from a first rebuff, he made no effort to offer consolation. There was none. He too well remembered the torment of youth's love life, before manhood's disillusionment encased the cynic in his shell. . . . Protective armour! Yes, but only hard experience could grow it, as the oyster, by an irritant deposit grows a pearl.

But how to tell her, Henry mused, that nothing dies? That all loves live on in some form or another, even after the first eager passion is burnt out; the love of books, of art, of beauty; any striving of the senses or mood of intellectual excitement, the ceaseless weaving and interweaving of the spirit's self in a colourful design of swift impressions,—that is love: the fruits of love made manifest in a thousand daily exquisite delights and quaint conceits of fancy. Yet, how could he reveal the compensations of life's variegated harmonies to one whose ears were closed, whose eyes were bound, in a child's game of blind-man's-buff? How convince her that the elements of which we are composed extend beyond the fading of a dream? . . . .

And: "How heartless cruel you are!" cried Arabella, when packed inside the coach that was to carry her to Hardwick she flung a last appeal at this unmoved, incalculable Henry. "Why must I leave London now? Why? I've done no wrong."

"No more," he answered her obscurely, "than did Psyche whom Venus put to death, poor girl, because she robbed the goddess of her son. . . . Drive on!"

The coachman whipped his horses, Henry mounted his, while Arabella, scarlet and ignoring Bridget's grins, sat biting at her fingers through her glove.

Thus Essex came from his retirement to miss her; but he was soon consoled. The Maids no longer mourned his inattention Mistress Brydges, Lady Mary Howard, and a gentle, pretty creature Elizabeth Southwell, were all recipients of something more than kisses. Each, so gossip verified, was with child by him, but to Mistress Southwell only was a child born. The other ladies may have been more knowledgeable or less fervent; and little Mistress Southwell fled the Court.

Poor patient Lady Essex wept bitter tears in private. Elizabeth less patient, and in public, poured her wrath on all her girls in

urn. Whether innocent or guilty they were branded, each, she
old them, bad as one another. Words led to blows. For the
smallest fault her Maidens had their faces smacked, and smartly.
More than ever must they fetch and carry for Her Grace. She
harried them from room to room with shrill commands, and with
biting sarcasm exhorted every one to remain 'in virgin state as
much as may be'. But these feminine absurdities, notwithstanding
that they vexed, did not agitate Elizabeth for long. Current events
of greater import more immediately engaged her. The Council
was pressing for a truce with Spain. It had come to her ears that
Henry of Navarre, despite the obligations of his treaty, had made
a separate peace.

To her Council the Queen expressed her discontent at such
betrayal from 'This Anti-Christ of base ingratitude!' . . . And
now Ireland, England's most troublesome offspring, was up in
arms again, and a Lord Deputy required to quell a threatening
rebellion.

Elizabeth had named Sir William Knollys, uncle of Lord Essex,
a man of tact and courage, as well suited to the post. Essex, however,
had in mind Sir George Carew, a young gentleman whom he
detested and wished to have out of his way. There followed loud
disputes and violent discussions. The argument waxed warmer;
neither Elizabeth nor Essex would give in. The Council stared
amazed at the mad youth's impertinence; and mad he must have
been indeed when, during further parley, he let his temper run such
riot that he turned his back upon the Queen of England. An
outrage, unprecedented and unpardonable, witnessed luckily by
only three: Lord Nottingham, a Clerk of the Court, and the
silent Cecil. But far worse was to follow.

If Essex had discarded the respect due from a subject to a
sovereign, Elizabeth discarded her dignity as much. Convulsed
with fury she sprang to her feet, yelled: "Be hanged to ye! Go
to the devil!" and fetched him a box on the ear.

For a second he stood, too astonished for speech; then beside
himself, livid, clapped a hand to his sword, and: "By God's
Soul!" he swore, "I would not have taken such an insult from
our father—and I will not take it from you!" With which he
came at her as if to strike her down.

The horrified Nottingham leapt at his throat; the Clerk of the
Court made a grab for the sword. Essex sheathed it. Cecil stayed

very still, his eyes on Elizabeth's face. She had sunk in her chair, unstirring, and after her outburst unstirred, yet so white one could believe the blood in her veins had frozen. Wrenching himself from Nottingham's hold, Essex made as if to fall upon his knees, hesitated, muttered something indistinguishable, and in a ghastly silence backed, and rushed out of the room.

The Queen in her chair sat like Medusa. Her gentlemen stood as if turned into stone. Cecil feared that the shock might have killed her. If not, he conjectured, her ' temerarious youth ' had done for himself this time. . . .

Talk of the appalling conduct of Lord Essex swept the country. At Hardwick Arabella heard it, and hearing, feared for him. No man, not even the prime favourite, could be excused the inexcusable. He had offended more than Majesty ; he had committed, or in his madness almost did commit, sacrilege against the Lord's Anointed. Treason !

The Cavendish boys laid wagers on the penalty that Essex, when convicted, would be called upon to pay. The block, the gallows—with its reeking death at the end of the rope—or the Tower ? Which ?

Arabella listened petrified, and in the quiet of her chamber prayed to heaven ; but it seemed to her that God was deaf, and the devil loosed about the house to play such evil with her cousins' tongues that they could gloat upon the end of him who was her life's beginning.

Meanwhile the Queen attended to affairs of state, and, her dignity recovered, with a sublime indifference to whispers in the Court, or out of it. The penalty that everyone believed and many hoped would descend upon Lord Essex, appeared to be suspended. Or was Her Grace preparing some malevolent revenge, some frightful torture to surpass the horrors of thumbscrew or rack ? Would she put out his eyes, tear him limb from limb, or burn him as her sister had burned martyrs at the stake ? Would she confine him to the darkest dungeon and starve him by slow inches to his death ?

What she might have done will never be decided. She may have planned for him a thousand torments while, in silence still, she brooded, or she may not have planned one. In the midst of nation-wide discussion, and suddenly, to sweep away all other cares, came the illness of the venerable Burghley. He was dying.

izabeth's beloved 'Spirit' was about to leave her Kingdom for
e higher. His long day's work was done. Nothing could stay
passing, not all the Queen's doctors nor all the Queen's prayers;
t even the Queen's most gracious Presence at his beside. He
is going. . . . And he went.

She wept for him as she had never wept for any man, not
en for Tom Seymour, her first love. What would she do with
gentle, wise old counsellor to guide her? She was like a rudder-
s ship on a stormy sea. She had lost her dearest friend; but
rcely had she buried him than she lost her greatest enemy.

Racked with pain and hope deferred, yet still upheld by the
ief that a fourth or fifth, or maybe sixth Armada, would conquer
ally that wretched little island in the North, King Philip lay
on his pillows, conscious of yet not afraid of death; fearing
thing save, in the secret places of his soul, 'That Woman' and
power of her Fleet; and the curse that seemed to fall upon
own.

There, sweating, shivering, oozing the foul pus of his disease,
watched his chanting priests and stared up at the long faces of
doctors. He raved that he, and he alone, was Spain. Without
n Spain would sink into obscurity, a third-rate nation. They
ist cure him of his seizure. He must live. They must make
n live, or . . . he smiled at them gently, they too, with him, would
. . . . While with potions, unguents, balm, they strove to soothe
n, a courier came panting to his bedside hot with news from
land. He lifted up his dying head to hear it. His secret ally,
rone, had risen to attack and annihilate 'That Woman's' armies
Blackwater.

A miracle. A sign from heaven! He, God's Chosen, had been
nted this answer to his prayers. Spain would live again!
Struggling for breath to gasp the words, he bade them send
porting armies to Tyrone.
The last rites were performed. The leaden shroud that he had
lered to enwrap his sacred body, was brought to him. His
nbling fingers stretched to stroke it. His priests surrounded
. His eyes rolled up; the candles blossomed into glory. . . .
e bells tolled, and Philip, festering and frightful, ridiculous and
at, sank back upon his pillows into peace. . . .

'How he loathed—and how he loved me!' sighed Elizabeth;
for him too she wept, a little. Of all her generation only she

was left. So old? No. . . . Peering in the mirror at her tim
seared face, she closed her lips and smiled. Never old. Etern
youth ran in her veins. Youth was all about her, the heroic you
of England at her feet. Yes, all but one, who had so shocking
offended and stayed outside the pale, or inside his house at Wanstea

Softened by the death of Burghley, thankful for the death
Philip—an ever-present menace now removed—she thought
would be gracious to send word to that impossible young ma
He had played upon her sentiment too long. She now wou
play a while upon his, and 'stand upon her greatness as he upon h
stomach'.

But if she looked for an apology she looked for it in vai
He remained aloof, the injured party, while weeks and months
indecision and countless irritations caused by faulty governance
Ireland, continued to perturb the harassed Council. Would H
Grace never be persuaded to make up her mind who, or who shou
not, be sent to Ireland? Why did she wait, and for whom?

Every man of them knew the answer, though it was past beli
that after the shameful episode of almost a year ago, to say nothir
of that ill-conditioned Island Voyage which had cost England
fortune, the Queen should choose Lord Essex for the Vice-reg
office! That and more. The command of an army in Ireland.
was hoped he would conduct a military campaign better than
naval one. Apparently all was forgiven—or appeared to be—whe
Cecil, urbane as ever, approved the Queen's decision.

And Essex, elated, vowed: ' By the Lord, I will beat Tyron
for nothing worthy of Her Majesty's honour has yet been achievec

His send-off was tremendous. All London watched him g
Accompanied by his troop of hand-picked followers, he roc
down Seething Lane, through Cornhill and Cheapside. Excite
town's folk, butchers' boys, apprentices, screaming drabs a
beggars, bakers in their white caps, brewers and soap-boilers, th
black-faced men who heaved the sea-coal, vintners who had le
their vats, their hands stained red as if with blood, all came out
cheer him on his way.

The sun stood high in heaven, but as he arrived at Islington
great black cloud obscured it. The skies opened and a storm
rain and hail deluged him and all his company. While old wiv
clacked of omens, Essex laughed. Then, of a sudden, there flashe
through his mind some lines from a play about Richard III he ha

en at the Globe Theatre: the work, or supposed to be, of that
ay-acting fellow—he had forgotten his name—with a slab of
forehead, pale as dough, and the prettiest taste in words.
ow the devil did that couplet run? 'Shine out . . . Shine
it . . .'

Snatching his hat from his head Essex dramatically waved it,
d, to the huge delight of the cheering crowd, bawled at the top
his lungs:

> ' Shine out fair sun till I have bought a glass
> That I may see my shadow as I pass ! '

*   *   *

News travelled slowly to Derbyshire, and the disastrous story
the Irish Campaign was already stale to Londoners by the time
reached Hardwick Hall.

The Lord Deputy who ventured forth with such high hopes had
led !

He began with a grievous blunder, for no sooner did he set
ot in Ireland than he made his friend, Southampton, Captain of
e Horse, and this in direct defiance of the Queen's command.
noring Elizabeth's infuriated message to have Southampton
prived of an office to which, with her consent he would not, nor
ver could, have been promoted, Essex marched on triumphantly
Leinster.

And the deeper he journeyed into that island of violet mists
d great grey mountains, the more did he fall to the spell of its
chantment: a traveller in a world of dewy twilights, of faery lore
d legend. The graver purpose of his coming was lost in pursuit
a song. Ragged women, lovelier than sin, with shawls on their
ads and no shoes on their feet, ran beside his horse. Their long
ack hair was straight as rain; the movement of their tempting
s interpreted the unintelligible gibberish that fell from them.
eir cheeks were tinted like the foxglove, their eyes blue as their
oon-shaped lakes. Every peasant was a bard and all the people
ets. All were poor and all were happy, a race of children lovable
d garrulous, who sang and jested, wept, were sad with the
dness of shadowy waters, and gay with the laughter of the winds.
d he loved them; drank with them in their taverns, travelled
and ever on through the emerald bogs of his illusion, followed
ere their women beckoned, bewitched, dream-ridden. . . .

And rudely dream-awakened by the crash of fallen horsemen ar the groans of his men who lay dying.

The faery songs, the passion-dimmed eyes and pale eyelids young girls whose beauty plucked at his heart-strings, melted awa before the spectre of Disease. It stalked beside his horse whe once fair women ran. His armies sickened, died. There was n enough food to feed them in that dank, hollow land. His ey were opened and he saw: starvation, squalor, all around hi The laughter and the singing turned to mockery. Behind eve thornbush men lurked, watching, evil-eyed. They knew him f their enemy and had led him on with gentle blandishment, to him down! Then they rose at him and fought like fiends agair his weakened armies. What hope had he now of crushing Tyrone His troops were on the verge of mutiny. He wrote, self-defendin to the Queen:

'These rebels are far more numerous than Your Majesty armies, and have, though I do unwillingly confess it, better bodies As for himself, he bitterly reminded her, he 'had received nothi from home but discomfort and soul-wounds'.

To which complaint the Queen preserved an inimical silenc The best, or the worst he could do, he decided, was to call f an armistice. So . . . he met Tyrone in parley at a ford, and the proposed a truce which was accepted.

No battle had been won, though many fought. His enem at home declared him a traitor, only waiting for the Spaniards descend upon the island. Certain now that his destruction w determined, he hastened back to London to vindicate himself.

Bit by bit the sorry tale pieced together, was retold, and nothi lessened by embellishment at Hardwick.

There, in the new house, Bess had assembled her family. T old Hardwick stood forsaken save for those quarters used by t domestic staff. But the tough old Dowager was not content rest upon her labour. She would build again. While stout, we filled, well-satisfied, she presided at her table, her restless mi pursued its next objective. Oldcotes, a recently acquired prope within easy drive of Hardwick, would need much reconstructic She would leave her mark throughout the length and breadth Derbyshire; the finest manors in the country would be hers hand along the centuries, to glorify the name of Cavendish and their progeny.

Her eye fell on Arabella, seated between her grandsons, Gilbert
nd William. How white the child looked—as if about to swoon.
ad she over-eaten? Was she drunk?

Bess raised her hand to quell the uproar. It seemed that her
oung people had each a thousand tongues. It might be an advantage,
ne dourly reflected, to grow, with age, a little hard of hearing.
ruly the deaf were to be envied. Some argument, to which, till
ien, she had paid little heed, was under forcible discussion among
he younger members of her brood. The ominous words, ' Star
hamber ', caught her ears. She bellowed :

" What damnifying talk is this ? "

" Damnifying, madam, so it is," answered Gilbert, grinning.
I've laid a bet with my brother Will that Essex will be brought
efore the Council. I say that he'll be hanged. Will lays his goshawk
) my jerfalcon that he won't."

" No, nor will he ! " William leaned across Arabella to shout.
So long as he lies at the feet of Her Grace for whatever *dis*grace
e may bring her, he'll receive nothing worse than a clout on the
ar—and then turn t'other cheek to her for more ! "

Bess hid a chuckle behind her rebuke at the laughter that
ollowed this sally.

" Hey now, you rogue ! Take heed lest you hang yourself for
uch malapert talk of your betters. Arbelle, my girl, you're pale
s milk. . . . Have you been gorging to sicken your stomach ? "

" No, madam, I . . ." Her voice sank to a whisper. Under
ne table she clasped her hands tightly together. The blood beat
n her ears like a drum, drowning the chatter around her. But
he must listen, must force herself to hear their ceaseless gabble
hough it sink her. She called the steward to refill her cup with
rine, and under her grandmother's searching look she drank,
ragged a smile to her stiffened lips, and said : " I have a slight
ain in my side, madam. 'Tis nothing. It will pass."

Would it ? Would this weight that lay like lead on her heart
ver pass ? How could she endure this torture of suspense while
er cousins played with words that spelled his death . . . or hers ?
f she could die now in this moment, and so be spared the agony
hat she must suffer every hour, every minute of each day until
he knew . . . Knew what ? It might be better not to know.
But for her life she could not hold herself from asking, with that
xed smile screwed upon her mouth : " What are the odds against

the Star Chamber . . . or hanging ? " And she shrilled a laug
so high and cracked that her Uncle Henry opposite, narrow
observant, called across the board to his nephews :

"Hold your tongues and keep your hawks ! There's no hazar
to be lost or won on Essex. He's too sure. And from what I'v
heard he's done as well in Ireland as any man could do again
such odds." Then to his mother, who was frowning, he sai
lightly : "Madam, these young rascals have construed fact int
fancy. The facts are these—so far as I can glean them—and th
offence, if such, of which Essex may be guilty, is a farce. I under
stand that when Essex returned in haste from Ireland to Nonesuc
he did not wait to be announced, but all muddied as he was, burs
into the tiring-chamber where Her Grace sat at her toilet. If
know the Queen she must have been delighted to receiv
him."

"What ! " crowed Gilbert. "Without her wig, her grey hair
all uncovered ? My faith ! She'll not forgive him that, thoug
she may forgive the mess he's made in Ireland."

"Go to, you heedless jolt-head ! " cried Bess, with ill-conceale
enjoyment. "May your tongue be slit for treason ! Grey ? He
Grace is red."

"Was," corrected Gilbert irrepressibly. "Red as a vixen, s
I'm told, some sixty years ago. Your ladyship forgets Her Grac
is . . . elderly."

Bess darted him a glance to freeze his marrow, then, her dewlap
quivering, silently she chuckled. The saucy young chip ! Elderly
. . . Old ! But not quite so old as herself, though she looked i
with her pomade and fandangles and gewgaws. . . . And grey
Very likely when near upon seventy. Surreptitiously Bess raise
a hand to the fearsome transformation of orange-coloured curl
that covered what nature had left of her hair. A laugh bubble
up in her throat as her gaze turned fondly upon Gilbert, who wit
jocular insistence was repeating :

"I am prepared to wager with any one of you that nothing no
can save him from the block. Her Grace will never pardon him tha
sight of her grey hairs. He'll hang or be axed for sure. Come
fellows ! Why so shy ? Put down your stakes. I'll make it mone
since young William is afeared to lose his hawk. He'd sooner los
ten angels. . . . Double or quits then. Are you game ? "

This was not to be borne ! . . . Arabella closed her eyes ; he

orehead dampened, and a coldness came upon her with a shrinking
f her flesh. She must get up or go out : or be sick.

"Madam." She stood. "I beg your ladyship's leave to . . ."

The massive form of her grandmother seemed oddly to swell
vhile the board and the faces around it diminished. The tapestried
valls advanced and encircled her, pressing her down. She struggled
1 a suffocating vapour, fought for breath . . . and fell.

And an hour later :

"I tell you I too ate of roast pig. Have I sickened ? " His
nother demanded of Henry. "There's more in this swoon than
neets the eye, believe me."

Henry did believe her, but : "The excellent good fare your
adyship provides," he insinuated gracefully, "might prove too
;reedy a temptation for a delicate stomach to——"

"Delicate stomach my —— May you grow horns ! " Bess
eturned with more vigour than modesty. "I'll have her examined.
;o fetch me the doctor. If she's got herself with child my grand-
on Gilbert looks to win his bet and t'other young whelp lose it.
/ou know as well as I how that dandiprat has played the leman
o her whoring. She's not the first nor yet the last he's
avaged."

"Madam," demurred Henry, looking pained. "You do sur-
•rise me. Is it possible you can suspect your own granddaughter's
nnocence ? "

"As much as I suspect my son's," retorted Bess, "and however
ou may hope to shield her, you cannot hide what's there for all
o see. Moreover, tongues are wagging—as will the tail of a dog
vhen its nose scents offal. Yes ! Though I live remote from dirt,
he stink of it is in my nostrils, and the sight of it—or I'm a noddy
—hid beneath a petticoat. Was I born yesterday ? "

Henry dropped his quizzing tone and raised an eyebrow.

"Madam, I protest that you lend too loose a rein to your
magination." He sincerely hoped so. Was it possible that the
•ld dame had more knowledge than himself of Arabella's secret ?
f secret still it were, and not holloaed loud in every mouth from
lardwick Hall to London. "Arbelle," persisted Henry, disdaining
nterruption, "like many other maidens not excluding——" he
lipped a smile, "the highest Maiden of them all, might be diverted
•y the persuasability of one who is a master in amative pursuit,

but such indecorous intention as this with which you woul
impute——"

"Go, blockhead!" barked his mother, pointing to the door
"You are too smooth and do out-talk yourself to further m
suspicions."

Which, as her temper cooled, might well have been allayed
had Bess not received a letter written by no less a person tha
the King of Scots to his spy and toady at Whitehall, Lord Henr
Howard. That good gentleman, with the kindest intent, sent
copy of the same to Bess at Hardwick. Fear allied to doubt rekindled
roused her to a frenzy as she read:

> 'I am from my heart sorry for this accident befallen to Arbell
> but as Nature enforceth me to love her as the nearest of kin t
> me next my own children, so would I for her own sake tha
> such order were taken as she might be prevented from evi
> company, and that evil inclined persons might not have acces
> unto her, abusing the frailty of her youth and sex. . . .'

Horror-stricken, Bess read again the sanctimonious words. . .
Were her worst fears to be realized and Arbelle disgraced befor
a sniggering world, to say nothing of a King?

It might have somewhat comforted the agitated Dowager i
she had known that James of Scotland was on another track
Rumour had reached his ears that his young cousin was incline
to Papistry: rumours doubtless due to the known influence o
Mary Shrewsbury, whose Popish predilections were no longer secre
but pronounced. Bess, however, saw in this grieved remonstranc
from King James, clear evidence of Arabella's guilt. 'Evil incline
persons . . .' Ah! Bess knew of one who was inclined to 'hav
access' to her. Abusing of her frailty, forsooth! The girl wa
anything but frail. A wanton skit. A strumpet.

Raging, Bess tore the letter into bits and flung them in th
fire. A tongue of flame shot up and licked the words 'natur
enforceth me to love her as the nearest of kin to me. . . .' Muc
love had James of Scotland shown his cousin. He had stolen he
lands and her earldom and he would steal a higher title yet. . .
"Misery, misery!" groaned Bess aloud, "that my grey hair
should be brought down in sorrow to the——" She clutched he
head; her wig tipped sideways. Impatiently she tugged it for
ward. "My mind will go," she muttered. "I am too old fo
this."

One thing was certain, for her own peace she must have the child medically examined, and if proven undeflowered, God be thanked; although, Bess sourly reflected, that would not prove her undefiled. But let the doctor be called and decide.

The doctor was called and decided; and Arabella's innocence established as *virgo intacta*.

This was not the first, though it may have been the worst indignity that Arabella suffered under the aged Countess's autocracy at Hardwick. Ever since Elizabeth had intimated that her young kinswoman would never, by her will, be named her rightful heir, Bess, while blaming Arabella for this failure of her life's ambition, felt that she had equally failed herself. She would not admit it, though the thought lay like a canker deep in her heart; and it festered. She sought in petty invidious ways to wreak vengeance on her once 'Beloved Childe' who had squandered her chance of a throne by playing the rig with the Queen's paramour. There must be no more flummery of head-bowing and kneeling; no royal state maintained towards one whom Majesty chose to ignore. Bess may have exaggerated Majesty's disfavour, yet it was evident the Queen did not encourage her young cousin's presence at the Court. And why should she indeed? If, fumed Bess, talk of her ruttish misbehaviour had reached the King of Scotland's ears to bring from him a sermon, how much more and how much worse had come to the ears of Her Grace? Wonder it was the girl had not been apprehended, seized, and flung into the Tower. At least at Hardwick, where Bess Shrewsbury was Queen in her own right, she could enforce a rightful punishment.

But the Lady of Hardwick had reckoned without her household, or without the Stuart charm that evoked from all who met with it a whole-hearted devotion, which even the weakling Darnley had inspired. So, while their mistress imposed upon her every possible severity, treated her as slave if not as hostage, there was no male member of the staff who would not have risked his life to do the bidding of the Lady Arabella. She still had for her attendant the ever faithful Anne, but, to her sorrow, Bridget Sherland was dismissed: another spiteful gesture from the vindictive Bess. Mary Shrewsbury, however, found a place for Bridget in her own house, and Arabella had the comfort of knowing she was not to be for ever parted from one who, since her birth, had been her second mother.

Thus her star, once so high in the ascendant, sank, or at the best was hidden, in that clouded dawn of the seventeenth century.

Chapter Five

HERS was not the only star to fall in the year 1600. While all over England festivities were held to welcome in the new century ; while the Court Circular announced : ' The Queen is in very good health and comes much abroad these holidays ' ; while Her Majesty deigned to accept, among other gifts showered upon her from every one of her subjects, high and low, a ' token ' from the Lady Arabella, ' one skarfe or head veile of lawn cut-worke flourished with silver and silks of all colours ', which had cost the donor more than a whole year's pocket-money, Elizabeth at the same time rejected an ' exceedingly rich present ' from Lord Essex. . . . ' The Queen is still very angry with him '.

Angry enough to order him into the custody of Lord Keeper Egerton : a virtual imprisonment. And no more than he deserved, muttered those who hoped to see him hanged. The chief opposing factors, headed by Cecil and Raleigh, watched and waited for the nearing crisis, the one on his own admission, ' merely passive and not active in action. I follow the Queen and I lead her not.' The other, impatient of Cecil's tolerant acceptance of ' this Tyrant's malice, which is fixed,' thus Raleigh to him in a letter which should never have been written, ' and will not evaporate by any of your mild courses, for Essex will ascribe the alteration to Her Majesty's pusillanimity and not to your good nature. The less you make him, the less he will be able to harm you and yours ; and if Her Majesty's favour fail him, he will again decline to a common person. . . . Lose not your advantage.'

The Secretary smiled his slow, melancholy smile, and sat, inscrutable. The Star Chamber had catalogued his lordship's misdeeds. It was not for a mere Secretary, no, nor yet a Raleigh to question justice or condemn. Let past mistakes and blunders be forgotten. And for the day, mused Cecil, as he shoved the letter in his sleeve, sufficient.

And the evil thereof might well have satisfied the few, so

soon to be the many, who sought the downfall of the hated favourite.

Like sparks from an anvil springing red-hot, recurred the heedless consequence of youth's unbounded folly. The iron waited, ready to brand him, but the hand that wielded it must stay for ever cautious, judging the moment when to strike.

Seated at his table, the taper light upon his beautiful calm brow, the hump-backed dwarf who was the master mind of England, recalled again the deplorable ear-boxing incident that he had witnessed, and which he foresaw to be the first knot in the rope of circumstance that would inevitably bring about an end. . . . And then this second and more recent episode, less deplorable, but never, if Cecil knew his Queen, to be forgiven. What ageing woman could forgive a young lover's sight of her person unadorned, with her grey hair in wisps about her face, unpainted ? Crude, reflected Cecil sadly, very crude. . . . How strangely, he philosophized, does history resolve itself upon the merest trifles ; a lady's garter, or a butt of wine, a bag of tennis balls flung as challenge from an insolent young dauphin to bring about the fall of France. . . . A Queen interrupted at her toilet might bring about the fall of pride when greater means had failed.

Had Essex failed ?

The whole country held its breath. What dreadful punishment awaited him ? None whatever it would seem, or next to none. Rumour gave it he was ill, and by the Queen's grace returned from the custody of the Lord Keeper at York House to his home at Wanstead. The Queen showed the deepest concern and sent him a basin of broth and eight physicians to his bedside. . . . He recovered, and was brought again before the Council whom Elizabeth empowered ' to censure and not judge him.'

A mock trial resulted and Essex was ordered to forfeit his every office, and forbidden entry to the Court.

If Elizabeth thought that this unkindliness would break his spirit to bring about an exquisite reunion, she was mistaken. His spirit was as high as hers, his obstinacy higher. While all appeared to be as she would have it, while letters poured from him : ' Haste paper to that happy Presence whence only unhappy I am banished. Kiss that fair correcting hand . . .' Essex schemed. His popularity among the citizens of London had been proven. Should he put it to the test ? ' That fair correcting hand ', no doubt to try him to the last extreme, had now denied him the renewal of his patent for a monopoly of sweet wines, which privilege brought him in a goodly income. Moreover, the Queen accompanied her refusal with the ominous remark : ' When a horse becomes unmanageable we must stint him of his corn. . . .'

But deprivation of his corn did not, as she imagined, tame her stallion : not at all. He fed upon his wrath, that boiled to consume him till his passion burst its bounds. He had humbled himself to her, had pleaded, asked pardon for his fatal mistakes in Ireland. No man is infallible. Any other, so he reasoned, would have failed under such conditions. His men were dying of disease. Let her curse the fates, the gods, or the treachery of those she trusted, but let her not curse him ! Her blood be on her own head. He had done with her whose mind, he declared to a roomful of men, ' was as crooked as her carcase '.

And those outrageous words of his were carried to the Queen. . . .

*   *   *

Arabella, chafing in her prison-house at Hardwick, heard first-hand of the desperate course that Essex now pursued. Mr. Starkey, returned from London where he had spent his annual vacation, may have found some slight macabre satisfaction in the account he gave of all that he had seen. She listened with the chill of death upon her, but showed no outward sign of her heart's anguish.

One gleam of comfort only had struggled through the clouds of her oppression during the whole of this last dreary year. Although she had received from him no letter in return for another she had written and delivered at his house by Mr. Starkey, that same messenger had brought her back a small sealed packet. It had been handed in, Mr. Starkey told her stiffly, at his lodgings the night before he left.

Later, in her room that gave access to Lady Shrewsbury's, and when her grandmother's sonorous breathing denoted that she slept, Arabella read what he had written. Headed ' York House ', and dated some months earlier—she presumed that he had penned it during his confinement there in the custody of the Lord Keeper —he sent her this poem.

'Made by the Earl of Essex in his Trouble.

> The ways on earth have paths and turnings known
> The ways on sea are gone by needles' light
> The birds of heaven the nearest ways have flown,
> And under earth the moles do cast aright :
> A way more hard than those I needs must take . .
> Earth, sea, heaven, hell, are subject unto laws
> But I ! Poor I ! must suffer without cause.'

Scarcely the effusion of a lover, nor, seek how she might, could she find in this cheerless dirge any sentiment warmer than self-pity ; but she treasured it, slept with it under her pillow, carried it hidden in the corsage of her gown. The parchment rasped her skin and crackled every time she moved, till she feared her grand-mother would find and tear it from her. Bess, however, was too busy at that time to give her mind to anything beyond the rebuilding of Oldcotes ; and none but Starkey knew her secret, saw her tears.

From him she extorted every scrap of news that she could gather, and which served her nothing save to deepen her despair.

Much that he told her she already knew. How that Essex had behind him a great following headed by his closest friend, South-ampton, who at his residence, Drury House, had for some time past been holding daily meetings. It was common knowledge—to Starkey with profoundest gloom pronounced—that every man of them, his lordship not excluded, was determined on extremest measures of revenge towards the Council and Her Grace. There were many who believed the noble earl had been most hardly used and cruelly misjudged. Some, it was said, favoured an attack upon the Court. Others went so far as to intimate that the sacred person of the Queen herself would not escape the violation of——

"And do you dare repeat such dirt to me ?" Arabella fiercely interposed. "I thought better of you than to listen to such evil."

"Madam", in pained protest Starkey moved his narrow shoulders, "I repeat only what is spoken loud in every street. The list of names attendant on his lordship number a hundred and twenty earls, barons, knights and——"

"I know who are his friends," said Arabella, sharp, "but I have still to learn who are his enemies."

"Ah ! They," with mournful relish stated Starkey, "must be legion."

She raised her eyes and looked him over coolly. He stood very upright at the table where she sat in the Long Gallery, a lexicon open before her, a pile of books beside it, to which, should her grandmother interrupt this session, she could at once refer. The light from a mullioned window fell full on the tutor's face. And she wondered how one part of her being could so detachedly observe while her soul screamed torment . . . Mr. Starkey's egg-shaped head with the sparse hair lying streakily upon it : his greenish rodent's teeth, the shabby black of his doublet, gone greenish, too, with age ; a very neat little darn in his hose. Who mended his stockings ? Doubtless himself. The Lady of Hard-wick would never allow him a servant. . . . And what pitiful legs, thin as a heron's with great knobby knees ; and his hands red and swollen with chilblains. Mechanically he rubbed them while he talked.

" These meetings, Madam, have aroused the gravest suspicions. I think his lordship has been ill-advised to hold such——"

" What you think", she told him clearly, " has no interest for me. What you have seen is more to my purpose. What *have* you seen ?

His eyes goggled, then shifted uncomfortably from hers.

" If I may tell your Ladyship that I was present at a play of Richard II at the Globe Theatre when Sir Gilly Merrick—one of the Earl's most faithful adherents—and a party of other gentlemen attended the performance——"

" What has this to do with Essex ? " asked Arabella through her teeth. " Get on, sir, with your story, if you have one."

" This is my story, Madam," Mr. Starkey said, aggrieved, " your Ladyship will allow me to tell it my own way. The performance, Madam, it appears, was commanded by Sir Gilly. I had come prepared to see Richard III and did confess to not a little disappointment, since Richard II is nothing near so fine a play to my mind as——"

" I do not care what is to your mind. Why did Merrick will the players to perform that particular play ? "

" Madam, the play in question is—" Mr. Starkey ceased rubbing his chilblains to finger his ruff—" is the history of a sovereign deposed."

She whitened. " Yes. . . . I had forgotten. I have read the play. But what if so ? Is that a reason why it should not be performed ? "

"The players, Madam," said Mr. Starkey, beginning again on
s chilblains, "did at first demur, then finally agreed to act the
ay for forty shillings. There was much applause to it among
e common folk, and among the nobles also. I myself was not
pressed with the acting nor the—hem! As I was about to say,"
continued in a hurry as he met his lady's eye, "the Council took
e matter very hard. It is believed Sir Gilly Merrick, at the
tigation of Lord Essex, did seek to stir the people in revolt
ainst our Sovereign and depose her Most Gracious——"

"Depose?" cried Arabella, springing from her chair. "Revolt?
ke back your words or be struck dumb! So you too—as all
e rest of them, would impeach him with false treason, kick him
en he's fallen. That's the way! Do you think I do not know
hy you detest him? Because, like every other man—if man you
e and not a rattlesnake—you envy him his power. Yes, Starkey,
en you can find it in your little mind to wish yourself a thousandth
rt as great as he."

Although not unaccustomed to his lady's variable humour,
r. Starkey could not let this pass without rebuke. His Adam's
ple swelled as if to choke him. He blinked; again he swallowed
d: "Madam," he remonstrated feebly, "you forget my calling."

"Your calling", she retorted, "is to serve me. What more
ve you to tell? But I warn you if it be of harm to him 'twill
ing more harm to you."

Mr. Starkey stole a glance and said with care:

"I can but repeat the evidence of my own eyes. It happened
was lodged at the house of a friend near Fen Church. He, like
yself, is a Clerk in Holy Orders, a fellow graduate with me
——"

"Will you, pray, keep to your point?"

"Why, Madam, certainly. But let me explain how I came to
lodged in the City when my good mother lives in—however,"
r. Starkey hastened to assure her, "that is neither here nor
ere, save that had I been lodged in the village of Chelsea I would
t have seen from my window at ten o' the clock in the forenoon
February the eighth—or was it ninth——?"

Arabella closed her eyes.

"The eighth," decided Mr. Starkey, "a great concourse of
me two or three hundred, on the march to Paul's Cross. I saw
s lordship, too, riding at the head of the procession—a magnificent

gentleman, Madam—so graceful—hem!—waving his sword and crying loud, 'For the Queen! A plot is laid for my life.' The city folk stood confounded, but none followed him. No," Mr. Starkey produced a pale smile. "Not one. His lordship appeared to be in an exceeding agitation."

"But," Arabella moistened her dry lips, "you have told me nothing that indicates revolt. If he had discovered a plot which might have endangered his life, he was justified in asking protection from the people. He was," she said warmly, "their idol. I have seen how they cried for him—worshipped him! Yes, I have seen it. And I know that the citizens of London will never countenance injustice done to one who stands in their esteem as high as or even higher than—Her Grace."

"Madam," Mr. Starkey backed in horror, "hush! Such words, if spoken to any other but myself would——"

"They are spoken to none other but yourself, and you will not repeat them. Am I not entitled to free speech?"

"No, Madam," Mr. Starkey was emboldened to remind her, "none but Her Grace is entitled to free speech."

"Yes," she nodded to him. "Such is the divine right of queenship. And the only regret I have in the deprivation of that glory," her soft mouth hardened, "on which my relatives have built their lives, and mine, is that I may never know the freedom of my tongue. . . . So what more did you see from your window?"

"No more, Madam, from my window, for the streets were empty. The people had been ordered to remain within doors, and when his lordship came to Paul's Cross where he had hoped to gather his insurgents, none was there to greet him save the beggars and their dogs."

"And is that all?" she asked him bleakly.

"Almost all, Madam." Starkey's eyes slid sideways. "Save that the Council is now sufficiently convinced of his misguided motives to apprehend his lordship as a rebel—if not as a traitor."

Her jaw clenched. "Careful, Starkey!" she managed to articulate. "Unless you know the truth of what you speak you may yourself be apprehended. If this is hearsay that you bring me, I'll not listen. And I see no evidence of treachery in anything you have, so far, related."

Mr. Starkey moved away and, his back half turned, he shot his final bolt.

"Madam, that the Council Chamber could but think the same! But alas——" from his meagre depths he sighed. "The news is bruited up and down the Kingdom that his lordship has already been arraigned. He with Lord Southampton and others of his followers await their trial in the Tower."

If he had intended to inflict on her whom he so hopelessly adored, a vicarious revenge for all the years that he had suffered her indifference, her chaplain in that moment knew himself repaid. But the knowledge brought him little consolation. So still she sat, so frozen white, he feared his words had killed her. . . . The room was cold, his chilblains itched. He wished he had feigned ignorance of this deplorable affair. Yet, if so, would that have spared her when she knew—as she must come to know—the worst?

He approached her chair into which she had sunk, huddled, her hands folded, and her lips, as if she never meant to open them again.

"I beg your Ladyship," he mumbled, "will not unduly grieve. His lordship will be given a fair trial. Be assured that justice——" Starkey paused. Her eyes were fastened upon his in a look to blast him where he stood.

"Out!" She rose and screamed at him, "out of my sight, you toad! I don't—I *won't* believe a word of it. You father the wish to the thought. But if what you tell me be truth and not a lie to slander his great name, then . . ." She sank to her knees, and lifting her hands bowed her face upon them, "then," the shattered Starkey heard her whisper, "God grant that if he dies I may die with him."

* * *

On February 19 he was brought to trial before his peers. While they read the indictment he frequently smiled and held up his hands in mock wonder at the monstrous crimes of which he stood accused.

No word of interruption passed his lips until Raleigh was called to take the oath, when he contemptuously exclaimed : ' What booteth it to swear this fox ? ' Nor at the end of that long day, when the verdict of High Treason had been passed and the hideous penalty pronounced, did he ask quarter of or make appeal to her, whose attitude throughout the whole proceedings had been that of an avengeful Aphrodite. But he had offended more than Love.

Like other of her victims he realized too late that he had never known her. No man could ever know her. While she melted to their flatteries, rapaciously absorbed their adoration, the inner fortress of her being stayed secure. Men might kneel before her, vow their vows, declare her beauty blinded them—she drank their words and sealed her heart, and smiled. Her capricious femininity, her paint, her gowns, her jewels, were all part of an elaborate pretence. Behind that flimsy barricade she stood, iron-bound and unassailable. For one sole purpose had she lived, and for that purpose would she die, inviolate. To one passion only did she dedicate her life and that was England; all else beyond it make-believe, a game of puff-ball played with partners picked for her amusement, till she tired of her pastime. Nothing more: no less.

That Essex, so desired and desirable, had uttered words, rash, foolish, cruel; that he had disgraced himself, insulted her, forced entry, travel-stained, into her presence; that he had failed in the trust she placed in his command, had bungled woefully in Ireland, and engaged in a preposterous flirtation—if no worse—with that flighty, insolent young person, her own cousin, none of these would, of necessity, have brought about his end. His offence lay deeper. He had struck at the core of her Kingdom, had sought to raise a following behind him, and so wrench the sceptre from her hand, the Crown from off her head. For that there could be no relenting, no redress; for that, and for no lesser deed, no spoken word, he stood foredoomed.

On the night before his execution he called to the guards below his prison casement: 'Tomorrow, my good friends, you shall see a strong god and a weak man! I have nothing to give you,' he grinned as he held up his empty pouch, 'for I have nothing left but that which I must pay to the Queen in the morning.'

Clear and cold broke that morning, with a high wind and a watery sun in the sky. His face was pale but his step firm as he mounted the scaffold, watched by the privileged hundred odd assembled there, and by Raleigh from a window in the White Tower above.

With consummate grace he bowed to his audience, and, not without a touch of conscious melodrama, he delivered his lengthy preamble. Confessing his sins, he admitted his pride and his love of this world's pleasures. He besought God, Creator of all things and Judge of all men, to 'lift my soul above all earthly cogitations and when my soul and body shall part, send Thy blessed angels to be near me which may convey it to the joys of heaven.'

So affected were the lords and knights and aldermen, who from their seats near the scaffold heard and witnessed this performance, that scarce a man among them could contain his tears. And when he asked the executioner how he should be disposed before the block, the aged Earl of Hertford, who, as the husband of Catherine Grey, had all but met with the same fate, shuddered and shook to such woeful extent that his few remaining teeth rattled like dice in a box.

Removing his black satin doublet, Essex startlingly revealed himself in a shirt of crimson cloth. The executioner begged and received pardon for what he was about to do. Then, kneeling, and in a low voice, his victim recited the Lord's Prayer, stretched his arms across the block and laid his head upon it. The breeze, light-fingered as a woman, played with his chestnut curls. The executioner whirled his axe . . . 'Strike home!' cried Essex loudly, 'Strike! Lord Jesus, come! Receive my soul. Into Thy hands, O Lord, I commend my . . .'

Three times the axe crashed down. The first stroke killed the words upon his lips; the second stroke killed him. The third severed the head from its body.

The blood spurted out over those brave crimson sleeves.

With a shout of 'God save the Queen!' the executioner seized the head by the hair and held it up to the silent watchers; the eyes were open still as if they saw.

Raleigh's face disappeared from the window.

Chapter Six

HE died on Ash Wednesday, 1601, and within two months of his passing none talked of it. Within two years only three women remembered it, but those three could never forget: his widow at Wanstead; the Queen on her throne, and a Princess, neglected, obscure.

She at Hardwick cherished sorrow that must lie for ever hidden, while her young life limped beneath a burden too great for it to bear.

She had prayed that she might die with him; instead she lived with him, went haunted. By day he talked and walked with her; at night he lay with her, ghost heart to beating heart, warm, seeking lips turned cold with unkissed kisses. His voice called to her through the darkness, his hands caressing, never touched. Such nights showed in her face: so pale, wan and fragile that Anne Bradshaw, seeing, sorrowed with but could not comfort her.

Yet the piteous spectacle of a young girl's heartbreak aroused no spark of sympathy in Bess. This long aftermath of suffering, so silently endured, indicated to the merciless eye of the Dowager no more than the end of a trivial intrigue; and her suspicion that the Queen must have been aware of her cousin's presumptuous infatuation for Lord Essex, was confirmed by the continued marked disfavour of Her Grace.

Like some once sturdy oak crumbling beneath its stranglehold of ivy, so was Bess warped in her rancour. The stricken, crushed young creature, once her pride, now stood for nothing but the one abortive failure of her life. She who had seen herself seated on a throne—or as near to it as blood-relationship could tie her—must watch that roseate vision fade, a mirage in the arid desert of her declining years; and in her embitterment she still maintained a systematic persecution of her victim.

But while Arabella outwardly submitted to her grandmother's cruel jibes and petty tyrannies, her spirit mutinied. The implacable old Dowager had not taken into account the streak of Tudor blood that flowed in the veins of an offshoot of him who had snatched the crown from England's King on Bosworth field. Nor did she reckon with youth's amazing powers of resilience. As snow will surely melt, so no grief endures for ever. Each season brought to Arabella its recurrent balm; each lingering day of golden summer, each ripening harvest, fall of leaf burnt red in autumn sunsets; white shroud of winter slowly passing into spring with its unfolded sweet deliverance of leaf and bud and blossom, lent each in turn time's gentle healing. . . . And then towards Eastertide the aching hurt of memory awakened to rebel.

On Ash Wednesday, 1602, Mr. Starkey wrote:

'The truth is she, seeming to be discontented, told me she had thought of all the means she could to get from home by reason she was hardly used (as she said) in despiteful and disgraceful words, and her most plagued withal which she could not endure; and this seemed not feigned, for oftentimes being at her book she would break forth in tears. Whereupon I promised that if it pleased her to use my service I would deliver her messages while I stayed in Town. . . .'

When he made that promise Starkey doubtless thought he would not be involved again in any other clandestine affair. There was no man to his knowledge in London now, nor out of it, with whom her Ladyship would wish to correspond.

He was mistaken.

To Arabella, chafing against and longing to escape from the miserable conditions imposed on her at Hardwick, an opportunity was suddenly presented. While Anne Bradshaw watched and suffered with her young mistress all the pangs of her unendurable existence, she was powerless to raise a finger to her aid. It needed the cunning of good Bridget Sherland to bring matters to a head and offer her the first loophole to freedom.

It happened that Bridget chanced to be at Hardwick that December, 1602, having been sent by Mary Shrewsbury with Christmas gifts from Sheffield. The night before she started on her journey back, she came to Arabella in her room.

In her forties Mistress Sherland had been plump; in her fifties she was fat. She had three chins, but her starched yellow ruff hid all save one of them. Her eyes, black and bright as a bird's, darted an inquisitive quick glance at Arabella where she sat, wan and drooping in her chair.

Bridget nodded to herself.

"Sure, me darling, you're pale as curds! And all for the want of a man. . . . No, not *that* man." Her gaze, impudent and meaningful, raked the girl's slim body as if to uncover its nakedness under the stiffened brocade. "Any man," declared Bridget, "who'd put flesh on your bones. You're too thin. If I had a voice in the making of laws I'd count it illegal that a maid once she's flowered should never be plucked. You're young and—" Bridget lowered an eyelid, "you're lusty, and you ask for what all women want who are as God made 'em—a husband to take to your bed."

"Well! I . . . you . . ." stammered Arabella, "you disgust me."

"Ho! Disgust you, do I? And what may I ask is disgusting

in nature? Every cow has her bull and every goose her gander, so why should Jill go starving for her Jack?"

"The way you talk," said Arabella, crimson, "one would think you kept a bawdy-house."

"Pity 'tis for your sake," retorted Bridget, "that I don't."

Arabella bit her lip. "Your speech has loosened since you left this place," she countered coldly.

"It would seem so since there's none to tighten it. But here! We're wasting time with words."

"You are," said Arabella. "I'll not listen."

"Nay, now," protested Bridget, "you shall listen, for I've a plan that if it carries will drive you out o' this living tomb and out o' that hippogriff's clutches. . . . Yes! And to her face I'd call her so. A fire-breathing monster is an angel next to her, but," Bridget declared grimly, "she will pay. We all pay for our sins upon this earth and not when we're beneath it. Have ye heard tell of the Seymours?"

Arabella stared.

"What in the world have the Seymours to do with——?"

"They have to do with what I say," Bridget sharply interposed, "if your Ladyship will let me say it. 'Tis a family almost, though not quite, as royal as your own. The old Earl of Hertford, who heads it, is now in his dotage. He was husband to Lady Catherine Grey. *She* died in prison, poor soul."

"I know her story," murmured Arabella, "'tis a sad one. Is that old man still alive?"

"Yes, and he's the grandfather of——" Bridget cast a hasty glance around the room. The window looked into the garden and was open. She went to shut it and in passing unfastened the door and peeped out.

Arabella watched these manœuvres uneasily, to ask: "What mischief are you hatching now?"

"No mischief, Madam." Bridget returned to her seat. On her face was a satisfied smile. "Unless it were mischief to offer you means of escape."

"Escape!" Arabella sighed. "If I could. . . . But I can't."

"Yes, you can." Bridget leaned forward. "Come close, and mark me what I say. My Lord Hertford long ago did ask for you in marriage to one or t'other of his grandsons. He has three."

Arabella's gaze upon her widened.

"Then it was true what my cousin Mary told me!"

"I know naught of what that chatterpate has told you and care less. What *I* tell you is on the best authority. Her Grace refused his lordship's suit as she refused all other offers for you—yes, even from the King of France himself. She'll not have you wed while she's alive and that'll be for ever. She is," said Bridget sombrely, "a female Methuselah. She'll not die till we're all dead before her."

"As we," said Arabella primly, "hope and pray."

Bridget snorted. "H'm! So do we? . . . As I was saying then, these Seymours would welcome you as wife to any one of them whom you may choose to fancy. I'd name my Lord Beauchamp, the old Earl's eldest son, but that he's already married, and I'm told, is dying o' the pox. Yes, I think I'd sooner mate you with young William, Lord Beauchamp's second son. He's more likely to succeed to the earldom than his brother, who's a weakling having been born deficient of one of his—um—and there it is," Bridget obstructively concluded. "You can take my advice for what it's worth."

"I cannot see", Arabella said unamiably, "that you've given me any advice."

"No, but wait. I'm coming to that. Here's what I suggest we should do. Write to the old Earl of Hertford yourself, and let him know that you are not unwilling to consider his proposal."

"That dried up old faggot! I'll be hanged if I do," exclaimed Arabella, dismayed. "I thought you were speaking of his son."

"His grandson, child! How ye twist my words. But the offer, don't ye see," said Bridget, urgently, "must come from the old one, himself. His grandsons are under age."

Arabella's lip fell.

"Under age! I'll not," she objected provokingly, "marry a suckling."

Bridget raised her eyes in despair to the ceiling. "Will ye hear it!" she entreated, "will ye hear how it puts me to cross purpose with cross questions? Suckling is it? And the lad handsome, golden-haired, and hearty and upstanding, and learned at his books—a scholar of Oxford Uni——"

"Have you seen him?" Arabella interrupted.

"Not to say seen—face to face," confessed Bridget undaunted,

"but I've made it my business to inquire and believe me he's ho
—and he's ready. He carries your likeness next to his heart."

"My likeness? And how did he obtain it? And how—"
with increasing suspicion Arabella demanded, "do you know
where he carries it?"

"It is my duty to know what may be to your advantage."

"Bridget, did you", sternly persisted Arabella, "send m
likeness to this young William Seymour?"

"What! I?" Bridget flung up her hands. "I did not! Ma
I be disembowelled and my quarterings thrown to the dogs if I di
—but I swear—" she profusely repeated, "I didn't. Would you
Ladyship accuse me of taking such unpardonable liberties with
your precious name. Why, Madam, what can ye think I am?"

Arabella wrinkled her nose.

"As near a good liar", she said silkily, "as a very bad lia
can be."

"Och, so! It's a liar you'd be calling me! That's prett
hearing from the babe I bounced upon me knee. Sharper than th
serpent's tooth is the ingratitude of—Liar," repeated Bridget with
a breath to burst her stays, "and me whole life dedicated to you
service, even though I'm hidden from the sight of ye, at all . .
Well now," with tactical inconsequence she added, "I have tol
you what to do, so go and do it."

Arabella heaved a triple sigh.

"For mercy's sake—do what?"

"Suffering Job!" ejaculated Bridget. "Here have I talke
meself hoarse and you ask me—do what? Why, write that lette
to Lord Hertford, to be sure! Place your case before him. Ar
ye not of the Blood Royal and distantly related to his grandson
through their grandmother, the old gentleman's dead wife, ow
sister to the Lady Jane? Go look at your family tree. You'll fin
it all there—how you descend directly from Henry Tudor, Kin
of England, as do the young Seymours. You have every right t
make the offer being as you are the highest in the land after He
Grace . . . And what's done," said Bridget cryptically, "canno
under Heaven be undone."

"It can," Arabella gave a little shiver, "with the axe."

"Blarney! To axe you they must find you. Once married yo
can get away to France. The French King will be happy to receiv
you who might have been his Queen. Lord, how Her Grace ha

wrecked your chances, but we won't let her wreck this . . . Now will you do as ye're bid ? "

Bridget left her and went to a cupboard, took from it parchment, an inkhorn, a quill. Placing these on the table she drew up a stool, then :

" Sit ye down," she directed, " and write."

Having urged her young mistress to this rash extreme Bridget departed next day in high fettle, leaving Arabella to deal with Mr. Starkey. He, they decided, should take and deliver the letter. But when reminded of his promise made some few months back, and which Arabella now called upon him to fulfil, Mr. Starkey, to her profound vexation, refused to be concerned in such an undertaking. In vain did she entreat and rail, threaten. He stood firm. He would have nothing to do with, " so ill advised an errand, which," he solemnly assured her, " is in deliberate defiance of Her Majesty's command."

" Her Majesty has never commanded me not to write letters."

" Madam, it is understood," lugubriously stated Mr. Starkey, " that the name Seymour is to Her Grace anathema."

" But *why* ? "

Mr. Starkey attempted to tell her. The Seymours were grandsons of the Lady Catherine, whom Her Majesty had very properly imprisoned as a menace to the throne, and for that reason——.

Arabella cut him short.

" Which is no reason why the Lady Catherine should have been imprisoned. She had no pretensions whatsoever to the throne. All she wanted was to marry the man of her choice. Is that a crime ? I could say a thing or two," she added warmly, " as to *my* opinion of that blot on Her Majesty's good name."

" Hush, hush." Mr. Starkey gave an apprehensive glance around. " My Lady ! I beg you will refrain from passing any such——"

" You make me sick ! " to Mr. Starkey's stupefaction his Lady interposed. " You profess devotion to my service, you come crawling for my favour, and when I give you a commission to perform, you place before me every kind of obstacle to balk it. I can only think that you're afraid to run the risk."

Mr. Starkey drew himself up.

"Madam," he protested, greatly injured, "such an accusation is unjust. Surely your Ladyship must know that when I advise you not to venture on so rash and dangerous a——"

"Rash!" scoffed Arabella, "dangerous! Here's a brave knight *you* are! I thought you were my servant and I find you are my fool."

That finished Mr. Starkey.

The stored passion of ten years broke through the fetters of restraint that had withheld it, to dissolve him. His head whirled; discretion fled. He fell upon his bony knees; he implored her to have pity. If she desired—and he knew that she desired—to escape from her unhappy circumstance, he would assist her by all means within his power, but never by such means as she suggested. There were other means and safer ways. He would take her to his mother's house at Chelsea. Such love as his, he urged, could not and *must* not be despised. He could give her happiness if she would only look on him as kindly as she would look upon her dog. He was her slave—her creature. His miserable fortune, his bleeding heart, his life's devotion, were hers utterly. He worshipped her, would live for her—and sooner than see her wife to any other he would die for her. He had suffered too long; he could suffer no longer. Would she not ease his torment with compassion?

Too horrified to stem the current of this blubbering recital, Arabella stood aghast and stared at Mr. Starkey where he grovelled. His lean body shook as if with ague. His fingers clawed her feet; his head was bowed upon them. His shiny scalp gleamed through dank streaks of hair; tears trickled down his furrowed cheeks and dripped upon her shoes. Disgustedly she backed, and on his knees he followed her, his eyes upturned to show the whites, and on his writhing lips a fleck of foam.

"You must be out of your senses!" she gasped. "Get up and go. You revolt me. Get up!"

He got up, but not to go. Seizing her hands he dragged her to him. His sour breath was on her face, his eyes glared, blood-shot, maniacal. "If I am out of my sense," he babbled, "then I must be excused that I take advantage of my lunacy . . . If I am mad then let me have what sanity forbids."

She screamed, and in her terror fought to free her hands, struck out at him blindly and made for the door. There she turned to see him in pursuit, his doublet unbuttoned, his hairy chest exposed, and a dreadful smile distorting his face. She screamed again and raised her arm to shield her eyes from that last horrid sight of him, fumbled for the latch, flung wide the door and fled.

So did Mr. Starkey.

He did not appear that day at dinner, nor when they searched could he be found, though none had seen him leave the house. His clothes had not been packed, and his horse was in the stable. He must have gone on foot.

Arabella, who might have thrown some light upon his disappearance, held her tongue, while for two days and nights the search continued, but produced no trace of Mr. Starkey. He appeared to have been spirited away.

The Lady of Hardwick finally ordered the hunt to be abandoned. He had been pestering her for a rise in his salary and she decided he had gone because she refused to grant it. Meanwhile Arabella, recovered from her shock, sent for her servant, John Dodderidge, and gave him her letter. She gave him also a paper of instructions which she bade him read, commit to memory and then destroy. He must go to the Earl of Hertford's house at Tottenham, deliver her message and return. He must make all haste on the journey, stopping only for food and change of horse, and give her note into the hand of the Earl himself. He was to inform his lordship that the matter had been thoroughly considered and approved by the Lady Arabella's friends. She furthermore impressed upon him that ' it will confirm their good opinion of me if you require them to bring all testimonies you can, as some picture or writing of the Lady Jane Grey, whose hand I know, or of the Lady Catherine, or of Queen Jane Seymour, or any of that family which none but they have.'*

It was unfortunate for Arabella that the worthy Dodderidge, mistrustful of his memory, and anxious only to obey, did not, as she insisted, destroy the paper but kept it for reference in his wallet, with disastrous result.

On Christmas Day when all the family were seated at dinner in the Great Hall at Hardwick, John Dodderidge, judging it the best time to go when he was least likely to be missed, set out upon his journey. To atone for the loss of his Christmas dinner Arabella gave him a purse of money with which to provide him a feast at an inn when his errand was done. It is evident that the personality

* The above is signed and endorsed by the bearer as ' the note which my Lady Arabella gave me for instruction in witness whereof I have put my hand.—J.D.'

of her selected bridegroom, a boy in his teens, concerned her less than her pressing desire for freedom ; and if marriage were the only means to it, she had arrived at such a pitch of desperation that she might have been induced to accept, had he offered his suit, the old Earl.

But the old Earl had no such intent. He had suffered sorrow enough in his early life from Her Majesty's displeasure, and he would not wish a grandson of his, any more than himself, to suffer the same. His tentative proposal for an alliance between the Lady Arabella and a member of the house of Seymour having been so unmistakably refused, he accepted without demur the royal mandate. He had been bitten once, and by nature, timid, he stayed shy.

When John Dodderidge, mud-bespattered with hard riding, arrived at his destination he was at first forbidden entry. His insistent appeal for a hearing, however, overcame the dubious reception of the steward, who brought him to the septuagenarian Lord Hertford, where he sat at table enjoying his dinner.

He was not to enjoy it for long.

Falling on his knees Dodderidge announced himself the Lady Arabella's messenger, at which the terrified old gentleman looked to throw a fit. Nor after reading the letter thrust into his hand was he in happier case. Summoning his servants, he ordered them to seize honest John and lock him away in an attic, where he passed a most miserable night.

So one may presume did Lord Hertford.

Believing himself to be the victim of a plot that would involve him, if not his grandson William, in disaster, he determined on the safest course. He would inform the Council of this distressful business, which after all was none of his, and let them shoulder full responsibility. So with Arabella's letter in his pocket and a speech of vindication on his lips, Lord Hertford called upon Sir Robert Cecil.

By her well-intended interference, Bridget, it would seem, had stirred a wasp's nest. The Queen was in a fury, the Council in a fuss, and poor Dodderidge still locked up in the attic.

Ten days had elapsed since he started on his errand, and Arabella, having heard no news of him, and unable to bear the suspense, confided her secret to Anne, to her uncles and even to Mary, her cousin, who was staying in the house. She, however, much involved in trouble of her own, paid but scanty heed to Arabella's. The Earl of Pembroke, hovering on the verge of a proposal, had not yet proposed; and the latest talk coupled his name with that of Mistress Fitton, one of the Queen's Maids, who, it was said, had recently borne him a child.

And: " O, Arbelle, to think I gave my heart to such a villain . . ." lamented Mary, when with Arabella, she paced the Long Gallery at Hardwick on the morning of January 9, " and here's Elizabeth married, as I knew she would be—before me—to Lord Kent. As if that weren't bad enough, without *this* blow. I shall take poison. I can't live and see my sister with her pie-faced Kent so happy and me a laughing-stock. O, yes I am ! But I don't blame *him* so much as I blame that demirep, his mopsy. Would you believe a girl could be so wanton and she a Maid of Honour, to be *dis*honoured in her bed ? "

" Not necessarily," said Arabella, " in her bed."

" O, Arbelle, you mock at everything," sobbed Mary, " and now Heaven knows what further misery you've brought upon us all. O, how could you be so foolish as to write that letter to Lord Hertford ? I can't think what possessed you. Surely you know that the Queen hates the Seymours almost as much as she hates you."

" A happy sort of comforter you are," Arabella dismally replied. " And if," her fingers closed on Mary's rounded arm and squeezed until she yelped, " if you repeat to any living soul what I've been fool enough to tell you, well—then you *will* take poison, for I'll give it to you myself."

" O, Arbelle ! " Indignation dried the tears in Mary's eyes. " You are so curst I'm not surprised that you are still unwed and must go begging to marry a schoolboy. I'd sooner stay a spinster all my life than sink myself so low. And what Lord Hertford and his family must think of——"

Any further retribution Mary might have suffered in return for this reprisal was suspended. The trot of hooves, the clink of steel, a stir and a shouting below, sent her in haste to the window.

" O, here's visitors ! . . . Arbelle, come quick and see ! "

Arabella came and saw : a stoutish middle-aged gentleman with mud on his boots, a plumed hat on his head, a flaxen-white beard on his chin, and a face plump and pink as a porker's ; before him stood the steward, bowing to the ground.

" O," whispered Mary, all eyes as he dismounted, "I wond
if he can be Lord Hertford."

Arabella, pale, wondered too.

" He looks like a pig," chittered Mary, pressing her nose to t
pane. "O, now he's taken off his hat *I* know who he is ! . . . I'
seen him at Court. He's the Queen's Commissioner, Sir Hen
Brouncker. . . . What can he want here ? "

" *Who* can he want here," Arabella muttered, " is more likely

She was not left long in doubt.

No sooner had he changed his clothes and been received by t
startled Bess, to whom he diplomatically presented the Queen
compliments, than he asked the favour of her ladyship's priva
ear.

In her sanctum the discomfited Dowager was handed a ste
letter from the Queen demanding instant explanation of the deceitf
practices to which the Lady Arabella had resorted.

Although on the verge of collapse, Bess gathered her forces
hurl at Sir Henry a fervent denial of any deceits practised—to h
knowledge—by her granddaughter. The girl had been guarded ar
watched day and night, ever since Lord Burghley—of treasur
memory—had warned her against the presence of enemy agents.

Enemy agents, Sir Henry assured her, had nothing to do wi
the case ; but if he might be allowed to interview the Lady Arabel
and put to her a question——

A dozen if he wished, Bess answered with immense relief
know that Arabella, not herself, had induced this ominous desce
upon her house.

To the Long Gallery, therefore, she conducted the Comm
sioner to find her granddaughters in a huddle on the window-se
her son William delivering a prolation to the pair of them ; ar
Henry on the settle playing with the cat.

At the entrance of his mother and her uninvited guest, he ro
to greet the Commissioner with every expression of welcome on h
lips and the cat in the crook of his arm.

While Bess sharply noted the interchange of greetings betwe
Sir Henry and her eldest son, who showed no surprise whatsoev
at this unforeseen intrusion, she noted also the presence of the c
It had no right to be there ; its place was below in the kitchen.

That disciplined command of her mentality, which cou
register minutest externals and at the same time obtain a cle

oncise view of an intricate situation, now stood her in good stead. he wasted no energy in spurious conjecture. If Sir Henry was here o call Arbelle to account for some misdemeanour of which the Queen, not herself, had cognizance, then so much to the good. If he had unwittingly been inculpated in her granddaughter's deroga-on, then so much to the bad—and the worse for Arabella. Mean-hile one must keep an open mind.

There, monumental in her black and her pearls, her snowy coif d starched white ruff accentuating the waxen pallor of her face, e stood observant and unbowed. She saw William come forward his turn, heard his speech, and, imperceptibly, nodded approval. e, her favourite son, could always be relied upon to make a good pression. Henry was too full of affectations. At Arabella she d not deign to glance, but beckoning Mary, she showed her the oor.

" You may go."

" O, madam, must I ? "

" You heard me."

Mary heard her ; and went.

Bess remained standing and spoke.

" Arbelle, Sir Henry Brouncker has journeyed from London to e you."

Arabella licked her lips, rose, curtsied, and sat down.

" Do not sit," Bess vibrantly commanded, " Sir Henry Brouncker presents Her Majesty the Queen."

Arabella got up again and achieved another curtsy. Sir Henry ssily advanced.

" No, no, I beg your Ladyship, do not derange yourself. My sit is—ah—entirely informal. I am come to ask your Ladyship's sistance in a matter that gives rise to some—hum—to some eculation. Her Majesty believes your Ladyship can assist——"

Her frightened eyes upraised to his, her face grown smaller, or Sir Henry fancied, at his words, made it difficult for him to ntinue in a cross-examination which might condemn her, who as no older than a daughter of his own, to dire punishment. But ith careful circumspection he proceeded.

" I assure your Ladyship there is no cause for alarm. Her ajesty enjoins me to deliver her earnest of goodwill to the Lady rabella, and to convey in Her Majesty's name her thanks for your dyship's New Year gift, which greatly delighted Her Majesty."

And having got that out, Sir Henry, perspiring, took his handkerchief and mopped.

"Her Majesty," panted Arabella, "is too gracious."

Sir Henry cleared his throat.

"Her Majesty also desires me to say that she is well satisfied
with the good accounts she has been given of the sheltered and
retired life your Ladyship is pleased to live."

To every one of us there comes, at some time or another, a
moment of significance at which volition halts, and impulse takes
the rein. In such a moment, when sense is devoured in nightmare
unreality, and passes even while we strive to apprehend it, Arabella
uttered the unutterable.

"I am not pleased to live. You may tell Her Majesty I would be
pleased to die."

If a fire-breathing dragon had hurtled through the window and
alighted at the feet of those who listened, it could not have aroused
more consternation. In the snoutish countenance of the Queen's
Commissioner the colour turned from pink to raspberry. The
Dowager laid a hand to her heart, or rather to the black-garmented
part of her anatomy which concealed that adamantine organ, while
from her lips issued a sound like the squawk of a wounded macaw.
William, whose mouth had opened to emit no sound at all, stood
visibly gasping for air. The shocked cat took a flying leap from the
crook of Henry's arm and landed on the settle, tail up.

Arabella slid a glance at Henry. A small muscle moved in his
jaw; his eyebrows twitched and into his throat rose a splutter
hastily repressed. His mother glared, and Arabella smiled and gazed
with limpid plaintiveness upon the Queen's Commissioner.

"Arbelle!" With a virulence hardly conceivable Bess
found her voice, to repeat: "Arbelle! You have surely run
mad!"

"Indeed, I was never more sane," serenely contradicted
Arabella, "as Sir Henry, I think will agree, if I were to tell him,"
a dreaming look came into her eyes, "which, out of consideration
to your ladyship, I do not intend to do, of the misery you,
madam, in the fulfilment of your duty, have imposed on me—an
orphan——"

Bess removed her hand from her bosom to clutch at her throat.
William rushed to support her. She sank on a stool. Her head
moved from side to side, strangely like that of a tortoise emerged

om its shell to investigate some new, surprising insect. Then,
rey-lipped, she muttered : " You lie ! "

" No, madam," the dreaming look deepened, " I do not lie.
Nor will I lie in answer to any question Sir Henry may ask me.
Perhaps your ladyship would care to hear——"

But Bess had heard enough. Yet, despite that the impossible
had happened and that this devil's spawn, this changeling, who in
the timid likeness of her kith had wrought upon her now as once
before, a cataclysm unexampled in the history of Hardwick, her
wits did not entirely desert her ; though to save the situation she
must feign as if they did.

To William's alarm, to Henry's admiration, and the concern of
Her Majesty's Commissioner, the redoubtable Lady of Hardwick
gave way to a fit of the vapours. She flung wide her arms ; she
appealed to high Heaven ; she called upon God to witness this
'monstrous perversion '. She shrieked and she sobbed and she
laughed and she wept—and collapsed on her son William's shoulder.
Nor, until Arabella, with praiseworthy presence of mind, had seized
a copper flower vase from the table and flung the water it contained
all in the poor lady's face, did her parlous condition show any sign
of abatement.

Gathering the scattered remnants of her departed grandeur,
Bess majestically rose. She disdained the assistance of the embarrassed Queen's Commissioner ; she spurned Henry's attempt to
condole. Accepting William's proffered arm, and with a look at
Arabella to spear her where she stood, the Lady of Hardwick,
oozing venom, dripping moisture, sailed, or more precisely, was
towed by her son from the room.

*　　*　　*

In that first interview between Arabella and Sir Henry Brouncker
we can properly assume that she was questioned and accused of
having, upon her own initiative, sent a letter to Lord Hertford.
No doubt, too, that she denied the accusation. Only when con-
fronted with the very document she had prepared for Dodderidge
and which had been abstracted by compulsion from his pouch, did
she admit that the writing ' appeared ' to be hers. Thus far committed, and in a great fright, she shed tears, not entirely pretended,
and begged the Queen's Commissioner's indulgence.

Torn between duty and sentiment, the worthy knight readily

gave it. She had meant no harm, she heartbrokenly assured him—
" no more harm than that I'd do it for a—for a wager—and I did ! "

Which preposterous prevarication even the susceptible Sir Henry
could not pass, but tactfully persuaded the tender young creature
to write him, in her own words, an account of her part in this
affair. Seriously alarmed, she sought Henry's advice, and between
them they concocted a statement of which the Queen's Commissioner
could make no sense at all. ' A confused, obscure, and in truth a
ridiculous paper ', he pronounced it, and finally suggested that her
Ladyship should ask Her Majesty's indulgence and not his.

Whereupon, again with Henry's aid and possibly at his dictation, Arabella wrote :

> 'May it please Your Most Excellent Majesty, Sir Henry
> Brouncker has charged me with many things in Your Majesty's
> name, the most whereof I acknowledge to be true, and am
> heartily sorry that I have given Your Majesty the least cause
> of offence. The particulars and manner of handling I have, to
> avoid Your Majesty's trouble, delivered to Sir H. Brouncker.
> I humbly prostrate myself at Your Majesty's feet, craving pardon
> for what is past, and of your princely clemency to signify Your
> Majesty's most gracious remission to me by Your Highness's
> letter to my lady my grandmother, whose discomfort I shall be
> till then. The Almighty increase and for ever continue Your
> Majesty's divine virtues and prosperity, wherewith you bless
> us all.
>> Your Majesty's most humble and dutiful handmaid,
>>> Arbella* Stuart.'

With this effusion in his hand and a purse of gold in his pocket
which he was not above accepting from his hostess, Sir Henry
Brouncker departed from Hardwick. This to the immense relief
of everyone save Arabella, to whom his presence had acted as a
buffer between herself and the Dowager's gall. Pending the few
days' duration of Sir Henry's visit, Bess had shown herself uncommonly forbearing towards the instigator of this latest malefaction,
but no sooner had he gone than the full torrent of her wrath was
unloosed upon her granddaughter. She had a score to repay and
with full measure she repaid it. The culprit was locked in her room
and none, not even Anne, permitted entry. The servants who

---

* In all her letters Arabella signs herself thus, though her baptismal name was
Arabella.

brought her food were forbidden, on pain of dismissal, to speak to her. Then to try her further the revengeful Bess deprived her of her books.

It may be that the solace of fiction denied her who fed upon romance, induced that astonishing series of letters in which there is frequent reference to one she loves and refuses to name, and whose advice, she declares, decided her 'to play the fool in earnest.'

Bess, the first victim of this enigmatic correspondence, was more than ever in a ferment at the oft-repeated, vague allusions to dear and powerful friends upon whose opinion 'I have laid the foundation of my life' . . . And further to increase the Dowager's bewilderment, Arabella offers the following excuse.

'. . . To employ any, much more such base unworthy persons in such a matter had been a blot to my reputation never to be washed away without floods of repentant tears, if my intent had not been to have it known to Her Majesty, and I thank God it fell out better than I and my dearest, best and trusted (whatsoever he be) could have devised or imagined. . . . With my Lord of Hertford I have dealt so precisely that it has not been in his power to do me more hurt than reveal all he knew by me. . .' Again alluding to her unknown friend, 'He', she avows, 'who trusts me with more than I would have him, even the secret thoughts of his heart, taught me by the example of Samuel that one might plead one errand and deliver another with a safe conscience; by the example of Samson that one might (and if they be not too foolish to live in this world) must speak riddles to their friends and try the truth of offered love in some matter wherein, if they deal unfavourably, it shall but make their ridiculous malice appear to their own discredit and no manner of hurt to others. . . .'

This oblique stab at herself and her autocracy threw the Dowager in a rare taking: the more so when she read that Arabella intended to plead with the Queen for one month's grace in which to clear her name of imputation.

'. . . for I am so far from being ashamed of my choice that even for my honour's sake I could find it in my heart to reveal him, and some secrets of love concerning myself which it will be delightful for Her Majesty to understand. And I vow as I shall be saved that I will be accountable to Her Majesty and not to your ladyship for all that I ever did in my life or ever will do. . . . These dark speeches will I never reveal but to Her Majesty whom the Lord bless and prosper for ever, every way I trust that your ladyship is now satisfied I am neither so disobedient and inconsiderate as your ladyship might think me. . . .'

Bess was far from satisfied.

While her immediate reaction to this egregious document was to regard it as no worse than an impudent hoax to annoy her, it renewed, none the less, her uneasiest suspicions. Was Arbell indeed so lost that she could contemplate a revelation to the Queen of her abandoned love for Essex? But—' delightful for Her Majesty to understand '. Was that a blatant sarcasm? Would she dare ' to play the fool in earnest ' to such lengths?

Seated at her table, Arabella's letter in her hand, Bess in some perplexity reviewed the situation. There was more of cunning than of folly in this rigmarole, which appeared to have been offered as a threat. Yes! Behind locked doors and in return for rightful punishment inflicted, the girl plainly was preparing to revolt. Were she not released the Queen would hear of it. . . . Had she not already stated, if her written word could be believed, that to none but Her Majesty would she disclose ' dark speeches '? Did this diabolic child hope to ask for and receive an audience, and with simpering lies and injured innocence upon her lips, complain of harshness and severity administered in the execution of her guardian's duty? Did it think to pit its puny brains against those of a Machiavelli—of Elizabeth of Hardwick? No knowing what abominations the sly creature would be at. She had already, so it seemed, bewitched Sir Henry, who even while he pocketed the gold bestowed upon him for his pains, adjured his hostess as he left her door ' to deal kindly with the Lady Arabella. She is so gentle, mild-mannered, of gracious disposition '.

Gentle! Gracious! Bess champed her empty gums. A good trouncing with the birch might give her grace, and as for manners . . . Then, while she considered what sterner methods yet might bring the miscreant to her knees, Bess was given inspiration. The penalty so well deserved would in due course be paid, but not to her. A hollow chuckle issued from the gaunt old woman's lips. No, not to her, but to one higher, one who might, or might *not*, readily appreciate the revelation of ' love secrets '.

Two could play the game of bluff and one could be fore-stalled. . . . Arabella's cunning had misled her.

And thus it came about that the Queen was sent a copy of that letter, which the writer of it not ineptly named, ' the first fruits of these my scribbled follies '.

Chapter Seven

THE Queen's Commissioner returned to Court with nothing great to tell; nor was he given opportunity of telling it. The Queen was indisposed and could see no one.

That unbounded vitality, which for so long had refuelled the ashes of youth, was now ebbing slowly away. She had never recovered from the loss of him whose life she had destroyed, whose death had left a scar upon her soul. Yet she still courageously performed her task for the benefit of those who watched, to wonder. She rode. She chased the fallow deer in Richmond Park. She danced. Her clothes, as ever, were a source of envy to the ladies and surprise to Scaramelli, the Ambassador from Venice, who wrote to his Doge that she received him ' attired in silver and white taffety, gold-trimmed. Her hair is of a light colour never seen in nature.'

But in the New Year of 1603, the gilded façade showed visible signs of decay. Court Circulars guardedly reported: ' The Queen is deprived of her sleep, lacks appetite and suffers from a sickness of the stomach.'

Since Her Majesty's Commissioner was unable to obtain an audience, he gave to his Queen a written account, more propitiatory than veracious, of his dealings with the Lady Arabella.

She, Sir Henry stated, had confessed that her regrettable proposal to Lord Hertford as a wife for his grandson, William Seymour, had been prompted by no worse intent than a wager. The young lady, he assured Her Grace, was grieved beyond all measure that by so ill-advised a prank she had caused offence to her beloved Majesty.

Mollified by her Commissioner's assurance and the humble tone of Arabella's letter which Sir Henry enclosed with his, Elizabeth dismissed the culprit with a warning. Such pranks as these might, if repeated, lose her more than she could win by any wager. The Queen also issued a command to Lady Shrewsbury, conceived no doubt of hints dropped by Sir Henry of conditions prevalent at Hardwick, that the Lady Arabella be freed from all restraint. She must, the Queen insisted, be restored to her rightful place and given precedence before all others of the household.

Such unlooked-for leniency from one who hitherto had treated her with marked disapprobation, encouraged Arabella to write again expressing her unbounded gratitude and the wish that she might be permitted to present ' my service and myself unto Your Majesty, whose displeasure and not punishment is the only thing I fear.'

Not content with leaving it at that, she proceeded, as excuse for her behaviour to catalogue her grievances against the luckless Bess.

'. . . For though I have done many things without her knowledge yet I call the Judge of all to witness they have been such that she should have had more reason to wink at than to punish so severely. . . . I have forborne till now to impart this much unto Your most Excellent Majesty, nor by way of complaint or moan have I disclosed my most distressed state to Your Majesty of whom I only have expected, and with silent and stolen tears, implore relief. . . .'

The same courier who went hurrying from Hardwick to the Queen with these specious protestations in his pouch, carried with him also the copy of Arabella's letter to her grandmother.

It was providential for the writer of both, that Cecil and not Elizabeth received them. Her Majesty's health had been causing concern. Her doctors enjoined her to rest. It is doubtful if she followed their instructions beyond handing all her correspondence to her Secretary, and he had more to do than waste his time on the plaints of hysterical girls, or the malice of wicked old women. The incident might well have been forgotten, but that a startling occurrence brought a trumpet blare of notoriety about the House of Hardwick.

The Lady Arabella's chaplain, Mr. Starkey, who had disappeared and none knew where, had at last been found ; or rather his body had been found—at the end of a rope, hanged by the neck in a woodshed !

The gossips were enchanted. Here was food to feed them for a month. A case of suicide, of course, and the reason for it obvious.

The Lady Arabella had led the poor man on above himself to plead his suit, and her rebuff had preyed upon his mind.

It preyed on Arabella's.

Though she guessed poor Mr. Starkey must have been deranged, he had sense enough to leave behind him a confession, that while exonerating him from any part in her negotiations with Lord Hertford, cast some doubt upon her earlier activities.

'She told me she had good friends and more than all the world knew of. . . .'

Arabella read this with dismay. Was the trick she had devised for her grandmother's confusion about to be repeated for her own? She hardly dared read further lest the wretched man had chosen, in his death pangs, to divulge how he had played the messenger between herself and Essex. But it appeared he had more personal intent.

For her birthday he had given her a Bible with his initials embossed in gold upon the cover. This gift, by the recipient forgotten, was in Mr. Starkey's statement, now recalled.

'The letters J.A.S.,' the poor gentleman declared, 'did *not* stand for John and Arabella Starkey'. Nobody till then had thought they did, but a certain curiosity was levelled at the case by the unfortunate assertion: 'For which gross error committed by me, though unwittingly, to the impairing of Her Ladyship's fame and good name I am so inwardly vexed, that if I had a thousand lives I would spend them all to redeem the least part of her reputation. . . .'

In spite of which it would appear he had done his best to damn it. If in life his hopeless love had been so ruthlessly disdained, in death it was exhibited for all the world to see. The country rocked with rumours. Old Lady Shrewsbury, more than ever convinced that she harboured in the image of her granddaughter a harlot and a sister of the devil, poured forth a daily torrent of abuse to that effect, and disregarding the Queen's orders relocked her in her room.

Furious at this renewal of imprisonment, and anxious to clear herself from implication in this latest scandal, Arabella wrote to Cecil begging him to intercede with the Queen on her behalf . . . 'When, if it would please Her Majesty to keep my council I will to her and her only deliver my mind.'

Than which nothing could have been more foolish.

Thus reminded of the recent unsavoury reports regarding her relations with her tutor, Cecil now began to think there must be something in them. A distracted letter from the Dowager in which she announced herself "wearied of life and Arbelle so wilfully bent that she has made a vow not to eat or drink in this house or where I am . . .' decided the Secretary that the case must be further looked into.

The soothing answer that he penned to the agitated Countess, for all its tactful tone, contained a caution. 'Her Majesty reiterates her gracious acceptance of your sincere and careful dealings with the lady, who, being young, is easily misled. Yet Her Majesty would have you only use her according to our last letter. . . .' In which Bess was commanded to treat Arabella with proper respect for her rank.

One can well suppose her mortified to receive these stern injunctions. In view of Arabella's self-inflicted hunger-strike, Bess had sent her off to Oldcotes where she hoped that she would eat. One could not see the child starve to death. She therefore took exception to the Secretary's hints that her treatment of her fractious charge was over-harsh.

Had the girl been telling tales? Apparently she had: 'Since seeing by the young lady's letters it is almost impossible to make a judgment who or what she means.' In conclusion Cecil added that Sir Henry Brouncker was on his way to Hardwick to resume investigations.

That announcement roused the much affronted Dowager to frenzy. . . . Let him send that hank of gammon then! And Cecil soon would see whether or no his 'young lady' (young hell-cat—young bawd!) Bess savagely amended, deserved the sort of usage best delivered at the whipping-post. Letters! So she'd been writing letters. . . . And I, said Bess, a-boil, can write a letter too!

Meanwhile a room must be prepared for the 'hank of gammon', and a feast. Feed him well. He liked his food. No treating with a man, experience had taught her who had knowledge of four husbands, till his stomach was well lined.

Bess hustled her household; she called for her steward. Four fat geese must be killed, two capons, a boar's head—if he'd eat his own kin—and enough wine to souse him—" Go see to it! And send a messenger to Oldcotes for her Ladyship."

Henry, who was staying in the house, offered himself for this service and was duly despatched in the coach.

On the way back to Hardwick with his niece at his side, Henry attempted a scolding.

"God knows what trouble you have brought upon yourself by your tomfoolery, and who or what persuaded you to do it is beyond my comprehension."

Arabella wept.

"Your mother's cru-cruelty," she whimpered, forcing tears. "If you'd been treated as you were gallow's meat, starved, beaten, and locked in a cell you might have been persuaded to do wor-worse."

"Keep the play-acting for Brouncker," Henry unsympathetically advised. "He may, but I do not applaud it, though I'll grant that if your sex were permitted to perform upon a stage you would likely make your fortune."

Arabella redoubled her sobs.

"I—I—I am not play-acting. Why are you so hard? Why is everyone so hah—hah—hard and cruel?"

Henry eyed her coldly.

"You have said that you would play the fool in earnest," he reminded her. "So go and play it, but I beg you not to me. The Queen's Commissioner will drink your tears and eat your words so long as you don't overstuff him. Have a care for that. Be simple. Act the fool for all you're worth, which," he added scathingly, "is less than the price of a bodkin."

She glared at him.

"Why, sir! Do you insult me—your own dead sister's daughter? Am I spurned by you as by your mother? Poor wretch, poor orphan that I am, exiled, maltreated—" she began again to snivel, "and des-despised."

"Stop that!" said Henry firmly, "or I'll slap you. We're almost home, and here's some good advice which you had better take, unless you wish to be escorted to the Tower."

That silenced her, and mindful of her uncle's threat she edged from him and listened.

"When Brouncker questions you again, as he most surely will, you answer nothing save these words: 'The King of Scots'. You understand?"

"I certainly do not. Such an answer," she objected, "makes no sense."

Said Henry sourly: "We do not wish it to make sense."

"But the man'll think I'm mad!"

"And if he does your recent actions would not prove him so far wrong."

"I may be taken up for treason," she cried in great alarm, "if I use the King of Scots his name in such a fashion."

"You may still be taken up for treason," was the comfortless reply, "if you do *not* use the King of Scots his name in *any* fashion."

It is likely that this sinister suggestion decided her to follow her uncle's good advice: which might indeed have turned out bad advice, had the Queen's Commissioner been less susceptible or the Lady Arabella less appealing. The fact remains that he, more mystified than ever, returned to London in a blizzard to find the Court removed to Richmond.

He was suffering from toothache, occasioned by exposure to the cold. For near upon a week and in a mild agony, Sir Henry Brouncker waited at his house in Lambeth in the hope his swollen face would soon subside. He did not care to come before the Queen with his cheek blown up like a bladder. But a message from the Secretary demanding the cause of his delay sent him in a hurry down to Richmond.

He found the Court in gloom and the Maids of Honour in hysterics, but whether from fear, or what other emotion, Sir Henry was loath to decide.

The Queen would eat nothing, drank little, and lay for hours speechless in her chair. Was she aware of a crisis impending? Did she watch and await the approach of a foe more powerful than any she had yet encountered? Was she mustering her forces to come at grips with Death? And would she emerge as ever, triumphant, unconquered from this battle, which, scorning aid from her auxiliaries, the Court physicians, she must and she would fight alone?

"We can but pray," pronounced Sir Henry, when Cecil told him of Her Majesty's precarious condition. "God Save our Queen her precious life. Amen."

Cecil narrowed his eyes to ask blandly: "What is amiss with your face?"

"The toothache, sir," the Commissioner tenderly patted his jaw, "which is the cause of my delay. I have been much incommoded." He produced a sheaf of papers. "Herewith is my report, but I fear it gives the least enlightenment upon the subject of her Ladyship's letters. Her persistence in the reiteration of one name, I confess, has greatly puzzled me."

Sir Henry paused. The Secretary's upper lip caught back on a dry tooth, gave to that sculptural countenance a sardonic expression belied by the calm benignity of his beautiful sad eyes. Puffing a little, Sir Henry proceeded.

"The young lady appeared to be tractable. She has, I think, been too severely used."

Since no purse of gold had been bestowed upon him this time, the Commissioner felt it but his bounden duty to express a fair opinion.

"I see she names the King of Scots," Cecil took a quill from the inkhorn on the table and made a mark in the margin of the document. "A name outside the realm, and one to which can be attached no whisper of intrigue."

A faint line like the markings on a coin appeared between the Secretary's brows. He laid down the grey goose-quill, spread his pale fingers on the parchment, and appeared to be engrossed in contemplation of his nails.

Sir Henry held his face. This infernal pain, and that infernal gentleman who sat as still as Egypt's Sphinx, and this whole infernal business into which he had been dragged, had not improved his temper.

Sir Henry cleared his throat.

"I have also brought—if you will pardon me a moment——" he leaned across the seated Cecil to fumble with the papers. "Ah, here we have it! A declaration signed by the Lady Arabella, and to this effect—if I may read it?"

The Secretary nodded.

Sir Henry braced himself and read:

"'I take Almighty God to witness I am free from promise, contract in marriage or intention to marry, and so mean to be while I live, and nothing whatsoever shall make me alter my——'"

"How many pages have you there?" asked Cecil gently.

Sir Henry pinkened.

"A dozen, sir, as near as I can count them."

"Then let us count them—" Cecil smiled, "as if read. This," he tapped his finger on the document before him, "is of more immediate concern. I see that you have cross-examined the young lady at considerable length, and with your usual exhaustive attachment to detail."

Sir Henry bowed.

231

"'Being demanded ',"' Cecil continued, reading in his turn, "' who that noble gentleman is by whose love she is so much honoured as cannot be ashamed of her choice, she saith it is the King of Scots.' '"

"As so she did." Sir Henry wincing, nursed his swollen jaw. "I admit it took my breath away."

"' And being demanded who that gentleman——' Pray sit, Sir Henry, I can see you are in pain."

"In *great* pain, sir," the Commissioner corrected as he took the proffered chair.

Cecil, with exquisite elocution went on reading :

"' —who that gentleman is that would forsake her rather than offend Her Majesty ever so little she constantly affirms it is the King of——' '" The Secretary let fall the parchment. "My good Sir Henry, I wish I had the leisure to pursue your careful questions to all of which the young lady gives you the same answer. Can it be possible that the Lady Arabella—" he paused before he ventured mildly, "plays a game with you—and me ? "

"I think, sir," returned Sir Henry with some heat, "that had you been in my place, which to your good fortune you were not, you would have found the situation as difficult as it was delicate. Could I openly accuse her Ladyship of a maladroit liaison with her chaplain ? "

"Her chaplain ? " Cecil gave the now much flustered Queen's Commissioner a meditative look that held, for all its gravity, a hint of ridicule, or so Sir Henry judged it. He twitched his snoutish nose. Confound the fellow and his subtleties—his smile !

"I had forgot the chaplain," and on Cecil's lips that smile reappeared. "So this noble gentleman, whom she consistently avows to be the King of Scots, is none other, think you, than the suicidal chaplain ? "

"Indubitably."

And with so much emphasis did Sir Henry nod agreement that the exercise induced a torment in his cheek. He clapped a hand to it and in a voice muffled with pain : "Indubitably Starkey," he repeated. "Who else in the world could it be ? "

"Who else," concurred Cecil, "indeed ? " His gaze slipped past the agonized Commissioner to focus on the wall above his head. The oaken panel, oddly, seemed to melt away in mist to reveal a scene by night of a gateway to a house along the Strand. . . .

A figure in the foreground, gay, colourful, beneath the torch-flare, young, and loud in laughter; a lean, grey shade beside him. 'By God's Beard, I've been mistook! You're Cupid's messenger and not my tailor's. . . .'

"Yes, indubitably Starkey," smiled Cecil, and he rose and bowed, a crooked figure of deformity, his splendid head so cruelly misplaced on hunchbacked shoulders, "which being so I need not trespass longer on your time or your good service . . . I hope, Sir Henry, you will call upon Her Majesty's chirurgeon to ease that abscess in your face. It should be cupped."

But long after the Queen's Commissioner had left him he sat studying, not that sheaf of documents, but a letter intercepted by himself and addressed in Arabella's hand to Sir Henry Brouncker. It covered more than twenty pages and was dated 'From Hardwick this Ash Wednesday'.

A bitter anniversary, mused Cecil as he read:

'. . . And the new dropping tears of some might make you remember were it possible you ever could forget. . . . Were I not unthankfully forgetful if I should not remember my noble friend who, in his greatest and happiest fortunes graced me, by Her Majesty's commandment disgraced orphan, unfound ward, unproved prisoner, undeserved exile, even to the adventure of eclipsing Her Majesty's favour so dear to him? Shall I say—now that I have lost all I can lose or almost care to lose— shall I *not* say that I never had nor never can have the like friend? . . . I have cast away my hopes, I have forsaken all comfort. What harm can the world do me now? You will say I occasion it, but my conscience will not accuse me, nor they in the end will not think so, whose malice extends so far every way as their base-bred suspicions can reach. The more you think to make, the more you mar. . . . When all is done I must shape my coat according to my cloth, though it shall not be after your opinion of this world, but fit for me and in every way becoming of that virtue, or an infective virtue of the Earl of Essex. . . .'

Cecil's finger hovered. He took up his pen, put a tiny cross against that name, and turning the pages ran his eye over each. Again he made a mark upon that paper.

'Had the Earl of Essex the favour to die unbound because he was a prince, and shall my hands be bound from helping myself in this distress? How dare others visit me when the

Earl of Essex, then in highest favour, durst scarcely steal salutation in the Privy Chamber, where it pleased Her Majest I should be disgraced in the Presence at Greenwich and di couraged in the lobby at Whitehall? . . . Does it please He Majesty to command me in her letter, and in Mr. Secretary hand, to be suddenly examined ? Yet your Commission was, seems, so strangely strait that it was not possible Her Majesty expectations could be better satisfied.

I have spent this day in portraying my melancholy innocenc in this undeceiving black and white, but I tell you true I thin it will not be your fortune to understand my meaning, for it not my meaning that you should. . . .'

" And I promise you that none save I ", the Secretary murmure " shall ever understand it, my poor child."

He folded his lips ; then he folded the letter and put it away i his pouch.

*   *   *

The strangest rumours floated through Court. Her Majesty mind was affected by the frightful spectres that appeared before he where she stood. She now refused to sit, but *stood*, so her scare Maids reported, for fifteen hours, fearing to sit again lest she shoul never rise.

The air was thick with portents of doom and awful omens. Sh spoke of apparitions that surrounded her, and inquired of he terrified attendants, ' Are you too in the habit of seeing suc things ? '

Sir Robert Cecil had urged her to take to her bed. Her Majest must, for her people's contentment, if not for her own, go to bec Her ladies told how she answered with lightning scorn and a flas of her old spirit : ' *Must* is not a word for princes, little man. your father had lived you durst not have said so much. Yo presume thus because you think I'm dying. . . .'

But still she stood in that same posture, all day and well into th night, disdaining help, immobile, dressed, bewigged and painted till her legs tottered and she sank down upon the cushions sprea on the floor to receive her. There for four days and nights she la speechless with her finger in her mouth. She would not eat, sh would not sleep, she lay . . . fighting her fearful combat, her eye fixed and, terribly, staring : at what ? At the crumbling structur

of her glory ? At England's future, or her past—a shifting cavalcade
of phantom lovers ? At the ghosts of those that she had done to
death : the gentle lovely Catherine Grey, whose grandson might
yet be a king ; at one who had aspired to be King and had laid his
rash temerarious ' head on the block, to come to her now with his
mockery ?

There were some who told the tale how the Queen had given
Essex a ring with the promise that if at any time he should return
it, he would be pardoned whatsoever fault he had committed. It
was said the Earl, leaning from his window in the Tower, had hailed
a boy and thrown the ring down to him, bidding him take it to the
Countess of Nottingham with the request that she should send it to
the Queen. But the Countess kept it and said nothing until, upon
her death-bed, she confessed. Did the Queen see with those fixed,
ghastly eyes, the spectre of a distraught woman in her shroud
begging on her knees forgiveness for a tragedy that might have
been averted ? Or what dark buried secrets did Elizabeth of
England resurrect from her dead youth as she lay, shrunken, on
those cushions with her finger in her mouth ? Some said she saw
her mother, Anne Boleyn, shrieking with witch's laughter as she
mounted to the scaffold. It had been known her mother had on her
right hand a sixth finger, small as the teat of a cat, with which she
could suckle the devil. . . .

One of her ladies who had left the Queen's chamber for less
than five minutes saw her gliding before her down the gallery, but
when in a panic she returned, there was the Queen, as ever, lying
on the floor ; nor had she moved so much as the lid of her eye.

Some said Her Grace feigned sickness while she devised some
dreadful punishment for the Lady Arabella, whose scandalous
behaviour had caused a mort of trouble to the Queen.

The latest news of her—the Maids of Honour had it pat—was
that Mr. Henry Cavendish, her uncle, had attempted to steal her
from Hardwick Hall with the assistance of one Mr. Stapleton, a
Papist. There had been a great to-do : forty horsemen posted
round about the house, and one led a horse with a pillion behind.
The Lady Arabella, still imprisoned, had stolen out in the early
morning—some gave it she had been lowered from her window by a
rope—and reached the gates of Hardwick, to be waylaid by that old
cockatrice, her grandmother, who harangued her there and slapped
her face and dragged her back into the house again for all the

villagers collected outside the gates to see. . . . If that were true, then it looked as if the lady and her uncle were in conspiracy with the Catholics to raise a following, and proclaim the Lady Arabella so soon as Her Grace should die. But Her Grace would never die while such a fear possessed her. It was to spite her cousin that she kept herself alive long after all her doctors gave up hope.

In taverns men laid odds on the chances that the Lady Arabella would take her rightful place; for who else within the realm was of the Blood, save those lesser branches of the Tudor kin, Lord Beauchamp and his three young sons, the Seymours?

Old men there were who could remember Lady Jane, the Nine Days' Queen. Was Lady Arabella destined for the same fate, or one more glorious than any fairy's tale?

And then the news, by best authority reported, that her Ladyship was now in custody and closely guarded at the house of her cousin, the Countess of Kent, lest the people should rise in her favour. None asked for a Seymour on the throne of England, still less did they ask for a Scot. There were those who asked, and openly, for Arabella.

Rumour had it that Mr. Secretary Cecil was in secret correspondence with King James, and that it needed all his diplomatic cunning to conceal the messages that he received and sent.

One day, at the offset of her sickness, and in the Queen's presence, a packet was delivered to the Secretary. The Queen ordered him to open it and read to her the contents. . . . The gossips chuckled in their ale mugs as they recounted how Master Secretary had saved himself exposure. Recollecting that Her Grace could not abide bad smells, and went in mortal terror of the Plague, Secretary Cecil cut the string and sniffed, and said the packet stank and had evidently been in contact with an infected person or a corpse. The Queen commanded he should have it purified, as no doubt, they hinted, so he did; and took the opportunity to purify what it contained before he read to her the message, which may, or may not, have come from Scotland. . . . Such talk was common knowledge within and without the Court.

The stakes rose high in all the taverns on the Thames; while in her chamber Bess of Hardwick sat and prayed, and wondered. . . . Had she miscalculated? Were her lost dreams, her buried hopes, to be at this eleventh hour disinterred? And if so, did she regret that she had not, of late, extended her indulgence to her 'Jewel', whose value now had soared from lowest ebb to astronomical proportions ?

But in her palace down at Richmond, she, who could have spoken, did not speak.

The nightmare horrors faded. They induced her to her bed. She asked for music. Sweet sounds eased her oppression. Her face beneath the daubs of paint showed wan and pale as a bone. The sunken eyes gazed out of it, unhaunted, at the bowing personages gathered round her bedside. The Lord Admiral stood at her right, the Lord Keeper at her left, and her Secretary at the foot of the great canopied four-poster.

Her eyelids wavered. Cecil dropped upon his knee. The momentous question must be asked, and who but he should ask it ? . . . Would Her Most Gracious Majesty be pleased to name to these her servants, her successor ?

The red-wigged head upon its pillows moved in negative reply.

"What of Henry," Cecil offered, "King of France ?"

The head stayed still upon the pillow ; the eyelids fluttered, sank.

The Lord Admiral stepped aside and Cecil took his place.

"What of her who is nearest of kin to Your Highness in this realm . . . the Lady Arabella ?"

The Lords at the bedside, the Councillors who listened in the background, pressed forward for the answer that struggled to those fallen lips, but scarce a breath came from them.

Then with infinite care, "Would Your Majesty consider," the Secretary asked, "the Lord Beauchamp or any son of his ?"

A narrow gleam appeared between the lifting eyelids, a gleam that smouldered like a faint blue spark, while the lips snarled back from the darkened stumps to give him answer clear.

"I'll have no rascal's son in my seat."

The Councillors and Lords exchanged swift looks. Cecil, his face inscrutable, knelt again, slowly to ask :

"Who then shall be Your Majesty's successor ?"

And of those who strained their ears for Elizabeth's last words none but Cecil heard her say :

"Only a King shall sit in my seat which is the seat of Kings. . . ."

The Secretary sat at his table. So through the night he had sat, driving his quill over pages of parchment, and when dawn shuddered into the sky of that grey March morning he still sat, his head sunk, his crooked body bent a little forward, his hands quiet on the chair-arms, his whole attitude that of one who waited for a summons.

Suddenly, from some outlying distance beyond the palace walls, rose the first triumphant cockcrow of the day.

Cecil pricked his ears.

Hurrying feet had stopped at the door. The arras was thrust aside to reveal Lord Keeper Egerton, breathing down his nose and sickly white.

Cecil stood, and at the question in his eyes the other bowed his head and answered him.

" The Queen is dead."

There was a second's silence, then :

" Long live the King," cried Cecil, " of . . . Great Britain ! "

BOOK THREE
(1605–1611)

> ' Droupsy and drowsy,
> Scurvy and lousy,
> Face all bowsy,
> Like roast pig's ear.'

MEN sang it in the taverns, lads sang it in the town   For two years
they had been singing it until its flavour staled. . . . ' All things work
together for good to them that love God ', croaked the Puritans,
who had calculated on the Presbyterian predisposition of King
James for adhesive favour to their own.

They were soon to change their views ; and the Catholics no
less when their Sovereign, after all his vows to grant them religious
toleration, broke his word.

And England mourned.

The last and greatest of the Tudors had left her country to an
alien : a gross untidy man, coarse-mannered, but though loud in
liquor never drunk, foul-mouthed but never obscene.

He had been loyally welcomed.   The Queen had named him her
successor, so let him succeed !

He was given every opportunity, notwithstanding that he started
handicapped by outward imperfections.   His beard was too thin,
his tongue too large, his skin ' soft as taffetas-sarcenet ', this from
one who knew him* and who declared he never washed his hands,
only rubbed his fingers lightly with a wetted napkin. . . . His legs
were weak that made him lean on other men's shoulders, his walk
circular, his fingers ever fiddling about his codpiece. . . .' And he
was mean with his own money, but ' had much use of his subjects'
purses '.   Still they made the best of him, and if they chose to adapt,
to their new King's disparagement, a rattling verse handed down
from the reign of old Harry, who cared ? Not he, whose sole care
was to make himself loved by his people.

He did not show tact in his method.   To appear bluff and well-
met to all men, he exploited his broad Scottish accent to the amusement of his courtiers and the wonder of the yokels, who lined the
village greens to watch him pass on his way to the chase.   He had a
passion for hunting the deer, yet in spite of his fondness for animals

* Sir Anthony Weldon.

—he loved his dogs, it was said, more than his wife or his children, or even his favourite boys—he showed no mercy in the killing of his prey. He would slit with his knife the belly of a dying stag, and plunge his arm up to the elbow in its carcase, dragging out its entrails with triumphant hoots.

The scholar, the pedant, the man of affairs, he at whose command England was given her authorized Bible, played the rôle of a hearty buffoon. Not unjustly named ' the wisest fool in Christendom ', he kept at his right hand, Robert Cecil, on the advice of whom he made peace with Spain and raised Cecil to the peerage.

But the popularity accorded him by these manœuvres, and the tactful guidance of that great little man behind his throne, did not conciliate the Catholics whom he hunted to their deaths under the assumption of a saviour.

Such false policy pursued in spite of Cecil's warnings, resulted in the Bye Plot in the first summer of his reign, and the Main or Spanish Treason in September.

This last, prompted by the Jesuits and divers English nobles— Lord Cobham and his brother, Lord George Brooke, Lord Grey of Wilton, Sir Griffin Markham, and by no means least, Sir Walter Raleigh, was yet another of those die-hard schemes to place Arabella Stuart on the throne.

The supposition that Raleigh could have been involved in such conspiracy was no less fallacious than that the Lady Arabella had promoted it. Both were accused of their share in the plot, but she was then in such high favour with her kingly cousin James, that she could afford to laugh at the letter she received from Cobham, preparing her to meet her trial bravely.

" Meet the devil ! Cross my heart," she swore, " if I had more to do with these abominations than has Your Majesty."

And she handed James the letter.

Conscious of his insecurity upon a seat from which high eminence he judged, not incorrectly, that half his subjects would have wished to see him fall, James was at greatest pains to fawn upon this troublesome young cousin. Although he insisted on a strict observance of her rank as Princess of the Blood, the knowledge that she was the one person in his Kingdom who could, (some muttered ' should '), claim right to supersede him, gave rise to an incessant apprehension. Moreover she had a disconcerting manner of address. She treated him with scanty reverence, held a look behind her eyes that in Scotland folk called 'fey', but which James, to himself, did not scruple to call insolent. While his wife sang her praises from morning till night, while his children adored her, James worried.... The throne was his, and he had two sons to inherit, and a daughter, yet here were plots and counter-plots, and treason, and this girl with dancing eyes, holding out a letter that in black and white informed her to prepare to meet her trial.

"So what," she dimpled at him, "does Your Highness say to that?"

And how she stressed it—*High*ness, for all the world as it were *Low*ness.

"Hoots, toots!" He patted her, a-goggle. "We say that ye're as gude a lass as ye are bonny. We say that ye speak truth and have no more to do with this than I myself, or my son Henry, or wee Charles, nor yet my wife and daughter, nor any one of us to whom ye are as near and dearly loved as——"

His loose tongue stumbled. She was laughing undisguisedly. At whom? At him? He stiffened. "We rejoice to see your Ladyship can jest at grievous matters."

"There are matters, Sire, so grievous, so injurious, so false, that only laughter can destroy them lest such matters destroy us. May I destroy the letter?"

And before his tongue could find an answer she took it from his hand, tore it into pieces and flung them at his feet. "Your Majesty", she said, "needs not the assurance of my everlasting fealty—and my devotion."

Then she curtsied low and bent her head to hide her eyes. Her lashes lay like gilded crescent moons upon her cheeks.

A saucy piece! James frowned, while furtively his fingers strayed to fiddle. Hell take the woman! Who could tell what she was at? The scattered bits of paper lay around his shoes. Looking down he noticed that the rosette on one was dangling. He stooped and plucked it off.

"Had I a needle and thread by me", he heard her say demurely, 'I'd put a stitch in that for you, Your Grace."

His Grace! No doubt she would, and stitch him up and truss him, too. And why the mischief was she kneeling?... He extended her a hand. She took it, kissed, and waited.

"Weel now!" With hearty gush he told her, "that's handsome of ye, cousin. But we'll take the thought for the deed, and we'll not ask assurance of your fealty. We know that ye're a richt brave lass. Would it please ye to attend the trials of these villains in this town?"

It would please her not at all, but since he had let her go so lightly when she might have stood condemned, she answered that nothing in the world would please her more.

The Court had moved to Winchester, in which city the trials were held. Escorted by Lord Nottingham she sat with other ladies in the Gallery, and heard, to her dismay, her name dragged dangerously forward. For all the King's adherence, a case might have been trumped up against her by insinuation if Cecil had not risen, suavely to declare : ' She is as innocent of all these things as I or any man here ; only she received a letter from my Lord Cobham to prepare her, which she laughed at and immediately brought to the King.'

That, while it cleared her of all imputation, did not silence chatter. Those ladies who, with agreeable titillations, had come to see her High and Mightiness disgraced—as she deserved—were in two minds about her ' innocence ' thus championed by Cecil. While she had been an outcast poor relation of the Queen, these Court beauties showed the friendliest compassion for her state— so hardly used, so cruelly maltreated, so put down and humbled, the poor thing ! But now that she was raised so high—(" and higher than she should be ", whispers flew behind the fans, " if His Majesty were known to favour women "), those who once had rallied round her turned their eyes to heaven. God save His Grace ! His Majesty was blind. He would live to rue such tolerance towards one who was undoubtedly a witch. She had for sure cast spells. Had she not brewed him a potion distilled from weasels' turds, toads' tongues and the guts of a black cat, stewed ? But she told His Grace that it would cure his gout.

" So *that* was why he never looked upon a woman ! "

" Yes, and short of murder done before his eyes he'd believe her nothing lower than the angels."

" Was she Cecil's mistress that he spoke so spry in her defence ? . . ."

The ladies closed their fans and dispersed, disappointed. The day had not brought with it much excitement, more than hearing the death sentence passed on the conspirators, and poor gallant Walter Raleigh committed to the Tower.

There, behind the same barred window where he had stood to watch the death of him he called his friend, Raleigh sat imprisoned.

His death on Tower Hill had yet to come.

If Arabella's rise to fortune as first cousin to the King was disparaged by Court ladies, her grandmother reviewed it with complacency. All was as it should be, and as it always should have been, had her 'Jewel' behaved in less besotted fashion.

While Bess continued to nurse rancour to the length of revising her Will, and leaving Arabella and her 'bad son Henry' out of it, she still could keep an eye on the main chance. Though all hope of glory direct was abandoned, one might yet bask in glory reflected. Her pride, if needs must, could be sunk to furnish her 'good son, William,' with a peerage. Lord Cavendish, Earl, even Duke. . . . Who could foresee what honour might be lavished upon him, her heart's idol ? If Henry, as his father's heir, must inherit Chatsworth, in which her interest only held for life, William should be compensated. . . . Yes !

Brooding in her fastness, the Dowager considered how best she could achieve her noble purpose. Until now Arbelle had rendered nothing but the coldest of receptions to every olive branch she had extended.

Cruel, cruel, quoth Bess, such base ingratitude, such harshness, from my own dear dead one's child ! Working a tear out of her eye that ran along the furrows of her face like silver treacle, she summoned William to her room. Would he write for her a letter ? Her hands were now so swollen with rheumatics she could not hold a pen. Moreover—she sighed deep—she had been given warning to believe her days were numbered. God's will be done. She was ready for her call.

William, greatly startled, sat, and at his mother's order wrote.

And thus came Arabella, hastening contrite, on an urgent message from her uncle to make all speed to Hardwick if she wished to see her grandmother alive.

She had no wish to see her dead, but Bess, although past eighty, was still no nearer dying than when she was eighteen. She found the venerable lady in the best of health and spirits, and her household gloomily rejoicing on their mistress's recovery.

"I have ate", Bess airily explained, "of tainted mushrooms.

But you know how William is, so very fond and anxious. And for you, my precious poppet, I have killed a dozen geese, two peacocks, and——" Bess cackled, wagging, very knowingly, her head, " a fatted calf."

The whole family of Cavendish, the Shrewsburys and Talbots, gathered at the table in the Great Hall to enjoy the feast prepared for their prodigal's return. Toasts were called; Bess beamed. Under the table William Cavendish linked hands with Arabella and whispered in her ear: " The old beldam will poison you, sweetheart, if you can't persuade our lousy monarch to hand a peerage to my father."

She flashed a look at him. " Which may be yours one day ? "

So that was why she had been brought from London to her grandmother's ' sick-bed '. Admiration struggled with resentment. The old tigress would fight to the death for her favourite cub. If it lay in my power, Arabella considered, I'd move earth and heaven to give Henry his rights, but as for the other . . . She turned to his son. " Feather your nest while you can," she said, cool. " What do you fancy ? The crown ? "

" I'd wear it better ", vowed young William, " than that bug-ridden——"

" Hey ! " She dug her nails fiercely in his palm. " I'll counsel you, my lad, to pick your words lest your tongue be blasted. Will I sit and hear a Cavendish talk filth against a Stuart ? He's your King. If his exterior be rough——"

" His hands are smooth." William pulled a face. " Which is more than mine'll be if you don't loose your claws. . . . Is it true that he has knighted Robert Carr ? "

She smiled at him, dangerously sweet. " Yes, His Majesty *has* knighted Robert Carr."

And of all those mincing courtiers who licked the feet of James, Arabella most detested him.

Formerly page to Lord Dingwall, he had pushed himself to the fore at a tilting match. In presenting his lord's shield, as was the custom, he manœuvred his horse to fall at the feet of the King, and fell with it. That fall was his rise. Struck by the lad's beauty James had him carried to a house at Charing Cross, and sent the Court physician to attend him. The visits of the King's doctor were soon replaced by visits from the King, and the erstwhile page soared to heights undreamed. While the Court snickered at the spectacle of God's Anointed hanging on the arm of a ladyish young gentleman with paint on his face and gold dye on his hair, Arabella turned from it revolted.

But her dislike for Robert Carr was nothing to the hatred the pretty youth aroused in the heart of his discarded predecessor.

'Ludo', Duke of Lennox, had accompanied his Sovereign on the journey down from Scotland to the Palace of Whitehall. The King, who once had loved him to distraction, now ignored him. True, he had a dukedom and he also had a wife, but the novelty of both had long since staled, and Ludo's plaints were bitter. He would sit for hours giving vent to them in Arabella's room, till she lost patience and had all to do to hold her hand from mischief to his ear.

Ludovic had altered little with the years. His voice was still half treble and half croak, his stature small, his figure dainty, his hair as gold as nature once intended it to be, or as Sir Robert Carr's. The King ever favoured the fair.

This rollicking new Court, its plays, its revels, balls and masques, its endless gaieties and banquets, were at first a welcome change to Arabella from the decorous magnificence that formerly prevailed. She, so long repressed, scorned, virtually exiled, was now accepted as one of the Royal Family. It is true she had never lacked cousins, but only as a child among children, did she feel herself whole-heartedly one of themselves. As she grew to womanhood, so was she uncomfortably aware that her rank excluded her from the intimacy that such close relationship demanded. With her fall from grace the younger fry, following their matriarch's example, cold-shouldered her, subtly, imperceptibly, yet none the less to hurt. But when James, King of Scots, ascended the throne, the ties of clanship proved stronger than fear. She might have a following, might still take his crown, yet in all this foreign land which now was his, she stood the nearest to himself of Stuart kin. Loyally the call of blood responded. None in her presence dared discuss, much less criticize his singular obsessions, mimic his walk and his manner of talk, mock at his fumbling habits.

It was not that she loved him. Who could? He was timid; all things to all men to suit his own purpose. He slobbered, was dirty, uncouth and undignified. Yet . . . he was chief of the Stuarts in Scotland, the land of her forbears, united for ever with England, the land of her birth.

Time came when he might have remembered—but by that time James chose to forget—that none in his realm was more staunch nor more faithful than she.

*   *   *

'Gunpowder Treason, Gunpowder Treason,
Gunpowder Treason and Plot!'

Quaking behind the windows of Whitehall, James heard the lads bawling it: *'Treason* and *Plot!'*

He was told how they had gathered rags and straw, fixed masks atop of bolsters with two pitch-balls for eyes, and paraded through the raw November dusk, bearing on their shoulders the wobbling effigies of Fawkes. At Paul's Cross they made a pile of their tarred and feathered Guys, set a light to it and danced, yelling round the blaze. The fun went on all night.

James in his palace sat and fiddled, and worried himself sick while he watched the red reflection in the sky. . . . Eh, this was all very fine, and proof no doubt of loyalty among the citizens of London, but his father had been blown to bits at Kirk o' Field, and now these goddam Sassenachs, Papists or whatever, were out to blow up him!

In vain did Cecil argue that he was never their objective. Such monstrous treachery, diplomatically he soothed, had not been levelled at the sacred person of the King, but at his House of Parliament.

"Hoots, man! And what is the House of Parliament but *my* house?" James demanded, "I dinna believe ye."

He regretted now that he had been so hasty to confer a peerage on this much too canny hunchback, with his beautiful Christlike face.

"I do not," James repeated loudly, "believe ye, my gude lord."

His 'gude lord' bowed.

James fidgeted.

"Our life," he pursued, "has been threatened."

"May," prayed Cecil softly, "God forbid."

James held his peace but still did not believe him. And when silence could no longer save his colleagues, and Fawkes, yielding to repeated torture, shrieked the whole horrific tale of the Plot to the shocked Council, James stayed unconvinced that the destruction of his Parliament, and not himself, had prompted their murderous scheme. What was Parliament without a King? If this abortive attempt had succeeded they would have massacred him and his children. Why attack a body of men and not their representative?

The King's terror was transmitted to his people. From Land's End to John O' Groats the country shook. But scarcely had the tremors ceased with prayers of thanksgiving for catastrophe averted, than the Court was in a buzz again. The Earl of Northumberland had been arrested as suspect of a share in the conspiracy. His name proved his undoing. One of the cut-throats in the plot was surnamed Percy, a relative—a cousin, of the Earl, and known to be a Catholic.

Aware, through all these years, of a devotion as silent as it was sincere, Arabella, while grateful for the 'Wizard Earl's' fidelity, had never yet returned it. Her heart was pledged—she thought it buried—in the grave of him by whom it had been utterly possessed. But the least that she could offer now as a token of her gratitude to friendship, if not love, was to plead his case to James for his release.

She did, and strongly, if to little purpose.

A name. . . . What was a name? On what proof, under Heaven, could they arraign Northumberland? . . . . "He stands above reproach. His loyalty has ever been unquestioned. I beg you, Sire, take my word for it, I know him. I have known him since I was a child. He is my friend."

James goggled at her.

"He's a bad man and a Papist."

"He is not—and if he were——"

"If he *were*!" James repeated, shying. "Woman! Durst ye utter to me face such heathen blasphemies? He's a warlock and has business with the devil. And moreover," added James severely, "'tis highly disrespectful to contradict the King."

"But Sire, this impeachment is unjust. I'll swear to it——"

"Ye'll swear your head on the block with his!" James shouted in a passion. "Hold your peace. Do ye presume upon our kinship to pass judgment on our justice? Wisht! You try our tolerance too far. Nay now——" for she had sunk upon her knees in a pretty show of tears, "we applaud your sympathy, but believe me what I say, it is misplaced. 'Tis a bad man, that."

"I—I——" sobbed Arabella, peeping through her fingers at her pop-eyed cousin's countenance, which for all its weakness showed a mulish obstinacy difficult to overcome, but she could try. "I woo-ould sooner perish here at Your Ma-jes-jesty's feet than displeasure Your Majesty, but——"

"But me no buts," James said testily, "and for God's sake dry your tears. Dinna vex me to extremes."

These women with their caterwaulings! His good wife now. . . . One and all the same. She would lie upon her bed and kick her heels for what she wanted. The late Queen's gowns, no less, to be brought from the Tower, a good five hundred of them that he'd hoped to have on show and charge admission for the sight—a pretty penny for his purse. But no! Tears, sobs and he gave in. . . . He'd not give in to this young baggage. He would not.

"God's life, lass, cease lamenting!" James implored her. "I promise ye this. We'll examine the case and give him opportunity to clear himself. As for justice," he reminded her sternly, "never question your King on that score. We are just. We luke upon both sides of the problem. Ay! The man'll get what he deserves. Begone wi' ye. I've spoken."

And when he did nothing on earth could move him.

Northumberland was convicted on a series of offences. Not the least of these were his endeavours to secure toleration for the Catholics. He had also been found guilty of negotiations with his friends to harbour Thomas Percy, his kinsman, and a recusant, 'when that same chief practicer and contriver of most horrible Treason was fled into the north' and for 'utterly neglecting to give commandment to apprehend that same Thomas Percy, being known as a damnable and dangerous Traitor.' The penalty adjudged was a fine of thirty thousand pounds to be paid to the King, the deprivation of his every office, including that of Privy Councillor, and his removal to the Tower, where he remained for fifteen years.

He may have been lucky to escape with the loss of a fortune, when he might have lost his head. James went in mortal fear of losing his. Not even that thirty thousand extracted from the 'Wizard Earl's' coffers to fill up his own, could banish his dread of conspiracy.

He had sustained a deplorable shock, was more than ever fumbling and nervous, until he devised a plan of wearing next his skin a padded shirt. Since they had failed to blow him up they might try to run him through, but no sword could pierce that thickness, He wore it to the dance, and he wore it at his dinner ;

e wore it to the chase and in his bed. His wife complained, but till he wore it. . . .

The pursuit of pleasure went its giddy round. The King's company of players were in great demand at Court. It was said the chief actor, Mr. Shakespeare, wrote most of the plays himself. A play of the Marchant of Venis ' was received with tremendous applause. Sundays and Holy days were entirely devoted to the drama, while James lolled in his seat and fumbled Robert Carr, and ' Ludo ', at his left side, sat and glowered. ' The Merry Wives of Windsor ' was played before the King on a Sunday in November, 605. The King guffawed, the ladies clapped, and Prince Henry crowed with laughter at the antics of the fat knight, but the Queen, who had not yet mastered English enough to follow a play, spoiled the fun for Arabella by requesting her throughout to explain every one of the jokes.

Her constant attendance on the amiable, empty-headed Queen who professed to dote on her ' sweet cousin ', kept her ever at her side. The lavish entertainments, the gifts she was expected to bestow upon each member of the Royal Family, soon became expensive. To her Aunt Shrewsbury she wrote : ' I mean to give Her Majesty two pairs of silk stockings lined with plush and two gloves lined, if London afford me not some daft toy I liked better. . . I am making the King a purse. This time (Christmas) will manifest my poverty more than all the rest of the year. My quarter's allowance will not defray this one charge, believe me.'

If Mary Shrewsbury believed her, she did not rise to this broad hint beyond sending her a ' share of our good cheer ' in the form of some venison pasties. The King doled her out a pittance scarce enough to clothe her. She had nothing left for presents.

Her steward, Crompton, a trustworthy, pompous person selected by her Uncle Henry for his unimpeachable good character, took full responsibility of her affairs, but he was greatly exercised to pay the wages of Arabella's servants, besides their food and clothing, after she extracted what she needed for her gowns. A different one for every function, as incumbent on her rank, soon swallowed what remained of her small income. So heavy were her debts that she was in two minds whether or no to sell the Lennox pearls ; these the only heirlooms left to her of her lost heritage. Her jewels had long ago been handed to Ludo's father, Esmé Stuart, with her earldom.

It was not easy to get money out of James, but by persistent badgering of Cecil she managed to obtain an increase in her allowance from six hundred to a thousand pounds a year. This should have well sufficed her needs, had she not been extravagant, and generous to folly. Crompton kept a list of her disbursements, and in this we see that not the least of them were gifts to the poor, and in addition, the too lavish tipping of her own and others' servants. A year after receiving her augmented income she was deep in debt again.

Marriage might have solved her difficulties, but James was no more anxious than Elizabeth had been to see his cousin married. Besides, as he continually reminded her, she had made a vow never to marry and had put it into writing. He meant to make her keep her word.

The King of Poland was the first of her royal suitors James rejected. Enamoured of her portrait, he had sent his Ambassador to England with an offer, though James doubted, so he did not hesitate to say, it was not her face but her fortune he desired.

" Fortune ! " Arabella's burst of laughter was a trifle shrill. " And where, Sire, is my fortune ? Where my lands ? And where my father's earldom ? "

She had never before dared broach that tender subject to the King, until, piqued now by this blunt disavowal of her charms, her temper ousted caution.

" Am I such a monster that no man could fancy my portrait which, if flattered as it may be, cannot hide my sad defects ? Does Your Majesty suggest I am a hag, decrepit, maimed and ugly ? "

James fingered his beard and rolled a shocked eye at her speechless. . . . No respect. She showed him not one tittle of respect.

" Eh, but ye're a handful," he said helplessly. " I'm not surprised Elizabeth, our cousin, kept ye in your place. I'm mistook in ye to raise ye up so high. Would ye queen it then in Poland A barbaric cold outlandish country from all telling. Nay, we' find ye a husband more to your taste and one of our church witha This Pollack is a Papist. As for your earldom—" James began to fiddle, " I'm distressed ye should mention it. However, sinc you'll have me tell ye, when Matthew O'Lennox, our grandfathe died, the earldom reverted to me, but by our favour," James sai grandly, " we bestowed our title and all that went with it on you

ather and our uncle, Charles Stuart. Ye were a bairn when
e died. We therefore decided that the Lennox estates would be
better controlled by one of our clan, and our kinsman. We do
ot hould wi' a woman taking to hersel' the prerogative of male
ssue. 'Tis to my mind unseemly. So these—" James glanced
uspiciously askance at the now smiling Arabella, who bent her
nee and bobbed, "so these," James repeated loud, "are the facts
' the case, and dinna speak to me agin upon the subject."

She never did, though she still pestered him, through Cecil,
or more money.

Her next proposal came from Duke Ulric, a younger brother
of the Queen, blond, loud-voiced and over-amorous. The King
might have considered him as a possible mate for this tiresome
ousin had she not flatly refused.

To Cecil, whom James had recently created Earl of Salisbury,
e complained: "What's to do wi' such a one? Will ye believe
he had the impudence to tell me, 'I dinna like the man', she
aid, 'he smells.'"

Salisbury composed his face to murmur, "Most irreverent."

"Ay!" James eyed him truculently. "She's sair difficult and
hrewish, my gude lord. We canna wonder that Her late Majesty
nsisted on strict dealing with the Lady Arabella. Would ye not
hink my own wife's brother would be high enough for her?"

"Her Ladyship," suggested Salisbury gently, "may aim
igher."

"Higher!" echoed James, extremely fussed. "Who, save
God A'mighty, or our own dear son, can be higher than a brother
' the Queen?"

There was, however, yet another brother higher still: King
Christian of Denmark himself.

In July 1606 he arrived at Gravesend, where he received an
uproarious welcome. Short, stout and amiable, he bore so singular
a likeness to his sister, Queen Anne, that they might have been
aken for twins. He professed himself delighted with his reception,
with the English Court, the English ladies and above all with
Arabella. For his entertainment, banquets, carousals and masques,
went on from early morning until late at night. His energy was
nexhaustible. Within three hours of his landing he hunted with
King James in Greenwich Park and killed two bucks. Then the
wo kings and their respective suites, the Queen and Arabella,

departed on a visit to Lord Salisbury at Theobalds. There they were greeted with an ode written by Mr. Jonson, and spoken by three boys disguised very daintily as Hours. In the evening another feast was held, followed by a masque representing Solomon (the King of Denmark) in his Temple, and the coming of the Queen of Sheba with her gifts. We can take it that Lord Salisbury, who had spared no time, expense, or thought on the production, must have been dismayed at the result. So lavish was the banquet, so various the wines, that the lady who had been called upon to play the Queen of Sheba carrying a salver laden with fruit, flagons, creams, jellies and other matters, forgot, or was too full of her feasting to see the steps that led to the platform where Solomon in all his glory, and in scarcely better case than the performers, sat arrayed.

Carefully advancing with her burden, Sheba missed her footing, and to the guests' delight and their host's horror, upset her salver and its contents into the royal lap.

Much was the hurry and confusion. Cloths and napkins were brought forth and the Danish King, loudly guffawing, was wiped down, but before he was cleaned he pushed the pages aside, got unsteadily upon his feet and insisted that Sheba should dance with him. As he approached her, however, he too slipped the steps and fell on the floor where he lay; nor could he rise.

They lifted him up and they carried him out and left him, still splashed with Sheba's gifts, to recover, snoring on a bed of state.

Yet still the show went gaily forward, ' while most of the performers went backward—' (thus we have it from an eye-witness's account)* ' or fell down, wine did so occupy their upper chambers. Now did appear in rich dress Hope, Faith and Charity. . . . Hope did essay to speak, but drink rendered her endeavours so feeble that she withdrew and hoped the King (James) would excuse her brevity. Faith then was alone and left the Court in staggering condition. Charity came to the King's feet and seemed to cover the multitude of sins her sisters had committed; in some sort she made obeisance and brought gifts, but said she would go home again as there was no gift which heaven had not already bestowed upon His Majesty. She then returned to Hope and Faith, who were both sick and spewing in the lower hall. . . . I have marvelled much at these strange pageantries.'

As no doubt did Arabella.

But of all her suitors, one, though least in rank, was in love
the most adoring : a wealthy dilettante, Mr. Fowler. As Secretary
Queen Anne he had nothing much to do save write and read
er letters, fetch and carry, tend her lap-dogs and make passes
the Lady Arabella.

He caused her some annoyance. He would stand and ogle
er as she came in and murmur in her ear as she went out. He
llowed her from room to room, was always ready at her elbow
run errands. The ladies whispered, Queen Anne giggled and
ased her for her conquest, and Arabella stormed to Mistress
radshaw.

"The man is making me ridiculous. He approached me in
e Ante Room, before those grinning Maids, struck an attitude
d said ' Behold the eighth most perfect wonder of the world '."

Anne suppressed a laugh.

"Yes, laugh," raged Arabella. "The whole Court holds its
des. I dropped my handkerchief. He sprang to pick it up and
hen he returned it to me I found folded in it—*this*."

Anne took the crumpled paper from her hand.

"Read it," commanded Arabella.

With laudable sobriety Anne read :

> ' Thou godly nymph possess'd with heavenly fear,
>   Divine in soul, devout in life and grave,
> Wrapt from thy sense and sex, thy spirit doth steer,
>   Toys to avoid which reason doth bereave.
> O graces rare ! Which time from shame shall save,
>   Wherein thou breath'st (as in the sea doth fish
> In salt not saltish) exempt from the grave
>   Of sad remorse the lot of worldlings wish.
> O ornament !——'

"O, stop !" cried Arabella. "Did you ever hear such stuff ?
That does it mean ? Can you make sense of it ? "

Anne, incurably romantic, sighed, " Poor fellow."

"Poor ass, poor zany, clown ! How the Queen's Maids delight
see me made a peepshow for this fool ! They are so full of
alice and derision that I think hate and envy are tied in serpent-
il around their necks to sting me to death—an they could."

They certainly were bitter. Two Kings and a Prince to her

bow, never mind that His Majesty refused them, they were offered. And how many more besides, to say nothing of poor silly Mr. Fowler? But would any give thanks to be courted by him who stood in corners mooing like a bilious calf at sight of her? . . . One would think to see her so set up that she, and not Her Majesty, was Queen of England, as she still might hope to be when Prince Henry came of age. . . . But what of hers? Well over thirty if a minute. *Quite* a crone. Some called her pretty. Who, the ladies loftily inquired of each other, could be pretty with that turned-up nose as freckled as a cowslip, and a figure like a child's, undeveloped? And the way she encouraged that innocent sweet boy was a scandal. . . . Everyone knew how she sought his society, walked with him in the gardens down at Hampton, played hide-and-seek for hours in the Maze, read with him in her chamber, and conversed in Latin. Did they conjugate the verb *Amo* together?

It was true Henry made no secret of his admiration for her. A handsome, intelligent lad, tall for his fifteen years, he resembled neither physically nor mentally his parents. The orgies he was forced to witness in his father's palaces, represented to the young prince, tutored by that rigid Presbyterian, Adam Newton, the worst excesses of the Romans on the eve of their decline.

Brought at the age of ten from the glens and braes of Scotland and the kindly discipline of Mr. Newton, to be plunged into a life where perversion, drunkenness and immorality were not only accepted as the standard mode of fashionable living, but encouraged by example of the King, Henry remained surprisingly untarnished through the years of adolescence.

Lacking the advice and guidance that his mother was incapable of giving or that his father would not give, he turned to Arabella the one woman at the Court whom he respected, and on her he lavished all his young affection. She, recognizing his rare qualities returned it, seeking his society in preference to others much his senior.

His father both feared and disliked his heir-apparent. He disliked him for his charm, his grace, his popularity, that James for all his hail-fellow heartiness never could achieve. He disliked him for the frank contempt in which he held his father's favourites and in more veiled, but no less degree, his father.

To be rid of that silent condemnatory reproach, the King set apart for his son's residence St. James's Palace.

The early death of this remarkable boy may have changed the fate of England by removing from the Stuart dynasty one who, had he lived, would unquestionably have been its greatest light. But if Henry was still too young at this time to be accorded political significance, he was old enough to air his views in support of his opinions, which he did not scruple to disguise, were directly opposed to the King's. With a perspicacity beyond his years he chose none but the cultured, more serious youth of the day to attend him. His establishment was governed by the carefullest regard for the proprieties, and doubtless in revolt from the corrupt extravagance of James, with as careful regard for his purse. He soon devised a scheme whereby, without unduly overdrawing from his personal exchequer, he could dispense alms to the poor. No gentleman or lady at his Court was permitted to swear, and for every oath inadvertently uttered, a fine must be paid into a box kept for that purpose. By this means he collected a good monthly sum to be distributed for charitable purposes. 'A holy paragon', some called him, while others did not hesitate more bluntly to add 'Prig'.

But his priggishness, if such, was no more than the natural reaction of any healthy-minded youngster from a surfeit of licentiousness, which may at first have amused before it sickened him. He excelled at tennis, loved horses, studied two hours a day and spent the rest of his time, when not in the tennis court, at tossing the pike, vaulting, tilting, shooting with the bow or galloping across the grassy spaces of his Park. He loved his fat and foolish mother for the love that she bore him, and loyally averted his eyes from the spectacle of the Queen of England tippling with her ladies, laughing uproariously at the ribald jests of the King's Fool, Archie Armstrong, or the lewdities whispered from behind the hand of some leering old rip, which, since her knowledge of English was limited, she may or may not have understood.

The Prince was not, however, entirely alone in his self-imposed aloofness. Between him and his sister Elizabeth, destined to be Queen of Bohemia, there existed the strongest attachment. With the relentless criticism of the very young they gravely disparaged their elders, not in their case without cause. Both determined to save their little brother, Charles, from libidinous contamination. The baby, Mary, Arabella's god-daughter, born in 1605*, was too

* The Princess Mary died September 15, 1607.

young, they decided, to be spoilt; but Charles must be dragged from the Pit.

He, a weakly, delicate child and difficult to rear, was his mother's favourite, perhaps because for the first few years of his life he suffered from rickets; nor, until he reached the age of five could he walk or talk. When he did at last speak it was with a deplorable stammer.

Arabella, on whom the little fellow doted, undertook, with indefatigable patience, to help him overcome his unfortunate impediment; but for all her care he showed little hope of any marked improvement. Deprived of the free action of his limbs he would sit for hours at the table playing with his wooden soldiers, his small pointed face propped in one hand, his flaxen hair about his shoulders, brooding on some knotty problem of warfare. He was meticulously careful in the placing of his men, and would give no unfair advantage to the side he represented.

"Ah—ah—I'll ber-ber-be a ser-soldier *if* I ler-live to be a ma-ma-man," one day he solemnly announced to Arabella.

"But of course, sweetheart, you'll live to be a man," she replied with haste, alarmed at that emphatic 'if', "a great man and a great prince."

"A ser-ser-soldier," Charles stubbornly repeated. "Ah—ah—I'll fer-fight for Ah-ah-England and for Ser-ser-Scotland too."

"There'll be no wars, please God, in your time," Arabella said, "we've had wars enough in mine. May you be spared all such, my dear."

"I der-do not wah—wah—want to be sper-spared sah—sah—such." Charles smiled, fingering his soldiers. "Wa—wars make mer-men ber-ber-ber——" His twisted tongue refused to speak the word. He tried again, and failing, buried his head in his arm and wept silently. That soundless, pitiful surrender to his infirmity tore at Arabella's heart. She raised him up, and stroking back the primrose silken hair from the flushed, shamed forehead: "Try again, my love," she whispered. "What is it you would say beginning with 'B'?"

Charles squared his chin, blinked the water from his eyes and smiled at her.

"B—Brave!"

She clapped her hands. "Bravo! And now again, so that another time you will not stumble when you say——?"

" B-brave," repeated Charles, and well-pleased with his success :
" B-brave. S-see how I am b-brave," he said. " *Brave* Charles ! "

That Arabella preferred to spend her time with Charles in his nursery than with his parents in the Court, may be gathered from this letter to her uncle, Earl of Shrewsbury :

'May it please your lordship to pardon me if I write now in haste with a mind distracted by the several cares of household and those that this remove (to Whitehall) may add thereto. . . . If you knew what business we have here! Yesterday the Spanish Ambassador, the Florentine, and Madame de Beaumont, took their leave of the Queen. There is an Ambassador from Polonia and fain would he be gone again because of the freezing of the seas, but he has not yet had audience. . . . It is said the Turk has sent a Chahu to the King in embassage. It is said the Pope will send a knight to the King in embassage. The Duke of Savoy's embassage is daily expected.

But out of this confusion of embassages will you know how we on the Queen's side spend our time? While I was at Winchester there were certain child plays remembered by the fair ladies: " Rise Pig and go," " One Penny follow me," etc., and when I came to Court they were as highly in request as ever cracking of nuts was. So I, as Mistress of the Revels, was compelled to play at I knew not what (for till that day I never heard of a play called "Fire") but was even persuaded by the princely example I saw, to play the child again. This exercise is most used from ten o'clock at night till two or three in the morning.'

We can take it that ' this exercise ' soon palled. As once she had chafed against restriction, so now did the lack of it prove wearisome ; and save for the company of the King's three children, and despite the King's high favour, she was friendless.

She had, however, after much tactful persuasion, managed to secure a peerage for her uncle, William Cavendish. As a result of this good deed, and in the hope no doubt that it might be repeated, her Cavendish uncles, with the exception of Henry, and every one of her Cavendish cousins, pestered her to visit at their various houses. But her constant attendance on the Queen kept her ever on the move from Hampton Court to Whitehall, from Windsor to Woodstock and Theobalds—which James had lately taken from Lord Salisbury, and given him the Royal residence of Hatfield in exchange.

Thus, year in, year out, she found herself at the beck and call of others. She had a staff of thirty servants and her ever-faithful gentlewoman, Anne; she had pages, grooms, a stableful of horses and a coach. She had a suite of state apartments in the Palace, but never a home of her own. Nor had she a will of her own. In return for all this splendour she must obey the behest of the King and his Queen, go where they went, dance her feet sore, laugh, chatter, amuse them, and gambol. There seemed to be no future for her, and she was not so young. Yet she grew outwardly no older. Her glass still gave her back reflection of a girl. It was as if her youth had been arrested in its flight, to brood, bewildered, in the debris of a passion that had stormed her citadel to leave her empty. Bereft of love she now believed herself untouchable, inviolate. . . . She did not know that her life's love was yet to come.

The year 1608 made an icy entrance with the coldest winter since the King's accession. James was forced to abandon his hunting. In Derbyshire the men, who at their mistress's direction were reconstructing Bolsover, were forced to abandon their work. The impassable conditions of the roads had delayed the transport bringing bricks, cement and timber. Drifts of snow rose higher than the walls, the hands of the builders were frost-bitten; icicles formed from their breath on their beards. They shivered, though less with cold than in fear of their lady, when, wrapped in a fur-lined cloak, her head muffled in a hood, she descended on them like a cyclone.

Undeterred by the elements, the aged, still indomitable Bess, cursed them roundly for a pack of lazy hounds, and shaking her fist in their faces, "Are ye snowdrops," she jeered, "to lay down your tools for a snowflake? The house must be built. Go, get begun! Hurry!"

But since they had nothing to build with they could not 'get begun'. They must wait for the thaw to bring the much belated transport from the south.

Meanwhile Bess, having spoken her mind, returned to Hardwick in her coach. The short journey took ten hours. Twice her men had to dig the wheels out of the snow. When at last she reached home she announced she felt chilly, drank a hot posset, felt worse. Assuring her servants she felt better, she took herself to bed.

All the next day and in a high fever, she issued her orders. Those Bolsover rascals must, *must* get to work. Never to stop. They must build. . . . A gypsy once had warned her that while she went on building houses she would not . . . she would *not* die.

Like a rusty bell the cracked old voice unceasingly tolled through the house. Her frightened attendants sent for her sons. They flocked to her bedside and fell on their knees. Her eyes, overbright, ever restless, surveyed them, looked through them. She gave them no blessing. She had a great pain in her side. She had a great weight on her heart, a great fear. . . . Her men had ceased their work. Her men must get to work. . . . Let them build her house of sand, of stone, of rock. Why wait for bricks when there were rocks upon the mountains? A pale-livered pack of hounds! Go, get to work . . . and *build*!

There, propped upon her pillows, blue-lipped and sunken eyed, her white hair springing fiercely from her unwigged undaunted head, she shouted her last breath away.

On the thirteenth of February, 1608, died Bess of Hardwick, Dowager Countess of Shrewsbury, mistress of many great mansions, in the 91st year of her life.

The gypsy's prophecy had been fulfilled.

* * *

The snows vanished and spring danced again, never surely with such lavish sweets to offer, as if to atone for winter's devastation.

In the Palace gardens the saffron crocus spread its wings and fled before the trumpet-peal of daffodils. At Hampton Court bleached alleys, greening joyously in April showers, let fall a lacy petticoat of starry bud and blossom. From her casement Arabella watched the promenade of strutting courtiers and their ladies; purple, red, or gold of gown and doublet flaunting a garish contrast to the flowerful delights of hyacinth and narcissus, and those recently imported cup-shaped plants from Holland that the gardeners called ' Two-lips '. Stately, tall, they stood and bowed all in a line like sentinels under Arabella's window, yellow, red and parrot-striped, or coloured like the lilac. On May Day there were celebrations, bear-baiting, tilting, Maypole jollity, Morris dancers, and, so Arabella wrote to her Aunt Mary: ' This everlasting hunting.'

The King did not always follow hounds in the orthodox sportsmanlike manner. There were occasions when, dressed very youthfully in a suit 'as green as the grass he trod on, with a feather in his cap and a horn instead of a sword at his side', he would ride in Windsor Great Park, dismount behind a tree and take pot-shots with the crossbow at the tame deer as they browsed.

Attended by the Queen and Arabella, his gentlemen and Robert Carr, the King, in his juvenile dress, set forth on a May morning in the greatest of good humours; he returned in tears.

The Queen, who had begged to be allowed to draw her bow, instead of shooting the tame and lovely startled stag at which she aimed, missed her mark and killed the King's favourite hound.

There followed the greatest to-do, with the King on his knees beside the limp body beseeching his 'dear Jowler, come speak to me. One word before ye die, dear lad, one word, my precious laddie. . . .'

"The King will kill me too for dis," sobbed the Queen. "My eyes deceift. I think I was clear aim at the stag. I would not wish to kill the dog—not for ten t'ousand crowns. The King will not belief. So you go tell the King, Arbelle, and say I sorry."

It is something to James's credit that he accepted his wife's apology in better part than might have been expected. Seeing her concern he assured her, as well-meaningly as it was ill-expressed, that: 'for her sad mishap he could not love her worse than he did now' and besought her not to grieve for his good Jowler, who, he declared, had with his dying breath pardoned his murderess, and bequeathed her by way of legacy a diamond ring valued at two thousand pounds. Whereupon Anne, all smiles again, mounted her mare and rode home with her ladies. The King and his gentlemen followed with the corpse.

Such and other incidents recorded made up the daily routine of Arabella's life. Aware of inward restiveness that was not wholly due to the monotonous frivolities of her existence, she continuously tasked herself for her ingratitude. What more could she desire after years of tyranny than the King's good favour, the loving-kindness of his Queen, and the genuine affection of their children ? A hundred and one compensations were offered in exchange for lack of intellectual companionship. What more, then, could she ask than the high position which she held, with her rank acknowledged and her life lived as should become it ? What more ? . .

hen spring breathed its perfumed message from every burdened
edge, to sun itself in glory of blue and golden light? Why, when
orchards flung a silver-petal fortune at her feet, should she com-
ain of money debts? Could money buy a blackbird's song more
lovely than the choristers' who hymned it in high heaven? Why
earn and lash yourself, she said, for more than God has given?
Have you not yet enough? Go ask the King to pay an increase
in your income, what could you buy more beautiful than that one
ranch of cherry-flower sweet against the sky? God shrive you for
our sins, she said, and save me from your moanings. Will you
ng: Magnify God and diminish my stiff-neckedness. . . . Am
not lower than the worms that crawl, purblindly praising a single
lade of grass as it were Jesus? Whereas I, a Princess, decked,
pparelled, bedded in a palace, tended, flattered, fawned on for
y good grace, yes . . . am I not shamed to ask God for the moon?
et must I so, since nothing else, I swear, will fill my craving for
. . the Lord alone can say!

Thus, in some such fashion, on some green afternoon, Arabella
may have sat and dreamed, touched by who could tell what magical
isquiet born of that fervent spring? And seated at her window
here, bemused and all alone, she scarcely knew that she was
nterrupted, thought she dreamed again when she heard approach-
ng footsteps in the grass. Nothing warned her, no pricking of
he thumbs, no premonition, recognition, no awareness, that all
he asked of life was in her hand.

"Arbelle!"

She leaned her head out of the window. His face upturned,
his eyes screwed against the sun, Henry called to her: "Hey!
Arbelle! We go to play at tennis. Will you come?"

We go to play at . . . 'We?' . . .

She was conscious of another who stood behind the Prince,
et conscious less of him than of his shadow.

"Will you come, Arbelle?" the Prince repeated gaily, "I
play better when you watch. You always spur me to my best
—and I must play my better best today!"

The game had already started when Arabella, with Anne
Bradshaw in attendance, took her seat in the dedans between
Princess Elizabeth and Charles, whose governess, Lady Carey, sat
beside him on his left.

Henry, from the hazard side, managed to win a short chase, and was gleefully applauded by young Charles, who watched every stroke, and, with undisguised partisanship, loudly cheered each time his brother scored.

The game proceeded, waxing faster. The players appeared to be well matched, and though Henry was the lighter on his feet, his opponent showed more skill in the placing of his ball, and with a fine stroke into the winning gallery brought the score to deuce.

"Ner-ner-ner-no!" shouted Charles. "It was thir-thir-thirty fif-fif-fif——"

"Hush, sweetheart," whispered Arabella "you disturb the players."

The late afternoon sun poured through the narrow openings set high above the main wall, emblazoning the gilt and scarlet crowns under the galleries, splintered into sparks of gold the rich embroidered doublets of the pages, and slanted a sword-thrust beam in Arabella's eyes, which might have distorted vision to see backward, or to see again.

What was it she saw? *Who* was it she saw, or for the first time closely noticed, when the other player turned to pick up his ball from the shallow trench in front of the dedans? Such light was in his eyes to dazzle hers that stayed a moment startled, held. . . . A young, too young, and laughing face with backswept unruly hair, chestnut-gleaming, tossed above a clear, high forehead; brows faintly tilted as the wings of a bird in flight, and lively lips that followed that same lifted curve. . . . Did the sun play tricks to call up ghosts long buried?

"He—he—he mer-missed!" cried Charles excitedly. "Ha-ha-Henry wer-wer-wins the a'vah-vah-vantage!"

And Henry won the game.

"Why, sir, you are not in your play to give me this," he chaffed "You, who can band a ball at six score paces mounting. Sir come on!"

And Henry won the next game.

As the pages ran forward to collect the balls, "Who", Arabella asked of Lady Carey, "is His Highness's opponent?"

"I have never seen him, Madam, here before. I canno say."

"I can tell you," said Elizabeth sedately, "he was presented to me by the King at Oxford. His name, as I remember it, is——"

Her words were interrupted by another cheer from Charles as a ball, just missing the tambour, crashed into the grille.

"Fifteen-love," called the marker.

Henry served again and the ball, heavily cut, seemed to die in its appointed corner.

"Thirty-love."

"Henry," said Elizabeth, "looks like to win the set."

And Henry did; and not till then did Arabella learn that the name of him who lost was William Seymour.

Chapter Two

DURING the summer months the gossips of the Court gathered a plenteous store of scandal for their garbage heap. Lady Essex, wife of the dead earl's son, had set her cap at Robert Carr, who was in the running for a peerage. Would he get it? Not likely, unless the King were too love-blind or deaf to see how those two sat in corners cooing, or heard them at their transports when they couched!

Worse still, Prince Henry had been caught, and carried the glove of Lady Essex in his pocket, mooned after her all day and night, which would sure disjoint the stuck-up nose of Someone. . . .

Would it?

The Queen's damsels bunched their heads together nodding.

"Has she not another if much lesser fish to fry?"

"What! That stripling, Seymour? Would she dare stir up that mud again?" Which the older maids declared, they'd heard their mothers tell had caused the greatest buzz when they were in their cradles. What had she to gain by chasing *him*, and he scarce out of swaddling clothes?

"Yes, but don't forget that Seymour is near as royal as herself. A pretty match they'd make of it between them to push the King from off his throne!"

"Would you believe! He can't be more than twenty-three, and *she* is long past thirty! Has she no shame?"

And: "O, Arbelle," thus Mary Talbot, married at last, and most unhappily, to Pembroke. "O, Arbelle, if you could only hear the half of what is said of you I think you'd never show yourself. . . . O, is it true?"

"Is what true, love?" purred Arabella.

"Is it true that you— O, I hardly care to say it—that you are courting William Seymour?"

"As true, my little dear," Arabella said with smiles, "that no man save your husband has ever courted you. And he, I'll swear, howsoever he may stray, will never be dubbed cuckold."

At which Mary sucked her underlip and reddened to retort: "Nothing in this life'll change your adder's tongue, Arbelle, but I'll excuse your sharpness. You are soured with long spinsterhood. O, yes!" Mary dolorously sniffed. "You may mock me for my virtue, but pity 'tis some others do not follow my example and blink an eye at their lord's peccadilloes. What man is perfect? Yet mine always returns loving to my bed, for I am broad——"

"Indeed," murmured Arabella, "so you are, and growing broader every time we meet."

"'Od's my life!" cried Mary, mortified, "you sure are contrary to snap me up before my words are out. I would have said my *mind* is broad. I am not petty, and as matron, which you as maid should not presume to understand, I can tell you that a wife with any wisdom will go so—" Mary covered her eyes, "to many things a virgin might think culpable. And," proceeded Mary, pouting, "as a married woman, allow me to advise you that it ill becomes a maiden to show herself so randy. . . . And O, Arbelle, upon my soul, you are a cat!"

"As you're a kitten, sweet, since we are of one family. Come, draw in your claws. I'll not contend against your scratching. I can see how you are swollen with your fur on end to spew the dirt you have collected in my name. Well now!" as Lady Pembroke with what dignity her plumpness could command, rose from her seat announcing she would not stay to be insulted, "why so tetchy? Will you go, having pricked my curiosity to leave me smarting and unsatisfied?"

"O!" Mary drew a breath. "You never will be satisfied, and that's a fact. 'Tis a sure sign how you are ageing that you must ever play the coquette with a boy. First the Prince and then his gentleman. Why not choose a man of your own years? I've sorrowed sore to see how the whole Court observes your want of taste."

"My taste," suggested Arabella meekly, "may have suffered from a surfeit of catnip."

"O, go shake your ears!" cried Mary, roused. "You should know that I speak only in your interest. You once before escaped a punishment that might have brought you to the scaffold when you offered yourself so barefaced to this very same young Seymour. Have you not learned your lesson that you go tempting Providence again? O, I'd not be in your place and have such talk around *my* name—not for a million units, no, I wouldn't."

And Mary left the room, well pleased with her success. She had obeyed her impulse, and relieved her mind, by offering good counsel in cousinly affection to Madame-Starchneck Arabella, who now, reflected Mary, may *stew* for all I care!

Since the King's accession, Mary, in accordance with other noble ladies, had agreed that it was irksome, if not utterly ridiculous, to bow the knee and scrape to one, who by the late old Queen's command had been disfavoured, disinherited by her own grandmother, and disgraced by her own folly. But now His Majesty, forsooth, needs must reinstate her with all the fuss of royal rank and precedence revived, claiming her his cousin, and nearest of his kin after his wife and children. A very different state of things, indeed, from the days when her Ladyship was looked upon with pity and disacknowledged by Her Grace's order. . . . And O, said Mary, much aggrieved, that I should pursue my way to warn her against her want of judgment and be jeered at for my pains. So let me die if I so much as *pip* at her which way the wind is blowing, and only wait until the King gets scent of what's afloat! O, yes! Then may she regret she paid so little heed to one who bears her naught but good will. Amn't I her kinswoman? And much benefit my lord and I have gained from near approach to royalty from *her*, I'll say! She has it in her power to lift my lord into a dukedom while the King goes so easy to deny her nothing. Would you not think that she'd have been more generous to me, her friend from birth? But no! She's so raised up that she'll not look down below her navel to those who shared her girlhood and her secrets. O, well, said Mary, flouncing, I can share a secret too. . . . *I* made her blush.

It would seem from these reflections, that marital disillusionment may have put a point on Mary's tongue, to prick.

The blush that she had marked still lingered hot in Arabella's cheek, when after Mary left her she sat long at her window. From behind the arras in an inner room she heard the voices of her gentle-women, hushed. Had they listened to her cousin's chatter, and now embellished it in whispers? Gaggling fools! They would not dare if Anne were in their midst, but Anne had been called to Derbyshire to attend her mother's sick-bed, and Bridget was content to wait, with the least work to do, on Lady Shrews-bury at Sheffield. So even here among my servants, thought Arabella, wryly, I have few save Anne and Crompton I can trust.

The Shrewsburys had lately taken a larger house, more suit-able to their requirements, in Broad Street. Having been granted a short respite from her duties as first Lady to the Queen, Arabella gladly accepted her Aunt Mary's invitation to stay at the Broad Street house for a few weeks while the Court removed to Wood-stock. But whatsoever she had gleaned, and that was not a little, of young Seymour's captivation, Lady Shrewsbury was too tactful to tread where her daughter Mary had rushed in. No comment passed those self-contained, thin lips, while keen-eyed and inscrut-able, Lady Shrewsbury observed the progress of events through that summer, 1609; observed too how Arabella bloomed afresh like an autumn rose.

And on that warm October afternoon when Mary had relieved her mind to vent her spleen, Arabella, left alone, surveyed the perturbation of her thoughts. It was as if by Mary's well-directed good, or bad, intent an ant-heap had been stirred and its inhabitants scattered helter-skelter, lost to all command.

Her window looked upon a garden, small, compact, with trim yew hedges framing an herbaceous border where michaelmas daisies rioted beneath burnt yellow spears of golden-rod. The sun was sinking and the scent of dew on flowers rose sweet above the acrid smell of ivy, of stray cats, and the stench of London's ditches. How soft and warm the evening, as if summer were loath to step aside for autumn as a woman will retrace the steps of youth long after youth has fled.

On her lips a smile came and faded with a sigh. Youth. . . . So cruel swift its passing, irretrievable its loss! Strange, she mused, how Time goes halting for the young; how the days, the hours, stretch farther; a month becomes a year, and in a year the whole of youth's impassioned race is run while Time stands still. And

ow cruel again, that at the downward crossroads of Life's journey
'ime's pace quickens, to speed the clock from dawn until sundown,
etween youth's yesterdays and all youth's dead tomorrows. One
ight well give up all hope of heaven to relive ten years of youth
nburdened by the spectre of old age. . . . Foh! Draw your
urtains! Why fret yourself for what must come to every one of
s as surely as the seasons come and go. You, timeworn, world-
eary, should know better than to ape the maid, as Mary rightly
inted. Mutton must not play the lamb, decked out in spring-time
nery, skipping after what is not for you. Chew the cud and feed
pon your memories. Let them suffice and leave youth, or young
anhood, to follow its fair game. Do you not know your age?
. . And O, did he?

This moment then had come when, without flinching, without
entiment, she must review these last gay, careless months of her
ool's paradise. Was she at fault in that, since their first meeting
n the tennis-court, she had not taken sterner measures to extinguish
is impetuosity?

Admit, she said, you might have quenched the smoke before
he flame. But how—when every movement, gesture, tone of voice,
rought back so poignantly that other lost young love—resist the
rresistible? Yet none the less and rigorously she had meted him
gentle series of rebuffs, which served nothing save to refuel
is fire.

She recalled that Maytime afternoon when he had been presented
vith the Prince's formal introduction. . . . "Madam, Mr. William
eymour craves the honour——"

His smile, exceedingly swift, uncovered teeth as white as
lmonds. No formality of etiquette could stay his flying look,
is eager, quick response.

"Surely we . . . have I not already had the honour? We have
net before."

"I think, sir, never."

He bowed; she passed. And that was all until the next day
when she walked in the garden with Anne Bradshaw: and was
ollowed.

"Look behind you, Anne. Do you not see——?"

Anne looked behind and closed her face.

"Do you not see a likeness, Anne?"

"Imagination, Madam——"

269

"Can play tricks—but not in this case. Admit that you observe it too."

Anne quickened her steps.

"Why this hurry?" smiled Arabella. "Do we run a race? Walk slower, will you? I am out of breath."

And breathless still, a little, when he joined them.

"Does your Ladyship grace the tennis-court again this afternoon?"

"No, sir, not this afternoon."

"I gave your Ladyship a most disgraceful exhibition. I am pledged to vindicate myself."

"You were faced, sir, by a powerful antagonist. The Prince is one of the finest players in the Kingdom."

"I still maintain—" his eyes gleamed in the sunlight, as with irrelevant audacity he told her, standing planted in her path, "I still maintain that we have met before."

"Mr. Seymour, we have never met before."

"Can you be sure? We may have lived a hundred other lives than this. Pythagoras believed in transmigration of the soul, and I am not unsympathetic to the contemplative mysteries. Are you?"

She stole a glance at Anne who was agasp. A bubble rose to Arabella's surface.

"Sir, your scholastic postulation puts my ignorance to shame, yet I might suggest that ethico-religious fragments of Pythagorean philosophy are not distinctly relative to your presumption."

"I could, were I permitted," said Mr. Seymour, undeterred, "prove that there is something in the Master's theories which has converted me from scepticism. Madam, will you walk?"

There was no crushing him. They walked; and Mr. Seymour, without ceasing, talked.

Of what he talked the better part, although extremely learned, had conveyed but little sense to Arabella. His mercurial dexterity of speech, leaping from Greek cosmology to Plato's *Timæus*, from thence to the moon by way of the astrologers, and returning in a trice to earth, amazed her with the inconsequent, surprising interjection: "If this is not your double, Madam, then it is yourself."

And from somewhere hidden in his tunic he produced, as if by sleight of hand, a miniature.

It lay there in his palm, gold-bordered set with pearls. Her portrait—hers! She gave one glance at it and, crimson, glanced away. Said Mr. Seymour, while his eyes enjoyed the charming contour of her half-turned cheek: "I see, Madam, that you recognize this portrait."

"I think, Mr. Seymour," she had kept her head to say, "you draw upon coincidence too far. The picture, I admit, resembles me, but how it came into your possession———"

"I can tell you, Madam," he coolly interrupted, still gazing, not upon the portrait but at her. "It was sent me when I was a boy, by messenger but with no message. I vowed to seek out the original if it took me my life long. I have been these six years seeking—and have found."

She steadied her lips and the laugh on them. "Sir! I prefer your dialectics to———"

"You do not believe me? You think that I presume on the chance likeness of this toy to win your interest. That, Madam, is not so, yet I confess I would not hesitate to murder, steal or renounce my faith in God, to win so much regard from you as you would bestow upon your page. Forgive me, but I think you can't deny that here is limned your every feature—this face, heart-shaped and so small a man's hand could span it. These eyes that in the sun are the clearest of things yellow and in the shade the deepest, coolest grey—or are they green, taking their colour from that jewel at your throat? This mouth, so exquisitely fashioned and childishly red. I think I never saw such———"

"Mr. Seymour, I have walked, and you have talked—enough. I will bid you a very good day."

He stayed where she had left him, staring after her. And: "O, my Lady, did you ever hear the like of it!" breathed Anne. "How in heaven did he obtain your portrait?"

"How in hell?" she had retorted. "Go ask Bridget Sherland. Here's the devil! I swear he thinks I sent it. Would you believe that I'd be faced with *him* of all the world . . . Anne?"

"Madam?"

"Do you not think him erudite?"

"I think, Madam, he is glib."

"That I grant you, but 'tis a change to hear some other speech than witless babble. He certainly is far beyond his years."

Anne put her lips together.

"Anne?"

"My Lady?"

" What would you guess his years to be ? "

" Somewhere in the twenties, Madam."

" Somewhere in the very *early* twenties, Anne. Be honest."

" I have no desire, Madam, to be anything but honest. I do not know the age of Mr. Seymour."

" A plague upon you! Why," demanded Arabella, " do you adopt this disapproving tone ? "

" Madam," Anne raised her steady eyes, " would I presume to disapprove by tone or word of your Ladyship's . . . amusement ? "

" Then take that look of a suffering spaniel from your face. Did I encourage this young—this *very* young gentleman—to follow me and speechify his learning and catalogue my charms ? Did I, Anne ? 'Od's body, how he talks ! And how the world will talk—to see me courted from the cradle. Here, let's in to dinner now. I'll hide my head for shame. And you go tell the Queen I'm indisposed." . . .

That was how it had begun and how, in some degree or other, it went on. At the dance, ignoring comment, he dared to partner her before all those of higher rank than he, taking the precedence which, unacknowledged by King James, was none the less his right as sixth in succession to the throne.

Educated at Magdalen College, Oxford, where he secured honours degrees in classics and theology, he had hoped, so to Arabella he confided, to have achieved the life of a votary and scholar.

" I had," he said, " determined to build myself an inner temple where I could pursue my avocations and retire from the world."

" Your outside," she told him gravely, hiding laughter, " does not bespeak the hermit, Mr. Seymour."

" If my exterior belies my heart's intent," he answered unabashed, " it is merely an assumed protection, as the skin of a chameleon which will take its colour from immediate environment. I confess that I believe myself superior to the falsities of an existence which is as foreign to my spirit—as I think it is to yours."

His egotism took her breath away, and seared her with renewed reminder of one who would have spoken with just this same assurance to reconstruct the universe, and tune it to his humour. She had held herself in check to return with some asperity : " I see, sir, that you criticize our modes and manners of today."

" Madam, I do not criticize ; I accept—with resignation—and

deplore the passing of an age which future generations may look back upon as the most enlightened, the most cultural, this land has ever known. Our rebirth—that renaissance which flourished in France and Italy two centuries ago—emerged somewhat belatedly from mediaeval ignorant obscurities, but although it came, and went unheralded, and almost unobserved, it may yet prove to be significant."

"You speak," she said, "as if our renaissance were past."

"Madam, can a lily grow to its perfection on a dung heap? The great matriarchal era of Elizabeth, so near to us, is all forgotten now. Can you wonder I rebel against the wanton dissipation of a cult that should have raised our generation to Olympus? Can you wonder I return into myself when I see genius decried, unrecognized and unacknowledged?"

He was tremendously in earnest, and mounted on his hobby, carried her along with him. She had no words to stem the torrent of hyperbole outpoured to her who wonderingly listened.

"You," he said, "of all these mummers in this merry-go-round of shiftless unrealities, are the one supreme among us with the eyes to see, the ears to hear. That much I knew before I met you. That much I gathered from the study of your pictured face. You may, Madam, believe I am a lunatic. Believe it, then, and call me moonstruck. Yes, I am! I am! For if lunacy and love are one——"

"Mr. Seymour, such high flights of fancy do not recommend your self-exploited erudition."

His boy's face, at that, had flushed.

"I see you jest at life——"

"Which is too serious," she had lightly intervened, "to be taken seriously, Mr. Seymour."

"There again," he said, "speaks the chameleon. That is not your true belief, nor is it mine."

She passed a hand across her lips to stay a sudden quivering. How cruelly he played upon her heartstrings to stir echoes long since silent.

"You spoke of genius unrecognized." With gentle irony she probed him. "Do you believe yourself so gifted, Mr. Seymour?"

"Madam, I cast aside your mockery. It does no more than scratch my skin. . . . If your Ladyship must know, there is one who in my esteem will survive the future, one who apes the play-man, and at the King's command writes the plays for his performers, one who is applauded by the gutter, brought before the Court and doled a pittance for his poesy. Does any living soul of us who tosses him a condescension of bravos recognize *he* is immortal ? "

"You speak of Mr. Shakespeare," she said calmly. "I have read his published works. But what immortal is ever recognized in his own time ? "

"How can you say that ! " he heckled hotly. "What of Plato, Aristotle, Socrates ? "

"They inhabited a world that was ultra-civilized. We, Mr. Seymour, are barbarians."

"Can we forget it ? Can we not hope and strive to justify our flesh-embodied spirits upon some higher plane, even as did the masters ? Can I persuade your Highness to believe that this encounter has embued me with so fierce a will to live, to gather and to cherish every moment I may share with you, that I think the days cannot contain sufficient hours to express my worship, adoration . . ."

She knew not what to do with him. He would not be put down, nor would he be at all put out by her refusal to allow a repetition of this scene. While she, at greatest pains, avoided him, he as determinedly pursued her. When the Court removed to Theobalds he again was there.

In temporary attendance on Prince Henry for his good play at tennis, he was received with scanty favour by the King, who regarded him and all his house with dour suspicion. Yet he came and went, undaunted, and still talking.

Before the Court returned to Nonesuch, and Arabella back to London, he had talked himself into a declaration.

She laughed at him ; he had, seemingly, laughed too, while with that in his eyes to startle her : "I know you, Madam, better than you know yourself," he said. "What made you write to my grandfather, Lord Hertford, years ago, naming me your husband ? . . . What made you do it, Madam ? "

She paled, had turned indignantly to parry and was halted.

"Do not misunderstand me. I would not have spoken on so delicate a point, but that your laughter goads me to it. Were you not prompted then, as I am now, by some time-embowered memory, to single me for honour ? I have two brothers. Why name me and neither one of them ? You had never seen me."

"That reminder," she said weakly, "is as ungallant as it is false. . . ."

He looked at her with his enchanting smile, his eyebrows tilted in a faint surprise. "It is not ungallant, nor, Madam, is it false. I did not lie when I told you we had met before. We have—though not in this life. Nothing is accidental. It is written in God's Book of Words that our destinies conjoin and run together. Not all your protests, no, nor mine, can change Fate's ultimatum."

That scene, etched in memorable detail, was now unwillingly revived. She had striven to forget it, but she could not. . . . How he had sought her in the gallery at Theobalds on an afternoon when the King, the Queen and all the Court were at the hunt. She had excused herself on plea of megrim and had taken a book and herself to a seat in an alcove where she had hoped to remain undisturbed ; but not for long. A footstep on the polished oak came treading softly. The sun-glint through stained glass dyed his gold-laced doublet crimson, blue, and purple, casting stranger colours on his hair. There he stood with no apology for his intrusion ; and there he sat, on the cushioned seat beside her, and, as if he were continuing an interrupted conversation, "Have you no heart ?" he had murmured. "Yet I know you are all heart. I love you so completely. Yes, I do presume to love you. For all your laughter— and you are full of laughter—I discern a sadness as of one who jests to hide a scar. You have been wounded, sweet . . . but I will heal you. Give me your life to mend. Give me your hands."

He knelt and took and held them to his heart. She felt the fever in his blood and her own leapt to meet it.

"Dear," he said, "my very dear. Give me to hope."

"What you ask," and how she found the voice to tell him this she did not know, "is the impossible. I ", unflinchingly she forced herself to say it, " am almost thirty-five, and you are twenty-three. Even were I disposed to countenance your over-bold assumption, disparity of years would render it ridiculous, and——"

"God be praised !" To her immense alarm he interjected, while his face expressed profoundest, gay relief. "Is *that* the obstacle ? Then I can hope—and dare to ask again. Unless—" he whitened in a sudden panic, "unless—— Do you mislike me ?"

That momentary betrayal of his depleted confidence had infused her with an urgent, mad desire to take his sensitive young face between her hands and comfort it.

But: "There can be no question," she had firmly said, "of liking or misliking. I have not considered——"

"Will you——" He dropped his eyes from hers, turned her fingers over in his palm, and lifted them lingeringly to his lips. He wore no beard upon his chin, no hair upon his cheek; his downbent head leaned nearer, his forehead touched her breast. "Will you," he whispered, "not consider now?"

His arrogance, and a something more about him that discovered in herself exquisite resurrections, was no longer to be borne. Half mesmerized she heard his words, muffled against her heart. "Age is man's counting of the years. Man has made time his own, defying God, within whose sight a thousand years is but a yesterday. Love is ageless. Dear . . . my dearest. . . . Do not spurn me for my youth."

"Not for your youth. . . ." She had raised his head between her hands and looked at him. All that he was feeling had carved faint furrows from his nostrils to the corners of his mouth, not tilted now; close-lipped. "Not for your youth," she said, low-voiced, "for mine, that I have lost."

"Not lost," he told her tenderly, "not lost, but only waiting. Your youth is here. I give it back to you for all you can give to me. A poor return, I grant. Mine is the advantage. I go starved for human contact, a mind to match my own. I read your thoughts. I think you can read mine. I can look up to heaven and say—there dances the same star that nursed us both. I seek for beauty and I see that the women of my age—since you must have it—are harsh, metallic, parrot-squawking drabs. Nothing to choose between them and the trollops of the town, save that they, poor wretches, are paid in coin for their attention to man's pleasures. . . . So must I be denied a wife because in our small, vicious circle, hemmed with whores who pass for virgins, I can find none that would not degrade my body or the name it bears? Would you have me mate with one of these, when here in you is beauty? . . . You have hands like flowers." He crushed her hands in his. "I ask you now to give me life. You *are* my life. If you have ever loved—men say you have —they say so, I don't care. But if you have suffered such a love as this, then bear with me in pity." His tears had fallen on her fingers. "You have me utterly," he whispered. "I am yours . . . and I am devastated."

So, with that, was she.

But from his too stormy kiss, from his sobbed gratitude, she bore herself away. This must not, could not go on.

She was thankful for her Aunt Mary's invitation. To the house in Broad Street he would never gain admittance. But he did . . . with stolen meetings in this very chamber, in this garden that her window overlooked, and which opened by a wicket-gate into a lane. That way would he come through the autumn dusk, and on that square of lawn would they pace together, he arguing, pleading, praying. . . . Would she not give him hope, a word, a sign, that he might live again? For her denial, her stern reticence, was death.

So here, now, in this room, where Mary, blundering had left her, she faced the crisis that all these last few weeks she had ignored.

A sickle moon, uprisen, hung low between the branches of a plane-tree; her gaze fixed on the silver-gilt edge of a cloud in the deepening sky, she relived the ghostly rapture of her first yielding . . . his wild kisses and his broken words. . . . To what was she committed? To what end this sweet, dark fever that immersed them both, and which she resisting, could not any more resist? What promise had she given? None, since he refused what she had offered.

Her face burned again with hot mortification as she recalled his answer to the compromise she recklessly devised to ease his passion and surfeit her own.

"I see now that I have spent myself upon the air. Is this no more to you than appetite to be assuaged by furtive sweets? I would not sully my love's honour by such means. *My* love, mark you, not yours, which I perceive to be a lesser thing than mine. You have never said you care for me. Why should you? Do you not understand?" . . . He had turned to take her by the shoulders, his lithe young body rigid with vital tension. "Do you not understand that what I ask of you is not a mere adventure of the alcove, as if I feared to shout my claim before the world? You think I am too young to be your husband. Will you not think, as I do, that time is non-existent? You are ageless,—yes, and I am young, but also I am old, for in my scheme of calculation the love I bear you is eternal. Is it not enough for you to know that I am yours? . . . Or are you afraid to take me? Do you fear the King's displeasure? He will be tolerant. I am so far removed from the succession that my royal taint can be discounted. Is that why you are adamant? If so, destroy your scruples. I will approach Lord Salisbury and will put my case before him. Dear heart, do not, I beg you, turn from me. . . . I want you. I must have you . . . for my wife."

This then was the sum of it; this was his demand.

Seated there beside her open casement, gazing out into the shadows, Arabella knew her call had come. All that she had sought in loneliness, in dreams, the shared, imperious delights of sense and touch, of thoughts united, was here, in her hands, surrendered. . . . Would she have the courage to renounce it?

She was conscious as she sat there of a mist around the moon, of a dampness rising, and of chill upon her forehead. . . . She shivered, rose, and shut the window, shutting out the night.

* * *

Early in January Mary Shrewsbury received a summons from her husband that brought her all haste from Sheffield to her London house in Broad Street.

Arabella was out of favour with the King and in disgrace again! Worse still she had been placed in temporary custody pending an examination in the Council Chamber.

On arriving at her journey's end, frantic with anxiety, frozen with the cold, her bones aching with the jolts and bumps of a three days' drive in a springless coach, Mary was met by her daughters, the Ladies Kent and Pembroke. The tale they unfolded nothing lessened their mother's disquietude, though Bridget Sherland, who attended her, did not appear to be unduly apprehensive at the startling intelligence that Arabella had, without the King's consent, betrothed herself to the Prince of Moldavia!

"O, and everybody," chattered Mary Pembroke, "thought that she was after—you know who."

Her mother begged her to be more explicit.

"Why, young William Seymour to be sure. 'Tis the talk of the town how she, at her age, is affected."

"An affection which," put in her sister sagely, "may be a screen to hide her true intent."

"Yes! But why Moldavia? She must have known the King would never let her marry him. A foreigner and Papist—and nothing of a principality. O, 'tis shocking how she shows herself so hot to get a husband, never mind that he be prince or pauper or a beardless boy. And now she's up before the Council for her sins. O, madam, can you believe it!"

278

Madam could not believe it. Nor seemingly did Bridget, whose philosophic phlegm in the face of pending danger exasperated Lady Shrewsbury as much as it surprised.

"Gracious heaven, woman, have you naught to say but wink the eye when Arbelle may this very moment be in prison ? Her Ladyship has overstepped herself this time, mark me !"

"Madam, I mark you very well," Bridget said with chuckles, "and I think my Lady Kent is not far out in her surmise. The screen her Ladyship puts up to hide her true intent is too . . . transparent."

"The Lord knows," murmured Lady Shrewsbury, distracted.

Her husband's arrival at the house, with a face as long as the account he gave of her Ladyship's examination before the Council of which he was a member, threw little light upon the case. It seemed that Arabella emphatically denied any association with, or intent to betroth herself to His Highness, the Prince of Moldavia.

The Prince had certainly made her an offer which, without first approaching the King, was an inexcusable breach of etiquette, though Arabella vowed she had refused him. It was also true that Moldavia had shown her marked attention, had sat beside her at a banquet and led her in the dance. "But," Lord Shrewsbury with a pale smile told his staring wife, "I understand the Prince was less imbued with love's persuasion than by Rhenish wine when he declared himself."

"Which being so," said Mary acidly, "I cannot see why your lordship has seen fit to bring me in this haste from home."

"I sent for you," his lordship proceeded to explain, "since as a member of the Council I am powerless to aid her. She needs advice and guidance."

"When," his wife snappishly inquired, "has she ever listened to advice ? And as for guidance—she'll take the bit between her teeth and bolt before she'll answer to the gentlest curb—as you should know, but that she plays upon your sentiment, if nothing more particular, to make a dandiprat of you—her hoddy-doddy ! Do you think," demanded Mary, "I have not observed, in all these years, how you have been attracted ? And do I care ? I know my duty to her, my dear dead sister's child, and I hope that you know yours—within *some* bounds. But let me warn you, Shrewsbury, that do you show yourself too eager to protect her, you may lose your seat upon the Council, and be hauled before the Chamber as a party to her tricks and malice—well-conceived—aforethought."

Which unkind interpretation of his genuine concern for Arabella's latest misadventure, so greatly discomposed the blameless gentleman that he refrained from further interest in the whole deplorable affair. Meanwhile Arabella, having cleared herself before the Council, was now called upon to clear herself before the King. Apart from her reported betrothal to the Prince she was more than ever heavily in debt, and had written to Lord Salisbury begging for a further increase in her allowance. It seemed she had been buying furnishings, upholstery, and gowns enough for a prospective bride. Moreover—there appeared to be no end to her demands—she petitioned that her father's house at Hackney, disused since his death, should now be rendered habitable.

It was obvious she contemplated marriage, but if not with Moldavia, with whom?

According to her Uncle Shrewsbury, when that point had been raised by the Council, the lady, with due reverence and humility had answered, " Ask yourselves, my lords, what subject in the realm would risk His Majesty's displeasure by approaching me, who by the King's command am placed beyond approach ? "

" As your Ladyship," Lord Salisbury replied in silky tones, " has been and ever will remain beyond reproach."

So much for the Council, but not enough yet for the King. She had still to account to him for herself, and the Prince of Moldavia.

What occurred between the cousins at that interview has never been revealed, save that Arabella returned from it restored to highest favour, with concessions. Not only had she wheedled out of James an income from the sole monopoly on sales of wines in Ireland, but she also obtained his promise, none knew how, to take as husband any subject in the realm on whom she laid her fancy, providing his estate and rank were suitable, and he was not a Papist.

That the King received her with an obstinate frigidity which exhausted all her charm to overcome, that she twisted him to penitence and melted him to tears, we may believe. But that James, when he pledged his promise she might marry whom she chose, had overlooked the one man in his kingdom whom he feared, is unbelievable. Yet thus it was, and for what followed James could only blame himself.

What did follow raised a hubbub, not only in Court circles but throughout the town. In alehouse and tavern, in mansion and market-square, tongues wagged for a whole week of nothing else . . . The Lady Arabella, first cousin to the King, was betrothed, handfasted, to young William Seymour!

The fat was in the fire, the Court was in a buzz, and Mary Pembroke smug and very knowing. *She* could have told a thing or two, but nobody would listen. Plain enough had been her cousin's motive in parading Moldavia as suitor, and thus bringing the attention of the Council and the King to bear upon her sad unmarried state. What cared she for His Majesty's displeasure, or any temporary punishment she may have suffered by this linking of her name with a principality abhorrent to the King? In so doing she had gained her ends and His Majesty's rash promise. . . . " O, yes," said Mary Pembroke, " and I knew so all along. You think I see no farther than my nose."

Indeed the Court, till then, had thought so. It was now inclined to change its views. Mary Pembroke's wit, it seemed, was sharper than her shape! The darkest hints were rife as to her Ladyship's decision in favour of a gentleman so very much too young for her, though not too young to win his way, it would appear.

The archest gossip of the Court, one Mr. Beaulieu, secretary to Sir Thomas Edmundes, the King's Ambassador in Brussels, lends a spice to his formal diplomatic correspondence, when he cattily remarks : ' These affectations of marriage in the Lady Arabella do seem to give advantage to the world of impairing the reputation of her virtuous and constant disposition. . . .'

So what would be the end of this beginning?

As might have been expected—immediate arrest. This time both offenders were brought before the Council Chamber for interrogation, which resulted in a pledge to King and Councillors that neither in this life would meet again.

They met again within the week at the house of a Mr. Bagge.

He, an advocate of some repute and a bachelor of means, was a friend of William's cousin, Edward Rodney.

On a February evening under cover of the dusk, Arabella, attended by her steward Crompton, Anne, and Bridget Sherland, left her aunt's house to walk, cloaked, hooded, masked, through London's streets : a bold adventure.

Crompton, stout, stately and black-bearded, walked a few paces ahead waving his wand of office against intruders in his path ; and notwithstanding the anxiety of this, her secret mission, Arabella's quick glancing, inquisitive eyes imbibed with interest the teeming spectacle of life abundant, and as far removed from hers as hell from heaven.

Twilight, draining colour from garish shop signs and mellowed brick and timbered house fronts, lent a dim enchantment to the scene. The orange glare of lanthorns flung an iridescent lustre like snails' slime on greasy cobblestones. From behind the closed red-latticed windows of inns and alehouses issued a bluster of voices, rowdy song and shouting. Every alley sheltered footpads on the watch for drunken roisterers, with one eye alert for the constables or catchpoles on their rounds, that, however, led them more often to the neighbourhood of tavern than of crime. In lurking shadows painted women plied their trade, hailing each other with raucous greetings from their posts. Their bold eyes unenviously raked the fine masked lady who betrayed her high rank by her dainty steps and a pucker of disgust under her nose, as she picked her way among the refuse where their feet habitually prowled.

A group of gnomish boys were playing shovel-board beside an open drain, while a noseless drab, half comatose with drink, her face scarred with disease, her grime-encrusted breasts protruding from her rags, sat among them crooning to herself unheeded, and unheedful of all but her concerns that were centred in an unceasing tuneless song, and an intermittent scratching of her parts. On perceiving the advance of Crompton and his party she produced a clapper-dish and banged on it for alms. But the pence that Arabella, holding her nose against the stink of her, flung the creature from her purse, were seized upon with hoots of glee by the urchins in the gutter, despite the shrieks, curses and buffetings bestowed upon them by the rightful recipient of charity.

As the evening deepened and lights festooned the dark like smoke-wreathed garlands, so did the pushing, jostling, shouting, scrambling of those who went about their lawful, or unlawful occasions, increase. The raucous parrot urge of ' what d'ye lack ? ' from the 'prentices at their doorways mingled with the bedlamite confusion of street criers, 'New brooms, green brooms', 'Buy a mat', 'Hot peas'—and the not unmelodious sing-song of fish-wives, 'Whiting, maids, whiting, who'll buy my sweet fresh whiting?'

As they passed the gates of the Fleet prison-house a piteous din rose up from the dungeons, moans, groans and howling entreaties: 'Bread and meat, for the mercy of God—bread and meat——'

Arabella halted, horrified. "Good God! Are those poor wretches living there below the earth like starving rats?"

"And rats they are," answered Bridget callously. "Why harbour criminals, at all? I'd hang the whole lot of 'em had I my way. Why keep them alive to feed and batten at the King's expense? They'd be less trouble dead. . . . Mind how ye step, here's a puddle o' mess."

With a stifled scream Anne Bradshaw raised her petticoats high above her ankles. "How much farther," she complained, "will Crompton walk her Ladyship through this disgusting filth? . . ." Another furlong, before he halted them outside a house in Fleet Street. This, somewhat larger than its neighbours, had an air of opulence in the ornate carving of its timber and the brightly painted gargoyles that grinned from every beam. A massive figurehead of monstrous ugliness guarded the iron-studded door, which, in answer to Crompton's imperious knock, was opened by a grey-bearded bald man in a bottle-green doublet and crimson hose. Myopically, but with undisguised suspicion, he peered at the arrivals.

Crompton importantly spoke.

"This, sir, I believe, is the abode of Mr. Advocate Bagge? Do I address Mr. Advocate Bagge?"

Intimating, with equal importance, that he did address Mr. Advocate Bagge, the bald-headed gentleman ushered them in, and led the way along a panelled passage into a room scarcely large enough to hold its wealth of furniture, joint-stools, tables, chairs, and a great dresser laden with pewter plates, cups and tankards. At a long trestle-table on which was spread a redundance of food and wine, sat William and his cousin, Edward Rodney: a keen-eyed, sharp-nosed young elegant, this, in a doublet of red satin laid with gold and silver lace.

As Arabella entered William went swiftly to meet her; taking

283

her hands to kiss, he turned to his gentleman: "Edward, you may leave us now; and you, my sweet," he dropped his voice, "send away your woman and—" his eyes crinkled into laughter, "your excellent Malvolio. Have you seen the King's company of players in 'Twelfth Night or What You Will'? He—" jerking his head in the direction of the much offended Crompton—"is the living spit of one of them for pomp and gravity—and as I live in almost the same dress! Your man wears yellow hose and is cross-gartered too. Are you, sirrah, a comedian?"

Disdaining this impertinence, "Sir," with immense hauteur, queried Crompton, "is it your wish that I also shall retire with the gentlewomen?"

"You read my thoughts, Malvolio! You may go until I call you back, when we'll all sup here together. I can recommend my host's metheglin, which I doubt not you'll sample while you wait. Mesdames," he bowed with a flourish to Anne and to Bridget, whose grin had broadened till it looked to split her face, "of your indulgence do you trust your lady to me. I must have her to myself for a short while. . . ."

What occurred in that 'short while' may be gathered from this letter which he and she devised, and presented as William Seymour's signed submission to:

'The Right Honourable, my most singular good Lords, the Lords of His Majesty's most Honourable Privy Council.

May it please your good Lordships: Since it is your pleasure which to me shall always stand for law that I should truly relate under my hand those passages which have been between the noble Lady Arabella and myself, I do here in these rugged lines truly present the same to your lordships' favourable censure. . . . I do therefore humbly confess that when I conceived the noble Lady might, with His Majesty's good favour and no just offence, make her choice of any subject within this Kingdom, I did plainly and honestly endeavour lawfully to gain her in marriage, which is God's ordinance common to all.

I therefore boldly intruded myself into her Ladyship's chamber, at what time I imparted my desire unto her which was entertained—but with this caution on either part, that both of us resolved not to proceed to any final conclusion without His Majesty's most gracious favour and liking was obtained. When I was convented before your Lordships I did deliver as much as I now write, before them; and now protesting before

284

God upon my duty and allegiance to His excellent Majesty, and as I desire to be retained in your Lordships' good opinion, there is neither promise of marriage, contract nor any other engagement whatsoever between her Ladyship and myself; nor was ever any marriage by me or her intended. . . .'

Having got thus far and doubtless at his love's dictation, we may take it William was unwilling to proceed.

"Neither promise, contract, nor whatever! By God's living soul," he swore, "I'll not sign my name to such a blatant lie. Would you have me play the cur and disclaim you to the Council? Be damned to them—and this!"

"You do no worse," she soothed him, "than did Abraham and Isaac, who both for a time disclaimed their wives."

"I am not a patriarch, nor yet am I a Jew," was the rejoinder. "For my honour's sake, if not for my love's, I'll tear this—burn. Let me!"

He seized the paper as if to throw it in the flames. She stayed his hand.

"So burn it and you burn our hope of life together. I know the King and how to treat with him. He's humoursome—as stubborn as a donkey and as fickle as the moon. But give him time to chew his wrath and he'll digest it—and forget it, and be kindly to our cause."

As she believed; and after some persuasion so did William. In his letter to the Council he specifically mentions that meeting at the house of Mr. Bagge; and it is not unlikely Mr. Bagge's professional advice was called to bear upon the legal aspect of the document, which after much re-writing was eventually despatched.

It served its double purpose, as Arabella had foreseen, in convincing James, not only of young Seymour's subjection to himself, but of a reassuring lack of ardour in his attachment to the 'noble lady'. Lulled into the belief that Seymour had now recovered from his infatuation, James speedily restored her to high favour, presented her with a cupboard of plate, and paid up the arrears of her debts to the tune of ten thousand crowns. Thus having settled the affair to his own and to her satisfaction, James returned to his boys and his hunting. . . .

Arabella returned to the Court.

Chapter Three

IN June of that year, 1610, Henry was created Prince of Wale
The rich gave balls and banquets to celebrate the great occasio:
the poor declared their joy no less sincerely in the sharing of the
cakes and ale among the beggars of the town. These, with a vag
bond mob at their heels, tinkers, cutpurses and doxies, pedlars ar
counterfeit cranks—those who with the aid of a mouthful of so;
lay foaming in well-simulated fits to play upon the pity of tl
gullible—all turned out *en fête*, along with the most respectable
citizens, to watch the Prince's barge come up the Thames.

London pealed its joy-bells; every street was gay with ga
lands, loud with cheers. From the river bank girls pelted him wi
flowers; lads yelled for him as he stood in the bows, his cap
his hand, his lips full of laughter, his eyes full of tears, emblem
England's youth: regeneration.

When his barge stopped at the steps of Whitehall the dee
throated love of a multitude rose to a roar as, rejoicing, th
welcomed him, laid their hearts' hope in him, heir to all Britai
their Prince . . . who was never their King.

From a window in the Palace Arabella watched beside tl
Queen, whose heart was big with pride; she blew him kisses. H
returned them, calling up a greeting to his mother as he passe
The King at his window, his eyes a-pop, stood in the fidgets, finge
ing himself. A pest upon the shouting! This lad of his receive
more favour from the people than was ever shown for him.
noise to blast your ears. . . . He closed the casement with a slam
but the noise went on all night. There were bonfires and dancir
in the streets and a banquet in the Palace. The Prince and h
gentlemen dined in the Great Hall. The King dined alone wi
Robert Carr.

The next day a grand masque was presented by the Quee
entitled 'The Queen's Wake, or Tethys' Festival'. The first ha
of the performance had been specially designed to give Charle
Duke of York, a chance to appear in a children's masque, assist
by twelve little girls of his age.

While all eyes were on the pageant, Arabella, with Lac
Shrewsbury, stood aside in an alcove, and hushed confabulatio:

"So," Mary said sepulchrally, "you need have no qualms.
our Uncle Henry and my sheepish husband, who trembles in his
oes to raise his voice for you, but yet works silently on your
half, both approve of your decision. You know my views—
t I do wish that Henry were here and not in France. For all his
ppancies, my brother is clear-sighted and shrewd enough in his
lvice, when called upon to give it. In his letter, received today
y courier from Paris, he expressly urges you to hold yourself in
tience both before and *after* the event. The King will never
and upon his order. You can twist him any way you will—but
ide your time."

"Dear Aunt!" Arabella caught gratefully at Mary's sleeve.
You take too much of my misdoings to yourself. I do not fear
e consequence for me, but if those I love should suffer for my
ult——"

"A fig for consequence!" hissed Mary. "Your happiness is
y first care, and you've had little happiness in your life to miss
hat God may give you now. And I'll warrant," she determinedly
lded, "that there'll *be* no consequence worse than a dust-storm
hich will settle so soon as the breeze has passed. You have the
ing's own word that you are free, and he cannot gainsay it."

"Yes." For a second, as a raincloud that will brighten to a
ash of sun, Arabella's face glowed, then as swiftly darkened.
But I've no right," she said, "to take *his* freedom from him.
e is young and I—" again that watery gleam—"I'm bound to
lmit I was cutting my capers before he was cutting his teeth!"

"Why will you harp on this note of your age?" Mary asked
ith impatience. "Forget it, but remember this. A woman is
ver as young as she looks, and a man is old—when he *ceases* to
ok. So keep yourself young for him while you've still some-
ing to show. . . . 'Sh!" Her quick eyes slewed round to warn
er: "No more now. Here comes Mr. Fowler. Why don't you
ke him? He's made of money and yours for the asking."

"Him!" rejoined Arabella with noiseless ferocity, "I'd as
ef bed with an eel."

Mary's lips quirked at the corners; then eyes and voice ecstati-
lly raised for the benefit of the approaching Mr. Fowler, "How
lightfully His little Highness dances," she exclaimed, "I declare
ever in my life I saw a cherub sent from heaven to bless us with
is beauty and his—— Why! If it isn't Mr. Fowler! Sir! . . .

You startled me. I did not recognize you in your merman's dress. Are you already costumed for the masque?"

"Madam, I am not," answered Mr. Fowler stiffly, "costumed for the masque. Nor do I represent a merman."

But anybody might have been mistaken that he did. His doublet of green satin was patterned in a jewelled device, representing what appeared to be fish-scales. His sleeves were slashed with cloth of gold and silver; his hair dyed flaxen, fell to his shoulders in lovelocks after the latest style affected by gentlemen of fashion. Ignoring Lady Shrewsbury's unconvincing murmurs of apology, Mr. Fowler elaborately bowed to Arabella.

"Madam, I am bidden by Her Majesty to remind your Highness that the masque which your presence will so gloriously grace, is due to be performed within an hour of midnight."

"Save my soul! And here am I not dressed. I'll have to hurry. . . ."

Her tiring-women had to hurry too, to have her robed in time for her appearance in the costume chosen for her by the Queen and designed by Inigo Jones. Extravagantly beautiful, it had cost whoever paid for it—but certainly not Arabella—something in the region of a hundred thousand crowns. From a helmet of coral and shell hung a thin veil of gauze. The bodice of sky blue taffetas was lavishly embroidered with every kind of maritime invention. A short tunic of cloth of silver cut in points to the knees, was inlaid with golden thread. Under this a lace petticoat, with nothing much beneath it but her bare legs, fell to her feet, and—so we have it on contemporaneous authority*—'waved round about them like a river, and on its banks and sedges, seaweed, all of gold. Her shoulders were embroidered with the same work as the short skirt of silver, cypress spangled and ruffed out to fall above the elbow, the undersleeves all embrodered as the bodice. . . .' The night was hot; her dress was cool. She made a great sensation.

The scene of the masque was set in a sea-cave with glittering stalactites composed of precious stones. In the midst of this, plump, smiling, resplendent, reclined Queen Anne as Tethys with her nymphs in groups and attitudes around her. Each represented a river of England: Princess Elizabeth the Thames; and Arabella the Trent.

So great was the press of people who had obtained invitations

* Nicholl.

o witness this magnificence that the Lord Chamberlain, to ensure seating accommodation for all, issued a command that no lady would be permitted to enter in a hoop.

The masque was followed by a banquet that went on all through the night till sunrise, when those of the guests who could walk went to bed; the rest of them stayed at, or under, the table until they were fetched by their servants.

That ended the season's festivities. Soon after the King, Queen, and the Court moved to Greenwich; and in their train followed, but at a safe distance, to lodge near the gates of the Palace, the ubiquitous and ever-hopeful Mr. Seymour.

The State apartments occupied by Arabella opened on a terrace that overlooked the Thames, divided from it only by a lawn. There in that strip of garden, enclosed by box and privet, she, with her gentlewomen walked, or sat at her embroidery under a sycamore tree; or sometimes she would sit alone, hands folded, idly watching the reflection of the willows in the river, musing on the strange, deep life that stirred unseen beneath it; musing perhaps on its unending, inevitable course that wound timelessly, for ever, to the sea.

And with that tranquil march of summer it seemed to those faithful few around her, Mary Shrewsbury, Anne Bradshaw, Bridget Sherland, that the restlessness by which she had been utterly possessed was calmed and she at peace, as if she had stolen from that shining drift of water something of its unconfused determination. And often too, it seemed to them that she had embodied in herself the very spirit of this nymph-like summer, its brightness and its gold . . . and its fulfilment.

Even the Queen, whose powers of observation had never been considerable, remarked to Mr. Fowler that her Ladyship looked young enough, of late, to be her daughter; and waited for her secretary's disavowal of this not at all exaggerated statement. But no contradiction came from him who in silence suffered, but with less tragic consequence, the same increasing unrequited passion for the Lady Arabella as had poor Mr. Starkey.

On the evening of the longest day, June 21, Mr. Fowler having noted that his lady loved to walk beside the river towards taper-time, decided he would walk there too on that midsummer night. Mr. Fowler recently had witnessed the King's players perform 'A Midsummer Night's Dream', and was filled with fantasy. If he could find ' that little western flower, called Love-in-idleness ', and touch Her eyelids with that same magic herb, a miracle might come to pass : or it might not.

Mr. Fowler was a poet, and he may have been absurd, but he had faith and he believed in fairies ; and if despite the spate of verse that poured from him in praise of Arabella, only the smallest fragments have survived, they were none the less inspired by whole-hearted adoration. Mr. Fowler was quite hopelessly in love.

With his writing tablets in his pouch, a silver ink-horn in his hand, and dressed in subdued moth-grey as befitting the occasion, he, on that midsummer evening, stole from his apartment in the Palace. Stepping carefully, tiptoe, he made his way to the river-lawn facing her Ladyship's parlour. There by the water on a bank he would sit and watch the fairies at their revels. On such a night as this Oberon, bestride a moonbeam, might well go courting his Titania. Mr. Fowler would go courting too. . . . She surely would be tempted out to take the evening air. Reduced to desperation Mr. Fowler would declare himself, confess his worship, grovel at her feet. At the worst she could but laugh at him and he was used to that.

Placing his ink-horn on the dew-wet grass he spread his hand- kerchief to save his suit, and sat. The air was still, unstirred by any whisper of a breeze ; gnats danced in the dying sunshafts across the dusky water where tree-shadows sank, drowning. From the fields, bereft of workers now, came the scent of hay and meadow- sweet and clover. In that brooding quiet sounds were hushed ; the twitter of a sleepy bird, the bark of a dog, the plash of a risen fish. Light deepened in a sky of rose and gold to spend itself in one last fierce embrace of warmth and beauty. The brightness sank, and behind the tender flush of its fading shone the first ray of the moon.

Spellbound, Mr. Fowler watched that slow uprising. . . . Gold. And full as the sun, but so soft the eye could rest upon it without strain. " O, wonderful," ejaculated Mr. Fowler, " Chaste Diana. Artemis. Goddess of the night. . . . Madonna."

He rose, and, solemnly, he bowed ; then took his tablets from his pouch, his quill from his sleeve, and in ecstasy he sat again and wrote :

' Great learned Lady whom I long have known, and yet not known so
    much as I desired,
Rare Phoenix whose feathers are your own, with which you fly and
    are so much admired,

Come like the golden moon, new out of bed, and cast your eye upon
  this little Book.
Although you be so well accompanied with Pallas and the Muses,
Spare one look upon this humble . . .'

A bat flew in his face, and inspiration fled. Mr. Fowler had a
mortal fear of bats. With a faint shriek he dropped his tablets, and
in his haste to rise and ascertain that the creature had not settled
in his hair, he knocked over the ink-pot. The contents were spilled
on his grey stockings, and on his shoes that had cost him a small
fortune. Rosettes were going out, buckles were coming in, and
Mr. Fowler had indulged himself in the last cry of fashion to
purchase silver buckles set with diamonds.

Horror seized him as he gazed at the hideous black stain
poured upon those jewelled trifles, and on his delicate silk hose.
How truly dreadful! He could not kneel before his goddess so
befouled. He was undone.

Dejectedly he stood considering. Should he return to his apartment and change his shoes and stockings, or hope that the darkness
would cover him? Or was it now too late to hope at all? If she
were coming she would have surely come.

"Hell's misery!" ejaculated Mr. Fowler.

He stooped and gingerly removed his soaking shoes, twiddled
his toes in his stockings that were wet through and black as——

"Hell!" repeated Mr. Fowler.

Darkness gathered round him. The moon hid behind a cloud,
through which gleamed a faint shiver of gold. . . . Midsummer
night indeed! Yes, Puck himself had jerked that ink upon his
shoes for mischief. So much for fairies. Demons more like. . . .
He would take himself home and to bed.

He picked up his tablets, and, catching sight of the ink-pot,
gave it an unpremeditated and quite savage kick. It went soaring
in a silver curve to fall with a plop in the water. He had not meant
to kick so hard. Certainly some superhuman force, hobgoblin, imp,
or whatsoever, was abroad this night to plague him. And his
precious ink-horn, ally of his pen, source of inspiration without
which his Muse was impotent, now lay at the bottom of the Thames
and irretrievable. . . . But was it? The water here could not be
very deep.

Mr. Fowler carefully descended the slope of the bank, and

holding on to the branch of a willow, he leaned over, peering down. From those beslimed watery depths the blurred face of the moon grinned up at him, then ducked again behind that cloud which was thin as a fairy's shift.

"What fearful pranks," groaned Mr. Fowler, "does this night play with me?"

For in that strange effulgence all things were magically distorted; the spear-like blades of rushes, the evil shapes of pollard trunks were black as a witch's cloak, their gnarled arms outstretched as if to clutch at Mr. Fowler. He trembled, but resolutely turning his back upon fear, he gazed down into the sluggish water in the hope of discovering a silver gleam that would indicate the whereabouts of his lost ink-horn. And suddenly he heard a sound—a very small sound, which might have been no more than the scuffling of a water-rat among the reeds, but in that eerie, ill-conditioned place it so startled Mr. Fowler that he had all to do to save himself a tumble in the Thames.

Regaining his balance he stood in vibratory palpitation, to see the prow of a boat come nosing round beneath the aspens, not twenty yards from him.

A boat!

Mr. Fowler experienced relief.

No unearthly visitant was he who invaded these private waters in a boat. No; this nocturnal trespasser was bent upon more mundane purpose. Robbery! Mr. Fowler could deal better with a thief than with a fairy.

Garnering his courage, he was about to leave his ambuscade and shout the alarm to the sentries, when even as he turned to clamber up the bank, he suffered greater shock than any yet imagined. He who with silent agility leapt from the boat was no thief; nor was he a stranger. The pale trick-light of the moon shining full on his face as he stooped to secure his craft to a projecting snag, revealed him plainly.

The eyes of Mr. Fowler almost started from their sockets; his receding chin fell till he looked to have none. Stunned, half-paralysed and open-mouthed, he watched the intruder draw his cloak across his face—too late; watched him creep, a solid shadow in the deeper shadows of the privet, till he reached the angle of the terrace that led to the apartments of the Lady Arabella. Mr. Fowler grappled with suspense. The blood beat in his ears to drown the

lamour of his heart, as in fearful agitation he stood, hoping against
ope that the window of a lady in attendance on his goddess, and
ot Hers, was this clandestine objective . . . Was it? Was it
ot?

A ray of lanternshine gleamed out between the stealthily divided
urtains. There for a second a woman's form appeared, outlined
gainst the light, her hand upraised in a gesture to beckon, her
oice hushed to a whispering call.

And the love-witched heart of Mr. Fowler froze. . . .

There was no man in Britain in more wretched case than he
/hen he wakened from his midsummer night's dream.

*   *   *

Nor was there a man in Britain in more wretched case than
3ritain's King when he heard the consequence of that night's
1eeting; but not from Mr. Fowler.

Though his divinity had basely fallen from her shrine, he
uffered disillusionment in silence. Mary Pembroke was the first
o voice the news, and to her mother, having found the burden of
er cousin's confidence too heavy to be borne.

And: "O, Madam," wailed Mary, "she is lost but she *is*
1arried."

According to this same informant, with whom Arabella had
ppeared to be uncommonly communicative, William Seymour, on
hat June night, had visited her in her chamber and stayed there
ll daybreak. Then a priest was called and in the presence of her
entlewoman, her steward Crompton, and William's cousin, Rodney,
he, who had been named prospective Queen of England; she
/ho might have been the Queen of Poland, of Denmark or of
rance, became the wife of Mr. William Seymour.

"Can you conceive such wickedness!" lamented Mary. "Only
1ink of her deceit—and the King so tolerant and generous towards
er. O, madam, I could no longer hold my tongue and keep my
romise not to tell a soul. I could not have it on my conscience.
Vedded and then wedded! O, the shame!"

"More shame, surely," was the dispassionate reply, "were she
edded and *not* wedded."

"O, madam," expostulated Mary, "how can you be so gentle
1 the face of such catastrophe! Do you not understand? She
as married Mr. Seymour without the King's *consent*."

293

But even this announcement did not appear unduly to disturb

"Go run and tell your sisters. Go tell the Maids of Honour Go screech it from the housetops, but do not," her mother begged her, "pester me."

Mary regarded her mother with dawning suspicion.

On Lady Shrewsbury's thin lips an evasive smile hovered; he low-lidded glance eluded Mary's.

"Is it possible," her daughter gasped, "that you alread knew?"

It was not only possible, but highly probable; and very soo the whole Court knew, the Queen, the Prince of Wales, and hi sister. The King was the last to know.

He eventually heard it from Ludovic of Lennox.

If Ludo, by the offer of so savoury a morsel, had hoped to regai his former place in His Majesty's affection, he was thwarted. Jame received the news, and Ludo, with a brainstorm. He thundered oaths; he called down curses on his cousin, Arabella. He praye the Lord destroy all issue of the hated house of Seymour. His eye bulged. A vein swelled in his forehead; his face became em purpled. He looked to have a stroke. He cuffed the Duke o Lennox, who turned white beneath his paint and fled the Presenc wishing he had never entered it.

The King raged on. His pretty pages slunk behind the curtain and stood quaking. Robert Carr administered a posset. Jame gulped it down and choked and blubbered on Carr's shoulder, an kissed him warm and flabbily, and bade him: "Go fetch my Lor of Salisbury. I must take counsel with my gude Lord Salisbury . . .' Then falling on his knees he prayed: "O God, confound thi Witch of Endor. May the Lord God Almighty give me guidanc to mete her a richteous punishment that she account for this misdee with her life's blood!"

A shocking exhibition. . . .

Thus returned to the quiet of Hatfield after a thunderou scene with his monarch, Salisbury reviewed it and the cause thereo

This young woman certainly had always been a nuisance. Fron her birth and through two reigns she had proved herself to be— "a most infernal nuisance," murmured Salisbury. But that th King should rave in so unseemly and undignified a fashion, and i a state that seemed to border on dementia was, to Salisbury' impartial reasoning, a trifle in excess of the situation's gravity

The case, without doubt, called for censure; yet the King admitted
—and had signed his name to such a pledge—that he agreed to her
marriage with any subject in the realm of high enough estate, and
Seymour undoubtedly was that. Perhaps, reflected Salisbury, of
too high an estate.

Opening a drawer in his table-desk he drew from it a parchment.
An almost imperceptible compression of his lips betrayed uneasiness as his eyes scanned his own careful presentation of a
genealogical tree. He took his pen and poised it above the name
of Arabella Stuart, and beside her name he wrote in his diminutive
clear lettering: 'Married William Seymour.' Glancing at the head
of that punctilious chronology, a tiny crease appeared between his
brows. From this same source, the seventh Henry, flowed these
twin Tudor streams—Stuart: Seymour: and his place in the
succession but twice removed from hers; both near enough, were
they sufficiently supported, to revive their mutual claim through
her by reason of her English birth, and, more indirectly, through
young Seymour. The obsolete Act of Attainder could, were it
brought forward, place her in priority for the throne of England.
The King had been born an alien, and as an alien he had ascended
without one voice raised against him. Would that voice remain
for ever dumb, or would it give utterance now that these two were
one, united? The late Queen had feared this girl—or rather she
had feared the interest of Spain that centred in this girl; and not
only Spain but France, and all of Catholic Europe. That fear had
been abolished by the peaceable accession of James Stuart. Yet
might it not be revived by those—and in particular the Papists—
who for so long had sought to press the Tudor right of Arabella,
and regain the throne of England for themselves?

If James suspected these rash young people of more than merely
amorous intent, then his fury, although uncontrolled, might not
have been unwarranted. Yet Salisbury, who had known the Lady
Arabella all her life, could not believe her capable of treachery.
Reckless, high-spirited, wilful—yes, she was that and more, but not
malevolent. Yet, what under heaven could have induced the
foolish couple so to deceive? Why, having recovered the King's
favour and his promise that he would not show himself inimical to
her desire for marriage, must she make a secret match of it? Why
could she not have put her case before him, and by so doing shown
that she had no dishonourable motive? Why go to such

meretricious lengths to gull the King, not only by presenting to the Council Seymour's statement that they would never meet again but his solemn vow that between the two no promise of marriage nor betrothal had existed ? Which was, on the face of it, a brazen lie. They must have foreseen that the King would be justly indignant at such sharp practice turned upon himself. It would appear they were content to take that risk, relying on his genuine affection for his cousin to condone this last extreme.

Frowning, Salisbury tapped an irritable finger on the document before him. . . . Fools ! Then as a ghost might have smiled so did he. His pale forehead poised beneath the grizzled hair was calm, his face unmoved, devoid of all emotion ; the eyebrows lifted, the lids lowered. They would likely find, he mused, their secret game was scarcely worth the price they'd have to pay for it.

Replacing the paper he had taken in the drawer where it belonged " Dear fools," he sighed, a very little, " and their folly. . . ."

Nor could all his intervention or plans on their behalf conciliate his outraged Sovereign one iota. The King had spoken and the graceless pair were brought before the Council and committed he to the Tower, she to the custody of Sir Thomas Parry, Chancellor of the Duchy of Lancaster.

Her steward, Crompton, and Seymour's valet, Reeves, both of whom had been present at the marriage, were sent to the Marshalsea in Southwark. Edward Rodney and Anne Bradshaw were brought before the Council and examined ; but luckily for Bridget Sherland she and Lady Shrewsbury, having sponsored the secret wedding from a distance, were not involved. After some close questioning Anne and Rodney were dismissed, but forbidden any communication with the chief offenders.

They, despite their separation, were not unduly pessimistic. Both believed the King's free pardon would be offered once his indubitably righteous indignation had been given time to cool. Neither had reckoned with, nor understood, the obstinate perversity of one whose very weakness was the direct result of that pre-natal psychological reversion, the murder of his mother' paramour before the eyes of her who held him in her womb. His mind was thwarted, and his crippled soul went shamed, seeking cover from its spiritual deformity in an introverted love for its own kind. The affection he hitherto had borne for Arabella needed but the slightest jerk to turn it into hate ; a hate that shadowed his unconscious life, a hate allied to fear—the buried voice of Darnley crying vengeance upon Woman. And in his heart he feared *this* woman who had strengthened her claim to his throne by taking for husband a Seymour.

The pair were a menace, a threat to his Kingship. If from this marriage issue resulted, he and his sons might well be deprived of their heritage, and a Seymour dynasty established. But more than all of these horrific possibilities was James shattered by the shock of her deception. She had deceived, not only him but the name she bore, the clan he represented. With fair promises and fairer words, she, nearest of kin to him after his children, had tricked him—played foul to the Stuart.

For that he could never forgive.

In justice to James he had reason to rage ; in justice to her she had done what she did with no motive behind it save love. She was blind ; and still blindly, her head in the sands of illusion, she wrote :

. . . 'and though Your Majesty's neglect of me and my good liking for this gentleman that is my husband drew me to a contract before I acquainted Your Majesty, I beseech you to consider how impossible it was for me to imagine it would be offensive to Your Majesty, having given me your royal consent to bestow myself on any subject of Your Majesty's . . . If Your Majesty had only vouchsafed to tell me your mind and accept the free will offering of my obedience, I could not have offended Your Majesty of whose gracious goodness I presumed so much, that if it were as convenient in a worldly aspect as malice may make it seem to separate us whom God hath joined, Your Majesty would not do evil that good might come thereof. . . .'

To this plausible petition, as might have been assumed, James maintained a lofty silence, while he hastened her removal to Sir Thomas Parry's house. There, for the present, and at the King's pleasure she would stay. Nor had he yet devised what further punishment he would inflict, while in silence still he brooded.

So far the penalty the King exacted from the two was not severe. The suite of rooms allotted to William in St. Thomas's Tower were in the same quarter as those then occupied by Raleigh, overlooking the Thames on one side and the inner court upon the other. His apartments, however, though large were unfurnished, a default that was soon to be remedied. Having wheedled from his grandfather, Lord Hertford, a substantial monthly sum for his maintenance, which Sir William Waad, Lieutenant of the Tower, was nothing loath to accept, William purchased tapestries at ten pounds apiece and sent to Arabella's house at Hackney for beds, linen, silver and all else that his comfort required.

She, meanwhile, had turned her charm with some success upon Sir Thomas Parry.

The rooms set apart for her in his house at Lambeth were luxurious. She ate off gold plate and slept in a bed fit for a queen, richly canopied and curtained. She was permitted to walk in the garden that sloped in terraces down to the Thames ; and although Anne Bradshaw had been forbidden to communicate with her, Arabella so played upon the tender heart and sentiment of Parry, that he contrived to find a situation for Mistress Bradshaw in the house and in, presumable, attendance on his wife.

Once assured that William in the Tower suffered as little material discomfort as herself, Arabella centred her immediate concern upon her steward, Crompton. He and William's valet, Reeves, were in grave danger of contracting prison fever, a plague of which had recently infected Marshalsea.

She wrote to the Council entreating their removal, for : 'I am informed that divers near that prison and in it are lately dead, and others sick, of contagious and deadly diseases. . . .'

Which request eventually was granted.

While her imprisonment and William's appeared to be so purely nominal and their jailors so ready to oblige, willing intermediaries were always near at hand to carry messages between the house at Lambeth and the Tower ; but only one of these, from her to him remains extant.

'I am exceeding sorry to hear you have not been well I pray you let me know truly how you do and what was the cause of it. If it be a cold I will impute some sympathy between us, having myself gotten a swollen cheek at this same time with a cold.

For God's sake let not your grief of mind work upon your body. You may see by me what inconveniences it will bring *me* to ! And no fortune, I assure you, daunts me so much a that weakness of the body I find in myself, for " Si nous vivons

l'age d'un veau " as Marot* says, we may by God's grace be
happier than we look for in being suffered to enjoy ourselves
with His Majesty's favour. But if we be not able to live to it
I, for my part, shall think myself a pattern of misfortune in
enjoying so great a blessing as you so little a while . . . Where-
soever you be or in what state soever you are it sufficeth you
are mine.'

But letters, however sweet, by no means sufficed William. He
must see her. . . . In his tower-room he raved to Rodney, whose
admittance there to him appeared to be as free as Mistress Bradshaw's to her lady. Rodney must—he positively must—bring
Arbelle to visit him. Impossible ? And why impossible ? Certainly
for William it would be impossible to visit her. The Tower gates
were too well guarded. But there could be found a way.

He dragged Rodney to the window, pointing down. " Do you
see here ? Under this archway is a postern, and when the tide is
low there is a beach—a yard or so of mud——"

He had discovered a stair—never mind how—that led from
his apartment to some sort of dungeon or cellar immediately below
the Traitors' Gate. The postern that gave access to the cellar was
always kept locked, but Arbelle could be brought there in a boat,
and through the bars he would talk with her. . . . " For the love
of God bring her ! She complains that I don't write enough, that
my letters are nothing but dirges. How can I write ? What are
words ? "

Poor food for lovers to feed upon apart ; nor could such frugal
fare for long content them.

On a night towards the end of September Arabella left the
house at Lambeth accompanied by Anne and Crompton. He and
Reeves, by her earnest intervention with the Council, were now
at liberty. The King bore no continued grudge against the Seymours' servants : his anger, undiminished, was directed to themselves, and it seemed his intention was less to persecute than to
ignore the pair. Their circumstances might have been much worse.

Crompton, now provided with accommodation in the kindly
Parrys' household, advised Arabella to wait until the moon had
waned before she undertook so perilous a venture. And never did
the moon shine so full and far beyond its span, or thus it appeared

* Clement Marot, popular poet at the Court of François I.

to her who nightly prayed for an eclipse. At last that clear, cruel light was dimmed and sank. Her spirits rose. A boat was commandeered and brought to the landing-stage at the end of Sir Thomas's garden. Arabella played cat's cradle with Lady Parry until ten o'clock, when, after a nightcap of mulled wine, Lady Parry curtsied to her guest, and went to bed. Her husband went to bed. Arabella went to bed; undressed, and dressed again. Anne gave her a cloak to wrap round her and a pair of thick stockings to pull over her shoes. Crompton had warned her of mud. She was finally handed a basket of eggs.

"For heaven's sake, why this?" she wished to know. "Do they starve him in the Tower?"

"In case," Anne explained, "we are seen by the Watch. We should be prepared for emergency. I'm carrying butter. We go as market women—but the Lord knows I do not want to go at all."

Anne disapproved: of Crompton and his high-handed manner —"Do this, do that, dress her Ladyship thus—bring butter and eggs and keep silent." She disapproved of the way her lady flirted with her host to dupe him, the while with artful condescension she transported his good wife by offering her royal cheek to kiss. She disapproved of Arabella's whispers, nods and giggles, as unbecoming to her lady's years and state. In fact, though heart and soul Anne Bradshaw loved her lady, she immensely disapproved of the whole business.

The night was close and warm, the sky a velvet vizard through which shy stars peered faintly. The river, dark and sluggish, and at that hour devoid of traffic save that of merchant-traders coming up or going down, reflected little light. On the palace side Whitehall lay wrapped in gloom. The Court had moved to Theobalds and with it all of fashionable London. The city folk were fast in bed, the risk of discovery slight; but not slight enough for Anne's composure. She clutched her basket, hoped for the best, and greatly expected the worst.

Beside her in the stern Arabella sat and hummed a song, and every now and then she laughed below her breath. She dabbled her hand in the water and withdrew it to fling drops in Anne's lengthening face. "Pooh, you! What a kill-joy you are to be sure. You remind me of that flower the French call mignonette—a prim tight-petalled little flower that never dares unfold itself for fear

300

lest a bee steal its honey. . . . O, God! Why so slow? Tell the boatmen make haste. We shan't be there till daybreak."

They were there within ten minutes. As William had foretold, the receding tide had left a narrow beach of mud and pebbles under the arch of the wharf. Directly above it loomed the Traitor's Gate and over that, standing out across the moat, the tower where William lodged. The river-wall, deep in shadow, cradled the skiff as it grounded. With one eye alert on the watch for the sentry, Crompton handed his lady out and led her, ankle deep in mud—she was glad of her woollen hose—to the postern where William waited.

A melancholy meeting-place for lovers. They dared not speak above a whisper, hands touching, lips fruitlessly seeking between the iron bars. But the dreariness of their surroundings, the musty smell of damp, the inky-black interior of that noisome cell, the squeak and scuttle of unseen rats, the slime of river-weed and refuse, and all their present danger, passed unheeded in the sweet surprise of passion re-aroused.

"O, to feel you," William breathed. "But I can scarcely see you. I dared not bring a light. I bribed my warder. He is cautious. He forbade me a torch or even a candle. . . . How I've starved for you!"

There was so much to say and not a word to say save love reiterated. Their eyes fed upon this darkened and divided image of each other, that mocked the longing thirst of flesh to flesh.

"Your mouth!" he yearned. "I want it. . . ." Rose-red and tremulously offered in the ghost of a kiss through a grating. His outstretched groping fingers touched her eyes. "Sweet one . . . I too have wept. I'm frenzied. This continued separation is torture's uttermost refinement. I plan, I scheme, and yet I see no way."

"Have patience," she guided his hand to her lips for comfort. "God will find a way."

"So you believe. I wish I could. I am so full of book lore and philosophy that I've forgotten God if ever I remembered Him. I can't—I cannot and I will *not*——" He broke off savagely to shake the bars as if he would uproot them. "I'll tear these down. I wish you hadn't come. You are my Tantalus. Here for my ease within an inch of me and my starvation is fruit and wine and——"

"Eg-eggs!" Laughter warred with her held tears. "I'll pass

them through to you. Do they feed you well enough in there, my soul?"

"Eggs!" He gazed at her despairingly, then laughter seized him too. Helplessly, hysterically, they giggled.

She wiped her eyes, "O mercy! I am glad that we can laugh. Is your cold better?"

"No. I'm full of cold. Only you can warm me."

"Here, love, take them. I only brought them as a blind, in case I might be . . ." her voice faltered to a memory of some such other time when in similar disguise and with a basket she had stolen out to meet another love.

Chapfallen and in silence she passed eggs to him through the bars. He dropped one and it cracked and spilled.

"I don't *want* eggs!" he shouted, "I want you!"

"Don't speak so loud. You will be heard."

"I wouldn't care. I *want* you. I must have you. I'll go mad if I don't have you. . . . Yes! Our canny monarch may deserve felicitation in having chosen this particularly subtle form of vengeance. I envy and admire his finesse. He is an artist, point-device in exacting the extreme of gentle torment without the use of rack or thumbscrew. I would welcome either in the place of this accursed separation. My nights are unendurable. I dream of you, exquisitely, and wake to find the bolster in my arms. . . . That amuses you. I too am glad that you can laugh."

"I am not . . . laughing."

"Only one so utterly perverted as our beloved King could have devised so delicate a punishment. I am given such unnecessary cruel reminder of your sweetness. Among the things your men delivered here from Hackney is a glove. Your glove. I found it in a box full of books and scented with the same perfume as that you used upon our wedding-night. I remember a mole beneath your left breast. . . . Must I never see or touch you? I'll break these!" With renewed vigour he again attacked the bars. The whites of his eyes glinted dangerously; there was wet about his forehead. She wriggled her hand through and touched it.

"How needlessly you do torment yourself. . . . We'll find a way. Tell me of your plans."

He glared at her.

"So! You think my torment needless. 'Tis evident that you have never suffered as I do. As for my plans—they soar with the sun and sink with the moon. Short of instigating regicide I *have* no plans."

"Be quiet!" Her face, moon-pale in the moonless dark, gleamed up at him. "You will most certainly be heard, and that'll be the end of you—and me."

"This *is* the end of me! This goddamned miserable situation, stuck here like a pig in a poke——" He ground his heel into an eggshell, "but I'll tell you this——" Fury was submerged in his mischievous, enchanting grin, "I've induced my brother, Francis," William said, "to shave his beard. Without it he resembles me enough to act my deputy. You shan't come here again. I'll come to you."

Her lips parted.

"If you could!" she breathed. "I can manage my Sir Thomas. My imprisonment is farcical, but yours——"

"I'll work it that my exit shall be greased. That villain, Waad, so worships money that he'd rob his mother's corpse for twenty crowns. I'll bribe him to the hilt to let me out of here upon parole. Others do, so why not I? I've not approached him yet, because I wait for Francis to remove his precious beard, which he has been at pains these last two years to grow. Even if Waad shows himself accommodating I must have a standby, since I'll only be permitted out by day and within bounds. . . . Hell! Here comes your man and there's the boat. You'll have to go. Give me your hand again."

She slid it sideways through the bars. He covered her palm with frantic kisses. "Such a little hand to hold me in its hollow. . . ." She felt his tears and stayed her own, and leaned her mouth to his between the rusted iron.

"God bless and keep you safe," she said, "my soul."

And then she turned and hid her face and went from him.

Huddled in the boat she sat, her eyes fixed on those great bastions and turrets of London's citadel. Seen in the night's un-glistening obscurity it looked to be a fortress of the dead, stark reminder to the living of the unrestful grey procession that trod this same unending path along the centuries, and through the Traitor's Gate.

She shuddered. In the tower-room above that gate her love lay prisoned, lost to her. No, never lost. . . . Behind her tears she smiled. Nothing is lost. The grass still sprang as bravely between those bloodstained stones. Birds mated in the buttresses that had frowned upon the murder of King Henry's wives, and of a gentle, innocent, uncrowned Queen, and on that other whom her heart shrank to name. They had said he died in scarlet. ' Though their sins shall be . . .' All now in memory as white as snow. . . . And within those walls the grandmother of him whose wife she was, had borne her sons. Life entwined itself with death, a passing in, a passing out, as certain and continuous as this unwearied river's journey from its eternal source down to the sea.

*   *   *

The autumn months dragged by; days shortened and nights lengthened while those venturesome two met and loved, and met, to love again.

The stone walls of William's prison could not encage him. Ready palms received his lubrication. His brother Francis shaved his beard and lay in his bed in his room, while Sir Thomas Parry's not too watchful eye avoided ladders hoisted underneath a window in the moonlight. And he, already slightly deaf, turned deafer still to sounds and murmurs drifting from the chamber of his charge, when she and all the household should have slept.

His good wife complained of ghosts. A housemaid saw one —the apparition of a monk in a cowl who crept across the lawn and vanished. So did all the servants who would not stay, they declared, to be haunted. Arabella kindly made up the deficit in the domestic staff by sending to her house at Hackney for her own.

Christmas came, but with it nothing more substantial than the echoes of carousal crossed the river from the Palace to the house on Lambeth Marsh. Yet if James were determined to ignore her, Arabella was equally determined he should not. She beleaguered him with more petitions for his pardon, and though none of these was answered she continued, optimistically, to write :

' May it please your most Excellent Majesty, the unfortunate estate to which I am fallen by being deprived of Your Majesty's Presence (the greatest comfort to me on earth) together with the opinion of me conceived by Your Majesty's displeasure towards me, hath brought as great affliction to my mind as can be imagined. Nevertheless touching the offence for which I am now punished, I beseech Your Majesty to consider in what a miserable state I had been had I taken any other course than I did. For my own conscience witnessing before God that I was then the wife of him that now I am, I could never have matched with any other man but to have lived all the days of my life as an harlot, which Your Majesty would have abhorred in any, especially in one (how otherwise unfortunate soever) to have any drop of Your Majesty's blood in them. . . .'

Impervious still to this plea, which was admittedly less humble than defiant, James continued to ignore her existence. To him, his Court, his Council, and to all intent and purpose, Arabella was not only banished, she was dead. But the house at Lambeth proved to be less of a tomb than a tryst. The unseasonable bitter cold that froze the Thames in early March could not freeze William's ardour. On the contrary it served to heat it more. He did not have to row across the river, he could walk, and with his wife, upon it. The icy dusk embalmed them in their bliss.

None came to that far bank, or none whose business it would be to recognize a pair of lovers wrapped in furs and lying on a bed of rugs spread beneath the willows. The drooping hoar-rimmed branches, like some chilled dryad's hair, enclosed them in an icicled oblivion. And in that amorphous world, wrought of brittle silver-white embroidery, where sunsets were redder, and shadows more vividly violet, seen now in oyster-coloured twilights under the ice-green stars, those two kissed and comforted each other, and talked the inconsequential foolishness that has been lovers' language since time immemorial.

And sometimes they talked of their future, made plans unsolid as the vapour that rose from the marsh, and melted with their breath upon the air.

When this cruel separation was forgotten and the King's pardon, so slow in coming, obtained, they would leave England. They would live in France. . . . Yes, but Navarre, who would have welcomed them, was dead. She sighed for him whom she had never known and now would never see. He had been assassinated in the streets of Paris in the May of the previous year.

"Which removes," said William jealously, "one more potential husband from your past. . . ."

Or they would live in Florence, the Flower City. On the Ponte Vecchio they would tread behind the ghosts of Dante and his Beatrice. They would dream before the frescoes of that exquisite immortal, Fra Angelico. They would go to Venice, Spain, America. The world was their adventure, a world wherein they two would voyage for ever . . . always. "No secrecies, no schemes, no shifts to hold you in my arms, no nights apart. . . . O, God," he groaned, "how long have we to wait?" He clutched her closer. "If I tell you something you are not to fret."

"I do not fret when I am with you."

"That's the point." His eyes left hers. "Francis greeted me this morning with a tale of his beard. Without it his resemblance to myself, or so he says, is too singular for safety. Yesterday in the Exchange a catchpole clapped him on the shoulder and would have walked him to the Council in the hope of a reward, but that he had, luckily, a letter in his pocket proving him to be my brother and not me."

"Does that," she asked him faintly, "mean——?"

"It means, my beautiful, that Francis is a craven-hearted cur whose first concern is for his skin and not my need. He told me straight enough he would no longer play my double—in such a double game. I wouldn't care if it were only warders I must pass. They're easy, though I'll warrant I'll not have a crown with which to cross their palms before I'm out of there. No, 'tis not my good jailors who present a difficulty, but that hell-hound Waad. He has been tightening his watch of late, yet so far he has not been unde-ceived by Frank's face upon my pillow when he's on the prowl o' nights."

"But," her startled gaze upon him widened, "it is not only nights you come to me. What of the days? Is Francis not standing deputy for you this very minute?"

"No," said William glumly, "that's the devil of it. Not now or any minute."

"There's a rat he is!" she breathed. "In that case I'll never see you. I'll not have you come here at such a risk. Why did you not tell me before?"

"Risk!" he scoffed; then violently kissed her. "I only tell you now lest I may not find my way here quite so often, since Frank decides to grow his mangy beard."

She laughed a trifle shakily.

"Pity 'tis that *I* can't grow a beard!"

"Thank God! But I—" he rubbed his chin against her cheek, "I can. Feel this."

" So that's it! I believed you careless, now you're wed, to come courting with a stubble. 'Tis golden as young corn. Hi! Don't! It pricks."

" It'll prick more when it begins to sprout, and 'twill serve as a precaution while I'm officially described as ' a fair smooth-shaven man, just under two yards high.' I read that notice in a list of us who lodge in Sir Thomas's Tower. We're docketed that all who read may know if one escapes, for what to search. Well! I'll no longer be smooth-shaven. I'll be hairy."

She sighed. " I'll hate you hairy."

" Will you so ? We'll see——" he caught her to him, bearing heavily upon her. From under their heaped rugs came an ominous, thin sound. " S'death ! " cried William, " now the ice is cracking ! "

In their absorption they had not observed that the fiercer cold had lost its sting, and that a low mist had gathered on the marsh as herald to a thaw.

William sprang to his feet, swung his wife off hers, carried her to the near bank, and set her down.

" So here is where I leave you, sweet," he murmured.

Crompton all this while had kept a faithful watch upon the pair. He now approached. His nose was blue, his face was pinched, his grievance bitter. He wished himself and his lady in the Indies and his lady's husband somewhere warmer still.

" I'll come again tomorrow," William promised.

Tomorrow and tomorrow came. . . . A succession of to-morrows came ; but to the house on Lambeth Marshes William came no more.

Chapter Four

THE thaw set in and the King set out—with his Court to hunt at Royston. There from early morning until dark he rode to hounds, shot several stags, played dice with Robert Carr—the recently created Viscount Rochester—danced reels and got mildly drunk. In such and other pleasant pastimes did he seek diversion from anxiety.

The King was greatly troubled. His Commons were causing

a pother, to plague him. They had refused his good Lord Salisbury's demand for six hundred thousand pounds to pay his debts; not that such a trifling sum would pay the half of them, when his good lord's accounts showed him to be one million and three hundred thousand down. He had, however, hit upon a scheme approved by his Lord Treasurer whereby he could raise money. Having discovered that the first patent of Baronet or little Baron had been granted to Sir William de la Pole in 1340, which title, not consistently hereditary had long become extinct, James decided to revive it.

At the charge of one thousand pounds per head he would confer baronetcies on sundry gentlemen of good estate, who would be willing to pay for the privilege.

But the Commons were as usual argumentative and captious, and moreover they had taken exception to his greatest, wisest, and most forceful speech delivered some few months since.

'Kings', he had told them, 'are justly called Gods, for they exercise a manner or resemblance of divine power upon earth. If you will consider the attributes of God you shall see how they agree in the person of the King. . . . They have power to exalt low things and abase high things, and make of their subjects like men of chess—a pawn to take a bishop or a knight. To resist the King,' he declared in a voice to shake the rafters, 'in any of his acts or impositions is sedition, for the King is above all laws. . . !'

He bit his tongue and swallowed blood and sat in deathly silence. His Commons stared astounded, then in a body rose, not to cheer but to utter their defiance. Yes! They dared defy Him! Calumny. And as near to it as made no matter—treachery! They had told him flatly he extolled his kingship to the detriment of Magna Charta, which, with unsurpassed effrontery they reminded him, had laid certain and eternal limits to the rights of kings. Finally, and in direct opposition to and disregard of Sovereign Power, they appointed a committee to question the points raised by His Majesty's speech.

He had never yet recovered from that insult, nor from the defeat of his bishops and lawyers in their loyal support of his dogma. A certain learned cleric, Doctor Cowell, who in his 'Interpreter, or Law Dictionary', had broached unmitigated maxims of Divine Righteousness, was received with loud vituperation when he contended that 'the King is Absolute'.

And even Francis Bacon, for whom James till then had entertained the mightiest regard, conducted the case for the Commons against Cowell to the ultimate suppression of his book, and his imprisonment.

James had been forced to eat his own words and condemn his own champion. Shocking! No monarch had ever suffered such indignity from Parliament. And in his heart James may have much regretted the failure of the Plot to blow it up.

So with his coffers low, his temper high, and his good Lord Salisbury looking, James was grieved to see 'most fearfu' frail', he retired in the month of March to Royston. There in bucolic rusticity he would forget his tribulations. He was not allowed forgetfulness for long.

An ever-present gnawing, miserable worry, which by sheer force of will he had relegated to a false oblivion, hurled itself into his holiday humour.

Sir William Waad, Lieutenant of the Tower, had sent a message to the King to the effect that Mr. and the Lady Arabella Seymour had, on several occasions, evaded custody and met in or about the vicinity of Lambeth.

This news caused James another brainstorm, which terminated in the adjectival, ultimate decision to deprive Sir Thomas Parry of his charge. Having exhausted his vocabulary, his Viscount and himself, the King sat down and signed a warrant for the transfer of the Lady Arabella to the care of:

' The Right Reverend Father in God the Bishop of Durham,
    We greet you,
    Whereas our Cousin, the Lady Arabella, hath highly offended us in seeking to marry herself without our knowledge (to whom she has the honour to be so near in blood) and in proceeding afterwards to a full conclusion of a marriage with the self-same person whom we have expressly forbidden her to marry, after he had in our Presence and before our Council forsworn all interest concerning her either past or present, and with solemn protestation upon his allegiance . . . we have therefore thought good out of trust in your fidelity and discretion, to remit to your custody the person of our said Cousin, requiring and authorizing you to carry her down in your company to any house of yours as unto you shall seem best and most convenient, and to take order for all things necessary either for her health or otherwise.

This being, as you see, the difference between me and her, that whereas she hath abounded towards us in disobedience and ingratitude, we are still apt to temper the severity of our justice with grace and favour towards her, as may well appear by this course we have taken to commit her only to your custody, in whose house she may be so well assured to receive all good usage, and see more fruits and exercise of religion and virtue. . . .

From Royston this 13th March, 1611.'

The Bishop of Durham was greatly dismayed on receiving this royal command. He had no desire to take to himself so rebellious and wilful a charge, but the King's word was law and his diocese at stake should he ignore it.

He departed for London. The journey was long, the Bishop of Durham was old. He arrived at Lambeth much fatigued, to find the household in confusion, the lady in hysterics, and Sir Thomas Parry in a huff. The Council had, that very day, issued him a warrant demanding instant delivery of the Lady Arabella to the care of the Bishop of Durham.

Sir Thomas took this action as a slight upon his trust and an insult to himself and his good wife, who for many anxious months had been at pains to guard and cherish, and with unstinted hospitality and considerable expense, to entertain the Lady Arabella.

When that morning he approached her to impart with gentle tact the Council's latest order, she made a fearful scene. She accused him of betrayal. She had believed he was her ally. She knew he winked at ladders and never stayed her going out or coming in. Had he not encouraged her to walk upon the ice? Did he not supply fur rugs for her convenience? Who in their senses would walk on the ice, bearskins or no bearskins, to freeze, unless reduced to desperation?

"As *we* were," she screamed, "torn apart, divided. Always scheming, planning creeping, like thieves, to meet for half an hour. . . ." Was she not bound by holy matrimony, for better or for worse, to William Seymour? Would Sir Thomas put asunder two whom God had joined? Would Sir Thomas welcome separation from *his* wife? Maybe he would.

Sir Thomas swallowed something, tried to speak, was interrupted.

Yes! No doubt at all he would. He had been married thirty years, she not half so many months. And sure to goodness any man whose heart was not a stone would be tolerant to aid her. Sympathetic. . . . "I'll be given to the devil," she heatedly declared, " sooner than the Bishop, for my sins ! "

She paused for breath. The scandalized Sir Thomas offered tentative persuasion, to no more purpose than to start her off again.

The Bishop in the meantime had arrived.

The interview that followed with the Lady Arabella has been recorded by the Bishop as 'most painful'. His announcement that the King had ordered her departure for Durham that same day occasioned shock. She had not thought to be so hustled ; she had hoped to play for time, gain some respite to send William a warning.

While the good old Bishop knelt and prayed the Lord, ' Dispel this wayward humour and induce a more resigned and humbled spirit ', Arabella wildly devised what next to do.

She decided there was nothing more she could do but to faint. And so she fainted.

Restoratives were brought, and in Anne Bradshaw's arms she whispered : " Get a message to the Tower for God's sake. He can't come here. And send for Doctor Moundford."

He, appointed her physician in attendance for some years, had at the King's request, visited her regularly while she stayed at Lambeth to ascertain that she was in good health. James was nothing if not ultra-conscientious.

The Bishop went from prayer to prayer and she from swoon to swoon. With tales of saints and martyrs and their tortures endured without moan in the service of God, the good Bishop essayed to revive her and make her see reason. He served only to make her see red.

Doctor Moundford arrived and was intercepted by Anne at the landing-stage. He examined the lady, administered doses, pronounced her condition severe. The Bishop rose from his knees, and extolling her Ladyship's virtue, bade her have patience and summon her courage and start on her journey to Durham. Her bags were not packed ; she must take what she could. The rest, he assured her, would follow.

Dr. Moundford emphatically objected. Her Ladyship was in no state, he said, to undertake the first stage of her journey in a day. Her pulse was slow, her heart was weak, her frequent swooning symptomized a fever, if not death.

The Bishop, much alarmed, sent a message to the Council

imparting the doctor's report. This brought a hasty warrant by return to the effect, that, since the Lady Arabella was unfit to take the first stage to Barnet in a day, she would be allowed to lie the night at Highgate at the house of Sir William Bond. A courier had already been sent in advance to advise Sir William of her Ladyship's arrival. Highgate was not an hour's distance from the Tower. And, "If I die," she told Anne, whispering, "I swear that I will not be further north from him than Highgate Hill. I'll *never* go to Durham. . . . So now I'm going to faint again, for luck!"

They carried her to Highgate in a litter.

*　　　*　　　*

The King returned from Royston, well content with his manœuvres to shape his irksome cousin to his will. His Council and Lord Salisbury had appeared to be in complete agreement with his plan for her removal from the danger of propinquity. Secret meetings, lovers' vows and any such romantic folly would henceforward cease, and the unrepentant pair be brought to heel.

One only member of the Council, Gilbert Shrewsbury, had the temerity to protest against, and voice appeal to the King for some mitigation of the penalty. The Lady Arabella, he reported, had been taken ill upon the journey from Lambeth to Highgate. Her doctor pronounced her too weak to be moved to Barnet from the house of Sir William Bond.

In his recounting Gilbert did not spare the King the least detail of Arabella's sickness, which was manifested in high fever, delirium and fainting fits. In truth, Lord Shrewsbury assured the King, the lady's condition was parlous.

"And how," with goggle-eyed suspicion, James inquired, "have you learned so much of her ill-health, my lord, since to our knowledge you have sat in conclave with the Council on the matter these three days?"

"My wife, sire," was the diffident reply, "is anxious for the welfare of her niece. I have this news from her."

James rolled his tongue around his lips, then thunderously he swore: "By Jesus! I'd forgot the kinship there. Let me warn ye, my Lord Shrewsbury, be careful how ye show yeself too ready to champion the cause of one who has so bitterly offended. The duty of a Councillor is to support the King. As for our cousin's vapourings, 'tis enough to make a sound man sick to be carried in a bed the manner that she was, to say naught of the impatient and unquiet spirits that possess her. So of your goodness, leave her to our Bishop's ministrations and our will."

This interview, when reported by Gilbert to his wife, decided that determined lady on an instant course of action.

After having duly rated her husband for a fool to show his hand and all but lose his post by seeming over-anxious, no matter his opinion or affection, or God alone knew what weak sentiment he suffered on behalf of her—disgraced, it was his game, if not his duty, to follow the King's lead, nor never lay his cards upon the table. So let him shut his mouth and keep his peace, and leave his wife, who had more sense in one small finger than he in all his parts, to deal with this appalling crisis—"which," concluded Mary, "will require woman's wit to resolve with circumspection. What you've to do," she intimated strongly, "is to hold your tongue, sign all decrees, and show some sense—you sheep! Unless you wish to follow William to the Tower."

Which sound advice induced from the greatly distressed Gilbert a doleful letter to his good friend, Dr. Moundford, in which he states, 'I can doe my niece small service more than by my prayers.'

His wife, meantime, was active and in daily touch with William.

When first acquainted that his love was to be taken from him and imprisoned in the Bishop's house at Durham, he fell into a frenzy. His friends and jailors, no less, had all to do to hold him back from breaking bounds and his parole, and to go riding hell for leather up to Highgate. Anne Bradshaw was admitted to his tower-room with Rodney. Letters passed from hand to hand, and verbal fond assurances, recited tearfully by Anne, of his wife's constancy. He was not to fret, she said.

"Not to fret!" roared William. "Does she think that I'm a slug to sit here in my miserable sloth and let her go? . . . I'll rescue her."

"You'll not rescue her by shouting, to bring Waad to put you down and send us out," drawled Rodney, who truth to tell was somewhat sick of the affair.

If Rodney was regretful that he had been embroiled in such complicated circumstance, Francis Seymour bitterly deplored his own support of it. He had sacrificed his beard, he had sacrificed his pleasure. He had a girl at Wapping whom for three weeks he had not seen, since his nights were spent in prison and in his brother's bed instead of hers. He had run the risk of gravest punishment had he been discovered. He was prepared, he said, to run the risk no more.

It is to Rodney's credit that, despite a no uncertain fear for his own skin, he did not desert his cousin in his need. When Francis, with those last words, had departed, Rodney promised William he would stand by him and by his lady to the end.

" To what end ? " retorted William. " To the block—or to our freedom ? " Of which he now despaired. Yet at all costs, and at all risks, if it meant murder, so he raved, she must not go to Durham. He could never reach her there. Or maybe he could. . . . He was past reasoning. He paced the floor. He gnawed his finger-nails. He presented to the languid Rodney the most astonishing outrageous schemes whereby to rescue her. He would strangle his keeper, leap from the window, shoot Waad—or the King—find a horse. " I must have a horse ! Get me a horse. I'll ride up to Highgate tonight. I'm allowed out of here on parole. For the love of Christ, Rodney, do *some*thing ! " He kicked at the stool on which Rodney squatted. " Don't *sit* ! "

Rodney rose.

" Her aunt, Lady Shrewsbury," he said, " may prove resourceful."

" Then go to her—go ! " implored William.

Lady Shrewsbury had already proved herself resourceful. When the alarming news had reached her of Arabella's illness she drove at once to Highgate to find her niece in bed and in a swoon, the Bishop on his knees, at prayer, beside her, and Dr. Moundford solemnly protesting that he could not vouch for her Ladyship's survival if she were moved from where she lay.

At which Mary, expressing profoundest anxiety, wept and begged for a few moments alone with her niece. The doctor withdrew, the Bishop got up. He was stiff. His knees ached. He had prayed himself hoarse. He assured the sobbing Countess that he would despatch a message to the Council with a further report of her niece's condition, and hoped he would obtain for her a few days' rest before proceeding on her journey.

No sooner had the door closed behind him than Mary's tears miraculously stopped. Approaching the bedside, she gazed down at the face of Arabella, so colourless, so deathly white, it seemed that the blood in her body had ceased to flow. Mary, leaning over, gently rubbed a finger on her cheek. It left a smear; she rubbed again and smiled.

"An excellent good paint, my love. Does it deceive your doctor?"

"'Sh!" hissed Arabella, sitting up. "Dr. Moundford cannot diagnose my case. 'Tis one unknown to medicine—may likely be a plague. And the Bishop is most woefully near-sighted." She flung her arms round Mary's neck. "O, God, I'm glad to see you! Bridget came in the dead o' the night before last, and I swear you could paint the side of a house with what she laid on my face. As for the stuff she gave me to drink, I know her possets of old. Dr. Moundford forbade her to double the dose, which is all to the good or I might have been dead. The Bishop believed I was dying. He asked would I wish to hear prayers. I said yes, and he preached me a sermon. He gabbled all night. Not a wink's sleep did I have—nor did he. Poor old man!"

She began silently to laugh; and then, less silently, to cry.

Mary shook her.

"Stop that! You've been brave. You'll be braver. I'm working for you, and my plans are now ready. You'll do nothing more than what you're told. We'll contrive to keep you here a week before you go to Barnet. The longer the time the better for us. I'll have a word with Dr. Moundford. He'll corroborate the Bishop's letter to the Council."

"I," stated Arabella, mastering hysteria, "will not go to Durham. On that I am determined. Send for William. Bring him here. He must—I must—we *must*——"

"Now, now!" said Mary sharply, "calm yourself. All will be arranged. He'll come. You must have patience."

"Don't you spout to me of patience," Arabella gulped a sob. "I've had patience poured upon me by the Bishop till I drown in't! But I swear——" she thumped the pillows. In her ghostly face her golden eyes burned dark. "I swear by all that I hold holy, on my life and his, that I will *not* go to Durham!"

Despite her efforts at control she was near to breaking-point. The excitement and shock of these last few days had told upon a highly nervous system. She had it firmly in her mind that if she went to Durham she would suffer the same long dreary martyrdom as had Mary Stuart. She would languish and shrivel, fade away, and be brought for her end to the scaffold. Death, however, she declared, would be more welcome than lifelong separation from her husband.

The return of the Bishop halted these gloomy forebodings and sank her back upon her pillows in a faint. . . .

The Bishop's second report, despatched and endorsed by Dr. Moundford, brought a grudging consent from the King and his Council for another two days' respite, pending the Lady's recovery.

Two days . . . Much can happen in a day and more in two.

What did happen was William's arrival.

Reduced to desperation he flung caution to the winds, his month's allowance to his keepers, and with none to answer for his absence save a bolster in his bed surmounted by a mop of tow, and wrapped around with blankets to deceive a cursory glance, he left the Tower at midnight and rode to Highgate, there to find his love and leave her comforted.

His agony of mind appeased, starved senses satisfied, his hopes ran high. Let the King and his Council do their worst. He would *not* be thwarted. With the optimistic confidence of youth he believed that love would triumph over obstacles. He infected her with his enthusiasm. They kissed and wept together, loved again and laughed . . . and parted when the dawn was in the sky.

She was carried off to Barnet in the morning.

According to the Bishop, who has left on record an account of her resistance, they took her ' so much against her will that he was obliged to have recourse to means which were employed with decency and due respect. . . .'

That these means, however respectfully applied, did not bring her to her senses is apparent. They seem indeed to have had reverse effect, for we have it on the Bishop's own authority that her condition became so much worse that the men who bore her litter were compelled to stop six times on that short journey. Arabella, swooning, lolled upon her cushions while the doctor endeavoured to revive her, and the Bishop said his prayers and may have wished himself most fervently in Durham, and her sickly Ladyship elsewhere.

When the party eventually reached their destination, ' a sorry inn ' at Barnet, it was evident to all, and Dr. Moundford, that her Ladyship's malaise would not permit her to leave upon the morrow.

Once more the long-suffering Bishop appealed to the Council and to his petition Arabella added hers:

'May it please your Lordships: I protest I am in so weak case that I verily think it would be the cause of my death to be removed any whither at this time though it were to a place to my liking. My late discomfortable journey which I have not yet recovered, almost ended my days, and I have never since gone out of a few little and hot rooms, and am in many ways unfit to take the air.

I trust your Lordships will not look I should be so un-Christian as to be the cause of my own death, and I leave it to your Lordships' wisdom what the world would conceive if I should be violently enforced to do it. Therefore I beseech your Lordships to be my humble suitors in my behalf, that I may have some time given to me to recover my strength, which I would the sooner do were I not continually molested. . . .'

Their Lordships may have been less moved than alarmed by the hints that this message contained. They could not very well ignore them, nor the lady's state of health if the Bishop's and her doctor's word could be believed. To avoid catastrophe it was decided to grant her a month's rest, in which to recover her health and then resume her journey.

But the Bishop had now had enough of it. He could no longer neglect his diocesan duties. He must travel to Durham without her.

With renewed prayers and a blessing, and the somewhat tactless reminder that they would meet in the north, the Bishop left her and hurried away.

She was now placed in the charge of one Sir James Croft, a kindly old gentleman and a most worthy knight, who had been appointed her guardian in lieu of the Bishop.

She could not, however, remain at the inn. A house must be found for her nearby. A cottage at East Barnet on the outskirts of Hampstead Heath, owned by a Mr. Thomas Conyers, was placed at her disposal at the rent of a pound a week.

In this rural retreat she was installed, and there for the next few weeks she stayed. James, having reluctantly granted her one month's sick leave, was by no means satisfied by the reports of Dr. Moundford and the Bishop. He told the Council flatly he believed his cousin's illness to be feigned. If she befooled the

Council she could not befool the King. He would send his own physician, Dr. Hammond, to examine her, and woe betide the lady should he find her shamming sick.

Prepared by Dr. Moundford for the Court physician's visit, she summoned all the Stuart charm to meet him. The result of these beguilements is manifest in Dr. Moundford's letter to Lord Shrewsbury, in which he tells him : ' Her Ladyship begged that Dr. Hammond should be given private access unto her before he spoke with me. He entered into discourse of her infirmities, and pronounced her as assuredly very weak, her pulse dull and melancholy and for the most part uncertain, her countenance pale and wan Yet was she, none the less free from any fever or any actual sickness, but on his conscience he protested she was in no case to trave until God restored her to some better strength.'

James, bound to submit to this report from his physician, must now wait for the end of the month to expire.

It was clear enough to all the Council and Lord Salisbury, who throughout these disputations between the King and Arabella, had shown himself impartial, that His Majesty would not be swayed by sentiment.

If her Ladyship were ill she would be given all attention, but the penalty demanded—her retirement to Durham—must be paid.

Leaving the Council to debate the question at their leisure Salisbury returned to Hatfield. There, with his books and his garden, he could rest. He had aged considerably these last few years. The foolish extravagance and vacillations of a King who believed himself a god, had laid too heavy a burden of administration on those stunted shoulders. Nostalgic memories obsessed him of a halcyon era, and the extraordinary being whom he so long and loyally had served, and who, despite her vagaries and vanities her superficial ardours, was England's strength, and England's greatness . . . lost, and fallen now. He had hoped, had worked, and schemed for the unity of his beloved country with that warlike dour land across the Border. He had achieved his purpose, had made the two Great Britain, but he knew he would not live to see the fruits of his success.

His inability to meet the King's abortive demands for more money when the treasury coffers were drained, all this combined with the increasing anxieties of office in which none would wholeheartedly support him, had told at last upon that dauntless spirit

. . . ' Care and pleasure quake,' he said, ' to hear of death, but my life now desires it.'

At his table, in his oak-walled room he gazed out upon the joyous green of early June. Spring had melted into summer, and still the Lady Arabella stayed remote and guarded in her cottage at East Barnet. He could not but applaud her fierce determination to circumvent tyrannical command. She had outwitted the King and his Council, but she had not outwitted him. He stood withdrawn from the contention that seemed to have possessed the whole of Government to the exclusion, for this present, of all else. Too small a matter for grave men to squander time and substance in debating. Had he the power, or the mind to speak (or would they listen ?), he would have urged them and the King, whose pride more than his reason had prompted him to these severe extremes, to give free pardon to those two who had, Salisbury would swear, no other motive in their marriage beyond love.

That the succession to his rightful heirs might be jeopardized by this alliance between two distant branches of the House of Tudor, was absurd. James had three children. The Stuart dynasty was well assured. Why then such fear that his or his sons' claim to the throne could be questioned ? Did he think that England saw in this romantic pair, or in her who had the power, it would seem, to win her way with all men, a monarchy more readily acceptable than his ? James was unpopular ; she was loved. The country, to a man, outside the Privy Council—and not a few within it— stood behind her. Knight-errantry aroused would need but little more persuasion to bring revolt against the King's harsh treatment of his cousin . . . How history, mused Salisbury, repeats itself. So had Elizabeth, his mistress, in her youth and in the same revengeful spirit, condemned young Catherine, grandmother of William, to a similar cruel fate. But unlike the gentle Catherine, Arabella would not, he reflected, give in without a fight. All her life she had shown herself rebellious.

A thread of a smile wavered on his lips. He guessed, as did the King, if the Council did not, the truth of her swooning and vapours. She had hoodwinked, or charmed, Dr. Hammond as she had charmed Moundford, and that confirmed misogynist, James Croft, to be her mouthpiece before the Council. No doubt she might present a problem were she dangerously bent, but was she so ? . . . Enchanting, incalculable creature. Who could tell ?

Leaving that question poised upon his smile, Salisbury turned to the sheaf of correspondence his secretary had placed upon his desk.

Taking the first from the pile there, he read the most recent letter from Dr. Moundford to the Bishop of Durham, which that greatly harassed prelate had forwarded to the Lord Treasurer for his consideration. It told him little that he did not know, since he had been present at the hearing of the case for Arabella, urged by her latest custodian and suppliant, Sir James Croft.

Salisbury lifted an eyebrow. In truth this bewitching young person might be best out of the country than in it. She was become a menace to all men, regardless of their years. Sir James must be sixty if he were a day, but he had pleaded her cause with an ardour that belied his grey hairs . . . Yes, undoubtedly a problem, and one which must be solved by a good riddance, and the sooner the better for all concerned.

With some misgiving Salisbury recalled her impish look, her provocative blunt-cornered mouth, and those cats' eyes of hers, yellow, green or grey ? Her freckled schoolboy's nose, her irresist-ible temptation . . . No beauty was she certainly, but more danger-ous than beauty was her charm. . . . The Lord Treasurer would urge the King to let her go in peace, and be quit of her and of her husband. The two might prove to be a devilish combination should the Catholics glean support from foreign powers to divide opinion in favour of an English-born princess . . . What now from Croft ?

His smile deepened as he read :

> ' She hath not walked the length of her bedchamber to my knowledge ; neither do I find her at any other time but in her naked bed, or in her clothes upon it . . . As for her going this journey, the horrors of her utter ruin which hourly present themselves to her phantasy, occasioned by the remoteness of the place whereunto she must go, drive her to utter despair . . . Whereas, were she left, as Her Ladyship says, in some place " not so clean out of the world as Durham ", she would gather to herself some weak hope of more gentle fortune in time.'

Time . . . Yes, and a cunning device to gain it ! Salisbury flicked aside the closely written parchment. Were Croft and the Council so easily beguiled ? Another month's grace, forsooth, had been granted, yet His Majesty's decision remained resolute. It was a clash of wills between these Stuart cousins. Which of them would win ? . . . 'If I am King,' so James had sworn, 'I will not alter this—my resolution.' She in her turn had written a humble letter of thanks to the King, full of promises that 'while she breathed she would yield His Majesty most dutiful obedience to undergo the journey after this month, without any more resistance or refusal.'

But this meek submission did not at all diminish the King's doubt of her. To ensure the strictest watch upon her movements, he had ordered her steward, Crompton, and her gentlewoman, Mistress Bradshaw, to be dismissed her service. They were too fond . . . and too faithful.

In their place a Mr. Markham and a Mrs. Adams, a minister's wife, had been approved and chosen by the Council as above suspicion, and of unimpeachable integrity, to attend upon the Lady Arabella; and on pain of severest punishment they had been warned to discourage any communication, either by letter or in person, between her and her husband.

He, it was reported, lay sick and in greatest distress of the toothache . . . Again Lord Salisbury smiled. It might, he cogitated, be advisable to send a surgeon to extract by force, if necessary, the young gentleman's teeth, and so put him out of his discomfort.

Lifting his velvety, sad eyes from the study of the document before him, Salisbury gazed far-seeingly out of the window . . . A marvellous sweet day, full of early summer's gay intoxication, with a clamour of birdsong, and burgeoning of blossom in hedge-row and thicket, and the last of the hawthorn shedding its exultant perfume as it fell. The late noon sun, slanting through a gap in the elms that bordered the lawn at its extremest length, divided the glowing green of park and meadowland as by a golden ladder, leading from earth to heaven. And as the whimsy caught him, a slight spasm nicked that inscrutable thin smile from those lips. . . . One might desire death, but while life offered this complete per-fection, who would chafe against the order of his passing, long delayed ?

He rose from his seat and walked, with his shuffling gait, to the door and out into the hall. A boarhound, guarding the entrance to his room, got up from where it lay, drooped its great head to its master's hand and followed him.

Through the portals flung wide by waiting lackeys, into the

321

radiant flower-bright garden they passed, man and dog, the strangest contrast : he stunted, withered, bent, and his creature in all its splendid strength and grace of movement, sinewy muscles rippling beneath its satin skin. So in the shade of a yew hedge those two walked. . . . A drift of scent from honeysuckle, together with the hum of insects, was borne upon the still warm air. The Lord Treasurer stooped to sniff a rose, low growing, dusky-red. A bumble-bee alighted on its outer petals. Clumsily it probed its way into the opening heart and clung, with amorous hairy legs, to suck. Amazing that such passionate fierce purpose was manifest in this, the humblest insect. . . . Then, while he mused and wondered, with that thin smile returned to his lips, the hunched shoulders of a sudden, stiffened ; the great dog at his side pricked its ears, nose quivering, and pointed to a sound, scarcely perceptible, that resolved itself into the distant thud of a galloping horse.

Laying a cautious hand upon the hound's bristling head, Salisbury raised his own. The dog growled, but subdued by that warning pressure, stifled the bark in its throat.

No mistaking now the haste of hooves on the bordering grass of the drive.

With slow deliberation Salisbury retraced his steps towards the house, as a servant crossed the lawn, accompanied by a courier whose boots were white with dust, his leather jerkin dark with sweat, his face begrimed with both.

Salisbury halted. The hound at his heels stood expectantly still, while he who now swiftly advanced bared his head, knelt, and delivered his message.

" My lord, I bring grave news. His Majesty bids you return at once to Greenwich. The Lady Arabella has —" his hurried breathing slurred the word—" escaped ! "

Chapter Five

THE five-roomed cottage at East Barnet to which she had been carried looked out, in the near distance, upon Hampstead's hills and heath. Far below, in smoke-befogged haze pierced by the steeple of St. Paul's, lay London Town.

At her casement she would sit for hours, her eyes fixed upon that mist-encumbered sprawling mass, which, at the time of sunset when the western clouds were parted, would reveal a silvery filament winding between a chimera of houses, and the topaz-pointed light of many windows. And sometimes, looming vague and vast, slate-coloured, high above that mirage of a city, she could see, or coaxed imagination to believe she saw, the Tower.

The accommodation offered her in this humble lodging did not exceed the use of two small rooms, one her bedchamber, the other adjoining it, her parlour, scarcely large enough to hold the table, a chair or two and the joint-stools it contained. But its latticed windows opened on a garden, and the air blowing up from the heath was heady and sweet as wine.

Sir James Croft occupied a closet that led from her bedroom, and so restricted was the space, that, despite the thickness of walls built in the time of Henry VII, she could hear his snores while she lay sleepless in the night.

Mrs. Adams, who now attended her, slept by the King's command on a couch at the foot of her bed ; and Markham, she imagined, did not sleep at all, unless it were upon the mat outside her door, for the house contained no room for him. But neither he nor Sir James Croft were proof against her tears, her pathos and her swoons, which occurred with such distressing frequency that Sir James believed her dying.

Mrs. Adams, a stony-featured, sour-visaged woman in her forties, showed, however, nothing in her face nor in her manner to indicate that her sense of duty might, by persuasion, be relaxed. Her orders were to keep the strictest watch upon her ward, and unmercifully did she keep it. Yet, despite her gaunt exterior and unrelenting guardianship, Mrs. Adams, as Arabella soon discovered, was possessed of a weakness, not uncommon to man—or womankind. She had no head, although much taste, for waters stronger than small ale—a taste in which, as the wife of an underpaid cleric, she had never been permitted to indulge.

The covert glances cast by Mrs. Adams at the flagons of good wine served with Arabella's meals, did not pass unobserved ; and the amount of liquor consumed by her Ladyship, not only at her mealtime but throughout the day, according to the weekly account rendered by the steward, Markham, caused some concern to her guardian, Sir James Croft. Markham, however, assured him that her Ladyship's low spirits and not insobriety were the cause of these unusual libations.

A retired colonel, Markham, who had won distinction in the wars with Spain, was burly, rubicund and uncommunicative; indeed he rarely spoke, but what he had to say was to the point. And to Arabella, straightly, within a week or so of his attendance at the cottage, did he say it.

One evening when she sat alone at her window, her eyes tear-blurred and full of dreams, fixed upon those low-lying huddled roofs and spires shimmering in heat-mist far below, Markham came to her; and without preamble, to her wonder, Markham said:

"Madam, I am bidden by my Lady Shrewsbury to advise your Ladyship that you may trust me with your life—and these."

With which he offered to her startled gaze, a casket. She opened it and blinked to see its contents, dazzled by the sparkle of jewels—pearls, rubies, diamonds, emeralds of rarest worth, and among them the gleam of gold coins.

"Heavenly grace!" she gasped, "what's here?"

"A token, Madam," Markham, glancing warily this way and that, sank his voice, "of your good aunt's contrivance, that you shall know she works in your behalf. My name was suggested to the Council by Lord Shrewsbury as eminently suited to this post."

Her lifted eyes caught his; she thought their guarded look concealed a twinkle. Her face that had paled, glowed again. "O, God!" she breathed, "a friend . . . Are you a friend, sent me by my lord and lady? Is it true?"

Her hand went out to touch his sleeve. There was something young and lost, so utterly confiding in her gesture, that case-hardened soldier though he was, Markham melted, dropped upon a knee, raised her hand to his lips and answered her.

"Your servant, Madam, to command. These jewels," he spoke rapidly and almost in a whisper, "and the money here contained have been collected by your steward from your Ladyship's own property, with some additions from my Lady Shrewsbury, who has in keeping for you the sum of fourteen hundred pounds, of which Crompton now has charge. You will be well supplied with all that you and your husband may require to make good your escape. My Lady Shrewsbury believed that if you saw this evidence of her endeavours in your aid, you would take courage to follow her instructions, though they may seem to you—" he paused to add, "fantastic."

But despite this reassurance as he got upon his feet, Arabella's look expressed some doubt. "Fantastic! . . . I do not ask for fantasy, I ask for fact."

"The facts, Madam, are not yet ready to present. Have faith —and still more patience."

"Patience!" Her lip trembled. "I have had nothing else but patience preached to me these twelve months." She gazed at him beseechingly. "What can you tell me of my husband? No word has come from him for three whole weeks, and I cannot—I daren't write now—nor can he, with none to take a message."

"Madam," Markham's voice rumbled surlily up from his beard, "you may write. I will deliver your letters to Crompton, who will convey them to the Tower. He bids me tell you this."

She caught his rough red hand in hers. "God bless him—and you! Is it too much to ask for more—that I may meet my husband?"

"Madam, you will meet him in good time. Trust me and those who work for you outside these walls. But I must warn your Ladyship to speak no more of this again—within them." Taking the casket from her hand, "I must return this now," he said, "to Crompton."

"Is he here?" she questioned eagerly.

Markham smiled.

"He is waiting not a furlong from the house."

"Can I not see him for one moment? . . . Let me see him."

"Madam, no."

He bowed and left her in a state that needed but little more inducement to send her off into a veritable swoon, from sheer relief and hope renewed. So this sullen jailor, this 'paunchy, red-faced Beast', so to herself and often she had called him, was a friend promoted to her service by the wiles of her Aunt and Uncle Shrewsbury. Tears gathered in her eyes and overflowed. She was immeasurably moved; had believed herself forsaken. She had thought her aunt and uncle too complaisant in their renunciation of their efforts to obtain release for her by foul means, since fair had failed.

And all this while they had been in league with staunch allies to help her . . . Her good Uncle Gilbert had gravely jeopardized his own position by this dangerous connivance. He it was who had suggested to the Council Markham's name. If it were discovered that he had deliberately chosen one whom the King would call 'traitor' to guard her here, then he was doomed. . . . She shivered. Heaven! To be rid of plots and plans, of fears and falterings: to be free, to live and love, even as peasants or the beasts of the field were free, to mate where they willed. Any such were to be envied. . . . But those jewels! They must be worth a fortune. And there were more besides, and gold. The sale of the gems alone would keep her and William in comfort on the continent for life . . . O, life! A sob tore at her throat, tears fell. She sank upon her knees and from her heart sent up a prayer that her hope was not in vain.

That night, and for the first time since she had left Lambeth, she slept, untroubled by her dreams, and undisturbed by the snores of Sir James Croft.

While those who loved her made their secret preparations for the deliverance of Arabella, Rodney was no less arduous in his endeavours on behalf of William. That he and she, despite surveillance, managed to communicate during the last month of their captivity is certain, though none of these messages smuggled to and from the Tower is extant. But that she wrote, and that Markham carried what she wrote to Crompton, may be assumed, for letters passed, not only between Arabella and her husband, but between herself and her Aunt Shrewsbury.

And from that day when Markham had revealed himself to her, events moved with meteoric hurry to their climax.

On June 2, Rodney paid a visit to a certain house near the Church of St. Mary Ovary in Southwark, much frequented by young gallants of the Court and their ladies. Having requested the madam to reserve a room for him and a 'gentlewoman of fashion', he told her he would send his servant with certain articles to be laid in the chamber prepared for her reception. The madam, well accustomed to these secretive transactions, returned him a wink and a nod, and made ready a bed to receive the lady—with the bill for the accommodation to be paid in advance. Upon this stipulation she insisted, since, she said, experience had taught her to make sure of her money before the event, "when gentlemen were hot, and not after it—when gentlemen were cold!"

Rodney, grinning, handed her the cash, but he did not return with his lady for the night. Instead he sent his servant with a sack containing certain items : 'a cloak, a cap, a cabinet, a fardel, all wrapped in a white sheet', to be placed in the room he had engaged,

The next day there appeared upon the doorstep a gentlewoman, certainly, but one who by no means represented fashion. Since, however, gentlemen were contrary and unaccountable in choice, the madam did not show surprise at Mr. Rodney's, whom she afterwards described as 'not richly apparelled, and pale, with a wart on her cheek and one under the eye'.

The lady having gained admittance to the room reserved for her, deposited there another package of her own. She then bade the madam—who in view of these singular proceedings was inquisitive—to call a wherryman to fetch the sack left the night before by Rodney, carry it with her things to Tooley's Stairs, and wait for her. She had no occasion now, she said, to use the room.

Greatly curious to know what all this indicated, madam sent her maid to follow the gentlewoman, who was met outside the house by a lackey, or so the girl judged him to be. She returned after a short time, breathless with her haste and all agog with her tale of the lady and her servant, who had, she reported, a flaxen beard, and wore a livery of green and purple velvet with silver buttons. She followed them as far as Pickle Herring over against the Tower, where they took boat and where she left them.

All of which conveyed nothing to the madam more than to mystify her further ; but she had the money paid her for the room, and she let it to another couple that same night.

Meanwhile, the 'gentlewoman', who we may take it was Anne Bradshaw, and the servant, who was William's valet, Reeves, were rowed to Tooley's Stairs where they were met by the wherryman with the sack, as Anne had ordered. Thence they went on to Blackwall and put up at the Old Swan Inn.

Rodney, placed in charge of these manœuvres and determined to take no risks, decided that young Francis, who lodged in the same house with him, must not be told of his brother's imminent escape. He had left, however, a letter to be delivered to Francis when William, it was hoped, would be beyond pursuit.

Mary Shrewsbury, also in constant touch with Rodney, had given him precise instructions to be conveyed to William, acting upon which William took to his bed for two days being greatly troubled, as he told his warders, with the toothache. The warders duly reported his indisposition to Waad, the Lieutenant of the Tower, who promptly sent account of it to Salisbury. . . . The young man's face most certainly was swelled, William having gone to some extremes to bulge his right cheek with a pad of cotton flax. He lay groaning on his bed in greatest pain, visited by Waad, who expressed sympathy, stayed with him for three quarters of an hour, when, after recommending a hot poultice, he retired.

No sooner was he gone than William jumped up to summon his servant. To him, a Frenchman, who had replaced Reeves during the latter's imprisonment at the Marshalsea, William confided that his toothache was a hoax, and that he had been given opportunity to see his wife. He must ride at once to Barnet, and in his absence the man must guard his room and permit none to enter it till his return.

With Gallic sentiment the valet swore upon his life that his master's secret would be kept. Whereupon William, unlocking the cupboard, brought out of it a countryman's smock, a peruke, a beard of black hair, and a carter's hat, all provided by Rodney and brought to him there in relays.

The Frenchman, scenting romance, expressed himself enchanted to assist Monsieur, but he deplored the dress, "which smelt," he declared, "like a——"

"Never mind how it smells. Get me into it quick, and hold you your jaw," muttered William.

The smock slipped easily over his suit; the hat pulled down over his wig hid his eyes, and in the false beard and peruke, the Frenchman, with voluble excitement declared, that Madame his wife herself would not recognize Monsieur, and certainly never those types of animals, the warders. What time would Monsieur be likely to return?

"When you see me," William told him, handing him a coin, "and here's for you to drink my health and Madame's." Cutting short the fellow's thanks, he opened the door, peered out, saw no one in sight, and left his room; this opened on a narrow passage, on the right of which a back stairway led down to the inner court.

By the West Gate of the Tower stood a wagon piled high with faggots. It came there every week to deliver its load. As the driver climbed back into his seat, the warders guarding that entrance took little note of a bearded fellow who followed the cart, presumably to help with its unloading.

Along Water Lane, through Byward's Gate, the wagon rumbled, and behind it, beneath the unsuspecting noses of the warders, William went in his carter's dress, cutting with his whip at the flies that buzzed about him for the stench of dried manure upon his smock. There had been no hitch so far, beyond the wasting of much time in getting rid of the Lieutenant.

Rodney had arranged to meet him with a boat at Tower Stairs at eight o'clock, but it was long past the hour and full dusk before William arrived. The wharf appeared to be deserted, save for some ragamuffins playing in the dirt. Still in his carter's dress, and with Rodney in the stern to keep a sharp look-out, William took the oars and pulled downstream for Blackwall.

*   *   *

When at his country residence, Sir James Croft had been accustomed to ride out each day at noon and in all weathers ; nor could his latest appointment under the Crown deflect the course of his bachelor existence.

On June 3, having seen his captive served with dinner in the presence of her woman, Mrs. Adams, Sir James left the cottage at East Barnet to ride on Hampstead Heath.

The day was fair, the sky without a cloud, the air without a breath, and the cottage rooms too hot, so Arabella found them, for her comfort. She made pretence of eating, watched by the sour Adams, and then declared herself so thirsty she could drink the sea, she said.

Summoning Markham, she asked for canary wine as cold as could be to be brought, and then bade him go down to the village and call at the mercer's shop for a skein of silk that she required. Not even under escort was she allowed outside the cottage garden, which consisted of something less than half an acre.

"I vow my legs will grow as weak as spindles," she declared, "from want of use. If only I could be allowed to ride a horse again." And then she laughed ; and for no reason that Mrs. Adams could perceive, she went on laughing.

"I am rejoiced," said Mrs. Adams glumly, "to see your Ladyship in such high spirits."

"One cannot be for ever in the dumps." Arabella poured herself a beaker of canary and held it, brimming amber to the light, before she drained the cup and set it down and smacked her

329

lips. "Delicious! This wine, Mrs. Adams, tastes of the sun, of heather, and of all good joyous things. Pray fetch yourself a cup, for 'tis no pleasure," Arabella said, "to drink alone."

Mrs. Adams made some feint of a refusal, but her lady showed herself so gracious that she needed little more persuasion to obey.

The cup was brought, filled, passed, as did the afternoon, while Mrs. Adams waxed by turn loquacious, confidential, cheerful, tearful. By the time she had consumed the better part of two quarts of canary she turned from tears again to laughter, and all but toppled from her stool.

Arabella shook her by the shoulder.

"Look you, Mrs. Adams. You have given me your confidence. I know you now for what you are."

Mrs. Adams lifted a cautious eye and hiccoughed. "What am I, m'Lady?"

"Though your looks belie your sentiment, good Adams, you're romantic."

"Ro . . . man . . . Nay now, m'Lady," Mrs. Adams burbled, "you make mock o' me . . . my head! Eh! . . . how it rolls . . ." And swayed from side to side; as so did she.

Arabella steadied her. "Yes, dear Mrs. Adams, you're romantic." She knelt and put her arms round Mrs. Adams' waist and laid her cheek to Mrs. Adams' gaunt one. "And since, from what you tell me, you have loved, and not in vain—— No! You can't deny it, Mrs. Adams—you have opened out your heart to me. I'll open mine to you. My husband . . . Can I trust you?"

Mrs. Adams nodded. "Truss' me, Lady. . . . Yes?"

"My husband is this very moment waiting for me not a mile from this house. I must see him, talk with him before Sir James returns. . . . Mrs. Adams, come with me into my chamber."

She helped her up, and guiding her into the bedroom, sat her down.

"If you can't stand, then you must sit. And not a word of what you see, if you *can* see, which I'm doubting. . . . Here take this, and keep your mouth shut."

And into Mrs. Adams' hand she thrust a purse.

Wordless, and in wonder, Mrs. Adams gazed at it. Lifting her eyes that were askew and her head which was a-nod, she blubbered, "May God reward you, Ma'am . . . am I dreaming?"

"Yes," said Arabella urgently, "you are. You're dreaming,

Mrs. Adams, and this that I do is all part of your dream. . . . O, Lord! Have I made you too whittled that you can't help me out of my dress?"

"Dress?" Mrs. Adams' loosened lips fell open. "Wha'—why—wha' dress, Ma'am?"

"Unfasten me the laces of my corsage," commanded Arabella, presenting her back to Mrs. Adams, "and don't fumble. Break them if you can't untie them. O, why did I pour so much into you? Leave it then! . . . Where are my scissors?" She ran to a table, pulled open a drawer, and began frantically to cut the front of her bodice, wriggled out of it, unhooked her farthingale and dragged her petticoats over her head.

Ignoring the now helpless Adams, she took from a cupboard a bundle of clothes which Markham had brought and hidden there the day before, and while her woman sat and stared and chuckled, raised her hands and dropped her purse, groped for it, laughed, burst into tears and laughed again, Arabella proceeded to exchange her petticoats for a pair of trunks, a doublet and French hose. She combed out her long hair and plaited it close to her head, put on a fair clubbed wig and a black hat. A pair of russet leathern boots with red tops completed the transformation.

"Mrs. Adams," she came and stood before her, "if you think I am a boy you are mistook, for you are dreaming. When you wake you'll *know* that you've been dreaming."

"Why? . . . Wha' . . . Lady!" Mrs. Adams made a gallant effort to recall her roving senses. "What is thish?"

"I've told you, 'tis your dream. You'd best lie down so you may dream more sweetly." She assisted Mrs. Adams to the bed and hoisted her on to it. "And you can tell Sir James that you've been taken sick, as sure you will be when I'm gone. Lie there. . . . Forgive me," she whispered, "and good-bye."

Tiptoe, in her boy's dress, leaving Mrs. Adams lying happily unconscious, she stole out of the front door, and away.

Her boots were much too big for her, the rapier in her sword-belt insecurely fastened, kept sliding down to trip her up, and the high-crowned hat rammed over her wig had given her a splitting headache. Markham had arranged to meet her a furlong up the road soon after three o'clock, yet by the sun's position she judged the time to be nearer four. Hampered by her boots she could make little haste, but the danger of discovery while still within sight of the house, drove her on. However, she passed no one on the way save a farm-hand, who, she was relieved to see, gave her a glance that had nothing in it of suspicion more than the inquisitive stare of a native to a stranger. With immense daring she attempted to whistle a tune, and stepped out taking long jaunty strides. The fellow touched his forelock and gave her a " Good-day, sir."

Suppressing a giggle, she returned him a nod and strode on, her hand clutching the hilt of her rapier to keep it in place. So, breathless with excitement and the unaccustomed exercise after weeks of none, she arrived at the bend in the road where Markham waited, skulking, in a ditch. She accomplished the remainder of the journey on his arm, exhausted, and for the first time without pretence, half-fainting.

" How men," she gasped, " can endure these stuffy clothes ! I'm all but roasted in 'em. . . . I suppose I may not unbutton my tunic for air ?"

" No, Madam," Markham told her gruffly, " you may not."

But when she saw Crompton mounted in the courtyard of the inn with two horses ready saddled, her spirits rose and she had all to do in her relief not to give herself away by calling out to him.

" Put on your gloves," Markham warned her. " Your hands can as little be mistaken for a boy's as could your voice."

" Now that," she gleamed at him, " I call uncivil, Markham, when I flattered myself I was playing my part as good as any lad at the Globe Theatre plays the girl. Would you say I look too ladyish ? "

" No more, Madam," Markham grinned into his beard, " than do the royal pages."

But now another fear possessed her.

" Heaven help me ! Must I ride astride ? I've never rode cross-saddle in my life. I'll give myself away for certain when I mount."

And indeed the ostler who held her horse's head remarked that the young gentleman looked mortal weak, and gave it his opinion he would not hold out to London.

" My son," Markham surlily vouchsafed, " has always been of this same frail build. He was born deaf and dumb."

And with a reassuring wink at her, whom the ostler's observation had greatly scared, he helped her up from the mounting-block. Open-mouthed, and staring after them, the ostler watched the deaf-mute clap spurs to his horse with such unnecessary vigour that the animal reared and would have thrown him, but that the gentleman, his father, caught at the bridle-rein and led him out of the yard.

Pocketing his tip the ostler shook his head. No doubt whatever that the poor young gentleman would not last to London. He could no more sit that horse than he could ride it.

He was wrong.

In spite of her unwonted seat, her good horsemanship did not now desert her. The rapid movement soon returned the colour to her cheeks, and within half-an-hour she was outriding her escorts, as much at ease in the saddle as they. . . .

The landlord of the old Swan Inn at Blackwall had a full house that evening. A company of travellers with their servants and luggage had arrived, and took possession of the parlour and the room engaged the night before by a thin lady in black. The first of these newcomers was an elderly stout lady who appeared to be on terms of the easiest acquaintance with the thin lady. A meal for seven persons was commanded and some several bottles of wine. Four gentlemen, they told the landlord, were due to meet them there at six o'clock. At which time, or shortly after, two men and a boy rode up. The latter the landlord described as fair-haired, of a slight build and pale countenance, wearing a high-crowned black hat, a light coloured doublet and russet red-topped boots.

Dismounting with some awkwardness, he walked mincingly into the parlour where he was greeted by the stout lady with embraces and loud expressions of delight. The thin lady showed more restraint, and dropping him a curtsy, kissed his hand with homage. The three then went together into a bedroom, for what purpose the landlord was at a loss to understand, as both gentlewomen, certainly, were old enough to be his mother. Since, however, he judged the youth to be of some importance, his eccentricities of taste could be excused.

At the inn at Blackwall, then, the party dallied, according to the landlord, for near upon two hours, by which time the young gentleman seemed to be in greatest perturbation. He refused to eat, of the best the house provided, and aroused the wonder of the landlord, who we may believe had his ear and eye alternately glued to the keyhole, by bursting into tears and exclaiming in a petulant, high voice that he would not go till William came. . . . "What!" he demanded of those whom the landlord assumed to be his servants, "do you think I've risked so much to play the coward at this eleventh hour? Come what may, I'll wait."

Meanwhile the watermen, who, with their boats, had been hired to take the travellers to Leigh, were getting restive. The night was overcast and moonless, and they did not relish the journey downstream in the dark with a swift current running. They had been told they must be ready to leave Blackwall at six o'clock, and it was now past eight. If they left at once they would not be back till morning.

The innkeeper brought out to them a tankard of ale and a pipe each of tobacco, hoping to hear more of these singular proceedings than was offered by the keyhole. But the watermen could tell him nothing of the gentlefolk, neither whence they had come nor whither, beyond Leigh, they were bound.

We may believe that Arabella, waiting in that tavern for her husband, suffered torments of anxiety. With her face convulsively pressed to the lattice, she watched the river whiten under the evening sky, while her mind presented horrors unimaginable to account for his delay. His flight had been discovered and he turned back and re-imprisoned; or he might even at this moment be undergoing cross-examination on the rack. His inquisitors would try to force from him her whereabouts by torture. . . . Her escape from Barnet by this time must have surely been reported to Sir James.

Bridget—without doubt the 'stout lady' remarked by the landlord—who had insisted on coming to the inn to bid Arabella godspeed, strove to quiet her alarms with the reminder that Mr. Rodney had decided not to hire boatmen from the Tower Wharf, since none there could be trusted. This being so, and neither he nor Mr. Seymour accustomed to the use of oars, their journey would on that account take longer than——

"*Will* you stop your clacking!" was all the thanks she got for this. "You know as well as I that he can row. Can't somebody go see if he is on the way?"

Reeves was sent to scout and returned with no news of his master's arrival, but the watermen had told him the tide was on the turn and if they did not leave at once they refused to leave at all.

"Then I," determined Arabella, "also will refuse. I'm here and here I'll stay."

Nor until Markham firmly indicated that if she did so she would not only endanger her own safety but theirs, and possibly her husband's, since the landlord had already shown himself suspicious, was she at last induced to go.

Having ordered one of the baggage-men to stay behind with Mrs. Sherland, and inform her husband when he came to follow after them to Leigh, Arabella took her leave of Bridget, who was now reduced to tears.

"No matter how old you are, my poppet, you'll always be the babe I nursed upon my knee, and if I were ten years younger I'd come with you to France, but—" Bridget achieved a watery chuckle, "I'm too fat."

Arabella hugged her.

"My dear old faithful! I'll send a ship to bring you over to me on a visit once I'm there. We won't be gone for ever. The King will pardon us in his good time. I cannot believe that he will hold this feud against us all our lives—and his."

"If you," Bridget, snuffling, blew her nose, "go plead his pardon in this guise you'll surely get it! You make a lovely boy. . . . God keep you safe and send you all the happiness that you deserve."

"I will not," whispered Arabella, "say good-bye. . . . God bless you!"

The sun had set, but crimson light still lingered in the sky behind a bank of cloud. Mist was rising, and the fields either side the river lay lost in vaporous green. Sounds were few, birds silent, save for the shrill cry of water-fowl feeding in the rushes Bats flitted through the dusk; there was no wind.

Arabella sat in the stern of the boat, Anne's hand held fast in hers, and her eyes searching backward along the waterway for him who soon, she prayed, would follow. Facing her sat Crompton, Markham, and, behind them, Reeves. The wherrymen, naked to the waist, their tanned skins glistening with sweat, pulled steadily downstream. The boat that carried their baggage had gone on ahead.

Her physical exhaustion, the utter weariness of over-tired muscles due to her long ride, were forgotten in the anguish of suspense. Again and again she entreated the watermen—"Turn back! I will not go. Wait here. Put up your oars."

But the men, possibly induced by Markham to believe the young gentleman out of his wits, took no heed of 'his' words and rowed on.

Night fell and she sat silent.

Her mind seemed now to have been strangled by the terror that crushed her spirit, so short a while since buoyed high with hope. Her escape had been accomplished without challenge as he . . . her fainting thoughts revived . . . as he too would escape. He would. He must! His exit from the Tower on parole had never yet been questioned, but would his disguise have tricked the warders as hers did those tavern folk? Or had Rodney bungled, mistaken the appointed time and arrived with his boat at the Tower too late and found William gone? And then, conspicuous in his carter's dress upon that wharf, what would he do? Hire another boat and go searching for Rodney up and down the river? . . . "Most likely that." . . . she heard her own voice say. "They've missed each other, and William may have forgotten, or may never have known at which inn we were to meet."

"Yes, my dearest, yes," Anne soothed her, "he will be behind us, never fear."

The boat moved swiftly onward, passing Woolwich, but at Gravesend the wherrymen insisted on a halt. The way was long, their throats were dry, and they must have refreshment.

After some haggling and the promise of a double fare, they were persuaded to go on to Tilbury. There, supported by their mates in the first boat, they halted again and refused to budge until they had a drink. Thus some good time was lost and the wind had changed, blowing east by south for a gale, when they came at last to Leigh; and still no sign of William, nor of the French barque ordered by Crompton to meet them. The fisherfolk along the quay had seen no craft answering to her description put in for the last few hours. It seemed that Corvé, her skipper, had played them false and sailed to Calais without them.

Moored close to the quay, however, lay a brig bound for Berwick, but her master, one John Bright, notwithstanding a substantial bribe, could not be persuaded to alter his course. Dirty weather was brewing, he said, and he would not make for France in such a sea. He knew those currents off the Calais coast. It would be folly to attempt a landing in unfavourable winds. His port of call was Berwick, and to Berwick he would go.

When asked by Crompton if he had seen a French barque put in a while since, he pointed to a ship riding at anchor a couple of miles out in the Roads.

" She flies the French flag," he vouchsafed, " but I've no knowledge of her."

" Wait," Arabella pleaded. " Let us wait. That cannot be our ship, and if it is I will not go aboard until he comes. 'Tis pitch dark. He will never see us all that distance out. . . ."

Her safety, however, was Crompton's sole concern. They must get her away at all costs. Ignoring her entreaties, he ordered the wherrymen to row within hailing distance of the vessel, which to everyone's relief save Arabella's, was found to be the ship they sought.

But the appearance of so mysterious a party arriving on such a night and at such an hour, with their servants and baggage, had aroused the worst suspicions of John Bright. Through his glass he watched them board the French boat, and won praise at his subsequent examination for his evidence promptly noted in his log-book, and produced.

Crompton, he described as ' somewhat corpulent, with a small black beard and wearing a black suit '; Reeves as ' flaxen-haired, in grey '—he had changed his purple and green livery for one more sober. Of Markham he made no note at all; and Anne Bradshaw he surprisingly mistook for one Moll Cutpurse, much in demand with the sailors at Wapping, since ' she went', he said, ' barefaced and with a black riding safeguard, having nothing on her head save a black hat and her hair '. But that which most attracted his attention was the ' marvellous fair white hand of one who sat wrapped in a hood and cloak, and who wore underneath it a man's dress ; yet no man, he could swear, had possessed so fair a hand.'

It was now near upon four o'clock in the morning, and every minute precious if they wished to get away before daylight. The sea, lashed to fury by the risen wind, tossed the barque as it lay at anchor and reduced Anne to prostration. Arabella, unaffected by the incessant pitch and roll, stood in the bows, her eyes straining over the crested waves for the scarcely discernible shore. Then while she gazed despairing, the haggard sky was cleft by a luminous streak that widened as she watched to a milky crystal, lit by one lone star.

"Madam," Crompton touched her arm, "it is the dawn."

"Yes . . . I see it is the dawn."

"And," persisted Crompton, "Captain Corvé bids me tell your Ladyship that he can wait no longer if we wish to make Calais tonight."

"We do not wish to make Calais tonight. I will wait."

Since it was useless to consult or argue with her, the captain weighed anchor and the ship, released, sprang forward, plunging like a stallion in the trough of the angry sea. She wept, she shrieked, turned madly upon Crompton and accused him of betrayal. This was a plot to take her from her husband. They were in league against her, but she'd escape—throw herself overboard! She ran to Captain Corvé and prayed him, "Of your pity, put into harbour and take me back up Thames to Tilbury. I cannot go without my husband. He'll come! . . . I will not . . ."

Her words were lost in the yell of the wind, as a wave crashed down upon the deck and flung her violently into Crompton's arms. He lifted her, and heedless of her cries, carried her, still struggling below.

It was ten o'clock when William, having thrown off his disguise and pitched it in the river, arrived at Blackwall with Rodney, to find Bridget waiting at the inn and his wife gone. And loudly, we may presume, did Bridget upbraid him for his negligence,—a fine gallant he to leave his wife in such a miserable plight. From six o' the clock, for two hours she stayed, and had at last to be taken by——

"*Six*, did you say!" shouted William. "The appointed time was eight!" He rounded in a fury upon Rodney. "Was not that the hour you arranged with Reeves?"

Rodney had certainly, he said, told Reeves that they would meet at eight o'clock. He knew, because he wrote it that there should be no mistake.

"You wrote it? How? In words or figures?"

Rodney, paling, admitted he had written it in figures.

"May you be cursed!" William groaned. "The fool has mistook your eight for a six. What possessed you, to write *any*thing? Why couldn't you have trusted to your tongue?"

Then, as further recrimination would only delay their much belated start, William swallowed his rage, and offered a couple of wherrymen ten pounds to take them down to Leigh. But although they rowed with a better will than those who had gone before them, when they came to Leigh in the dawn they were told that the Frenchman, with his passengers, had sailed.

What now to do? It was unlikely they could charter a ship to carry them over to Calais at short notice, and in such a gale. William was for making the passage in a fishing-boat whose skipper seemed inclined to take the risk, for a consideration, but that Rodney, sighting a vessel of some size lying to in the Roads, suggested that the trawler should take them out to her and ascertain her course, which he argued might well be France for all they knew.

Her course was Newcastle, she a collier, and her captain much astonished at being hailed on such a howling night by two gentlemen of quality, one of whom made a trumpet of his hands to shout above the wind : " Will you carry us to France for twenty pounds ?"

" Make it thirty," came the answer, " and I'll do't!"

They went aboard.

Before weighing anchor the skipper insisted on seeing the cash, and the sight of it no less than the splendid attire of Rodney in his ' full suit of red satin laid with gold and silver lace ', gave him uneasily to question : Were they fugitives flying from justice? He'd no wish to be a party in a crime.

" No crime, my good fellow," William heartily assured him, " but an accident," his grin disarmed the honest skipper, " for which I blame my sword—or the wine I drank before I used it in the settlement of an affair of honour. I meant to prick and not to kill my man. So I'm advised to bide my time awhile on the French coast till the noise blows over."

Flattered to receive the confidence of one who carried money in his pouch, fought duels in his cups, and whose clothes were of an elegance that bespoke his high degree, the skipper was emboldened to ask the name of his distinguished passengers. William, about to answer, was stopped by a warning glance from Rodney, who gave his own name, and William's as ' Mr. See '.

" And if you take us now," he said, " you'll get what you've been promised, and ten pounds more besides."

The skipper, thinking it were better business in such case to mind his own, pocketed the money that had been already paid, and refrained from further question. He had some doubts, however, about making Calais that same night if he made it at all. Nor was he disposed to risk his ship in the teeth of the gale. Though the distance to Belgium was farther than France, he would prefer, he said, to make for Ostend, and safety.

William at first demurred, since Arabella, he presumed, would be awaiting him at Calais. But when Rodney suggested that, so soon as they arrived, a courier could be sent ahead to advise her of their coming, he agreed to go.

They sailed—and were driven into Harwich.

From there, against all argument, the skipper refused to venture out again until the wind dropped.

They had to wait for that, and finally were landed at Ostend on June 8.

* * *

When Francis Seymour read the letter left for him by Rodney he was panic-stricken. Although Rodney guardedly had given him to understand the barest facts of his brother's escape, Francis gathered that both William and Arabella had fled in disguise, and were by that time well on their way to France.

While he hesitated, in two minds whether or no he should hold back this information for a day or two and so give them the chance to evade pursuit, fear of the consequence that would befall him as accomplice to their folly, over-ruled his better impulse. And so, as his grandfather, Lord Hertford, ten years before had betrayed Arabella, did Francis, to save his coward's skin, betray his brother.

He hurried to the Tower, and despite the protest of the loyal Frenchman who guarded William's room, forced entry there, to find his worst fears realized and William gone. It was his bounden duty, thus he consoled his conscience, to inform Sir William Waad. The Lieutenant, equally as terrified as Francis, at once took Rodney's letter to the Council.

Great was the consternation that prevailed in the Chamber. How to break the news of this calamitous occurrence to the King? Salisbury was called upon to stem the shock and run the gauntlet of His Majesty's displeasure. Having despatched a messenger to Hatfield, the Councillors, with qualms, awaited the Lord Treasurer's arrival; and to pass the time reduced the wretched Francis to a pitiable state by putting him through strict examination.

On his knees in tears before them, he declared his innocence. 'I am as clear of their release or of any practice, as is the child but yesterday born.' . . . No, William had never communicated to him his intention, nor had he ever once essayed to impersonate his brother. . . . Yes, he admitted he had shaved his beard; he had a skin eruption, but on his life he swore that he was no party to these wicked undertakings. In the midst of his avowals, and to his inexpressible relief, Lord Salisbury appeared to take command. Francis was dismissed, but placed under arrest at Hertford House pending a further inquiry.

When told of the flight of his captives, James showed more fear and less wrath than Salisbury expected. In terror lest this double flight threatened his life and his dynasty, he raved of Catholic plots to dethrone him. That evil woman, Mary Shrewsbury, was known to be a Papist. She harboured priests and had amassed much money, for some ill use he would not doubt. She should long ago have been put down or put away, but that his trust in and affection for 'that traitress', his own cousin, had blinded him to danger.

"You, my gude lord," he clutched at Salisbury's hand, "arrest all persons suspect of aiding and abetting the escape of these miscreants. Her claim to the throne is supported by the Pope, and those two, now united, are a double threat to me and to my kingdom. What if a son be born to them? Or a daughter! 'Twould be worse. Women are the mischief. . . ." He raised himself from where he sat. "Go you, my lord, and tell the Lord High Admiral we command he chase them in the Channel with his fleet. We'll capture them yet!" Then in a fidget James plucked at his beard, rolled his tongue round his lips and said, "Ay! We'll have them shrieking mercy for their sins before we've done. They've had a gude day's start, but we will get them. . . . Hey!" He clapped his hands and bawled again! "Page! Hey! *Page!*"

The arras parted to admit a dainty boy.

"Go you, my dear," James bade him, "and bring me pen and ink. I'll write a proclamation, my gude lord."

And that same day, throughout the city, royal heralds cried:

'Oyez! Oyez! Oyez!

Whereas we are given to understand that the Lady Arabella and William Seymour, being for divers great and heinous offences

341

committed the one to our Tower of London and the other to a special guard, hath found the means, by the wicked practices of divers lewd persons to break prison and make escape on Monday, the third of June, with intent to transport themselves to foreign parts, we do hereby straitly charge and command all persons upon their duty and allegiance whatsoever, not to receive, harbour, or assist them in their passage any way, as they will answer for it at their perils.

Given at Greenwich this fourth day of June per ipsum regnum."

The whole town was in a stir. The cobbles rang with the clatter of iron hooves as the King's messengers went galloping from the aged Sea Lord, Nottingham, to his Vice-Admiral, Sir William Monson, and back again to Salisbury, with 'Haste! Post haste! Haste for your life', on their despatches, together with the sinister impression of a gallows, as reminder of what might come to them if they did not obey the King's command with speed. Scared citizens, peeping from their windows, thanked God that they were not concerned in this most sorry circumstance. The Queen, surrounded by her Maidens, outwardly condemned the Lady Arabella, and inwardly prayed she would go free. Prince Henry, it was noted, would not commit himself to pass opinion for her or against; but Charles went running to his mother, loud in tears, to implore her intercession with the King for his "Ser-sweet Arbelle and Mr. Ser-Seymour, who had shown him how to play at ser-ser-soldiers when he came to Hampton Ca-Court, and Arbelle had ta-ta-taught him not to ster-stutter. He would always love her and rer-member. . . ."

Nor when he was King did he forget.

Meanwhile the Lords of the Council were reassembled to confer. The Lord High Admiral Nottingham, taking into account the contrary winds and tides, felt assured that the fugitives would not reach Calais that night. He may have hoped they would. He had watched her grow up and it went much against his heart to commission Monson to pursue the reckless pair, in whose absence, he told Salisbury, 'England will find no loss' . . . 'Nor any gain', was Salisbury's rejoinder; and he smiled. 'So hot an alarm is taken in this matter as will make the couple more illustrious than ever in the world's eyes.'

'Yes, one might believe,' glumly assented Nottingham, 'that

their offence is nothing short of Powder Treason, to put the King in such a fearful imagination.'

Indeed Doctor Hammond, his physician, was alarmed for the King's reason. He refused to go to bed; he paced his room, he bit his fingers, would not—and this most alarming of all—receive his Viscount, Robert Carr, but ordered him sharply, "You can go tak' yeself to your whore, Lady Essex. She'll gladly pass the night wi' ye, and welcome!" ... And every quarter of an hour he would call to his yawning pages. "Holloa there! Hey! What news? Look out o' the window and watch ... Any sight of them yet? Has Sir William Monson gone?"

Sir William Monson had been gone some hours. He hastened down to Blackwall, where judicious questioning among the loiterers upon the wharf, revealed that if not Arabella, a lady who answered to the description of her gentlewoman, Mistress Bradshaw, and another, fat and elderly, had arrived there and departed with two men, and a youth whose girlish looks and manner had aroused remark.

Then, while Monson sorted evidence from the varied accounts supplied him by the wherrymen and the landlord, some fisherfolk, just come from Leigh, told of a strange company that had boarded a French barque skulking out in the Roads, and which had headed off for Calais at daybreak.

Enough for Monson; he would wait to hear no more.

Marshalling his men, he put six of them in an oyster-boat with ammunition and the order to pull down Thames for Leigh. He was then rowed back to Greenwich, where he commanded the pinnace, 'Adventure', to put out for the Flanders coast.

He followed in the rear to watch events.

*   *   *

The wind had dropped, and, as if wearied of its fury, the sea lay sullen as a sheet of lead under a fitful sun. The gale of the night before had compelled Captain Corvé to stand to under Sundhead, and he was still some distance off from Calais; nor in that heavy calm could he make way.

Arabella had resumed her watch on deck, her eyes achingly fixed upon these pallid waters, where spectral ships that had been sheltering in harbour, dipped on the rim of the horizon to vanish like lost birds. She had removed her cloak and wig, and stood in her boy's dress leaning on the gunwale, her loosened hair about her shoulders. Her face, drained of all colour, was carven to an immobility as lifeless as the sea.

So, unheedful of the entreaties of Anne and Crompton, to rest, to eat, she stayed. She would not rest, she told them quietly, until she sighted the ship that would bring her husband to her. If only the winds would rise again to drive this crawling boat! He might well have reached Calais before her and would be suffering the same anguish of mind—"As I did," she said, "last night. But I am hopeful now."

The barque, all sails spread, moved stolidly beneath its weight of canvas. The scream of a gull, piercing that torpid stillness, was like the cry of a soul in pain.

An involuntary shudder shook her body. Then, her head upraised, she stiffened, and her eyes were lit as if a flame had leapt behind them.

"Look! . . . A sail!"

Low-lying in the Channel's curve a sudden whiteness flashed, caught by a gleam of sun that struggled through a blanket of thick cloud.

"I knew it," she whispered. "Yes . . . I knew that he would come. He is behind us! See!"

Sure enough, like a gigantic swan, proudly skimming those numbed waters, a tall ship bore down upon them.

Captain Corvé, on the bridge, put up his glass and shouted a rapid order. There was a stir and gabbling in French among the crew, a hauling in of ropes, a heaving of the top'sle . . . "Why this?" cried Arabella. "Tell the Captain to stand in. Why put up more sail?"

"Madam," Markham laid his hand upon her shoulder. "She flies the Royal Ensign. Get below." But she stood rooted, her eyes still lit and her lips eager.

"The Royal Ensign! . . . Surely. She is an English ship. How swift she moves. She carries more canvas than we. Do you think that he can hear me if I call?" And over the sea she threw her voice in a joyous shout of: "William . . . Ahoy! William . . . *Will*iam!"

For answer, as if it mocked the echo of that yearning cry, came the harsh, staccato crack of gunfire and the hiss of its fall in a shower of spray.

Her face whitened.

"Get below, Madam," doggedly reiterated Markham.

"We are followed," she said slowly, "but not by him . . . No, I'll stay on deck."

Markham's groan of impatience was converted to a cough.

"I beseech you, Madam, for your safety. There is danger here."

She gave him a frozen look. "What do I care for danger?"

"Your husband, Madam, would not have you risk your life to no good purpose."

"My life," she answered tonelessly, "is of no purpose without him."

Another shot and then another barked from the pinnace that flew the King's flag. In a gallant effort to evade his pursuer, Captain Corvé threw out all his sail, but he had little chance to make headway with no wind behind him. Only when the alternatives of capture or sinking were certain, did Arabella allow herself to be hustled below.

In the cabin, dazed, half-deafened, she sat locked in Anne's arms, while flash after flash spurted from the pinnace, splitting the breathless air in a frenzy of sound.

Thirteen shots in all were fired, most of which fell short, but one struck the deck amidships, shattering the porthole of the cabin that sheltered the women; a second caught her in the stern, a third tore a hole in her side, wounding one of the crew. Water poured in, flooding her hold. The crippled barque keeled over.

Perceiving that further resistance was useless, Captain Corvé struck his flag and surrendered his ship to the King.

An account of the capture was sent to the Lord High Admiral by Captain Crockett, in command of the pinnace 'Adventure'. He laconically states:

'Under the South Sundhead we saw a small sail which we chased. We sent our boat with shot and pikes, and half Channel over our boat did overtake them, and making some few shots they yielded, where we found divers passengers, among the rest my Lady Arabella, her three men and one gentlewoman. But we cannot yet find Mr. Seymour here. My Lady saith she saw him not. . . .'

And thankfully she said it. If Captain Crockett believed they

345

were together it could only mean that he was still at large; and in the intensity of her relief she had no thought for herself. No matter now what might befall her, William still went free! . . .

*   *   *

From the deck of ' Adventure ' she watched the sun rise over London. The airless calm of yesterday had passed, and the morning was sweet with the savour of wind from the south. Along the city's waterway the huddled houses of the poor, the mansions of the rich, the belfries and church steeples, the dirt and squalor of the wharf, all looked to have been washed in opalescent light. Gold-pointed, dimpling under beam and breeze, the river hummed with the noise and bustle of its traffic. The sound of hammers from the dockyards mingled with the voices of shipwrights and wherrymen, the creak and groan of heavy freights loading, and the chuckle of wind in the sails.

A lovely day. . . . A lovely world!

She stood in the bows of the ship that was taking her out of it, and yet, although defeated, she knew no pang, no bitterness, no fear of what might be. The unendurable suspense of these last, long crowded hours had been lifted. She rejoiced to know him safe—and free! Her mind pursued that hope and hugged it to her heart. And detachedly, in some faint wonder that she could at such a moment accept her revelation, she saw the meaning of her whole life's unfulfilment.

One can only grow to knowledge through frustration, and learn the way of life through life's awakening. . . . For in life she said, we sleep. Pain, pleasure, sorrow, joy, all earthly passions and desires, brave lusts and dear delights of flesh, must die or be renounced if the human spirit seeks release from bondage, to dwell for ever unextinguished, and unidentified with an illusion. For what is life but an illusion ? And love . . . Elysium.

As a girl she had clipped love's wings with contraband embraces, and meetings made more poignant by their stealth. As a woman, as a wife, she had been given a glimpse of all that makes life bearable, yet what if her secret marriage were allowed to take its natural course ? Would time not stale its first rapture ? He was young and ardent now, but in their years together she would grow old and older, and the time might come when she would whisper to him in the night . . . and find him gone. A sigh escaped her lips,

346

but her eyes held a clear startling brilliance. God send him safe, she prayed, beyond despair and loneliness, beyond a lover's dream. . . .

"Madam," the voice of Crompton roused her; the face she turned to him was radiant, lit by the sun's dazzle on the water.

Clearing his throat of a rock, Crompton said : "Captain Crockett has orders to take you to the Tower. Mistress Bradshaw will attend your Ladyship, but I and Markham——" his words ran down in silent tears. She stayed her own.

"Don't grieve for me, dear Crompton, I have no grief for myself. . . . Others have lived and died there."

He dashed his hand across his eyes. "I am unmanned, my Lady, by your courage."

She echoed wonderingly, " Courage ? I need no courage when I have no fear. While my husband is at liberty and so long as he goes free, I too am free—in spirit. Crompton, my dear friend." She touched his sleeve. " My one regret is that I bring you and all who love me into danger. But," her smile dawned again, " I think 'twas worth it. We gave them a good run ! This I promise you," she raised her chin, " that come what may I'll see you righted. Not you, nor any who has aided me shall suffer for my fault. . . . And here's my hand on't."

Too moved to speak, he kissed it, turned, and left her standing there, her hair all loose about her face, and on her lips that smile.

Light caressed the turrets of the Tower, silvering its steel-grey walls in a pattern carved from shadow, as the King's ship, all sails furled, moved slowly in and anchored under the Queen's Stairs.

On the wharf, Sir William Waad stood waiting.

One hand she gave to Markham, one to Crompton, in farewell. They watched her go . . . a gallant figure of a boy, her head flung high, her step unfaltering, her shoulders squared beneath that rakish doublet.

With Anne behind her and no glance nor word for the Lieutenant ceremoniously bowing, she passed along the gangway of 'Adventure', and in through the open gate.

September 1946—*September* 1947.

AFTERWORD

Arabella Stuart died in the Tower on September 25, 1615. She was buried in the Henry VIIth Chapel of Westminster beside her kinswoman, Queen Mary of Scotland and her grandmother, Margaret of Lennox. William remained in enforced exile for a number of years. His desperate efforts to return to his wife met with no success; but after her death, which finally dispelled the King's groundless fears of that ill-fated marriage, James allowed him to come back to England. His elder brother having died during his banishment, William succeeded his grandfather to the Earldom of Hertford in 1621. A devoted adherent to Charles I and the Royalist cause, he distinguished himself in later years as a General in command of the King's forces, and won the highest praise for his strategy and courage in defence of Sherborne Castle and at the Battle of Lansdowne.

As if to atone for the cruel injustice of James, his father, towards his much loved cousin, 'Arbelle', and her husband, Charles I created him Marquis of Hertford. It was he, who, with four faithful others, carried the snow-covered coffin of their murdered King to the Royal Chapel of Windsor on that bitter day in February, 1649.

At the time of the Restoration and by special Act of Parliament, Charles II bestowed upon William Seymour the title and estates of his great-grandfather, the Protector, and made him Duke of Somerset.

By a strange coincidence he took as second wife, Frances Devereux, daughter of the Earl of Essex. He named his eldest child Arabella.

In telling this story of Arabella Stuart, I have not drawn upon imagination more than is compatible with the reconstruction of those scenes that must, of necessity, be fictionized. The main events of her life have been closely followed, and wherever possible I have reproduced the actual dialogue from eye-witness' accounts and the wealth of correspondence left to us.

All characters, names of characters, verses and letters quoted, although much abridged, are entirely authentic.

I am profoundly grateful to the Dowager Duchess of Devonshire for her courtesy in permitting me access to Hardwick Hall and the rooms in which Arabella lived her youth; to Ralph Straus for his expert advice on and demonstration of the royal game of tennis at Hampton Court; and to the officials of the London Library for their unfailing assistance in my research.

DORIS LESLIE

AUTHORITIES CONSULTED

Life of the Lady Arabella Stuart	E. T. Bradley
Arbella Stuart	B. C. Hardy
Life and Letters of Arabella Stuart	E. Cooper
Bess of Hardwick and Her Circle	Maud Stepney Rawson
Elizabeth and Essex	Lytton Strachey
Queen Elizabeth	E. R. Neale
Lives and Letters of the Devereux, Earls of Essex	Walter Bouchier Devereux
The Court of James I	Godfrey Goodman
The Secret History of James I, containing Osborne's Memoirs and Sir Anthony Weldon's Court and Character of King James	
Shakespeare's England	Clarendon Press, Oxford
The History of Hampton Court Palace	Ernest Law
The Cavendish Family	Frances Hickling
Lives of the Tudor Princesses	Agnes Strickland
Harrison's Elizabethan and Jacobean Journals, State Papers, etc.	

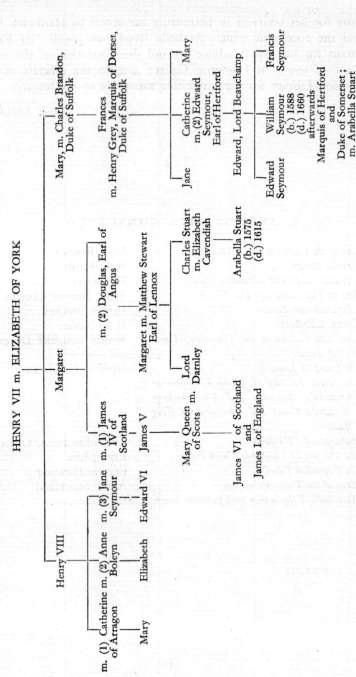

GENEALOGY OF ARABELLA STUART AND WILLIAM SEYMOUR

HENRY VII m. ELIZABETH OF YORK

Also by **DORIS LESLIE**

POLONAISE
A Romance of Chopin

Over a quarter of a million copies sold

"It will bear the re-telling, more especially when, as here, the available facts have been so carefully studied and from them has been built up a sympathetic record at once so ordered and so vivacious . . . an admirable example of the now very popular 'novelised' biography."

RALPH STRAUS in the *Sunday Times.*

"A fine realization of an artist by an artist."

SYDNEY CARROLL in the *Daily Sketch.*

"A convincing portrait, artistically executed. Her suggestion of the contemporary scene is excellent." *The Scotsman.*

"This is a beautiful book written with artistry and insight, and I cannot praise it too warmly."

H. S. WOODMAN in the *Manchester Evening Chronicle.*

"A really brilliant study in imaginative reconstruction."

L. P. HARTLEY in the *Sketch.*

ROYAL WILLIAM
The Story of a Democrat

"Miss Doris Leslie writes so invigoratingly about William IV, she makes the whole period exciting and fills us with her own enthusiasm for the Sailor King."

GEORGE W. BISHOP in the *Daily Telegraph.*

"Doris Leslie, an accomplished novelist, has made admirable use of her carefully gathered material . . . most entertaining."

RALPH STRAUS in the *Sunday Times.*

"Uncommonly well written. . . . This delightful and delightfully uncommon book." PHILIP PAGE in the *Daily Mail.*

"So interesting . . . so sympathetic. She has rescued the 'mountebank' from the grimy paws of Greville and Creevey."

Punch.

"A ready biography in the post-Strachean manner, readable and humane . . . decorated with innumerable happy glances at a richly romantic period." FRANK SWINNERTON in the *Observer.*

"A triumph." *Saturday Review of Literature, New York.*